JUL. 10.1985

D0343608

COMMERCIAL BANKING IN AN ERA OF DEREGULATION

Emmanuel N. Roussakis

PRAEGER SPECIAL STUDIES • PRAEGER SCIENTIFIC

New York • Philadelphia • Eastbourne, UK
Toronto • Hong Kong • Tokyo • Sydney

850588

Library of Congress Cataloging in Publication Data

Roussakis, Emmanuel N.
    Commercial banking in an era of deregulation.

    Bibliography: p.
    Includes index.
    1. Bank Management. 2. Banks and banking—United
States. I. Title.
HG1615.R68   1984   332.1'2'068   84-6763
ISBN 0-03-063654-X (alk. paper)

To Marina, Nicholas, and George

Published in 1984 by Praeger Publishers
CBS Educational and Professional Publishing,
a Division of CBS Inc.
521 Fifth Avenue, New York, NY 10175 USA

1984 by Praeger Publishers

456789 052 987654321

Printed in the United States of America
on acid-free paper

Commercial banks constitute the core of a nation's financial system. They are the depositories for the funds of numerous individuals, business units, and the government itself. Through their lending and investing activities they provide substantial financing to all major sectors of the economy: the household, the business, and the government. By extending credit to these segments of the economy, they facilitate the flow of goods and services from producers to consumers and affect the financial activities of the government. They provide a sizable portion of the money supply in the form of demand deposits, and are the means through which monetary policy is effected. All these services add up to one thing: no financial institution contributes more markedly to the successful functioning of a nation's economy than do its commercial banks.

The 1980s is a period of dramatic transition in the commercial banking industry, a period in which the nature of the banking industry is changing more rapidly than at any other time in its history. The combined forces of deregulation and electronic data processing and telecommunication are changing both the nature of commercial banks and the competitive environment within which they operate. These forces have broken down the traditional barriers that both restricted the activities in which banks could engage and protected their position within the prescribed areas of activity. As a result, banks can now offer more services and higher interest rates than before; at the same time they now compete directly with a variety of other financial and nonfinancial institutions for both savings and loan customers. In addition, computer-mediated information transfer is bringing banking services into customers' homes and altering traditional mechanisms of payment. The increasingly competitive environment makes skill and efficiency in bank management more important than ever. Indeed, it is efficient management that underlies the effectiveness of commercial banks in meeting the demands of the society, and hence in stimulating the development and growth of the economy. It is essential, therefore, that bank management be prudent, safe, and profitable if it is to have a strong and adaptable banking system capable of meeting the needs of a growing society. This book reviews the management aspects of commercial banks, with special attention to the challenges presented by the ongoing changes in the financial marketplace.

As in any other type of business organization, the ultimate function of management rests upon the bank's board of directors. The board, which is elected by bank stockholders, has the ultimate responsibility for formulating bank policy and establishing the managerial framework within which such policy is to be executed. In the formulation of a sound and flexible policy, the board is assisted and guided by the bank's senior management. And since the object of this policy is the efficient utilization of commercial bank funds and the optimization of bank profits, top management's role is to provide directors with an accurate picture of the bank's goals and requirements. Bank liquidity requirements, the ability to accept risk based on capital adequacy (solvency), the bank's income performance (profitability), and an appraisal of the market's position and outlook constitute the major parts of this picture. On the basis of these considerations, the board assesses the position of the bank and establishes policy directives for funds management in the ensuing period. And as long as these policy directives, and the necessary procedures for their implementation, are in written form, they clearly delineate the nature and limits of both responsibility and authority. Once established, these policies must be periodically reviewed and adapted to changing conditions so that optimal results can be achieved.

This book was originally intended as the second edition of my earlier book *Managing Commercial Bank Funds*. However, the vast changes that have taken place in the commercial banking industry in the intervening years made necessary not only a thorough revision of large sections of the book but also the writing of several entirely new chapters. The title *Commercial Banking in an Era of Deregulation* reflects these changes. Like the earlier work, this book has been written with the objective of providing professionals and students alike with a description and an analysis of the problems faced in the management of banks. In principle the problems bank managers face can be easily identified and rationally considered. In practice, however, solutions are anything but watertight. Indeed, in the real world in which the banker operates, application of the relative principles discussed in this book becomes an exercise in informed judgment. The principles presented therefore must be viewed as the guidelines that will assist the banker in the systematic evaluation of the relevant facts. This book does not provide the final answers, which vary among banks, and even for the same bank over a period of time.

From an organizational standpoint the material is divided into four parts. Part I provides an overview of the U.S. commercial banking system and the financial environment in which banks operate.

Part II deals with the sources of bank funds, and Part III with the policy objectives in the employment of bank funds. Part IV examines the uses of bank funds and describes the character of bank assets. Because of the quasi-public character of commercial banking, pertinent laws and actions by regulatory bodies are given due consideration throughout the book.

In the preparation of this book, I received important help and advice from a number of individuals. I am particularly indebted to my colleagues professors A. Prakash and R. Daigler for their helpful comments and suggestions on specific points in the manuscript. Special debt is also due to Ms. Caroline Ciancutti, instructor in English at Florida International University, Miami, for her valuable editorial assistance. The author would also like to express his appreciation to the many finance students at Florida International University who offered helpful suggestions in the preparation of this book.

Finally, I am deeply indebted to my wife, Sophie, for her unfailing patience and support.

CONTENTS

LIST OF TABLES AND FIGURES

1
SCOPE OF
COMMERCIAL BANKING

GF

'The U.S. financial system includes a variety of financial institutions, the oldest of which are the commercial banks. The first modern type of bank was chartered in 1781 at Philadelphia, and many of those established in the nineteenth century are still in operation. Perhaps because of this head start on other intermediaries, banks have grown to be by far the most important intermediary. Indeed, with assets in excess of $1.5 trillion, banks constitute the largest type of U.S. financial institution. But commercial banks are important also in terms of employment. With over 1.5 million employees, they are among the country's largest employers. Banks perform a variety of functions. Although lending and investing have been the epicenter of commercial banking, the last few years have witnessed a general surge in bank services. This surge reflected the expansion of both the types and the volume of services that banks extend to the communities or markets served. This surge has been induced in part by government regulation, but most importantly by competitive pressures. This chapter describes the major functions performed by banks and reviews some salient features of bank financial statements.

FUNCTIONS OF COMMERCIAL BANKS

GF

Commercial banks perform many functions, some central to their main role in the economy and others more peripheral. The three main functions of commercial banks are interrelated: the creation of money, accomplished through lending and investing activities; the holding of deposits; and the provision of a mechanism for payments and transfer of funds. They all relate to the banks' critical role in the overall management of the flow of money and credit through the economy.

1

Other services are offered primarily to draw customers by providing complete money management and ancillary services through a single institution. Some of these services, such as trust management and leasing, may themselves be profitable; others may be loss leaders offered solely to attract depositors to the institution.

Money Creation

Banks are unique among financial institutions in their ability to create money.* When banks extend credit in the form of loans and investments, they create demand deposits that result in an increase in the supply of money. Banks hold almost all business deposits and the majority of individual and government deposits. Thus, although thrift institutions offer demand deposits, the banks' supremacy in this area remains unchallenged.

Money creation is performed within the framework provided by law and regulation. The process of lending and investing builds up deposits against which banks must maintain sufficient reserves to comply with the requirements of the Federal Reserve System. Ultimately, expansion in the total deposits of the banking system is dependent upon the willingness of the Federal Reserve System to permit creation of additional reserves in order to stimulate economic growth.

The ability of banks to create money in this way results in a flexible credit system that is critical to the functioning of the economy. Without the availability of this credit, much economic activity would either become impossible or would be dependent on the ability of producers to amass capital from past sales before undertaking expansion or the production of goods for future sale. The existence of such a credit mechanism allows much economic activity to be financed through loans in anticipation of repayment from future proceeds. It also obviates the need for individual businesses to maintain large working balances at all times to meet changing needs for available funds.

Beyond the needs of individual businesses or other entities for flexible credit, the banks' role in credit creation is an essential component of the Federal Reserve System's objective of controlling the

---

*The Federal Reserve's most recent definition of the supply of money in its narrowest sense, M_1, includes currency outside the Treasury, Federal Reserve banks, and the vaults of commercial banks; traveler's checks of non-bank issuers; demand deposits at all commercial banks other than those due to domestic banks, the U.S. government, and foreign banks and official institutions, less cash items in the process of collection and Federal Reserve float; and negotiable order of withdrawal (NOW) and automatic transfer service (ATS) accounts at banks and thrift institutions, credit union share-draft (CUSD) accounts, and demand deposits at mutual savings banks.

supply of money for the economy as a whole. The Federal Reserve System attempts to maintain a money policy consistent with stable prices, sound economic growth, and minimal unemployment. In this way the attempt is made to avoid both inflation (which results when increases in money supply surpass increases in production of goods and services) and deflation (which results when the money supply increases at a slower rate than production).

Payments and Transfers of Funds

An important function of banks, one that provides an invaluable service for depositors, is the provision of a mechanism of payment and transfer of funds. Transferring balances among accounts is an activity that banks perform when directed to do so—that is, upon receipt of checks issued by deposit holders. Banks provide a payments and collection mechanism primarily to attract deposits.

Efficient funds management calls for keeping as much of the funds as possible profitably invested while the minimum necessary to cover current expenses is kept liquid and available upon demand. Recent years have seen a gradual reduction in money holdings compared with the gross national product, attesting to an economywide increase in the efficiency of funds management. This increased efficiency has been made possible largely by improved technology for effecting transfers of funds, along with increased sophistication in the management of funds by both businesses and individuals.

Providing for a payments mechanism is a costly activity. Indeed, managing the payments mechanism can absorb up to a third of total bank costs. Cost items include wages for tellers and bookkeepers, computer purchase and maintenance, advertising, and substantial equipment and supply costs. A large portion of employee time is spent performing the payments mechanism function. Services charges do not cover all of these expenses; in fact, competition for customers at times when interest rates are high (meaning high yields for invested and loaned deposits) leads many banks to offer free checking services.

The procedures for effecting the actual transfers of funds are undergoing rapid change with the introduction of technological advances in the storage and transfer of information. At present transfers of funds occur primarily through clearinghouse arrangements for the exchange of checks. These are city-wide within individual cities. Transfers between cities are routed either through large banks in major cities or through regional banks of the Federal Reserve System.

However, the expansion of computerized payment systems promises to reduce the employee time and paperwork involved in transferring funds. The recent introduction of automatic teller machines

(ATMs) heralds the inauguration of computerized systems that create the possibility of electronic withdrawal of cash from one's deposit account, making deposits and loan payments, and transferring funds between accounts. ATMs have been introduced by banks in many cities. To further expand their retail services, banks throughout the country are joining forces to share their ATMs. Although no deposit taking across state lines is yet allowed, various banking groups are developing plans to link their existing networks into a nationwide network of ATM systems. Eleven multibillion-dollar banks have established a shared network named Cirrus that will link more than 4,000 ATMs throughout the country. Another, the Regional Interchange Association (RIA), is the joint effort of several networks for providing internetwork, national switching for more than 2,500 ATMs. These networks would provide 24-hour banking services on a nationwide basis, at a minimal cost to the customer.

Another related development is the trend toward in-home banking. Banks are already offering services via two-way cable television hookups through which, for example, a bill can be paid directly. In addition, the customer can transfer funds between checking and savings accounts, and make balance inquiries.

The Chemical Bank, through its in-home banking system known as Pronto (introduced in October 1982), offers its customers home budgeting, checkbook balancing, electronic messages to and from the bank as well as between customers, and electronic statements. Chemical is franchising its in-home banking to other banks, an action based on a study indicating that by 1986, 4 percent of the U.S. household market (about 3 million households) will be using in-home services. Wider use of such systems will take people out of the bank and reduce the paperwork load of the bank.

Providing Credit

The extension of credit is the central activity of a commercial bank. Not only is it the primary source of bank income, but it provides financing for productive activity throughout the economy. Virtually every phase of the manufacture and transport of industrial products benefits from the availability of commercial bank credit. The purchase of raw materials and equipment, the manufacturing process itself, and the transport of goods must all be financed in advance of the sale of the goods, and this is frequently done through bank loans. When goods are to be stored for future sale at times of high demand (such as the Christmas season for many retail products), the lag between expenditure and sales revenue is even longer and the need for credit greater.

The agricultural industry, through improved transport, processing, and storage of foods, has freed man from dependence on seasonal availability of foods and mitigated the impact of climatic and other damage to harvests. Food production is a lengthy process, in terms of the time it takes to realize a return on the agricultural investment. This industry illustrates well the role of bank credit in financing productive activity through loans against its future revenues. The farmer, the processor, the transporter, the wholesaler, and the retailer all rely on bank credit to finance their activities.

Bank loans are also used to finance growth and expansion, to start new businesses, and to pull businesses through periods of unexpected loss or reversals. Finally, banks make loans to consumers for major purchases, such as homes and automobiles. Consumer loans allow individuals to improve their standard of living in the present by borrowing against future earnings.

Many government activities are financed through bank loans and through bank purchase of bonds issued by municipalities, states, or the federal government. Short-term loans are issued to government bodies to cover cash-flow contingencies. When banks buy bond issues, they help finance government capital development in the form of construction, purchase of capital equipment, and other activities.

Depository Function

Banks are in the business of borrowing money, principally in the form of deposits; therefore they offer different kinds of deposits in a variety of forms. Commercial banks hold depositors' funds as demand, time, or savings deposits. The purposes for which funds are deposited with banks vary. One of the primary reasons for holding bank balances is to use the payment facilities of the banking system. Balances held for this purpose take the form of demand deposits. Predictable daily cash-flow needs obviously call for immediately available funds in a checking account. Because of the purpose for which they are held, balances in these accounts are referred to as transaction or working balances.

In other cases deposits are used as a reserve against contingencies. Whether maintained by individuals or businesses, these precautionary balances can take the form of demand, time or savings deposits. For example, individuals may hold balances for the possibility of an unexpected emergency, to provide for retirement, or for other, nonspecific needs. Businesses maintain such balances to offset disruptions in production caused by strikes or recession. Many companies do well in periods of prosperity, but in periods of recession their incomes decline and their capital may dissipate.

Funds may be accumulated in demand, time, or savings deposit accounts to fund future expenditures. Such funds are usually accumulated by individuals for a planned purchase of a big-ticket item or service. Businesses may accumulate funds to finance acquisition of fixed assets or a new facility.

Funds may also be deposited in commercial banks simply because the depositor chooses this form of claim over other financial assets. Some of these assets may be money-market instruments—instruments of less than one year maturity, such as commercial paper, bankers' acceptances, or government securities; other assets may be capital-market instruments—longer-term debt instruments and stocks; still others may be in the form of claims on other financial intermediaries. The choice of a bank deposit over other options is affected by a number of considerations, including the saver's expectations regarding changes in economic activity, interest-rate trends, and movements in the general level of prices. For example, in periods of recession savers might prefer bank deposits to equity and debt instruments because of declining interest rates and depressed stock market activity. By contrast, when the economy enters the recovery phase, savers might prefer stocks to deposits, in anticipation of increased stock activity.

Last, funds may be deposited with banks because of a compensating-balance requirement. Banks require businesses to carry a deposit balance with them in order to be considered for the extension of credit. After all, businesses carry a deposit balance somewhere, so why not with the lending institution?

From the bank's point of view, accumulation of deposits expands reserves, which in turn enables the bank to make loans and investments and, in the process, to create money. Clearly, banking policy must determine what portion of deposits must remain available for withdrawal upon demand and what portion can be considered reserves.

Trust Services

For a great variety of reasons, individuals or corporations may desire a reliable outside entity to administer their assets. To meet this need, and to attract large depositors, banks offer trust services. As wealth in the United States has increased, the need for trust services has grown. Management of trusts involves both investing the funds for growth and carrying out specific instructions regarding them.

Personal trust services are available through many banks, and the assets held in trust in some cases exceed those of the bank. Estate planning and serving as executor/trustee under a will are the most common forms of trust service; others include administering funds for a minor or someone judged incapable of managing his or her own financial affairs, holding securities, and collecting interest or dividend income. Ancillary services such as tax counseling and tax return preparation may also be offered.

Although corporate trust services are becoming more common, they are still offered primarily by large banks in major metropolitan areas. Management of pension funds and profit-sharing plans is a leading function in this area. Banks may administer bond issues for corporations. Besides receiving the funds from the corporation and making the necessary interest and principal payments, the bank also must ensure that the corporation meets all the obligations created through the issuing of the bond. Banks may act as stock transfer agents, maintaining stockholder records and carrying out transfers. Again, the bank assumes responsibility for the corporation's obligation, seeing to it, for example, that the stock is not overissued. A related function is the administration of corporate stock-purchase plans intended to allow one corporation to gain a controlling interest in another or to absorb it altogether. Funds are deposited with the bank, which uses them to purchase the desired shares from stockholders.

International Services

Continued growth of the international economy since World War II has contributed to an ever increasing demand for international financial services. Responding to this demand, U.S. banks have focused not only upon developing an extensive network of international banking facilities but also upon expanding the types of international services offered and increasing the volume of these services. Of the international services that U.S. banks offer, some are an extension of those they provide in the domestic market and others are unique to international banking. Among the more important services offered by U.S. banks are transfer of funds, deposit and loan activities, purchase and sale of foreign exchange, and collections. A new dimension in the role of U.S. banks in international banking is their newly authorized participation in export trading companies. These activities are described below.

One of the basic services offered by banks engaged in international banking is the transfer of funds between parties residing or traveling in different countries. This transfer can be effected in any of three ways: air mail remittance, cable remittance, or foreign drafts.

Air mail and cable remittances both involve a bank, at a customer's request, notifying its correspondent bank in a foreign country that funds are to be paid to a specified individual or firm. Upon receipt of this communication, the foreign bank verifies the authenticity of the instructions and contacts the beneficiary. After payment of the funds (in local currency), the account of the instructing bank is charged for the amount of the payment. Unlike the air mail and cable remittances, which are bank-to-bank instructions, a foreign draft is a negotiable instrument drawn by a bank on its foreign correspondent bank.

One of the most widely known and used means of transferring funds abroad has been the traveler's check. Traveler's checks are negotiable instruments of worldwide acceptability. Although few banks issue these checks, virtually every bank maintains a large inventory to accommodate the needs of its traveling customers.

Another international activity performed by U.S. banks is obtaining foreign deposits and making foreign loans. In performing this traditional function, banks always strive to acquire deposits at a minimal cost and to lend these funds out to relatively low-risk customers. The banks most active in international lending are usually those maintaining branches or other types of vehicles that ensure a presence in foreign markets. Banks having only international departments generally concentrate on financing the export and import activities of their clients. Although there are several ways of financing international trade, one of the oldest and safest ways is acceptance financing. In domestic trade shipments are usually made on an open-account basis and bank financing of accounts receivable is a generally accepted practice, but in foreign trade this is hardly practical for an exporter because of the problems it entails. To circumvent the exporter's difficulties in checking the creditworthiness of a foreign buyer, the banker's acceptance has been developed. Under this arrangement the importer's bank will substitute its own credit standing for that of its customer, accepting a time draft for the price of the goods. Upon maturity of this draft the customer pays the bank in full. This procedure works as a short-term loan, with the difference that no funds are actually advanced. In place of interest the bank charges its customer a fee for the use of the bank's credit standing.

Foreign-trade financing is but one type of international lending. Since the late 1960s international lending by U.S. commercial banks has emerged as a significant activity. Foreign loans are of different types, each requiring various credit skills. Yet foreign credits share some characteristics with the domestic. In general, foreign credits may be broadly classified into three distinct types: loans or placements to foreign banks or foreign branches of U.S. banks (interbank lending), loans to governments and official institutions, and loans to businesses (such as loans to foreign companies; to U.S. corporations' foreign branches, subsidiaries, or affiliates; project loans). New and specialized patterns continue to emerge, but the above general categories still apply.

Still another service offered by U.S. banks is foreign-exchange trading. All international business transactions, as long as they involve foreign payments, will entail the exchange of one currency for another. Since there is no single central marketplace for this exchange (equivalent to the New York Stock Exchange for bonds and stocks), trading depends upon direct communications among the parties involved. The market is thus very informal, with no official setting of rates or trading rules, and is generally guided by a code of ethics that has evolved over time. In essence, this market is not a place but, rather, a mechanism that brings together a few foreign-exchange brokers and a small group of large domestic and foreign banks that take a position or maintain an inventory in foreign currencies.

An activity closely related to foreign exchange and funds transfer is international collection. Collection is the process of presenting an item for payment to its maker or drawee. There are basically two types of collections, clean and documentary. Clean collections include such items as checks, traveler's checks, and money orders, which, sent to a foreign bank to be paid or collected, are unaccompanied by any shipping documents. Documentary collections consist of payment instructions along with shipping documents (such as invoices, bills of lading, and insurance certificates), which, routed through banking channels, require the buyer to pay or make arrangements for payment before title to the goods is relinquished. Documentary collections are especially profitable because they represent an opportunity for collecting banks to earn fees for foreign exchange, for settlement of international payments, and for handling all items promptly and properly in accordance with instructions.

A new horizon on international banking for U.S. banks is establishment or participation in export trading companies. Recently enacted legislation seems to recognize the trend of greater liberalization in U.S. international banking activities. The Export Trading Company Act of 1982 provides for the formation of export trading companies by U.S. banking institutions. Clearly, the objective of the legislation is to boost U.S. export activity. The rationale behind bank ownership of, or participation in, trading ventures is that U.S. banks are already in the business of researching foreign markets, evaluating risks, and understanding the subtleties of international finance. A number of U.S. banks are considering establishing such companies, following the precedents set in Brazil, France, Great Britain, and Japan.

Safekeeping

Banks maintain vaults and elaborate security systems to safeguard their own stores of cash, securities, and other negotiable instruments. A traditional bank service has been to make this security available to customers for the safekeeping of their valuables. These services are of two types: safe deposit boxes and safekeeping.

Safe deposit boxes are metal compartments stored within the bank vault and rented to individual customers. This arrangement gives the customer both control over access to the stored valuables and privacy. The bank protects the goods from theft or damage, and guarantees that only the customer or authorized representatives shall have access to the box. The customer's right to the privacy of the safe deposit box is guaranteed by law: the bank may open the box only by court order following the death of the boxholder.

Safekeeping, by contrast, calls for the bank to exercise custodial functions over the valuables and to act as agent for the customer. Securities such as stocks and bonds are the items most commonly held under this type of arrangement. Individuals or corporations owning large amounts of securities commonly keep them in banks. Securities pledged as loan collateral are frequently held by banks.

Leasing

Many large banks, primarily through their holding companies, are involved in the leasing of equipment to customers. Although this consists mainly of leasing transportation equipment, heavy machinery, or computers to businesses, some banks lease automobiles to individuals.

The leasing arrangement benefits both the bank and its business customers. Businesses are able to acquire the use of equipment without making the capital investment necessary to purchase it; thus they realize a financial benefit and increased flexibility. Since banks are able to obtain funds at lower interest rates than those available to their business customers, the interest component of equipment purchase is less when the bank does the buying. The lessee realizes this saving by bearing the reduced interest cost through the lease arrangement. The leasing expense is wholly tax-deductible; there is no need to calculate interest payments or depreciation schedules.

The bank, meanwhile, benefits from retaining ownership of the equipment. In case of default by the lessee, the bank can reclaim the equipment without going through the legal steps involved in foreclosing on a purchase loan.

Other Functions

Banks offer many other services in addition to those discussed above. To consumers, banks offer credit cards, Christmas Club accounts, certified checks, and traveler's checks. To their business customers, they provide credit information, account reconciliations, inventory-control accounting, billing, lockbox plans, counseling on the investment of corporate funds, and business and financial advice on a wide range of matters, including foreign markets. For example, for companies that want to develop export activity, banks provide information about quotas, duties, health regulations, legal problems, and related issues associated with selling in specific countries. They can also provide market information on incomes, tastes, and existing competition in these markets. If the business customer is interested in establishing a physical presence overseas, banks can offer advice on locating plants or even purchasing foreign companies.

Apart from their services to consumers and businesses, commercial banks cater to the needs of the government by underwriting security offerings. Some large money-center banks, acting singly or in combination, frequently underwrite federal government issues and general obligations of state and local governments. In addition, they may make a market in such securities, standing ready to buy or sell particular issues at established bid and ask quotations. These operations, although conducted by the investment department are customarily reported in specially designated accounts to distinguish them from a bank's own investment account.

To their underwriting and marketing of government securities some banks have recently added a complementary function, brokerage service. In late 1982 some major banks announced their intention to act as brokers for their customers (to buy and sell stocks, bonds, and options), offering discount rates for the service. This move came in response to stockbrokers' encroachment on traditional banking territory through the rapid growth of money-market mutual funds. The latter, which are not subject to government ceilings on the interest they can offer the customer, have drawn savings dollars away from banks. The decision of some banks and bank holding companies to engage in brokerage services was an attempt to gain a competitive advantage by offering a complete range of financial services. Such was, for example, the case with Bankamerica Corporation, the holding company of Bank of America, which acquired Charles Schwab Corporation, and of Security Pacific Bank, which acquired the Boston firm Fidelity Brokerage Service, Inc.

Some of the services discussed above are provided by banks directly, while others are offered indirectly, through holding company subsidiaries and affiliates that enable banks to enter product and geographic markets from which they are barred by laws and regulations. Banks have used these vehicles to provide their customers with data-processing services, courier services, travel services, factoring, mortgage banking, and management consulting. In early 1984, banks devised still another vehicle for expanding the scope of services offered to their customers. The Chemical Bank, for example, announced plans to rent the lobby space of some of its branches to one of the nation's largest marketers of real-estate and other tax-shelter investments. In a similar move, the Bank of America rented branch space to an insurance company. Other banks are expected to follow the lead of these institutions and expand the scope of their services without running afoul of the law.

Even more significant are the services that banks offer abroad, where they are permitted a much wider scope of activity. Thus, through foreign subsidiaries and affiliates, banks engage in stock brokerage, direct equity investments, commodity trading, insurance operations, underwriting or private placement of public and private issues, and an array of other services that, though prohibited in the United States, are permissible in foreign countries.

BANK FINANCIAL STATEMENTS

Many of the commercial banking functions discussed above are reflected in a bank's report of condition (balance sheet). However, since size is an important determinant of the magnitude and variety of functions performed by a bank, rather than review the individual asset and liability items of a single bank, it becomes more meaningful if such examination is based upon an aggregate, all-inclusive balance sheet, such as the one presented in Table 1.1, which identifies the magnitude and scope of activities of all insured commercial banks in the United States. Since many of these activities are income-generating, no balance-sheet analysis can be complete without a corresponding review of the aggregate income statement. Brief explanation of the various items included in both statements will contribute to better understanding of the U.S. banking system and will highlight much of the material presented in the following chapters. The following sections thus provide a brief description of the various items in the balance sheet and income statement of all banks by referring to 1981 data for U.S. insured commercial banks.

Table 1.1. Aggregate Balance Sheet of All Insured Commercial Banks,*
December 31, 1981

Item	Amount (millions of dollars)	Percent of Total
ASSETS		
Cash and due from banks	$ 197,110	11.7
Cash items in process of collection	79,092	4.7
Currency and coin	18,714	1.1
Demand balances with domestic banks	36,333	2.2
Other balances with depository institutions in the U.S. and with banks in foreign countries	37,726	2.2
Balances with Federal Reserve banks	25,245	1.5
Securities	341,801	20.2
U.S. Treasury	103,382	6.1
Obligations of U.S. government agencies	69,101	4.1
Obligations of states and political subdivisions	151,182	9.0
All other securities	18,136	1.1
Federal funds sold and securities purchased under agreements to resell	90,664	5.4
Loans, net	901,226	53.3
Plus: Allowance for loan losses	11,118	.7
Unearned income on loans	19,322	1.1
Loans, gross	931,666	55.1
Commercial and industrial	329,533	19.5
Real estate	283,523	16.8
Consumer	186,789	7.8
All other loans	131,821	11.1
Lease-financing receivables	13,127	.8
Bank premises and other real estate	31,555	1.9
All other assets	114,233	6.8
Total	$1,689,718	100.0
LIABILITIES		
Business and personal deposits	$1,125,518	66.6
Government deposits	85,541	5.1
All other deposits	65,419	3.9
Total deposits	1,276,478	75.5
Demand	384,952	22.8
Savings	223,743	13.2
Time	667,783	39.5
Federal funds purchased and securities sold under agreements to repurchase	163,501	9.7
Other liabilities	125,229	7.4

Table 1.1. Continued

Item	Amount (millions of dollars)	Percent of Total
Subordinated notes and debentures	6,222	.4
Equity capital	118,306	7.0
Total	$1,689,718	100.0
MEMORANDA		
Number of full-time-equivalent employees at end of period	1,505,888	
Number of banks	14,415	

*Data do not include domestic branches of foreign banks and foreign branches of domestic banks.

Note: Details may not add to totals due to rounding.

Source: Federal Deposit Insurance Corporation, *Statistics on Banking* (Washington, D.C.: FDIC, 1981), pp. 34-36.

Balance Sheet Items

As shown in Table 1.1, the assets, liabilities, and capital of all insured commercial banks are composed of many categories, each of which encompasses subcategories.

The first component of the combined balance sheet for all insured commercial banks is "cash and due from banks," which at the close of 1981 amounted to $197 billion, 11.7 percent of total assets. This category, also referred to as "cash assets," is the most liquid of the assets held and goes to meet banks' working and legal reserve requirements. It includes checks that are drawn on other banks and are in the process of being presented to those banks for payment. As indicated earlier, in connection with the payments mechanism, these checks may be cleared through a local clearinghouse, a correspondent bank, or the district Federal Reserve bank. Increasing use of electronic transfer will significantly reduce the number of checks in process of collection. Other items considered as cash assets are coins and currency kept in the vault to meet the needs of depositors, demand balances kept with domestic correspondent banks, other balances with U.S. depository institutions and foreign correspondent banks, and balances that the law requires banks to maintain at the district Federal Reserve bank.

"Securities" is the next category of items, and the second major class of assets after loans. It includes both debt instruments and stocks. As implied by the term, debt instruments are evidences of indebtedness issued by borrowers and acquired by banks either at the time of issue or later, by purchasing them from other investors. Because of the variety of borrowers and their differing needs, a bank's investment portfolio contains debt issues that differ by issuer, maturity, stated rate of interest, and marketability. Debt issues are generally classified, according to obligor, into obligations issued by the U.S. Treasury, federal agencies, state and local governmental units, and other.

U.S. Treasury issues are the direct debt of the U.S. government. Because these obligations are virtually free from risk of default, they are generally considered of prime quality. Federal agency issues include the obligations of a number of agencies, such as the Federal National Mortgage Association (FNMA or Fannie Mae), the Federal Home Loan Mortgage Corporation (The Mortgage Corporation or Freddie Mac), the Federal Home Loan Bank, the Federal Land Bank, and other farm credit agencies. State and local obligations, often called municipals, account for the largest portion of commercial bank investment portfolios. Their major attraction is that the interest is exempt from federal income tax. This is especially important for commercial banks, which have relatively high marginal tax brackets compared with other financial intermediaries (such as pension funds and thrift institutions). The item "all other securities" includes obligations of domestic corporations, foreign governments, international institutions (such as issues of the International Bank for Reconstruction and Development), and foreign corporations. Also part of "all other securities" are bank holdings of stock. When a bank joins the Federal Reserve System, it is required to purchase stock in its district Federal Reserve bank in an amount determined by its capital. Other stock holdings include shares in subsidiary corporations (such as safe deposit companies and affiliated banks) and shares acquired as a result of borrower default on a loan for which those shares served as collateral. In the latter instance the stocks must be disposed of within a reasonable time.

Another component of the "all other securities" category is trading-account securities. Securities held in trading accounts are customarily those federal and municipal securities (general obligations) that large money-center banks underwrite; issues in which banks make a market—that is, they stand ready to buy or sell at established bid and ask quotations; and various securities that banks buy and sell in a nondealer capacity.

"Federal funds sold and securities purchased under agreements to resell" involve very short-term loans of funds to other banks and security dealers. A bank sells federal funds when it lends another bank its excess reserves on deposit with the Federal Reserve bank. Except for weekends and holidays, a federal funds transaction is normally for one day, which means that a bank experiencing an unexpected outflow of deposits may enter the market on an overnight basis to adjust its reserve position. A similar transaction is the lending of federal funds to other banks and U.S. government security dealers through the purchase of securities under a repurchase agreement. Under this agreement the seller (borrower) makes a commitment to repurchase these securities on a particular future data for a specified sum. The repurchase agreement thus makes the entire transaction functionally equivalent to collateralized borrowing.

"Loans" is the largest category of assets held by commercial banks and the main source of their income. Although loans may be classified in a number of ways (by security, by maturity, by repayment), their most commonly employed classification is by type of borrower or purpose for which the funds are used. The largest and most important type of loan is loans to businesses or, according to banking terminology, commercial and industrial loans. These loans are predominantly short-term, although in recent decades banks have been increasingly extending intermediate-term credit. The second largest type of loan is real estate mortgages: on residences, farmland, and large multifamily, commercial, and industrial properties. Next in importance are consumer loans, which include credit to households for various purposes. Finally, banks hold a variety of miscellaneous loans, among which are loans to financial institutions, farmers, and individuals or firms purchasing or carrying securities. Two accounts customarily reported with loans are "allowance for loan losses" and "unearned income on loans." The former reflects the amount of reserves set aside for possible loan losses; the latter, the unearned interest on loans that were recorded on the banks' books in amounts including such interest. Eventually, as interest is earned, appropriate transfers are made out of this account and into the current income.

"Lease-financing receivables" reflects the size of the banks' direct lease-financing activity (banks usually engage in lease financing indirectly through leasing subsidiaries).

"Bank premises and other real estate" represents the depreciated value of the bank building, furniture, fixtures, and equipment used in the conduct of the banking business. Although many banks own their building and equipment and depreciate them over time, some banks—especially those in bigger cities—prefer to lease part or all of the fixed assets they use. Bank ownership of "other real estate" may represent property that was foreclosed to protect against greater losses on bad real estate loans. In other instances it may represent purchases of property that was intended to become a bank's new site or to open a branch or otherwise to expand operations (for instance, to establish drive-in facilities). Sometimes a bank's ownership of real estate may take the form of shares in subsidiaries formed to hold titles to the bank's premises, parking lot, and other real estate, in which case such ownership would be reported under "securities."

Banks providing international banking services usually include in their balance sheet the item "customer liability on acceptances." This represents claims of banks against their customers arising from bank acceptance of drafts and bills of exchange, generally issued in connection with foreign trade. Lack of individual reference to this item in Table 1.1 implies that it has been incorporated in the "all other assets" category. This is a catchall category found on any balance sheet, and covers assets that defy classification in any of the groups mentioned above. Typically it includes such items as prepaid expenses and accrued items.

On the liability side of the balance sheet, the largest item is "total deposits" or just "deposits." Deposits are accounts representing the different forms through which funds are placed with a bank. They are customarily listed by ownership and by type. In terms of ownership, "business and personal deposits" constitutes the largest category of deposits (it is also referred to as deposits of individuals, partnerships, and corporations [or IPC deposits]). "Government deposits" are deposits held by the U.S. government, states, and political subdivisions for the carrying on of their activities. "All other deposits" include domestic interbank demand deposits, held mainly for check-clearing purposes; foreign government deposits, which are maintained for the purpose of facilitating the financial transactions of foreign governments with domestic entities; and foreign bank deposits, which are used by foreign banks in their customary international department transactions.

In terms of type, deposits are classified into demand, savings, and time deposits. Demand deposits are deposits that may be drawn upon or transferred at any time, without prior notice. Since withdrawals or transfers are usually effected by check, these deposits are also referred to as checking accounts. This type of account is customarily sought by depositors who wish to maintain an account for transaction purposes. Savings deposits, also known as passbook savings, legally require the depositor to give the bank at least 30 days' notice prior to any withdrawal, although banks hardly enforce this requirement.

Time deposits, as the name implies, are funds left with the bank for a specified period of time. Banks offer a range of time-deposit accounts to individuals, businesses, and governments. One popular form of time deposit is the certificate of deposit (CD), which derives its name from the fact that it is evidenced by a certificate. These CDs, especially the larger negotiable ones (over $100,000), have become an important part of the U.S. financial system in recent years.

"Federal funds purchased and securities sold under agreements to repurchase" is the reverse of "federal funds sold and securities purchased under agreements to resell." This item represents borrowing to cover a reserve deficiency or to acquire additional funds to lend. Its size is always larger than its counterpart on the asset side, because bank borrowing may be done not only from other banks but also from securities brokers and dealers, and from corporations that possess temporarily idle funds.

"Other liabilities" consists of a number of items that, for the purpose of our analysis, may be distinguished into two subgroups: "other borrowings" and "all other liabilities." "Other borrowings" reflects funds borrowed by banks for short periods from such nondeposit sources as the Federal Reserve discount window, a bank's overseas branch network (Eurodollar borrowings), and commercial paper (short-term, unsecured promissory notes). "All other liabilities" represents such diverse items as taxes and other expenses that, though incurred before the end of the accounting period, have not yet been paid. As these items are paid, new accruals replace them.

In recent years banks have been raising funds by relying increasingly upon the issuance of subordinated notes and debentures. These are intermediate- or long-term debt instruments subordinate in priority of payment to payment in full of all deposit and nondeposit liabilities. These issues may be utilized as a normal means of raising capital. "Equity capital" is a composite of the following capital accounts: preferred stock, common stock, surplus, undivided profits, reserves for contingencies, and other capital reserves. The sum of these items, excluding preferred stock (if any), is significant to a bank's common stockholders. This figure, divided by the number of shares of stock outstanding, gives the book value of each share, which relates to the price at which shares may be bought or sold.

Income Statement Items

In performing their various functions, banks generate revenues and incur expenses. Over time, the flows of these revenues and expenses determine the profitability of bank operations and the rate of return on capital accounts. Just as with any other business, so with a bank: unless it is profitable and provides a reasonable return on capital, it will be unable to continue as a going concern. Hence the importance of income statements in appraising the financial position of banks. Table 1.2 identifies the income and expense items of all insured commercial banks, and the profitability of their operations throughout 1981.

The single largest source of operating income for banks is interest and fees on loans. Indeed, as Table 1.2 shows, interest on loans provides two-thirds of the gross income for insured banks. The relative importance of this source is generally attributed to the large volume of loans made by banks, and the rates charged, which in the course of the last few years have reached all-time highs. Another source of income is interest on balances with banks, which is essentially interest on loans. This income is derived primarily from the redepositing (placement) of Eurodollars with other banks. This item is of importance especially to large banks that have international operations. Income on federal funds sold and securities purchased under agreements to resell is realized from the lending of excess reserves and the purchase of securities under resale agreement. Since both transactions technically involve the lending of bank funds, here too the income earned is basically interest on loans.

Investment income is the second most important source of income for banks. Interest from U.S. government, state, and local obligations accounts for most of the banks' investment income. Clearly, the total amount of income derived from investments at any one time depends upon such factors as size of the investment portfolio, security mix, and rates of return on the various types of issues. "Income from direct lease financing" identifies the amount of income that banks realized from their involvement in the leasing business. Because of the growing popularity of this form of financing, the importance of this source of income should increase significantly in the years ahead. Another source of earnings is income from fiduciary activities—that is, from the banks' trust operations. Trust department income is most significant to large banks because of the sizable amounts of trust assets they hold.

Service charges on deposit accounts are imposed by banks on demand deposits to cover the cost of handling these accounts. The faster growth of time and savings deposits, as against demand deposits, and the trend toward lower or no service charges by banks in competing for demand deposits, have generally contributed to a reduction in the importance of this source of income. Other service charges,

Table 1.2. Aggregate Income Statement of All Insured Commercial Banks, 1981

Item	Amount (millions of dollars)	Percent of Total
OPERATING INCOME		
Interest and fees on loans	$163,510	65.7
Interest on balances with banks	24,297	9.8
Income on federal funds sold and securities purchased under agreements to resell	12,270	4.9
Interest on U.S. Treasury securities and on obligations of other U.S. government agencies and corporations	18,107	7.3
Interest on obligations of states and political subdivisions	9,704	3.9
Income from all other securities	1,639	.7
Income from direct lease financing	1,746	.7
Income from fiduciary activities	3,179	1.3
Service charges on deposit accounts	3,920	1.6
Other service charges, commissions, and fees	5,308	2.1
Other income	5,119	2.1
Total	$248,800	100.0
OPERATING EXPENSES		
Salaries and employeee benefits	$ 28,044	11.3
Interest on time certificates of deposit of $100,000 or more issued by domestic offices	39,301	15.8
Interest on deposits in foreign offices	46,696	18.8
Interest on other deposits	53,450	21.5
Expense of federal funds purchased and securities sold under agreements to repurchase	23,879	9.6
Interest on other borrowed money	5,904	2.4
Interest on subordinated notes and debentures	617	.2
Net occupancy expense	8,598	3.5
Provision for loan losses	5,069	2.0
Other expenses	17,018	6.8
Total	$228,576	91.9
Income before income taxes and securities gains or losses	$ 20,224	
Applicable income taxes	4,624	

Table 1.2. Continued

Item	Amount (millions of dollars)	Percent of Total
Income before securities gains or losses	15,600	
Securities gains or losses, gross	−1,583	
Applicable income taxes	−726	
Securities gains or losses, net	−857	
Income before extraordinary items	14,744	
Extraordinary items, gross	68	
Applicable income taxes	12	
Extraordinary items, net	55	
Net income	$ 14,799	

MEMORANDA
Number of banks and full-time-equivalent
employees same as reported in Table 1.1

Note: Details may not add to totals due to rounding.
Source: Federal Deposit Insurance Corporation, *Statistics on Banking* (Washington, D.C.: FDIC, 1981), pp. 75-76.

commissions, and fees are a diverse source of income. This broad category includes commissions, charges, and fees associated with collection of checks, promissory notes, and other matured items; sale of bank drafts; acceptance of bills of exchange; servicing real estate mortgages; data-processing services; safe deposit boxes; and loan commitments. "Other income" is a catchall category for all other sources of operating income not specifically mentioned elsewhere, such as income from securities held in trading accounts.

On the expense side, "salaries and employee benefits" refers to payment of salaries, wages, and fringe benefits by banks. This item constitutes the second largest category of bank expenses after interest on deposits. As Table 1.2 indicates, the largest source of bank expenses by far is interest on deposits, accounting overall for 56 percent of the operating income of all insured commercial banks. The size of this expense reflects the higher rates that banks have been paying to attract funds, especially time deposits.

As banks obtain funds from sources other than deposits, several interest expense items figure prominently in their income statement. The item "expense of federal funds purchased and securities sold under agreements to repurchase" represents the interest expense that banks sustained in purchasing federal funds and selling securities under repurchase agreements. "Interest on other borrowed money" comprises the amounts of interest paid by banks for short-term borrowing from the Federal Reserve discount window, a correspondent bank, or the Eurodollar market, or by issuing their own commercial paper. "Interest on subordinated notes and debentures" is the interest that banks paid to holders of their notes and debentures. "Net occupancy expense" includes depreciation of furniture, fixtures, office machines and equipment, rental expenses, maintenance and repairs, and related items. "Provision for loan losses" is self-explanatory. "Other expenses" include items not elsewhere classified, such as cost of the examinations conducted by supervisory agents, premiums to the Federal Deposit Insurance Corporation for the insurance of deposits, other insurance premiums (for risks associated with the nature of the banking business), office supplies, and advertising.

"Income before income taxes" is arrived at by deducting operating expenses from operating income. Banks—like all other business corporations—are profit-oriented institutions, and thereby are subject to federal income taxes. The resulting after-tax income, adjusted for losses from securities transactions and for extraordinary income, determines net income, which, as shown in Table 1.2, amounted to $14.8 billion, 5.9 percent of operating income. Banks usually distribute part of their net income as dividends and retain the remainder.

SUGGESTED REFERENCES

Auerbach, Robert D. *Money, Banking and Financial Markets*. New York: Macmillan, 1982.

Nadler, Paul S. *Commercial Banking in the Economy*. 2nd ed. New York: Random House, 1973.

Robinson, Roland I., and Dwayne Wrightsman. *Financial Markets: The Accumulation and Allocation of Wealth*. 2nd ed. New York: McGraw-Hill, 1980.

Rose, Peter S. *Money and Capital Markets: The Financial System in the Economy*. Plano, Tex.: Business Publications, 1983.

Roussakis, Emmanuel N., ed. *International Banking: Principles and Practices*. New York: Praeger Publishers, 1983.

The present structure of the U.S. banking system has been shaped by historical forces and the needs of the economy. In addition, banking functions within a regulatory framework that is in part a direct response to these forces and in part a reflection of the U.S. political system. This chapter will review the history of banking in the United States and examine some of the salient features of the U.S. banking system. We will review how legal and historical developments have influenced the chartering of banks and discuss conditions for entry into the banking industry. Our discussion will highlight the number and relative size of banks in the industry and examine the development of correspondent banking, through which banks maintain reciprocal relations with banks in other cities.

Although the diverse vehicles through which banks may expand, and hence change their organizational form, are features of the banking industry, they are discussed in Chapter 3. The transitional state of these organizational forms and the changing competitive environment in which banks operate warrant treating them separately. Chapter 3 also examines the scope and structure of bank regulation.

We will begin our discussion by looking into the historical background of the U.S. banking industry.

U.S. COMMERCIAL BANKING: ITS ORIGINS AND DEVELOPMENT

Early History of Banking

Though moneylending and money changing are very old activities (there are records of loans by Babylonian temples as early as 2000 B.C.), the early beginnings of commercial banking may be traced to the growth of Italian coastal cities as maritime powers and the rise of Italian merchant banking houses that dominated high finance from the twelfth through the fifteenth centuries. These family-owned and -managed firms are generally viewed as the direct ancestors of modern commercial banks. Italian banking houses accepted deposits; financed foreign trade; made a market in foreign exchange; met the short- and medium-term credit needs of entrepreneurs, rulers, noblemen, and the clergy; and invested in industrial and commercial ventures.

From the sixteenth century on, as the winds of economic prosperity moved from one European country to the other, so did the development and growth of commercial banking activity. The discovery by the Portuguese of the trading routes to the Indies and the opening of the markets of southern Asia brought a shift in European trading patterns from the Mediterranean to the Atlantic seaboard. This shift led to the rise of Antwerp, and subsequently of Amsterdam, as important financial centers that contributed further to the development of banking. The history of international trade reveals that the center of commerce never stayed long in one place. Thus, in the early eighteenth century Great Britain, which had begun to flourish through the growth of large-scale industry and capitalistic enterprise, started challenging Holland for economic leadership of the world, and sometime during the second half of that century, London emerged as the financial and banking center of the world. This development was of no little consequence in the evolution of banking activity. In fact, it was in Great Britain that the term "commercial" bank came into wide usage because of the general belief that banks accepting demand liabilities should limit their lending to highly liquid, short-term commercial loans.

Banking During the Colonial Period

As Western European nations were transforming themselves from agrarian societies into complex economies with thriving industry and commerce, colonial America was experiencing financial stringency as a result of a severe shortage of money in circulation. Much of the gold and silver coinage brought by the early settlers gradually found its way back to Europe in payment for imports. The shortage of money became so severe that barter transactions were quite common. Thus, in 1618 tobacco became a legal tender in Virginia, and in 1641, corn in Massachusetts.*

---

*In Virginia during the administration of Governor Samuel Argall, the value of tobacco was set at three shillings per pound. His administration went to great lengths to define commodities both in specie and in tobacco. The list included wine, vinegar, cider, beer, bread, butter, cheese, fish, corn, and meal—and the price of young women brought from England to become wives of local planters. Initially the price of a wife was set at 100 pounds of tobacco; as the number of wives grew scarcer, the price was raised to 150 pounds of tobacco. Any debt incurred in the purchase of a wife had precedence over all other debts.[2]

The first bank to be established in the colonies was started in Massachusetts in 1671 by Rev. John Woodbridge. A variety of problems led the bank to close shortly afterward; in reopened in 1681 as a private bank of credit.[1] This bank and several that followed it became known as land banks, which were private associations that made loans by issuing bank notes on the security of real estate. Land banks were unincorporated, were usually formed to finance specific needs, often lasted only for the lifetime of the loan, and did not accept deposits. They justified their operations on the ground that they remedied the shortage of specie from which the colonies allegedly suffered. In time many of these banks failed because of the unsound manner in which they operated and the limited liquidity of land, which constituted the security for their loans.

An important stage in the early banking history of the United States came in December 1690, when the General Court of Massachusetts empowered a committee of individuals to establish a public bank. The purpose of this bank, the first such bank in the colonies, was to provide the means to meet the expenses of the ill-fated expedition the colony had mounted against Quebec at the urging of King William III. The Provincial Bank of Massachusetts was formed and issued "bills of credit" to cover the £40,000 cost of the expedition. A large portion of this amount was to be paid to the soldiers, who were to have been paid in loot. The bills were issued in anticipation of tax revenues and promised payment in hard coins. Although initially many of these notes were called in by the payment of taxes, eventually they proved such a tempting expedient that many new issues followed, and by 1704 the policy was adopted of postponing their payment.[3] By 1713 these notes had become accepted as a medium of exchange and a store of value, thus qualifying as the first paper money to be introduced in the colonies and, for that matter, in the British Empire. From then on, it was only a matter of time before other colonies followed the Provincial Bank's example and issued their own bills of credit to fund government expenditures.

As the colonial period drew to a close, the banks in existence were both public and private, the latter consisting of land banks, merchandise banks, and specie banks, depending upon the nominal base against which notes were issued. None of these banks were commercial in nature; their only function was the issuance of notes. The original conception of banking in the United States was thus synonymous with paper-money issuance.

The Emergence and Growth of Commercial Banking Activity

The first commercial bank to be established in the United States was the Bank of North America, which was chartered by the Continental Congress in December 1781 and opened for business in Philadelphia the following month. Questions regarding the legal power of the Congress to charter a banking institution led the bank to obtain a charter from the state of Pennsylvania, and later from other states as well. Within a few years the Bank of North America was a financial success. It accepted deposits and made loans to the government and the general public. Specifically, the bank made substantial loans to the national government and the state of Pennsylvania during the closing phases of the Revolutionary War. Loans were also made to businesses to enable them to expand the scope of their operations. The bank rendered an important service by issuing a high-quality currency that was redeemable in specie on demand. In 1863 the Bank of North America joined the National Banking System, on the ground that it already had a national charter.

Shortly after the establishment of the Bank of North America, several states, including Massachusetts, New York, and Delaware, followed the example of Pennsylvania in making provisions for the state chartering of banks. As a result, within two and a half years of the opening of the Bank of North America, two state-chartered banks were formed: the Bank of Massachusetts in March 1784, and the Bank of New York in June of the same year. The lead of these early institutions was soon followed by a large number of state-chartered banks. From 1784 to 1800, for example, the number of banks in operation increased from 3 to 28, and by 1811 it had risen to 88. The size of these institutions varied, as evidenced by the amount of their capital, which ranged between $25,000 and $3,000,000.[4] They were all banks of deposit and issue, and were located predominantly in states along the Atlantic seaboard. Many of these banks were quite successful and most are still in operation, either under the original name or under a different one as a result of merger, addition of trust activities, or reincorporation under the National Banking System.

The federal government entered the bank-chartering field in 1791 with the issuance of a 20-year charter for the establishment of the Bank of the United States. The bank's creation was promoted by Alexander Hamilton, first Secretary of the Treasury, who intended this institution to have central banking powers and to function as a fiscal agent of the government. Since the bank was meant to be of national character, it opened branches in the leading cities in addition to its head office in Philadelphia. The bank was capitalized at $10 million, one-fifth of which was subscribed by the government, which thus became the bank's largest stockholder. The government raised the $2 by borrowing it from the bank and agreeing to repay it in 10 annual installments.

Although the bank was charged with a variety of duties (including such commercial banking activities as accepting deposits and making loans to individuals and businesses), its greatest contribution was regulating the amount of money in circulation and controlling inflationary pressures. This it did in its capacity as a fiscal agent of the government. As depository of the government, the bank received on deposit tax revenues, which it held for disbursement by the Treasury. Since these revenues were paid in notes of different state banks, it followed the practice of presenting these notes to the banks of issue for redemption in gold or silver. By reducing the specie that the state banks held as reserves against their notes, the bank was able to control the quantity of notes they issued. Control of the volume of bank notes in circulation restrained lending activity and eased inflationary pressures. Conversely, to create easy monetary conditions, the bank would either hold the state bank notes that it had or hand them out to its own customers.

Despite the bank's aloofness from politics and its success as a banking institution, Congress refused renewal of its charter when it expired in 1811. Criticism of the bank came from various quarters. Some critics attacked the bank on constitutional grounds by questioning the authority of Congress to issue a charter for a national bank. State banks opposed it for restricting their note issuing and controlling their freewheeling. Agricultural interests denounced it for failing to pursue a liberal extension of credit. Most detrimental, however, was the criticism of those who opposed the extent of the bank's foreign ownership, which had grown to almost three-quarters of the total stock. Although foreign investors could not vote their shares, national feeling ran high and was quite powerful in public affairs. This state of events led the officers of the bank to apply for a charter from the state of New York and thereafter to operate the bank as a state institution.

The lapse of the charter of the Bank of the United States led to a quick deterioration of economic conditions. The number of state-chartered banks increased significantly (from 88 in 1811 to 246 by 1816), contributing to a rapid increase in the amount of notes in circulation and a concomitant depreciation in the value of those notes. The War of 1812 compounded the country's economic problems by forcing most banks, except for those in New England, to suspend redemption of their notes in specie. These developments set the stage for the reestablishment, with almost unanimous support, of a national bank, which was expected to restore an orderly currency and contribute to the growth and stability of the economy. In 1816 the second Bank of the United States was established by a federal charter that ran for 20 years.

The bank had a total capital of $35 million, one-fifth of which was subscribed by the government and the remainder by the public. The bank's charter provided for essentially the same functions performed by the first bank. Despite some difficulties and significant mismanagement in its early years, it functioned soundly from 1819 on. The bank achieved great success by 1823, when Nicholas Biddle became its president. Its success was such that by 1825 it had as many as 25 branches and controlled one-third of the country's bank assets. Unfortunately, this success incurred the wrath of the same forces that had been responsible for the demise of the first bank. As a result, when a bill was enacted in 1832 to extend the bank's charter, which was due to expire in 1836, President Andrew Jackson vetoed it. The following year Jackson arranged to have all government deposits with the bank transferred to various state banks, also referred to as "pet banks." This move ended the bank's role as the fiscal agent of the government and virtually deprived it of its central banking powers. Upon expiration of its federal charter in 1836, the bank was able to secure a charter from the state of Pennsylvania and to continue in business until 1841, when it failed.

A review of the banking conditions in the pre-Civil War years reveals that the banking system, consisting of the separate state systems, was in a chaotic state. All the state systems suffered, although unequally, from defects in banking law, supervision, and practice, with conditions being especially bad in the South and West. The extent of variation of state banking systems may be demonstrated by prevailing differences in their requirements for entry into the banking business. By 1860 more than half of the states continued to cling to the practice of chartering banks by special acts of the legislature, while the rest had adopted free banking acts that permitted the chartering of banks upon compliance with certain general provisions of law. But even among the states that had passed free banking laws, there was a considerable difference in chartering requirements. For example, to protect depositors, the bank charters of some states called for a maximum ratio of bank liabilities to capital (generally between 3:1 and 5:1), while other charters made no mention of such provisions. (The practice of stipulating capital requirements was borrowed from the charter of the Bank of England.) Some state charters required specified amounts of specie reserves (gold and silver) against notes issued, but others only provided for certain types of bonds.

This general lack of uniformity among states was not limited to requirements for entry into the banking field but also extended into the relationship between banks and states. Specifically, some banks were privately owned, others were wholly owned and operated by states, while still others were owned jointly by state and private interests. Wide variation was also encountered in the responsibilities of the privately owned banks to their chartering state. In some states, for example, bank chartering was just a matter of compliance with the various provisions of the banking law. In other states, however, chartering was also conditional upon the bank's commitment to finance certain projects that the state legislature viewed as of utmost importance (canal companies, railroads, and other enterprises).

Equally chaotic during the pre-Civil War years was the country's currency condition. Although the banking system comprised both private (unincorporated) and state-chartered banks, it was only the latter that had the note-issuing privilege, and hence supplied the country with paper money. With some 1,600 state-chartered banks in operation by 1861 and each of these banks issuing its own currency in different denominations, the country had a currency mosaic. One estimate places the total number of different types of notes issued by these banks at about 10,000. Since these issues varied in size, material, and design, distinguishing the degree of protection to the note holder presented a serious problem. The issues of northeastern banks were generally of good quality, whereas many of the notes issued by western banks were of questionable value. Some shrewd promoters in the West had established banks in remote areas, rendering it virtually impossible for note holders to redeem their notes. This practice became known as wildcat banking from the fact that in the area where these institutions were located, there were more wildcats than bank customers. Apart from wildcat currency, note holders were exposed to counterfeits, notes of banks that had ceased to exist, and notes that, although issued by solvent banks, had depreciated in value. The situation became so bad that in time specialized publications, known as bank note detectors, appeared, purportedly to provide note holders with up-to-date information on the quality of the currency in circulation.

This state of the country's currency, along with the need to finance the Civil War, led to the passage of the National Bank Act of 1863. This act, repealed and superseded by a law of similar title in 1864, became the banking code of the United States until substantially replaced by the Federal Reserve Act of 1913. By providing for the granting of national charters by the office of the Comptroller of the Currency, which was set up under the Treasury Department, it marks the beginning of the National Banking System. The provision for incorporation of banks under the National Bank Act established the dual banking system, in which banks have a choice between a national and a state charter. The intention of this legislation was to form a system of national banks that, under the supervision of the federal government, would issue a safe and uniform currency to replace that of state banks; assist in the financing of the war by purchasing government bonds, which were to be used as security against their national bank notes; and provide a reliable depository for government funds. When initial hopes for bank conversions from state to national charters proved disappointing, Congress moved in 1865 to impose a 10 percent tax on any individual or bank using or paying out notes of state-chartered banks. This tax, by rendering the note-issuing privilege of state banks unprofitable, proved effective in inducing many state banks to join the National Banking System—so much so that between 1864 and 1866, the number of national banks swelled from 139 to 1,582, while that of state banks decreased from 1,089 to 297. From then on, the formation of national banks progressed rapidly, providing the country with a safe, uniform currency: the national bank notes. These notes remained in circulation until the creation of the Federal Reserve System in 1913, when they were supplanted by Federal Reserve notes. Thus, until 1913 the chartering and supervision of national banks constituted the means through which the Comptroller of the Currency controlled the amount of money.

Despite loss of the money-issuing privilege, state banks did not disappear; instead they developed as banks of deposit. Realizing that they did not have to issue notes to operate profitably, they started accepting demand deposits—merely an alternative form of obligation —which they used in the funding of their loans. National banks shared in the growth of deposit banking because of statutory limitations on their note-issuing privilege. Deposit banking grew significantly in subsequent decades, and so did the number of state banks, which benefited from essentially less stringent requirements than those for national banks. By 1890 state banks, after a strong comeback, took the lead over national banks and have maintained it.

Prior to the passage of the National Bank Act, the United States had a good number of private banks along with state-chartered banks. Many of these private banks engaged in limited commercial banking activities that were conducted from frontier mercantile stores. Their activities included accepting deposits, buying bank notes at a discount and then presenting them to the banks of issue for payment, and extending credit. Some of these private banks obtained state charters to enjoy the note-issuing privilege. The National Bank Act and the 10 percent tax levy forced many of them to join the National Banking System, and limited the activities of those that remained. Subsequent legislation further restricted the activities of private banks, and their formation is no longer feasible because of the formal chartering requirements for newly organized banks.

CONDITIONS FOR ENTRY INTO COMMERCIAL BANKING

From 1838 on, one state after another began to adopt free banking acts, which provided that charters would be issued almost automatically to any group of individuals capable of meeting certain minimum legal requirements. The chartering process instituted by these acts made entry into the banking business easy, and resulted in the establishment of thousands of commercial banks. In the 60 years between 1840 and 1900, the number of commercial banks increased from about 900 to approximately 13,000. By 1920 there were 30,000 banks in the United States, operating 1,300 branches. Much of this spectacular increase was a product of the rapid economic development experienced from the latter part of the nineteenth century on. These were years of rising productivity in agriculture and increasing efficiency in industry that propelled the United States, just before the outbreak of World War I, into the position of the world's principal economic power. These conditions were responsible for the unprecedented increase in the number of banking facilities, most of which were unit banks located in farming regions.

This expansion in the number of banks suffered important setbacks during the 1920s and early 1930s (see Figure 2.1). Mergers and, most important, failures during 1921-33 were responsible for the disappearance of about 15,000 banks and losses to depositors in excess of $2 billion. Sizable losses were also sustained by the owners of bank stock, who in addition to loss of their investment often paid voluntary assessments to meet claims of bank creditors, in an effort to avert the closing of their bank.

Available data indicate that many of the banks that failed during this period were small unit banks in the agricultural and rural regions of the country. The sharp postwar deflation of 1920-22 and the recession of 1923-24 caused a general retrenchment in economic activity that hit the agricultural sector especially hard. As a result many banks suspended operations, with the greatest number of bank failures registered in the agricultural states of the Midwest, Southeast, and the Rocky Mountains. The renewed collapse of agricultural prices in 1929-30, accentuated by severe drought, accelerated the pace of bank failures in farming areas. These failures tended to undermine further the depressed state of economic activity, precipitating a general distrust of banks and widespread panics. On March 4, 1933, declaration of a national bank holiday by President Franklin D. Roosevelt restored public confidence in banks and averted the collapse of the banking system.

Apart from the effects of recurring contractions during 1921-33, the survival of banks in agricultural and rural regions was also affected by the changing economic conditions. For example, the building of good roads and increased transportation to nearby large centers have caused population shifts and broadened existing markets, with detrimental effects on small community banks. Moreover, where the scale of local business activity increased, so did the demand for services offered by adjacent larger-city banks. The inevitable result was the failure of many small banks and the absorption of a number of them by larger institutions.

The poor performance of the banking system during the 1920s and early 1930s convinced legislators of the need to eliminate free banking and subject the activities of commercial banks to extensive government controls. As a result, near the bottom of the depression, Congress passed the Banking Act of 1933 (Glass-Steagall Act), which was followed two years later by an equally comprehensive piece of legislation, the Banking Act of 1935. Some of the key provisions of the former included the introduction of a temporary plan of federal deposit insurance; prohibition of interest payment on demand deposits and the setting of maximum interest rates on time and savings deposits (Regulation Q); subjection of branching by national banks to state legislation and on the terms applicable to state banks; and the strengthening of the control of the Federal Reserve System over diversion of commercial bank funds to speculative and investment uses.

The Banking Act of 1935 addressed issues that covered virtually every aspect of banking. For example, it provided for the organization of the Federal Deposit Insurance Corporation (FDIC) on a permanent basis and granted it supervisory authority over all insured banks that were not supervised by a federal agency (the Comptroller of the Currency or the Federal Reserve System). This meant the extension of federal regulatory standards over all state-chartered banks that did not opt for Federal Reserve membership. Other provisions of the Banking Act of 1935 changed the legal title of the Federal Reserve Board to Board of Governors of the Federal Reserve System; revised the structure and functions of the Federal Reserve System; increased the control of the Federal Reserve System over commercial banking activity; and strengthened the influence of the government over the Federal Reserve System.

As the effects of the depression began to fade and economic recovery set in, the banking structure emerged at the end of 1934 with about 15,400 banks and 3,000 branches. During the next two decades, as shown in Figure 2.1, structural changes in the banking industry were characterized by a gradual decline in the number of banks and a rapid increase in the number of branches as their operations became increasingly important. The bank attrition was essentially due to mergers, while the phenomenal expansion in branching activity was a product of various developments, the most important of which were the liberalization of state banking laws on branching, population shifts from rural areas to urban centers, movement of industry out of central cities, and growth of suburbs. The attrition did not reverse itself until James J. Saxon was appointed Comptroller of the Currency in 1961. Recognizing the stimulus that new banks would provide to competition, Saxon adopted a more liberal entry policy that resulted in the chartering of over 600 new banks. This move more than offset bank attrition through the mid-1960s and strengthened the competitive climate of the banking industry. A similar liberalization of chartering requirements by state banking authorities in the early 1970s contributed to a gradual increase in the number of banks throughout that decade. At the close of 1981 there were 14,882 chartered commercial banks in the United States, a number significantly below the number of banks in operation in 1934. However, these banks operated 40,405 branch offices, which, in order of magnitude, was greater than the number in existence in 1934.

Classification of Banks

As implied by the preceding discussion, the U.S. commercial banking system is composed mainly of banks that survived the depression. Two-thirds of present-day banks are state-chartered, and one-third hold national charters (see Figure 2.1); however, the latter hold the majority of bank assets. Although the United States still has a dual banking system, differences in the powers and responsibilities of banks, which were so pronounced in the late nineteenth century, have been greatly reduced as state banking regulations have been patterned after federal legislation. An important factor in this respect has been

Figure 2.1. Number of Banks and Branches, and Classification of Banks, 1911-82

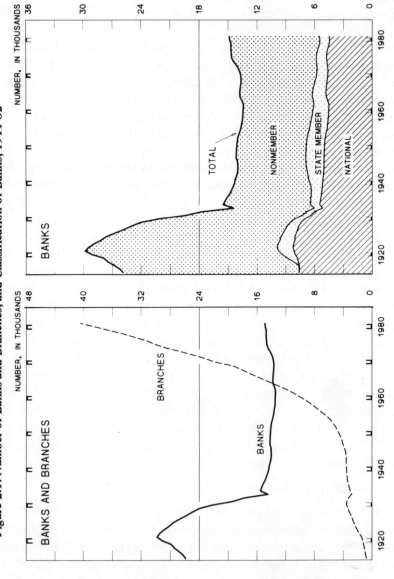

Source: Board of Governors of the Federal Reserve System, *Historical Chartbook* (Washington, D.C.: Federal Reserve System, 1982), p. 82.

the freedom of banks to switch charters from one regulatory agency to the other. This fact has exerted significant pressure toward more uniformity in bank regulation between national and state banking authorities. This point is well illustrated by an action of the Chase Manhattan Bank, one of the major U.S. banks and the largest of the state-chartered banks. In 1965 Chase, having failed to persuade the New York State legislature to revise its banking laws, decided to switch from a state to a national charter. However, a more significant factor tending toward greater standardization of banking practices among state and national banks is that virtually all commercial banks have come under federal authority through the influence of the Federal Reserve and the Federal Deposit Insurance Corporation.

This regulatory climate has accentuated the dual banking system to the point that the only area left completely to the discretion of individual states is whether, and to what extent, to permit bank branching within their jurisdiction. State regulations on this point apply to both federally and state-chartered banks.

Although the relative importance of the states in bank regulation is decreasing, the dual banking system continues to play an important role in U.S. banking. Several factors explain its durability in the face of the growing standardization of banking practices. To some extent it continues to provide a check against unduly restrictive regulation by a single authority. Also, in many states rural legislators hold disproportionate political power. They represent the interests of rural bankers, who tend to favor the status quo, and often prevail over the interests of large-city bankers who may favor change or innovation.

The distinction between state-chartered and nationally chartered banks is but one of several ways of classifying banks. They may also be classified as members or nonmembers of the Federal Reserve System. Federal Reserve membership is required for national banks but optional for state banks. State banks have the option of becoming members of the Federal Reserve System upon the approval of the Board of Governors, which considers such factors as financial history and condition of the applying bank, general character of its management, the adequacy of its capital structure and earnings, and whether its corporate powers are consistent with the purposes of the Federal Reserve Act.

An important characteristic of membership is that each member bank is required to buy stock in its regional Federal Reserve bank by paying in 3 percent of its capital stock and surplus, with another 3 percent being subject to call. Ownership of Federal Reserve bank stock entitles the member bank's stockholders to receive an annual 6 percent statutory dividend on the paid-in capital stock. Beyond this stipulated rate of return, however, member banks' rights as shareholders are subject to important limitations. For example, Federal Reserve bank stock is nontransferable; it entitles a member bank to a single vote, regardless of the number of shares owned; and voting is conducted only once every three years for the election of two of the nine directors of the district Federal Reserve bank, one of whom must be a banker (class A director) and the other a nonbanker (class B director), to represent the member bank's size class.

Until enactment of the Depository Institutions Deregulation and Monetary Control Act of 1980 (DIDMCA), a bank's decision to be a member of the Federal Reserve System was primarily influenced by reserve requirements against deposits. Although in many states the percentage reserve requirements for nonmember banks were comparable with those for Federal Reserve members, their definition of the form of reserves was generally more liberal. In many states the reserves required of nonmember banks could be in the form of correspondent balances or even of certain earning assets, such as short-term government securities. The consequence of this differential was that during the 1970s many newly formed state banks chose not to join and an increasing number of members withdrew from the system.

This development raised serious questions as to the effectiveness of the Federal Reserve's control over the monetary aggregates and led to calls for regulation. As a result, the DIDMCA extended, effective November 1980, reserve requirements to all banks, requiring them to maintain reserves against their deposits in the nonearning forms of cash and balances with the Federal Reserve bank of their district. Nonmember banks and thrifts were given an eight-year phase-in period, ending September 3, 1987, to build their reserves up to the requirements applied to members. The provision for uniform reserves has resulted in greater equity and has allowed the Federal Reserve System to implement monetary policy more effectively. At year-end 1981, Federal Reserve member banks numbered 5,474, 81 percent of which were national banks and 19 percent were state banks. These banks, though accounting for almost 37 percent of all commercial banks in the United States, held 74 percent of all bank assets.

Banks may also be classified as insured and noninsured, depending upon whether their deposits are insured by the FDIC. Membership in the FDIC is mandatory for all national banks and those state-chartered banks that are members of the Federal Reserve System. State-chartered nonmember banks interested in federal deposit insurance are also eligible to join the FDIC, as long as they are willing to subject themselves to its supervision. A bank's annual insurance premium amounts to 1/12 of 1 percent of its total deposits in return for a coverage of up to $100,000 per account. The effective cost of this insurance to the bank has been reduced by the FDIC's practice of using part of the premium as a credit against the next year's assessment. In recent years the net assessment paid by insured banks has been as low as 1/27 of 1 percent of assessable deposits. At the end of 1981, about 98 percent of all commercial banks in the United States, holding approximately 99.9 percent of total deposits, were insured by the FDIC.

Classifying U.S. banks by origin of charter, Federal Reserve membership, and insurance helps to identify their regulatory status. However, we can further enhance our understanding of the structure of the commercial banking industry by examining banks in terms of another important characteristic, size. The U.S. banking system differs from all others in that it is composed of nearly 15,000 banks. As a corollary there is enormous variation in the size of U.S. banks, with the large majority falling into the small category. This is readily apparent in Table 2.1, which categorizes all insured commercial banks according to asset size. At the close of 1981, 6,703 banks had assets of $25 million or less, whereas 392 banks had assets in excess of $500

Table 2.1. Size Distribution of Insured Commercial Banks

Asset size	Number of Banks	Assets Total per Category (billions of dollars)	Percent of Total
Less than $5.0 million	470	$ 1.7	0.1
$5.0 to 9.9 million	1,675	12.7	0.8
$10.0 to 24.9 million	4,558	76.9	4.6
$25.0 to 49.9 million	3,660	130.9	7.8
$50.0 to 99.9 million	2,186	150.2	8.9
$100.0 to 299.9 million	1,284	203.5	12.1
$300.0 to 499.9 million	190	72.5	4.3
$500.0 to 999.9 million	188	127.6	7.6
$1.0 to 4.9 billion	169	353.7	21.0
$5.0 billion or more	35	551.3	32.8
Total	14,415	$1,681.1	100.0

Note: Details may not add to totals due to rounding.
Source: Federal Deposit Insurance Corporation, *Statistics on Banking*, (Washington, D.C.: FDIC, 1981), p. 19.

Figure 2.2. Status of States According to Branching Laws, October 31, 1982

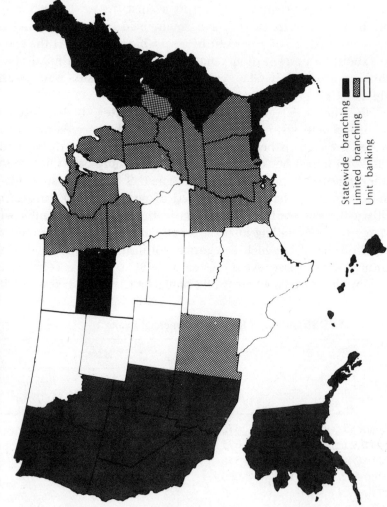

Statewide branching
Limited branching
Unit banking

Source: Prepared by author.

million. Stated differently, banks having less than $25 million in assets accounted collectively for only 5.5 percent of all bank assets, while banks having over $500 million accounted for 61.4 percent of all bank assets. This pattern of asset distribution is largely accounted for by the prevalence of unit banking, which gives rise to a proliferation of small banks. This pattern will change as more states change their laws to permit branching, for such a move will result in fewer banks with many offices. However, sentiment in favor of small locally run banks persists, for banks continue to be seen as symbols of a community's development and local pride. At the close of 1981, about 13 percent of all banking offices in the United States were single-office institutions or unit banks. By contrast, at the turn of the century 98 percent of all U.S. bank offices were unit banks. The intervening decades have seen a steady decline in the relative importance of unit banks. The states still favoring unit banking are shown in Figure 2.2. A closer look at Figure 2.2 reveals a marked regional pattern in the structure of the banking system. Unit banking predominates in the Midwest, while statewide branching is found principally on the East Coast and the West Coast. In states between the Mississippi River and the East Coast, limited branch banking is prevalent. In these states branching is limited to a relatively small geographic area, such as a town, city, or county. Unit banking, limited branch banking, and statewide branch banking are discussed in Chapter 3.

CORRESPONDENT BANKING

The correspondent banking system has been the dominant form of interbank relations for most of U.S. history, and it continues to play an important role. Correspondent banking involves a small bank's maintaining deposits with a larger bank in exchange for a variety of services. The larger bank may, in turn, have as correspondents larger banks in money-market centers. By means of this pyramidal structure banks throughout the country are linked in an informal network. The chief, but by no means only, service provided by correspondent banks is the clearing of checks. In the nineteenth century, prior to the creation of the Federal Reserve System, correspondent banking flourished because of the need for banks to maintain funds with other banks for the redemption of bank notes. Later, as maintenance of deposits became an acceptable practice, the major service performed was check clearance. Although smaller banks received services in exchange for maintaining deposits with their correspondents, in the nineteenth century the correspondents also paid interest on the deposits they held for other banks. During the 1930s the payment of interest on these deposits was prohibited; additional services replaced the interest compensation.

The National Bank Act of 1863 allowed national banks to include balances with correspondents in their required reserves. With creation of the Federal Reserve System, this practice was prohibited for member banks, although many states continued to allow it for their nonmember, state-chartered banks. Then the enactment of DIDMCA in 1980 extended the Federal Reserve System's control over reserve requirements to nonmember banks and other depository institutions, including foreign banks.

The chief function of correspondent banking has been to provide a channel for check clearing. Prior to the creation of the Federal Reserve System, virtually all checks written on one bank and deposited in another were cleared through exchanges among correspondent banks in an informal network that often involved roundabout routing of checks. Even after the Federal Reserve offered this service, many banks continued to rely on their correspondent banks for check clearing, since this channel was often considerably faster. In the early 1980s the Federal Reserve began charging for its check-clearing services, reinforcing the preference for correspondent banks.

Correspondent banking allows small banks to overcome many of the limitations imposed by their size. First, it enables small banks to offer their customers services that would otherwise be prohibitively expensive. Second, it provides direct services to the small banks themselves.

A small bank in effect purchases from its correspondent services that are too expensive for it to offer on its own. If a customer wishes a larger loan than a small bank is permitted (or considers wise) to make, the small bank may share the loan with its correspondent in an arrangement known as loan participation. Small banks may also participate in loans originated by their correspondents. In addition, the correspondent relationship makes it more economical for a small bank to extend to its customers services, such as trust management or international banking, that it lacks the expertise and funds to provide.

The correspondent bank relationship also helps small banks perform many internal functions in which economies of scale can be realized. At any particular time a small bank may have a relatively small amount of cash to place in the federal funds market or may need a small amount of funds. Trading in small volumes is expensive, however, and by going through its correspondent, the small bank can participate in this market more effectively. Banks may also loan to or borrow from each other, or buy and sell earning assets from each other. This service is especially important to banks that wish to avoid borrowing from the Federal Reserve System. In addition, the correspondent may provide management and investment counseling. It may help the small bank manage its assets and acquire capital. It may share credit information, evaluate loans, perform audits, purchase and hold securities, or, through electronic data systems, process the small bank's installment loans, deposit accounts, and other information. Some of these services are similar to those provided by a home office for its branches. However, the correspondent bank system provides the advantages of communication and pooled resources without creating a risk of overcentralization.

Maintaining a profitable correspondent bank relationship requires careful management by both parties. Payment for the services rendered by the correspondent may be through direct fee or through maintenance of compensating balances. In the latter case the level of balance required fluctuates with changes in the interest rate, since the cost of the services the correspondent bank provides must be covered by the dollars of interest the deposited funds earn for the correspondent. Alternatively, the respondent bank may receive fewer services in times of low interest rates and more services when interest rates are high.

The correspondent banking system provides an elaborate web of communication among U.S. banks. New York banks may act as correspondents to hundreds of banks in cities across the country because of New York's importance as the leading financial center of the country. Banks in other cities may have as customers many smaller banks in their region. In addition, many U.S. banks have correspondent relationships with banks in foreign countries. They maintain accounts with these banks in order to facilitate conversion of currency for their customers who travel or conduct business abroad. The correspondent bank network is thus an integral part of the U.S. banking system.

NOTES

1. Adolph Oscar Eliason, *The Rise of Commercial Banking Institutions in the United States* (New York: Burt Franklin, 1970), p. 9.

2. Herman E. Krooss, ed., *Documentary History of Banking and Currency in the United States,* 4 vols. (London and New York: Chelsea House and McGraw-Hill, 1969), II, pp. 838-39.

3. Eliason, op. cit., p. 12.

4. Krooss, op. cit., pp. 857-60.

SUGGESTED REFERENCES

Friedman, Milton, and Anna Schwartz. *A Monetary History of the United States, 1867-1960*. Princeton, N.J.: Princeton University Press, 1963.

Hammond, Bray. *Banks and Politics in America from the Revolution to the Civil War*. Princeton, N.J.: Princeton University Press, 1957.

Knight, Robert E. "Correspondent Banking. Part I, Balances and Services." *Monthly Review*, Federal Reserve Bank of Kansas City, November 1970, pp. 3-14.

————. "Correspondent Banking. Part II, Loan Participations and Fund Flows." *Monthly Review*, Federal Reserve Bank of Kansas City, December 1970, pp. 12-24.

Studenski, P., and Herman E. Krooss. *Financial History of the United States*. 2nd ed. New York: McGraw-Hill, 1963.

THE BANKING INDUSTRY IN TRANSITION

The structure of the U.S. commercial banking system is undergoing changes of unprecedented magnitude. Several factors are responsible, including changing laws and regulations and technological developments. In addition, market forces, in the form of public pressure on the demand side of the market and competition on the supply side, are altering traditional practices. Whatever the driving forces, these changes constitute a revolutionary departure from the past. They are transforming the structure of the banking industry and bringing about the integration of the U.S. financial system.

Specific aspects of this transformation will be highlighted in this chapter as we examine some key characteristics of the banking industry. We will first consider the diverse vehicles through which banks may expand, and hence change their organizational form. These vehicles include branching, merging, and group banking. Since the different aspects of banking activity are subject to regulatory control, we will also examine the structure of bank supervision and the scope and character of bank regulation. In recent years banks have been experiencing increased competition from other financial institutions. We will therefore describe the competitive environment in which banks operate and identify current developments and emerging trends in the financial services market. Last, we will review the activities of foreign banks in the United States and the various organizational forms under which they operate.

UNIT AND BRANCH BANKING

The U.S. Constitution granted powers of incorporation to the states, and each state, in turn, chartered banks that were authorized to operate within its borders. In addition, the federal government, through the office of the Comptroller of the Currency, has chartered banks in many areas. This had led to a proliferation of banks in the United States, in contrast with most countries, where only a few banks exist and are permitted to branch nationwide. Throughout much of U.S. history, branching has not been allowed in most states. Fear of banking monopoly by the large northeastern banks, some of which were branch institutions, led most states to prohibit branching —so much so that by 1910, only 12 states permitted it. As a result the vast majority of state banks were single-office institutions (unit banks).

National banks enjoyed no better status than state banks. Indeed, because the National Bank Act of 1863 did not address the branching issue, officials believed that it prohibited it. Moreover, the Federal Reserve Act of 1913 did not authorize national banks to establish branches; but it did not prohibit the state banks that joined the system from operating existing branches. It was not until 1922 that a

Table 3.1. Status of Branch Banking by State, October 31, 1982

Statewide Branch Banking	Limited Branch Banking	Unit Banking
Alaska	Alabama	Colorado
Arizona	Arkansas	Illinois
California	Georgia	Kansas
Connecticut	Indiana	Missouri
Delaware	Iowa	Montana
Dist. of Col.	Kentucky	Nebraska
Florida	Louisiana	North Dakota
Hawaii	Massachusetts	Oklahoma
Idaho	Michigan	Texas
Maine	Minnesota	Wyoming
Maryland	Mississippi	
Nevada	New Mexico	
New Hampshire	Ohio	
New Jersey	Tennessee	
New York	West Virginia	
North Carolina	Wisconsin	
Oregon		
Pennsylvania		
Rhode Island		
South Carolina		
South Dakota		
Utah		
Vermont		
Virginia		
Washington		

Source: Division of Research and Statistics, Board of Governors, Federal Reserve System.

ruling by the office of the Comptroller of the Currency led to the issuance of individual permits that allowed national banks to establish branches only within their home cities, provided state banks already operated branches in the same cities. This authorization was legalized in the McFadden Act of 1927. The collapse of the banking system in the early 1930s led to reevaluation of the prevailing anti-branching sentiment. As a result, when the McFadden Act was modified by the Banking Act of 1933, national banks were placed under the same restrictions regarding branching that governed state banks. Thus the U.S. Congress placed in the hands of state authorities determination of the branching activities of national banks. Subjecting national banks to state branching laws prevented these banks from branching widely within and across state lines.

It was not until after World War II that substantial numbers of states changed their laws to permit branching. A number of types of arrangements emerged. These fall into three broad categories: statewide branch banking (branches are permitted throughout the state); limited branch banking (some branching is permitted but only within specified geographic limits); and unit banking (branching is not permitted). The relative importance of each category is shown in Table 3.1. On October 31, 1982, 24 states and the District of Columbia permitted statewide branching, 16 states permitted limited branching, and 10 states permitted unit banking.

Unit Banking

Although branch banking continues to gain ground, one-fifth of the states still have unit banking laws. All unit-banking states allow the operation of auxiliary tellers' windows. These differ from branches in that, while branches can perform all the major banking functions, such as making loans and investments, the auxiliary teller's window can perform only the teller's function of accepting deposits and exchanging currency. There are generally restrictions, varying from one state to another, on the number of auxiliary tellers' windows allowed and how far from the bank building these may be located. For example, Oklahoma allows banks to operate auxiliary tellers' windows within 1,000 feet of the bank's main office; West Virginia sets this distance at 2,000 feet; and North Dakota goes as far as 35 miles from the main banking office.

Unit banking was well suited to the smaller, more homogeneous, and more far-flung communities characteristic of the nineteenth and early twentieth centuries. Improved transportation and communication, the growth of businesses, and the increased interdependence of communities have changed this profile. In addition, the population is now more mobile and more concerned with convenience. As a result unit banking is gradually giving way to branch banking, which better meets the needs of today's more heterogeneous and interdependent towns and cities. However, in the states where unit banking is still entrenched, a combination of tradition, vested interest, and special customer demands has kept unit-banking laws in place.

Branch Banking

As indicated by Table 3.1, most states now permit branching. The term "branch banking" is usually used when banks are permitted to branch throughout the state. Even states permitting statewide branching impose some conditions, such as capital requirements, population size, and limits on the number of branches. "Limited branch banking" refers to branching that is permitted only within narrower geographic limits. For instance, some states (such as Tennessee) allow branching only within the county in which a bank's head office is located. Other states (such as New Mexico) permit branching only within a certain distance of the home office, while others (such as Mississippi) may, in addition, place a ceiling on how many branches a bank may have. Still others (such as Georgia) use city limits as a geographic criterion to limit branching. Sometimes capital requirements, population considerations, or both are used to restrict branching. Banks vary in terms of the services their branches provide, some offering all the services the head office does. Branches have managers who direct their operations in accordance with policies set by the head office and the board of directors. Some basic functions, such as managing the reserve position and investment activity, are performed by the head office.

Arguments For and Against Branch Banking

The debate over unit versus branch banking has continued since the founding of the United States. Alexander Hamilton, one of the first to criticize branch banking, feared the weak branches might undermine the whole banking system. The most durable argument against branching has been that, by edging out small individual banks, it makes possible the emergence of banking monopolies. Small banks have supported unit banking because they have feared branch banking would place them at a competitive disadvantage. An additional argument against branch banking has been that, as parts of a larger institution serving a wider area, branches are less personal and less sensitive to the needs of individual customers and particular communities than unit banks.

Many arguments have been made in support of branch banking, most of these centering on the idea that branching allows for better management. Larger banks have more resources to invest in training. Larger staffs make possible more specialization. A second theme in the arguments for branch banking relates to asset management. Larger banks can achieve greater diversification of assets, thus spreading risks and reducing the danger of failure. A related advantage is that a large bank with branches in several areas has more sizable resources and is therefore in a better position to meet the seasonal needs of one branch or of particular localities; moreover, in case of emergency, these resources can be more rapidly mobilized to weather specific problems. In addition, branches have higher legal lending limits than unit banks, allowing them to make larger loans to customers. Finally, there are arguments regarding improved service to customers. They include that branch banks can be established in new areas more quickly than unit banks and that branches can offer services in areas that are not economically strong or active enough to support unit banks. Large banks with branches can take advantage of economies of scale and pass these savings along to their customers.

Although these debates continue, a number of regulatory and technological developments are creating a de facto predominance of branching and branchlike extensions of bank activity. For example, some states that prohibit branching by individual banks allow multibank holding companies to exist, making possible some of the advantages of branching in a nominally unit-banking system. Loan production offices represent another departure from strict unit banking that provides some of the flexibility of branch banking. These offices solicit loan customers and promote other forms of banking business for the home office. Other vehicles for expanding a bank's range of activity include traveling officers who visit major corporations in other states to solicit business; Edge Act corporations, which are allowed to cross state lines for the purpose of conducting international banking; and subsidiaries engaged in bank-related activities. All of these avenues allow banks to participate in interstate, national, and even international banking activities while conforming to unit-banking laws.

The advent of automatic teller machines (ATMs) illustrates the interplay between technological and regulatory forces. ATMs allow a bank to offer deposit-taking and check-cashing services without constructing and staffing a branch. Placing these machines across state lines is economically feasible and, where economic communities or metropolitan areas spread over state lines, desirable. However, court challenges based on the McFadden Act resulted in a decision equating ATMs with full-fledged branches, thus subjecting them to the branching laws in individual states. This action has not stopped banks from seeking to cross state lines. For example, in an effort to provide 24-hour service at minimal cost in many convenient locations, they have created interbank ATM networks. These networks represent a new challenge to the McFadden Act. Electronic transfer of funds is relatively inexpensive, it is technically feasible, and it is well suited for a banking public that values convenience. The flow of economic activity is not channeled by state boundaries, and it becomes increasingly unrealistic for banking activity to be so channeled. Because of the strength of market forces, banks anticipate further liberalization of laws governing branching and geographic extension of services. The building of ATM networks attests to this expectation. In addition, some large bank holding companies have made long-range acquisition agreements contingent on expected legal changes. Some have bought shares in bank holding companies in other states in anticipation of the possibility of closer interaction in the future. An example is Texas Commerce Bancshares of Houston, which acquired 1.5 percent of Orlando-based Sun Banks. Similarly, in late 1983 Southeast Banking Corporation in Miami and First Atlanta Corporation in Georgia announced their intention to buy just under 5 percent of each other's stock.

The momentum for nationwide banking is receiving additional impetus from the growing acceptance of the regional banking concept. Bank bills have been submitted to, or have been approved by, the legislatures of several southeastern states in an effort to promote regional banking on a reciprocal basis. This development has as its precedent the New England states, which permit banks in one state to own banks in another. The regional banking concept is also being considered by states in the Midwest and the Pacific Northwest.

In the face of these pressures, it is inevitable that legal restrictions on nationwide banking will continue to ease.

BANK MERGERS

A merger occurs when a bank ceases to exist as a distinct entity because of its acquisition by another bank. A related type of arrangement is consolidation. This term is used when a number of banks combine to form a new bank, with each of the combining banks giving up its corporate identity. Although "merger" has a technical meaning, it will be used here to mean any form of combination in which two or more banks join to form a single bank under a single management.

There is no single reason for bank mergers. In fact, a variety of factors have been responsible for bank mergers in the United States. First, the move toward branch banking has provided the impetus for mergers in which large banks create branches by merging with smaller ones. The merged bank then functions as a branch of the larger one. As both individuals and businesses have moved from the city to the suburbs, city banks have wanted to follow their customers. Merging with small suburban banks and maintaining them as branches has allowed them to do so. Second, if a bank wishes to offer a new form of service (for instance, trust services), merger may be the most expeditious way to acquire the facilities to do so. It is frequently more economical to buy a going concern with the desired area of expertise and an established market than to build such an area from scratch, recruit the necessary personnel, promote it, and operate it profitably. Third, economies of scale provide a motive for mergers. Spreading overhead costs over a larger volume of business reduces unit costs. Fourth, mergers allow banks to increase their capitalization and deposits. This is significant because legal limits on the size of loans made to one borrower are based on the size of the bank's capital (15 percent to any single borrower on an unsecured basis and, under certain conditions, an extra 10 percent on fully secured loans). With a merger the newly enlarged bank has a larger capital base and can make larger loans. Since growth in the size of businesses has increased the size of the loans they wish to negotiate, these larger maximum loan limits based on expanded capitalization are important. Finally, other factors motivating banks to merge include the urge to accelerate growth, the desire to improve earnings, and the need or desire to provide better service to existing businesses.

On the other side of the transaction, there are a number of reasons why smaller banks may find it advantageous to be absorbed by larger ones. If a bank encounters difficulty in acquiring capital it needs, or if it faces failure, merger may provide the solution. During the depression many banks consented to their takeover by strong banks in order to prevent their failure. But in times of high economic activity, too, financially weak banks may agree to acquisition in order to avoid failure. In 1981-82 the high levels and volatility of short-term interest rates presented important difficulties for banks lacking the skill to manage interest margins. Another very important reason for agreeing to be absorbed has been the problem of management. Small banks are often at a disadvantage in trying to attract highly trained and skilled management personnel. As current executives reach retirement age, merger or absorption by a larger bank may seem the best way to secure top-quality management skills. Stockholders in small banks may desire mergers in order to trade their shares for those of the larger bank, which often yield better earnings and sell for higher prices.

Although acquisition of banks has been a recurring phenomenon in the banking history of the United States, the 1950s saw a wave of mergers, almost 1,600, that aroused Congressional concern over preservation of competition in banking. This concern culminated in the Bank Merger Act of 1960, which assigned authority over bank mergers to federal banking agencies and introduced specific standards for exercising this authority. This act requires approval of the Comptroller of the Currency if the acquiring bank is a national bank, of the Board of Governors of the Federal Reserve System if the acquiring bank is a state member bank, and of the FDIC if the acquiring bank is an insured nonmember bank. In deciding on merger requests, each agency is to consider the financial history and condition of each bank involved, the convenience and needs of the community served, the character of the bank management, and the effect of merger on competition. Each agency is also required to consider the advisory opinions of the other two and of the Justice Department.

Before long it became apparent that certain provisions of the Bank Merger Act of 1960 lacked clarity or were too general. For example, the act did not assign relative weights to the individual criteria that regulatory authorities were to apply to merger applications. As a result, federal banking agencies emphasized banking factors, convenience, and community needs, whereas the Justice Department stressed competition, relying on the provisions of the Sherman Act of 1890 and the Clayton Act of 1914, the country's federal antitrust legislation. This conflict became evident in the first bank merger case to come up, that of Philadelphia National Bank and the Girard Trust Corn Exchange Bank. Their merger was opposed by the Justice Department, although it had been approved by the Comptroller of the Currency. In 1963 the Supreme Court ruled that the proposed merger violated antitrust legislation despite its approval by federal banking agencies. This case had a number of far-reaching effects. First, it stressed the overriding importance of competition over the other considerations that figure prominently in regulatory approval. Second, by using concentration ratios, it estimated the impact of the proposed merger on local competition (it identified a combined control of 36 percent of total deposits over a four-county area), rejecting the contention that these banks competed with other banks nationwide. Third, by identifying banking as a line of commerce, it concerned itself with competition within commercial banking, thus treating the services of nonbank financial institutions as not a close substitute.

Attempts to formulate a more coherent public policy for bank mergers led to enactment of the Bank Merger Act of 1966, an amendment to that of 1960. This act stated that the federal banking agencies could not approve a merger that would lessen competition or result in a monopoly, unless the anticompetitive effects were outweighed by the needs and convenience of the community. In the latter instance the burden of proof rested with the defendant banks. In addition the Justice Department was given 30 days following approval by a banking agency to contest a merger, in which case such a merger could not be consummated until a final court decision was reached on the case.

Since enactment of the 1966 law, a good number of cases have come before the courts. In all cases the courts conducted their own merger analysis without feeling bound by the opinions of the banking agencies. As might be expected, the courts' primary consideration has been the competitive effects of mergers. This stance led banks to abandon horizontal mergers (mergers between banks offering similar services in the same locality) in favor of market extension mergers, which involve banks not in direct competition with each other.

During the 1970s many of the antitrust cases brought by the Justice Department relied on a new criterion, the doctrine of potential competition. The Justice Department argued that an acquisition or a merger should be denied if either bank is a potential entrant into the other's market or a common third market. In other words, there was an attempt to assess not only the impact on the current market situation but also the likely impact on competition in the future. The obvious difficulties in making the clear forecasts necessary for such an assessment led to the rejection of this doctrine by the courts.

One of the most contested issues today is whether banking can still be viewed as a line of commerce. In the Philadelphia case, the Supreme Court interpreted the concept of commercial banking very strictly, segmenting the financial services industry into rigid categories. However justified such interpretation may have been in the early 1960s, it is far from true at the present time. In performing their basic functions, banks today compete not only with each other but also with other financial institutions. To secure time deposits, they compete for a share of the savings market with such financial institutions as savings and loan associations, mutual savings banks, and credit unions. In raising funds through negotiable certificates of deposit they compete with other participants in financial markets and, at times, even with Treasury securities. Banks also compete with other institutions in the granting of loans. Loans are of different types, each of which has different kinds of customers and hence is subjected to a different degree of institutional competition. Each of these types of loans can in itself be considered a line of commerce.

The Supreme Court's contention that banking as a whole is a separate line of commerce was undoubtedly influenced by the fact that only commercial banks produced demand deposits. However, that situation has changed. In 1976 Congress authorized all commercial banks and thrift institutions in the New England States (Maine, Vermont, New Hampshire, Massachusetts, Connecticut, and Rhode Island) to begin offering negotiable order of withdrawal (NOW) accounts. Enactment of DIDMCA authorized the offering of NOW accounts on a national scale. In addition, credit unions can now issue demand deposits through share-draft accounts.

Just as the concept of "industry" has changed dramatically over the years, so has the concept of "markets." Indeed, the evolution of the banking industry since the 1960s has rendered extremely difficult any definition of the relevant market in geographic terms. Banks are multiproduct firms, with each product having a different market, some extending beyond the geographic boundaries of the local area. Although real estate loans are typically made locally, business loans extend across regional, state, or even national boundaries. Also, consumer loans, because of national and regional mailings of credit cards, cannot be classified in their entirety as local. Similarly, large negotiable certificates of deposit may be held by distant individuals or businesses, but passbook savings depositors are usually local customers. Although banking business does not conform to geographical boundaries, competition is generally gauged by comparing a bank's assets or deposits with the total bank assets or deposits held in the area where it operates. Although concentration ratios were useful in earlier decades, when banks were more likely to serve primarily the area in which they were located, they are no longer a just measure of actual competition. The concepts of "markets" and "industry," with respect to banking, have altered dramatically in recent decades, but the Supreme Court has failed to keep up with these changes. Today's banks in fact deal in a variety of products and compete directly with other financial institutions. Any accurate measure of competition in banking must take these factors into account.

As the 1980s unfold, indications are that the number of bank mergers will increase significantly. They are an inseparable part of U.S. economic development. Since the 1960s there has been a considerable change in the business environment of most U.S. communities. Increasingly communities are served by businesses that are not locally owned. The large retail chain stores, service stations, insurance companies, manufacturing concerns, and other businesses serving the needs of these communities are owned by regional or national concerns. The emergence of larger businesses has led to a rise in corporate financing demands and an increase in the size of individual loan requests. This development and the widening scope of banking services demanded by the public are exerting important pressures on commercial banks, and will have decisive effects upon bank mergers in the years ahead.

Another factor conducive to increased mergers in the years ahead is the gradual easing of regulatory restrictions. The DIDMCA of 1980 and the Garn-St. Germain Depository Institutions Act of 1982 are two cases. These enactments have reduced regulation and expanded the operating powers of thrift institutions, blurring their traditional distinctions from commercial banks. As a result, mergers will be easier to accomplish not only among banks but also between banks and thrifts, with this process eventually extended to include all other kinds of financial institutions. Indeed, as the trend to reduced regulation continues, the competition among financial institutions will heighten. Those institutions not able to weather this challenge will likely be acquired by more successful ones. Institutions facing failure do not simply dissolve, but are absorbed in some manner by other institutions.

Anticipating these problems, the Federal Home Loan Bank Board has already eased regulations restricting mergers among savings and loan associations in order to allow thrifts to adapt to technological advances and new competitors. Although some of the mergers among thrifts occurring in 1981-82 were voluntary, a considerable number were prompted by supervisory action. These mergers, some of which were interstate, were ordered by the Federal Savings and Loan Insurance Corporation (FSLIC) because they were much less costly to it than having to function as a receiver and provide direct payoffs to insured depositors. Since these mergers involved failing institutions, they were not contested by the Justice Department. What is significant about these merger cases, however, is that until then interstate mergers among thrifts were not allowed, nor was the acquisition of thrifts by holding companies. The Garn-St. Germain Depository Institutions Act introduced an important departure by permitting the in-state and out-of-state acquisition of failing institutions in emergency situations. In essence, this legislation implicitly allows the affiliation of the two kinds of institutions—commercial banks and savings and loan associations—under a holding company. Due-process procedures are waived in these cases, permitting immediate consummation of the merger.

As the competitive climate among financial institutions improves, the merger trend will gain additional momentum, putting an end to the further compartmentalization of these institutions and paving the way for more interstate and interregional consolidations among them.

GROUP BANKING

Ownership or control of two or more banks by an individual, group of individuals, or corporation is called group banking. When an individual or a group of individuals controls (through stock ownership, common directorship, or other means) more than one bank, the term chain banking is used. A bank holding company is a corporation that owns one or more banks. These categories and their many subdivisions, as they have evolved over the years, are charted in Figure 3.1.

Chain banking first appeared in the late nineteenth century in northwestern and southern agricultural states. It developed primarily where branching and multibank holding companies were not permitted. Chain banking is usually fairly localized, involving a few small banks in a region. Often the chain includes one focal bank that is larger than the others. At times, chains may spread across state lines. The chain is built through acquisition in any legal manner of a controlling interest (ownership of 50 percent or more of common stock) in each member bank. The member banks retain their separate identities and boards of directors.

Although chain banking has been in existence for years, comprehensive statistics are few. However, it is clear that it is of small significance as a form of bank ownership. Chain banking is regulated under the Bank Control Act of 1978 (Title VI of the Financial Institutions Regulatory and Interest Rate Control Act of 1978). Any transfer of 25 percent or more of a bank's voting stock to an individual or a group of individuals acting together comes under regulatory review.

Unlike chain banking, bank holding companies are a dominant industry feature. This form of bank ownership has evolved in response to the increasingly complex competitive environment in which banks operate and to increased public demand for varied banking and financial services. In addition, bank holding companies represent a response to legislation prohibiting branching and regulations limiting growth of individual banks.

The growth of bank holding companies and the extent of their importance in the banking industry are reflected in the following

Figure 3.1. Types of Group Banking

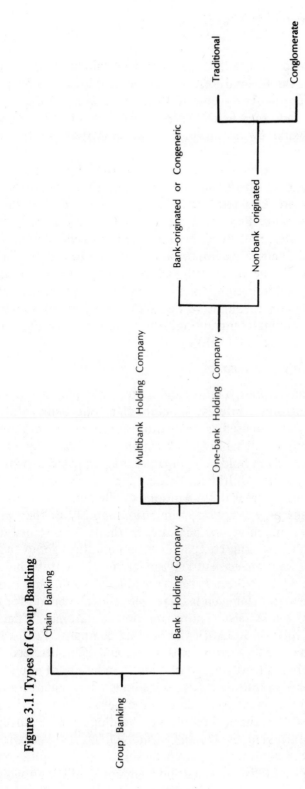

Source: Prepared by author.

55

data. At the end of 1957, there were 50 bank holding companies registered with the Federal Reserve System, and they held 7.5 percent of all bank deposits. At the end of 1981, there were 3,702 bank holding companies, and they held 99 percent of all deposits in the nation. Some of the banks owned are unit banks and others are banks with branches.

Just as in chain banking, each bank owned by a bank holding company retains its own name and its own board of directors, which is liable to the stockholders and to supervisory agencies for the functioning of the bank. Bank holding companies are generally divided into two categories: multibank holding companies and one-bank holding companies. The relative importance of each type is shown in Table 3.2. As shown in the table, although multibank holding companies trail one-bank holding companies in terms of total banking offices, they control a larger volume of deposits. The scope of activities of each type of holding company and the factors responsible for their development are discussed below.

Multibank Holding Companies

As the name implies, a multibank holding company is a company that owns controlling interest in more than one bank. Multibank holding companies are used as a substitute for branching in states that limit or prohibit branch banking. For example, in Texas, where branching is prohibited, bank holding companies are permitted to own banks throughout the state. Multibank holding companies vary in terms of how tightly they control the operations of the banks they own. The individual banks may function quite autonomously or they may be run from above, much as branches are. In the latter instance subsidiary banks enable holding companies to extend throughout the state a full array of specialized banking services (such as trust and international services) that these banks individually would find economically prohibitive to offer even if there were a local demand for them.

Subsidiary banks also enjoy certain operational efficiencies through their relationship with the holding company. For example, subsidiary banks benefit from centralized and computerized bookkeeping, auditing, advertising, marketing, purchasing of supplies, research, personnel recruitment, group insurance, retirement programs, tax guidance, investment counseling, and other advisory services. The economies of scale realized through their holding company affiliation could not be attained by the banks individually. Subsidiaries also benefit from the holding company's better access to capital markets for the raising of funds. As small independent banks they would be

Table 3.2. Banking Offices, Assets, and Deposits of Banks in Holding Company Groups: December 31, 1981

	Number of Bank Holding Companies	*Banking Offices*			*Amounts (billions of dollars)*	
		Banks	*Branches*	*Total*	*Assets*	*Deposits*
Multibank	511	2,607	14,746	17,353	$ 886.1	$ 669.0
One-bank	3,191	3,082	14,328	17,410	756.1	587.3
Total	3,702	5,689	29,074	34,763	$1,642.2	$1,256.3
All commercial banks		14,882	40,405	55,287	$1,675.5	$1,264.3
Holding company banks as a percent of all banks		38.2%	72.0%	62.9%	98.0%	99.4%

Source: Board of Governors, Federal Reserve System.

57

unlikely to receive a quality rating for their security issues. Moreover, holding companies facilitate mobility of funds through loan participations among members of the organization. In this way returns on the aggregate loans of the system are maximized. In addition, the returns on bank assets can be spread over all members of the holding company.

Although multibank holding companies date from the turn of the century, it was in the mid-1950s that federal legislation was enacted to regulate them. This legislation was prompted by the activities of a West Coast multibank holding company, the Transamerica Corporation. As early as 1948, the Board of Governors of the Federal Reserve System initiated antitrust proceedings against Transamerica, which controlled the Bank of America in addition to 46 other banks in a five-state area (Arizona, California, Nevada, Oregon, and Washington). When the court ruled in favor of Transamerica (instructing it to divest itself only of its Bank of America stock and allowing it to expand into other states), public pressure for regulation began to mount.

This pressure culminated in the Bank Holding Company Act of 1956, which provided for the registration of all multibank holding companies with the Federal Reserve Board and gave these companies the option of divesting themselves of all their nonbanking business or of all their banking business. Board approval is required prior to the formation of a bank holding company. It is also required for mergers among bank holding companies and for a company's acquisition of over 5 percent of the voting stock in a bank. In evaluating any of these actions, the Federal Reserve Board is required by law to consider the financial history and condition of the company or companies and the banks involved; the convenience, needs, and welfare of the community; and the degree of economic competition and concentration. Since the Bank Merger Act of 1966, with its emphasis on the competitive climate, this consideration has been of primary importance in evaluations of the acquisition requests of bank holding companies.

A provision of the Bank Holding Company Act of 1956 states that bank holding companies may not acquire banks outside of their home states without the permission of the state in which they propose to make the acquisition. Since at that time no states had laws authorizing this practice, the act thus both prevented expansion of bank holding companies across state lines and protected each state's banking community from incursions by companies from other states.

There is wide variation in the size and geographic spread of bank holding companies. Aggregate total assets range from under $100 million to over $1 billion. In terms of assets held, the largest multibank holding company in the country, with assets in excess of $128 billion in 1982, is Citicorp of New York, owner of Citibank. In terms of geographic area served, the largest is the First Interstate Bankcorporation of Los Angeles (formerly Western Bankcorporation), which succeeded Transamerica Corporation in holding this distinction. By the end of 1982, First Interstate Bankcorporation had assets of $39 billion and operated 22 banks in 11 western states, with 900 branches and several hundred ATMs. The latter represent the beginnings of a proposed nationwide ATM network. In addition, First Interstate Bankcorporation intends to sell its services nationwide through franchises bearing its name. The first bank to adopt this arrangement was the First National Bank of Golden, Colorado, now known as the First Interstate Bank of Golden.

The Bank Holding Company Act of 1956 was intended to regulate the growth of multibank holding companies. The language of the law failed, however, to bring one-bank holding companies under the purview of the act. This loophole was a key factor leading to the spectacular growth of one-bank holding companies in the 1960s. It offered banks the opportunity to extend their operations to include insurance, real estate, and data processing.

One-Bank Holding Companies

Unlike multibank holding companies, which have developed primarily in unit-banking and limited-branching states, one-bank holding companies have become a significant force on the banking scene. As the name implies, one-bank holding companies control a single bank. They fall into two types: bank-originated and nonbank-originated. The bank-originated one-bank holding company occurs when an existing bank creates its own holding company, thus placing itself in a subsidiary status. This type of one-bank holding company is also known as congeneric, since it is formed by a bank to engage in related financial activities such as mortgage banking and factoring. The nonbank-originated holding company does not draw its origin from the bank that it owns and controls. This type of holding company can be further divided into traditional and conglomerate. Traditional one-bank holding companies are corporations established to control a small bank; they may also be involved in real estate, insurance, and finance. Conglomerate one-bank holding companies are corporations that own a bank but engage in other activities or have subsidiaries that are nonfinancial. Examples include Hershey Foods, Goodyear Tire and Rubber Company, World Airways, charitable trusts, non-profit foundations, and labor unions.

Of the different classifications of one-bank holding companies, the most important is the congeneric because it enables a bank, or a bank-originated holding company, to establish a nonbank subsidiary and enter product and geographic markets from which banks are barred. It was precisely this prospect that induced bankers to take advantage of the loophole in the Bank Holding Company Act of 1956 and launch, in the 1960s, a number of bank-originated one-bank holding companies. The bank-originated one-bank holding company also offers bankers other advantages, such as greater flexibility in fund raising. This aspect became significant during the tight money periods of the late 1960s. The holding company could raise funds by issuing its own commercial paper and then funneling these funds to the bank by purchasing loans from its portfolio or bank-issued stocks and bonds. This technique was advantageous because the holding company, which was not subject to interest ceilings, could pay higher returns than the bank could offer its depositors. In addition, these funds were not subject to reserve requirements and did not have to be insured.

The rapid growth of one-bank holding companies in the 1960s led to calls for control by competing firms. As a result the Bank Holding Company Act of 1956 was amended in 1970 to cover one-bank holding companies. The 1970 amendments to the Bank Holding Company Act called for the Federal Reserve to regulate the activities of these companies, including placing limits on the nonbank activities in which these companies can engage. These activities must bear a close relation to traditional banking activities. Table 3.3 lists the activities in which one-bank and multibank holding companies may engage with permission from the Board of Governors of the Federal Reserve System, as well as activities in which the board is considering allowing these companies to engage in the future.

Examination of Board of Governors' rulings reveals the criteria used in approving or denying requests by bank holding companies to enter nonbanking activities. To determine whether certain activities are closely related to banking, the Board of Governors considers whether the proposed activities are similar to bank lending or operationally integrated into the lending process. Similar to bank lending are activities that involve extension of credit, such as factoring, leasing, and mortgage banking. And such activities as bookkeeping, data processing, and underwriting credit life insurance are judged to be operationally integrated into the lending process. There are other criteria as well, such as public interest and convenience, efficiency of management, conflict of interest, and competition versus concentration. The latter issue is an especially important consideration. De novo entries into new areas of activity are generally favored because they add another competitor to the scene. Thus, the Board of Governors might approve a holding company's application to create, rather than acquire, a factoring company. By contrast, moves to acquire existing concerns are rejected if they will have a negative impact on local competition. As a result, the acquisition of a small company would be favored over that of a large one.

Apart from charging the Board of Governors with regulating one-bank holding companies, the 1970 amendments include more substantive sections. One confers automatic approval on any application that the board has not acted on within 90 days following submission of all the requisite forms. Another, which spells out tie-in restrictions, reflects Congressional concern that the spread of holding company activities into nonbanking areas might adversely affect competition. These restrictions forbid any bank from making the availability of its services contingent on the customer's purchase of other services from the bank, its holding company, or its affiliates. In addition, a bank cannot require that its customers not do business with the bank's competitors, their holding companies, or affiliates. These restrictions do not apply to requirements intended to assure the soundness of loans or to traditional bank services such as deposits or trusts. Finally, a grandfather clause exempts some nonbanking subsidiaries acquired before June 30, 1968. However, the Board of Governors was given ten years to review any subsidiary, even if acquired before this date, and call for its divestiture if it was judged to inhibit competition unduly. Remaining nonbanking subsidiaries were to be divested before December 31, 1980.

Bank holding companies continue to engage in nonbanking activities as permitted, but the list of allowed activities consists almost entirely of activities in which banks are already permitted to engage directly. The list is so restrictive that, for instance, bank holding companies are not permitted to operate savings and loan associations even though banks are permitted to do everything that savings and loan associations can do. The Federal Reserve's conservative stance in this regard is motivated not only by concern over competition but also by pressures from other kinds of businesses fearful of takeovers by bank holding companies.

Table 3.3. Permissible Nonbank Activities for Bank Holding Companies under Section 4(c)8 of Regulation Y, April 30, 1982

Activities Permitted by Regulation	Activities Permitted by Order	Activities Denied by the Board

1. Extensions of credit[a]
   Mortgage banking
   Finance companies: consumer, sales, and commercial
   Credit cards
   Factoring
	1. Issuance and sale of traveler's checks[a,e]	1. Insurance premium funding (combined sales of mutual funds and insurance)

2. Industrial bank, Morris Plan bank, industrial loan company	2. Buying and selling gold and silver bullion and silver coin[a,c]	2. Underwriting life insurance not related to credit extension
3. Servicing loans and other extensions of credit[a]	3. Issuing money orders and general-purpose, variable-denominated payment instruments[a,c]	3. Real estate brokerage[a]
4. Trust company[a]	4. Futures commission merchant to cover gold and silver bullion and coins[a]	4. Land development
5. Investment or financial advising[a]	5. Underwriting certain federal, state, and municipal securities[a]	5. Real estate syndication
6. Full-payout leasing of personal or real property[a]	6. Check verification[a,c]	6. General management consulting
7. Investments in community welfare projects[a]	7. Financial advice to consumers[a]	7. Property management
8. Providing bookkeeping or data-processing services[a]	8. Issuance of small-denomination debt instruments	8. Computer output microfilm services
		9. Underwriting mortgage guaranty insurance[b]
		10. Operating a savings and loan association[d]

9. Acting as insurance agent or broker primarily in connection with credit extensions[a]

10. Underwriting credit life, accident, and health insurance

11. Providing courier services[a]

12. Management consulting for unaffiliated banks[a]

13. Sale at retail of money orders with a face value of not more than $1,000, traveler's checks, and savings bonds[a]

14. Performing appraisals of real estate

15. Audit services for unaffiliated banks

16. Issuance and sale of traveler's checks

17. Management consulting to nonbank depository institutions

11. Operating a travel agency[a]

12. Underwriting property and casualty insurance

13. Underwriting home loan life mortgage insurance

14. Orbanco: investment note issue with transactional characteristics

[a] Activities permissible to national banks.
[b] Board orders found these activities closely related to banking but denied proposed acquisitions as part of its "go slow" policy.
[c] To be decided on a case-by-case basis.
[d] Operating a thrift institution has been permitted by order in Rhode Island and New Hampshire only.
[e] Subsequently permitted by regulation.
Source: Board of Governors, Federal Reserve System.

One facet of the 1970 amendments to the Bank Holding Company Act of 1956 gives bank holding companies an avenue for significantly broadening their activities. Nonbanking activities of bank holding companies are not restricted geographically. Thus, while banks cannot open branches across state lines, bank holding companies can operate nonbank subsidiaries engaging in the approved bank-related activities without geographic limits. Citicorp and Bank of America, for example, both own finance companies in Oklahoma. Each of these companies, in turn, operates a network of offices in major cities around the country.

Bank holding companies have also tried to go across state lines by taking advantage of the Douglas Amendment to the Bank Holding Company Act. Section 3(d) of this amendment allows bank holding companies to acquire out-of-state banks wherever state laws permit them to do so. After South Dakota enacted legislation in 1980 permitting limited out-of-state bank holding company activity within its borders, Citicorp of New York moved its credit card division to that state. Similar legislation enacted by Delaware in 1981 made possible the entry of such out-of-state bank holding companies as J. P. Morgan, Chase, and Chemical. A more recent example of this trend is Alaska, which on July 1, 1982, allowed the unrestricted entry of out-of-state bank holding companies. These changes in the laws of individual states are paving the way for more interstate acquisitions by bank holding companies.

BANK REGULATION

Regulation of commercial banks in the United States has grown from a limited, ad hoc activity to a system in which three federal agencies and each state's banking authority undertake to ensure banks' compliance with many volumes of laws and regulations. Before 1830 bank examinations were not made on a regular basis, nor was a specific body charged with the task of conducting them. When rumor or a disturbing financial report suggested that a bank might be in trouble, a group of prominent citizens or a committee appointed by the governor or the state legislature looked into the situation. The regulations were comparatively few, calling for periodic reports and imposing some restrictions on the kinds of activity in which the bank could engage. The issuance of state regulations was motivated in part by the fact that many states were bank stockholders.

The development of bank regulation has occurred largely in response to financial crisis rather than through constructive planning.

The financial crisis of the Civil War gave rise to the National Bank Act; the Panic of 1907 led to the creation of the Federal Reserve System; and the Great Depression spawned the Banking Act of 1933 and the Banking Act of 1935. The last two pieces of legislation established the Federal Deposit Insurance Corporation, separated commercial banking from investment banking, and introduced interest-rate ceilings on deposits. These measures mark the point at which bank regulation was most aggressive in its efforts to protect the depositor and ensure the safety of banking.

The subsequent decades saw few changes in the regulatory picture. Preservation of competition was the dominant concern during this period. The major pieces of legislation reflecting this concern were the Bank Merger Act of 1960 and the Bank Holding Company Act of 1956 with its 1970 amendments.

Most recently we are witnessing a trend toward reduced and streamlined bank regulation as part of a shift toward less government control in many areas. The DIDMCA of 1980 is the first legislation to reflect this change. Factors bringing about the shift in attitude include high interest rates, tight money conditions, and disintermediation (withdrawal of funds from financial intermediaries and their direct investment in higher-yielding marketable securities). Because of bureaucratic inertia, changes come slowly. However, just as the dramatic technological advances of recent years are transforming many aspects of banking activity, so they are likely to speed up the process of regulatory change in the near future.

Commercial bank regulation today covers nearly every phase of banking activity. Although there is some degree of variation between federal and state regulation, the overall purpose—to ensure the soundness of the U.S. banking system—does not vary. Some of the more important regulatory activities include passing on applications for the chartering of new banks; issuing and enforcing laws and regulations; periodically examining the conditions, operations, and policies of individual banks; passing on applications for changes in banking powers, such as the offering of trust services; and passing on applications for branch offices, proposed mergers and consolidations, acquisitions by existing bank holding companies, and the formation of new holding companies. Other issues coming under regulatory purview include bank capital requirements, the maintenance of reserves against deposits, types and amounts of assets banks may hold, and liquidation of banks.

Evaluation of individual banks is carried out by means of the bank examination. Approximately twice a year examiners arrive unannounced at a bank and spend days or weeks, depending on the size of the bank, going over its operations. Bank examiners make sure that the bank is in sound condition and that it is in compliance with all applicable laws and regulations. They assess the bank's assets, capital, and liquidity.

The loan portfolio is gone over in considerable detail, since it is the area of greatest potential vulnerability for a bank. Each loan above a minimum size is examined individually. Again, compliance with regulations regarding loan size and eligibility of the borrower is assured. Adequacy of the financial information on the borrower is also checked. Then loans are classified according to the level of risk they represent. Loans judged to be uncollectable are classified as "loss" and may no longer be listed among the bank's assets—that is, they are charged off. "Doubtful" loans are those expected to result in partial loss. Loans considered unduly risky, and therefore calling for careful monitoring to avoid loss, are labeled "substandard." In addition, the examiners assess the quality of the bank's management and assure themselves of the absence of fraud.

The bank examination culminates in the preparation of a formal report, copies of which are placed in the files of the regulatory agency and submitted to the bank's directors. The report lists all problems or failings uncovered during the examination: instances of noncompliance with laws or regulations; problem loans; inadequacies in the capital base. In addition, the report may comment on specific management practices that are considered unsound or problematic. It is the responsibility of the directors to see to it that the report's recommendations are implemented. If the management is recalcitrant in carrying out these recommendations, regulatory agencies can, under authority granted by the Financial Institutions Supervisory Act of 1966, obtain cease-and-desist orders against specific bank practices. Failure to comply can result in the removal of the officers or directors involved.

Following the failure of the Franklin National Bank in 1974, Congressional hearings were held to look into the procedures of bank evaluation. It was found that these procedures varied considerably in terms of what aspects of banking activity were examined and how performance was rated. In effect, different standards were being applied to different banks. This lack of uniformity meant that aggregate evaluation activity was not yielding a coherent assessment of the health of the banking system as a whole. In addition, it was found that the examining agencies devoted more or less equal attention to all banks rather than focusing more intensive and frequent evaluatory effort on banks with demonstrated weaknesses. To remedy these faults, the Uniform Interagency Bank Rating System was introduced in 1978 to provide a general framework for the evaluation of all federally regulated and supervised deposit institutions. This system identifies five distinct areas of bank operation and conditions for evaluation: Capital adequacy, Asset quality, Management and administration, Earnings quantity and quality, and Liquidity level. These are commonly referred to by the acronym CAMEL. Each of these areas is rated on a scale of 1 ("strong") to 5 ("unsatisfactory and in need of immediate remedial attention"). In addition, the bank as a whole receives a composite rating on this scale. Banks with composite ratings of 1 are examined relatively infrequently, while banks earning the 5 rating undergo continual scrutiny.

The National Bank Surveillance System (NBSS), another approach to bank evaluation, has been in operation since 1975. The NBSS is administered by the office of the Comptroller of the Currency and is used to assess the ongoing performance of national banks. It originated in recommendations made by the accounting firm of Haskins and Sells, which had been retained to make a thorough study of the workings of the office of the Comptroller of the Currency. The NBSS consists of a computerized surveillance system that monitors the performance of banks and gives early warning of developing problems. It has four basic components. First, the Bank Performance Report (BPR) is compiled from balance sheets, income-expense statements and national bank examination reports. This report is made available to bank managers as well as bank examiners. Second, the Anomaly Severity Rating System (ASRS) assigns scores to various aspects of bank performance for the purpose of detecting problem areas and measuring their severity. Third, NBSS specialists (designated bank examiners) compile a report based on the BPR and the ASRS and submit it with recommendations to the Regional Administrator of National Banks. When actual or potential problems have been identified, the bank undergoes further scrutiny and a correction plan is devised in consultation with the bank's management. Finally, the Action Control System (ACS) monitors banks' progress in correcting identified problems.

The NBSS is a useful tool for bank directors and managers as well as for regulatory agencies. Because the performance of each bank is compared with that of other banks operating in similar competitive environments under similar branching laws and offering similar services, bank managers can use this information to judge their own performance. The Federal Reserve System uses the same system in monitoring state-chartered member banks, and the FDIC has developed a similar system of bank surveillance, the Integrated Monitoring System (IMS).

A distinctive feature of the American banking system is that supervisory and regulatory functions are carried out by a number of different agencies. The agencies involved in commercial bank regulation at the federal level are the Comptroller of the Currency, the Federal Reserve System, and the Federal Deposit Insurance Corporation. Each state has a banking commission charged with monitoring and regulating banking activity within its borders. In addition to these agencies, which constitute the predominant source of regulatory control, commercial banks are also subject to rules and regulatory decisions of other government agencies, such as the Securities and Exchange Commission (SEC), which provides for the registration of bank-issued securities and the full public disclosure of corporate information. As might be expected, there is considerable overlap in the jurisdiction of these agencies. The complexity of the U.S. regulatory system and the degree of overlapping jurisdictions are depicted in Figure 3.2. State member banks, for example, are subject to the banking laws of the state in which they are chartered and operate, and to all applicable federal legislation by virtue of their membership in the Federal Reserve System and the FDIC. By the same token, national banks are supervised by their chartering agency, the Comptroller of the Currency, and, because of their national charter, are required to be members of the Federal Reserve System and the FDIC. In addition, national banks are subject to the laws of the state in which they operate (for instance, laws on branching and legal holidays).

Proposed changes in banking structure may require approval from more than one body. The Board of Governors of the Federal Reserve System must pass on all holding company transactions, even when nonmember banks are involved. Merger applications by national banks require the approval of the Comptroller of the Currency, while those of state banks require—in addition to the approval of their respective states—that of either the Board of Governors or the FDIC, depending on their membership status. In evaluating the competitive implications of such transactions, the federal agencies involved must confer with each other and with the Department of Justice.

To eliminate some of the overlap and duplication of their activities, regulatory agencies have established a framework for cooperation. For example, they have divided among themselves the responsibility for conducting bank examinations, and the examination reports are made available to the other agencies having jurisdiction over the bank in question. According to this arrangement, the Comptroller of the

Figure 3.2. Structure of Bank Supervision

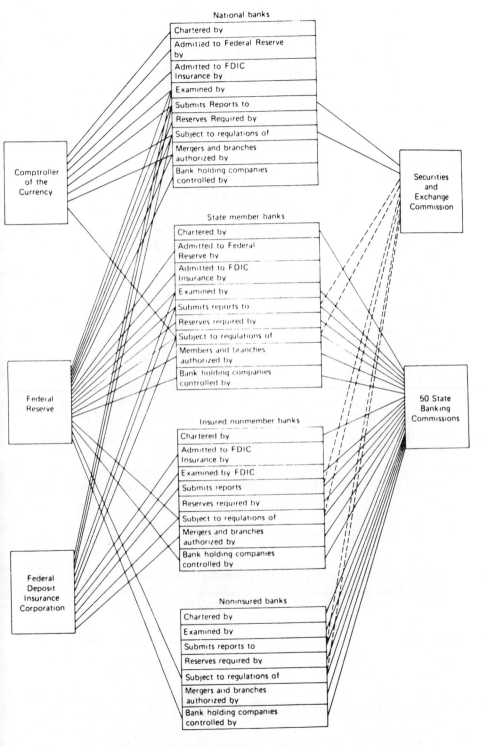

Source: Tracy G. Herrick, *Bank Analyst's Handbook* (New York: John Wiley and Sons, 1978), p. 266. Reprinted by permission of the publisher.

Currency examines national banks, the Federal Reserve System examines state member banks, and the FDIC examines insured state nonmember banks. State banking agencies examine all state-chartered banks and often coordinate their examinations with those of the federal agencies. Cooperation among regulatory authorities has also extended to exchange of information on chartering and branching.

In spite of this cooperation among regulatory agencies, the prevailing division of authority and responsibility has stimulated a number of proposals to reform and consolidate the regulatory structure and make it more efficient. These proposals have originated from a variety of sources, including administrative officials, committees, commissions, and the U.S. Congress. In 1961 the Commission on Money and Credit recommended that the supervisory powers of the Comptroller of the Currency and the FDIC be transferred to the Federal Reserve System. In the following year the Comptroller of the Currency's Advisory Committee on Banking proposed that all supervisory and regulatory authority over banks be vested in a single administrator under the Secretary of the Treasury. That same year (1962) J. L. Robertson, vice-chairman of the Board of Governors of the Federal Reserve System, recommended the establishment of a new governmental agency—the Federal Banking Commission—to assume all the supervisory powers of the Federal Reserve Board, the Comptroller of the Currency, and the FDIC, with the latter two being completely absorbed in the new commission. In 1971 the Commission on Financial Structure and Regulation—also known as the Hunt Commission—recommended the creation of a tripartite regulatory structure. It called for one administrator to oversee national banks and another to oversee state banks, while deposit insurance functions for banks and thrifts would be performed by a single deposit insurance agency.

In 1976 the U.S. Congress made its own recommendations in the study *Financial Institutions and the Nation's Economy* (FINE). These recommendations sought to stimulate competition among financial institutions by granting the same powers to all depository intermediaries. Thus, savings and loan associations, credit unions, and federally chartered mutual savings banks would be permitted to perform all the functions of commercial banks except making commercial loans. The authors of the study recognized that as the intermediaries become more homogeneous, separate regulatory agencies would cease to be practical. Thus they called for the creation of a Federal Depository Institutions Commission, which would assume the regulatory functions of the Federal Reserve System, the Comptroller of the Currency, the Federal Deposit Insurance Corporation, the Federal Home Loan

Bank Board, and the National Credit Union Administration. The commission would regulate state-chartered as well as federally chartered depository intermediaries. Only the very few noninsured banks would fall outside its jurisdiction. The Federal Reserve System's activities would thereafter be confined to the formulation and implementation of monetary policy.

The FINE recommendations were too sweeping to gain favor with the many agencies that were to be abolished or drastically altered under the proposed changes. Banks did not support the granting to other kinds of institutions powers that had been exclusively theirs. Savings institutions worried about the proposed abolition of interest-rate differentials that gave them a competitive advantage over banks in attracting deposits. Credit unions feared the loss of their special tax status.

An important step toward the reform and consolidation of bank regulatory authority at the federal level was taken in March 1980, with the enactment of the DIDMCA. As mentioned earlier, this legislation brought all depository institutions under uniform reserve requirements administered by the Federal Reserve System. This provision had immediate effects upon bank regulatory structure. An important motive for choosing a state charter rather than a national one prior to the DIDMCA was that state reserve requirements were typically more liberal than those of the Federal Reserve. That motive has now been removed, and more new banks are likely to choose national charters, which will allow them to deal with a single regulatory agency, the Comptroller of the Currency, rather than a combination of federal and state authorities. In addition, as banks contemplate the possibilities of interstate branching activity, national charters will appear more advantageous. State-chartered banks are governed by the regulatory bodies of their home states. For a bank chartered in one state to establish branches in another would raise thorny jurisdictional problems regarding supervision of its out-of-state activities: which state would oversee these? A national charter would obviate these difficulties. These trends will further attenuate the dual banking system and will tend to increase the Comptroller of the Currency's influence compared with that of the Federal Reserve System and the FDIC. Such a shift is bound to result in the concentration in a single agency of the authority to pass on applications for mergers and holding company acquisitions.

There are some additional economic forces that are likely to provoke further changes in the regulatory system. Currently, savings and loan associations are regulated by the Federal Home Loan Bank Board.

Recent attempts to help the thrift industry out of its difficulties have included giving them powers more like those of commercial banks. In addition, some thrifts have merged with banks in order to avoid failure. As depository institutions become more alike in their functions, it will become increasingly necessary to consolidate their regulation.

It follows from the preceding discussion that the overall trend in bank regulation is toward consolidation of regulatory authority and uniformity in the regulations. Inevitably, these reforms will lag behind the actual changes in the industry that are blurring the distinctions among kinds of depository institutions. The lingering existence of different regulatory bodies, state versus federal or those overseeing one type of institution versus those overseeing another, creates inequities as the variously regulated institutions move into more direct competition with each other. But the direction of change is clear. It will be toward increased consolidation of regulatory authority.

COMPETITION IN FINANCIAL SERVICES

Until quite recently the financial services market in the United States was divided into a number of discrete components that did not compete directly with each other. Each type of financial institution attracted certain kinds of deposits and made rather specialized forms of loans. Commercial banks largely concentrated on catering to the credit and other needs of businesses and were the only institutions to offer checking accounts. Savings and loan associations and mutual savings banks received time deposits and offered mortgage loans. Credit unions provided a means for members to pool their savings and take out installment loans. The division of function was fairly clear. Banks did not compete for time deposits, and savings institutions were not permitted to offer checking accounts. That banks and thrift institutions were viewed as separate "lines of commerce" was substantiated as recently as 1963 by the Supreme Court's landmark decision concerning the merger of two Philadelphia banks.

Since then, technological and regulatory changes have made these different institutions more alike, and thus have brought about more direct competition among them. Thrift institutions have taken advantage of technological advances that were developed by large commercial banks. As a result, savings and loan associations, mutual savings banks, and credit unions have been actively engaged in electronic funds transfer.

Recent regulatory changes have also intensified the competition between banks and thrift institutions. The changes resulted primarily from legislators' concern about the cyclical problems of thrift institutions and the mortgage markets. These problems became apparent during the monetary restraints of 1966, 1969, and 1973, when the market rates of interest rose above the maximum rates payable by thrifts. In these years thrifts suffered sharp contractions in the growth of mortgage funds and increased vulnerability of deposits. These factors, in turn, undermined mortgage lending ability and depressed the supply of housing. Moreover, the combination of volatile short-term deposits and relatively illiquid long-term assets (mortgages) made thrift institutions financially vulnerable. These experiences led thrifts to push for legislation that would provide them with greater freedom in determining the composition of their assets, in an attempt to correct the maturity imbalance between their assets and liabilities.

Since the mid-1970s several pieces of legislation have amplified the operational powers of thrifts and increased the variety of services offered. As a result, savings and loan associations and mutual savings banks have expanded their traditional role of home mortgage lenders and are now making more consumer and business loans, issuing credit cards, exercising trust powers, and investing in sell or hold commercial paper and corporate debt securities. The Federal Home Loan Bank Board is considering implementing the expanded range of powers for savings and loan associations authorized by the Garn-St. Germain Act. These include liberalized consumer and business lending limits, issuance of letters of credit, leasing, and lending for manufactured homes. This act also authorizes the conversion of savings and loan associations to federal savings banks, thus further promoting homogeneity among deposit institutions. Credit unions have also expanded beyond their traditional role as consumer lenders and are making home mortgage loans; issuing money orders, traveler's checks, and credit cards; and participating in loans with other credit unions. In addition, they have been calling for federal legislation to expand their activities to include trust and international services.

The centerpiece of deregulation for deposit institutions is the DIDMCA. In addition to some of the above reforms of the scope of services offered by thrifts, it deals with such supervisory areas as the introduction of uniform reserve requirements for all deposit institutions, with such reserves to be held at regional Federal Reserve banks; use of the Federal Reserve discount window by all depository intermediaries; pricing of Federal Reserve services; and gradual phaseout of interest-rate ceilings on deposit accounts (Regulation Q) through 1986. Moreover, the DIDMCA is credited with the removal of another important line of demarcation in the activities of banks and thrifts by authorizing all federally insured deposit institutions to offer negotiable orders of withdrawal (NOW) accounts, also referred to as interest-bearing checking accounts.

As follows from the preceding discussion, banks currently operate in an environment characterized by increasing competition. Through the immediate postwar years, banks competed only among themselves, as did each of the other types of deposit institutions. However, the technological and regulatory changes initiated in the 1970s have blurred traditional differences and are producing more competition among deposit institutions. In recent years this competitive climate has further intensified for commercial banks as a result of the expanding activity of foreign banks operating in the United States.

Apart from thrifts and foreign banks, commercial banks have been facing increasing competition from other participants in the money and capital markets. In their attempts to attract funds, as well as to lend and invest these funds, banks have been competing with other financial institutions, nonfinancial businesses, and the government. On the liability side banks must compete with the short-term and long-term debt instruments of financial institutions, nonfinancial corporations, and the government. In recent years a new competitor has entered the fray in the form of the money-market funds. The money-market funds are mutual funds (formally known as open-end investment companies) whose objective is to invest the funds raised from the sale of their own stock in negotiable CDs of large banks and commercial paper of large, well-known corporations. The emergence of these high-yield instruments enabled money-market funds to subtract a management fee equal to 0.5 percent of the assets managed and still compete effectively for household savings.

To the consumer who wanted to earn a market return on liquid funds, money-market funds offered an instrument that paid a more attractive rate than did the time and savings deposits of bank and nonbank depository institutions, which were subject to interest-rate ceilings. In addition to the higher rate on funds, this instrument offered some checking privileges and required no minimum maturity period. As for the absence of any government insurance or guaranty on the shares, this risk was minimized not only by the reputation of the firms offering the funds but also, more important, by the short-term and high-quality assets these funds held. These qualities of money-market fund shares have been responsible for the spectacular growth of those funds from almost zero in late 1974 to a record $232 billion in assets by December 1, 1982. Most of that amount was drained from thrift institutions and medium-size and small banks. For big banks, by contrast, money-market funds were a source of funds, since they invested a major share of their assets in the negotiable CDs of those banks.

The net effect of money-market funds was thus a shift of funds from smaller to bigger institutions, with this shift becoming more acute as market rates of interest increased. Such increases underlined the spread differential between money-market fund yields and the rates that banks and thrifts could pay. To remedy this situation, the Garn-St. Germain Act permitted banks and thrifts to introduce, on December 14, 1982, a money-market deposit account that offers consumers the same features (limited checking privileges, no minimum maturity period, and no interest-rate ceiling) as money-market fund shares, plus the same insurance coverage (up to $100,000) as all other deposit accounts. This account will enable banks and thrifts to recapture some of the funds that they lost to money-market funds; however, earnings will be hurt in the short run as consumers shift funds to these accounts from lower-cost passbook savings.

On the asset side (lending and investing), banks compete with a host of institutional and corporate lenders. On the institutional level they compete with such financial intermediaries as insurance companies, pension funds, commercial factors, and finance companies. On the corporate level banks compete with large manufacturing corporations—such as auto or farm equipment manufacturers—whose captive finance companies (finance companies they own) have expanded their traditional equipment-financing function to offer receivable and inventory financing as well as leasing. However, while they are making the same kinds of loans that banks do, they are not subject to the same regulatory constraints that banks are. Firms like General Motors or General Electric may extend loans anywhere in the country, while banks must conform to branching laws. Likewise, brokerage firms, insurance companies, and retailers are not subject to geographic restrictions. Since brokerage firms and money-market funds have begun to offer competitive financial services, the edge created by their geographic freedom becomes even more significant. Sears Roebuck competes directly with banks by offering consumer credit throughout its nationwide chain of retail stores. Moreover, through various financial companies it has acquired, Sears has diversified and now offers checking, time, and savings deposits; business loans; insurance; stocks; bonds; mutual funds; and real estate. Thus the potential exists for Sears to offer a full line of banking services at each of its retail outlets.

Nonfinancial corporations may also conduct banking activity across state lines by putting together corporate structures that do not meet the legal definition of banks, and thus are not subject to state branching laws. A commercial bank is legislatively defined as any organization that offers both demand deposits and commercial loans. By separating the lending and deposit functions, it is possible for organizations to circumvent interstate restrictions and provide financial services on an interstate basis. One way to accomplish this is through subsidiaries that offer a more limited array of financial services than commercial banks, and specifically exclude either the deposit-taking or the lending function. There have been numerous examples of nonfinancial corporations entering the financial services market on an interstate basis through such arrangements. Gulf and Western, a $5.9 billion conglomerate, offers commercial loan, deposit-taking, factoring, and insurance services; but since each service is offered by a separate subsidiary, the conglomerate is able to provide this array of services without conforming to laws affecting interstate activity by commercial banks or bank holding companies. No single subsidiary meets the legal criteria for the definition of a commercial bank; thus a true bank is not deemed to exist. Like Gulf and Western, Household International (formerly Household Finance Company) added deposit taking to its financial services by purchasing a bank that had divested itself of its commercial loan portfolio.

Nonbank and nonfinancial contenders in the financial services market have become such a significant force that Merrill Lynch's managed money-market assets, totaling $41 billion, are exceeded only by the holdings of the four largest banks in the country. Similarly, Sears, excluding its real estate and securities subsidiaries, would be the twentieth largest bank in the country. Figure 3.3 traces the changes in patterns of service offered in the financial market. The trend is toward a broader range of services offered by fewer, larger institutions. Although in the past the dominant pattern was one of institutions concentrating in a limited service area, now a few firms offer a full product line of financial services.

Why has this wave of new competitors been so eager to enter the banking business? The answer lies in the profitability and the stability of the commercial banking industry. The net earnings of commercial banks, as illustrated in Figure 3.4, increased by an average of 19 percent a year between 1975 and 1980. The return on assets (ROA) for commercial banks has held steady at 1 percent since the early 1970s, a level thrifts could not match. The high interest rates of the late 1970s caught thrifts in a bind of paying higher interest rates on savings while they continued to collect on fixed, low-interest mortgages issued in earlier years. Some thrifts lost money as this squeeze became too tight. Life insurance companies have also suffered an erosion in

Figure 3.3. The Financial Services Market, 1960-82

	Banks	S&Ls	Insurance Companies	Retailers	Securities Dealers
Checking	■ ●	●	●	●	●
Saving	■ ●	●	■ ●	●	●
Time Deposits	■ ●	●	■ ●	●	●
Installment Loans	■ ●	●	●	●	●
Business Loans	■ ●	●	●	●	●
Mortgage Loans	● ●	■ ●	●	●	●
Credit Cards	●	●	● ■ ●	●	●
Insurance		■ ●	●	●	●
Stocks, Bonds		●	● ■ ●	●	●
Mutual Funds		●	● ■ ●	●	●
Real Estate		●	●	●	●
Interstate Facilities		●	●	●	●

■ 1960
● 1982

Source: Donald L. Koch and Delores W. Steinhauser, "Challenges for Retail Banking in the 80s," *Economic Review*, Federal Reserve Bank of Atlanta, May 1982, p. 14. Reprinted by permission of the publisher.

earnings. Voluntary terminations of life insurance policies increased from 5.8 percent to 8.1 percent per year in the 1970s. The vicissitudes of the stock market led to corresponding fluctuations in the ROA for member firms of the New York Stock Exchange. These fell below zero in the mid-1970s but rose to 3.5 percent as the economy improved later in the decade.

The multidimensional competition that banks now face will no doubt intensify in the years ahead. At the same time, gradual deregulation of financial institutions is expected to widen the powers of commercial banks, broaden their geographic spread, contribute to

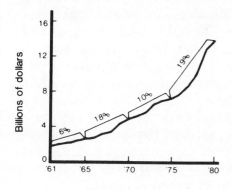

Figure 3.4. After-tax earnings of commercial Banks and Average Annual Percent Change, 1961-80

Source: Donald L. Koch and Delores W. Steinhauser, "Challenges for Retail Banking in the 80s," *Economic Review*, Federal Reserve Bank of Atlanta, May 1982, p. 14. Reprinted by permission of the publisher.

innovative financial arrangements, and result in more competitive pricing of financial services. Although the long-run implications of growing competition will be positive for the U.S. financial system, in the transitional stage it promises significant challenges for most of the nearly 15,000 commercial banks and 80,000 or so depository institutions. As nonbank competitors close in and legislative deregulation of financial services proceeds, banks may suffer some grief in the years ahead unless they plan carefully for the rapid change. Three major types of response to these emerging challenges appear likely: electronic banking, specialty banking, and the financial supermarket. These approaches may be employed singly or in combination.

Electronic Banking

Not so many years ago, bankers labored over detailed accounting books called Boston ledgers, manually posting every deposit and withdrawal from a customer's account and squaring each one individually with the bank's own books. By the end of the twentieth century, by contrast, a piece of electronic equipment in the living room may produce a kind of scrip that will be used like cash. Banks have come a long way. Many of the tedious tasks that bankers once loathed are now done electronically, and one of the chief beneficiaries of the electronic revolution in banking is the bank customer. And as deregulation of financial services proceeds, banks will increasingly emphasize customer needs and convenience in the design and deployment of electronic banking technology. Catering to the customer becomes increasingly necessary as the competitive environment stiffens and competitors of many types vie for banks' traditional customers.

For banks to survive in an era of deregulation and growing competition from financial service companies, it is imperative that they make increasing use of available electronic technology, and stay flexible and creative enough to incorporate new advances into their service offerings. We have already noted the growing use of electronic funds transfer systems (EFTs), which combine both cost savings and increased convenience to customers. The most visible effects of EFTs are occurring in the payments mechanism. In recent years a growing number of banks, concerned with the declining profitability of additions to their brick-and-mortar branch networks, have been developing extensive systems of automatic teller machines (ATMs). In some instances these ATM systems are proprietary (a system serves only the institution that owns it); in others they are shared by several participating banks, with transactions routed to the appropriate institution by a switch. At the end of 1981 there were 26,800 ATMs in operation, with the number expected to rise to 38,000 by the end of 1982.

A more dramatic breakthrough for customer convenience is the advent of in-home banking. As home computers become more prevalent, this service will become increasingly important. A limited number of banks are already extending services to their clients through two-way cable television hookups.Telephones can also link the home computer with that of a bank. The future will see most banking transactions conducted as information transfers between the customer's home computer or a terminal at a retail outlet and the bank's computer. As increasing energy costs make it more expensive for people to move about, the ability to conduct banking transactions without leaving home will seem more attractive, despite the reduced personal contact with bank employees. Bank costs, meanwhile, will shift, to some extent, from salaries to the substantial fixed costs involved in acquiring and maintaining electronic equipment. Since large numbers of transactions will be necessary to bring the cost per transaction to a profitable level, the trend toward electronic banking will favor large banks over smaller ones. Thus electronic banking represents one more force in the trend toward fewer, larger banks in the United States. Citicorp represents an example of a banking organization that has already invested heavily in electronic technology with the view that before too long, all types of financial service transactions will be conducted electronically. Citicorp data indicate that as of 1981, it had invested $500 million in research on communication systems and electronic banking technology. A key component of Citicorp's vision of a bank of the future is the widespread use of satellite transponders in the relay of data. Citibank and other major banks have already initiated use of such technology.

Specialty Banking

Deregulation of financial institutions and increased competition from financial service companies will prompt some banks to take a path chosen by firms in other deregulated industries, such as securities brokers, airlines, and trucking. These banks, rather than offering a wide variety of financial services over a large geographic area, may choose to retrench from their full-service offerings and concentrate on a more attractive product or customer segment of the market. This move will mark the emergence of specialty banks, institutions that will compete aggressively in a narrower range of financial services or in specific segments of the market, usually segments with a high customer-service preference (such as developing special service packages to cater to the needs of high-income customers). Geographic boundaries will lose their significance as deregulation proceeds and electronic banking becomes more prevalent; thus geographically defined market niches will cease to provide security for banks.

Banks that wish to create a secure position by becoming specialty banks should position themselves to selectively acquire competitors that will deepen rather than broaden their expertise, thus better equipping them to provide the more specific services on which they have chosen to focus. Commercial banking has been said to consist of five separate forms of business: retail, domestic wholesale, international wholesale, trading, and trust. Each of these is large enough to be considered an industry with room for a limited number of banks to emerge as leaders exercising substantial control in that area.

Financial Supermarkets

While some banks will deal with the coming challenges by narrowing their service offerings or focusing on electronic in-home banking, others will enlarge and broaden themselves to create "financial supermarkets." These will aim to provide customers with a complete range of financial services from a single institution. Since mergers will be a central vehicle in building these large and diverse institutions, the trend to financial supermarkets will reduce the number of depository institutions, which currently number about 95,000 in the United States.

As was noted in connection with Table 2.1, two of the distinguishing characteristics of the U.S. banking industry are the great variation in the size of the banks and the large number of relatively small banks. Besides varying in size, U.S. banks differ markedly in organizational form, management philosophy, and in-house talents and skills. Few would disagree that the decades ahead will be a period of consolidation for U.S. banks. Although it is unclear to what extent this consolidation will have a regional emphasis, it will nevertheless represent a trend toward a national banking structure.

This structural change in the banking industry has already begun as some banks have positioned themselves for acquisitions to expand their capabilities. These banks have acquired partial ownership of other institutions with agreements to acquire complete ownership in the event of changes in banking laws. A long list of examples could be provided, but a few will suffice to illustrate the trend. Citicorp has made a substantial investment in Central National Chicago Corporation by acquiring $12 million of the latter's nonvoting preferred stock. North Carolina National Bank has taken advantage of a grandfather privilege to acquire banks in Florida, its acquisitions at the close of 1982 amounting to four banks. In some cases the affiliation extends beyond partial ownership of one institution by another. Texas Commerce Bancshares of Houston not only has acquired partial ownership of banks in Wyoming, Colorado, Louisiana, and Oklahoma; it also has other business relations with each of these banks designed to increase their profitability. In a related move AmSouth Bancorporation, Trust Company of Georgia, and South Carolina National Corporation have made preferred stock investment in each other. Not only does this action protect each institution from acquisition by other interests; it also paves the way for the emergence of a regional interstate bank holding company should merger become legally permitted. These and other regional consolidation moves may act as models for the creation of national bank holding companies.

As partial affiliations and consolidations are taking place, many large banks, despite interstate banking barriers, are establishing an extensive national presence through a variety of other vehicles. This is being accomplished through automatic teller machines (ATMs), loan production offices, Edge Act corporations, and bank holding companies, which enable banks to diversify into such activities as consumer finance, factoring, investment companies, real estate, and insurance.

Just as banks are positioning themselves for consolidation of services and a stronger national presence, so are financial service companies. A significant example of this activity is the purchase of large retail securities brokers by major financial service companies. Examples are numerous: Sears has acquired Dean Witter Reynolds; Prudential has acquired Bache Halsey Stuart Shields; and American Express has acquired Shearson Hammill. The acquired brokerage firms benefit from the greater capital resources and broader management skills of the parent corporation; thus, their ability to compete successfully may lead to more acquisitions of this type. Because these combined institutions will be able to offer a range of financial services closely related to those offered by banks while enjoying freedom from the legal restrictions under which banks operate, this trend provides an important motive for deregulation of banks. The Glass-Steagall Act calls for the disengagement of banks from the securities business. However, a number of large banks are challenging this ban with moves to acquire interest in or to create working arrangements with securities brokers. For example, Security Pacific has purchased Fidelity Brokerage Service, Inc., of Boston, and Citicorp has announced plans to affiliate with Quick and Reilly, Inc., a discount broker. Other banks are attempting to circumvent Glass-Steagall restrictions by acquiring limited-purpose brokerage firms.

No one doubts the outcome of these developments. As financial service companies undergo the same consolidation process as banks, and as both types of institutions continue to invade each other's traditional type of business, the end result will be the integration of financial markets across institutions and space. What will emerge from this integration process will be a financial supermarket offering a smorgasbord of financial services. "Supermarket banking," "supermarket of financial services," and "financial supermarket" are all terms that have been used loosely in the last few years to describe one-stop shopping for financial services, similar to supermarket retailing of food and other products.

A comparison with the Japanese *zaibatsu*, powerful commercial and financial combines, suggests a possible future scenario for the banking industry as the financial supermarket trend continues to develop. *Zaibatsu*, including such giants as Mitsui, Mitsubishi, and Sumitomo, combine industrial, commercial, and financial activity. Before World War II a few major *zaibatsu* accounted for one-third of all bank deposits, one-third of foreign trade, and over one-half of heavy industry in Japan. Although *zaibatsu* have become somewhat less influential in recent decades, they continue to represent a major force in the Japanese economy. While there is nothing comparable in the United States, there are giant financial institutions that dominate significant markets. Of the almost 15,000 banks, 208 held 58 percent of all bank deposits at the end of 1981. All but a few of the 100 largest mortgage banking companies are controlled by commercial banks. Factoring is dominated by commercial banks. As the homogenization of depository intermediaries continues, we will see the emergence of giant concerns, each offering the gamut of financial services.

FOREIGN BANKS IN THE UNITED STATES

A number of foreign banks operate in the United States alongside the domestic ones. In November 1982 there were 265 foreign banks in the United States, operating through a total of 500 banking facilities and holding total assets in excess of $271 billion. These banks engage in a wide variety of activities in addition to commercial banking. For example, they provide investment banking services, venture capital financing, and real estate development.

The presence of foreign banks in the United States is generally attributed to a variety of factors. One consideration prompting foreign banks to establish U.S. offices was the need to facilitate foreign trade and the flow of long-term investment between the United States and other countries. Another motive was to follow their domestic clients to the United States or to extend to the corporate headquarters of U.S. multinationals the relationship these banks had established at home with the U.S. companies' local subsidiaries and affiliates. Other reasons for the presence of foreign banks include developing a retail banking business; gaining access to the largest money and capital market in the world; assuming the settling, or clearing, of all dollar transactions involving the foreign banks and their non-U.S. customers; and engaging in securities trading and underwriting activities.

Foreign banks may operate in the United States under a variety of organizational forms. These include the representative office, the subsidiary, the branch, the agency, and the investment company. The form chosen is often dictated by what state banking laws permit.

The representative office is not really a bank, but simply an office that assists clients of the parent bank in doing business in the United States and solicits U.S. customers for the parent bank. It does not conduct any actual bank operations. This is the most restrictive form of foreign bank organization.

Some states allow foreign banks to own subsidiaries in the United States. These are wholly or partly owned by foreign banks or by foreign bank holding companies. Subsidiaries offer most banking services. Foreign banks are subject to the same regulations and procedures as domestic banks in creating or acquiring subsidiaries. One form of subsidiary is the Edge Act corporation. The Edge Act privilege was extended to foreign banks by the International Banking Act of 1978. Edge Act corporations have their origin in a 1919 amendment to the Federal Reserve Act, proposed by Senator Walter E. Edge of New Jersey, that expanded the original provisions of the act to allow subsidiaries to be chartered for the purpose of engaging in international or foreign banking. Edge Act corporations generally require a minimum capital investment of $2 million and have relatively broad powers to conduct international business. They are permitted to open branch offices, and a number of Edge Act corporations have offices in various cities. Major disadvantages of an Edge Act corporation, compared with an agency, are its lower legal lending limit (due to its smaller capital base, compared with that of the agency's parent bank) and the limitation of domestic lending ability to import/export-related loans. Effective March 12, 1982, the Federal Reserve approved expanded powers for Edge Act corporations. In addition to activities ordinarily considered incidental to international financing, an Edge

Act corporation may provide investment and financial advice and portfolio management with respect to securities, financial instruments, and real estate interests.

Foreign banks operating in the United States enjoy the most flexibility when they are permitted to operate branches; however, few states currently allow this. Branches may offer the full range of banking services. Like branches of domestic banks, they function as direct extensions of their home offices. Thus, while the loan limit for a subsidiary is based on its own capitalization, the limit for a branch is based on the broader capital base of the home office in the foreign country. Foreign bank branches must comply with the same regulations as domestic branches.

An agency resembles a branch except that it cannot accept deposits from U.S. residents. The agency is well suited to foreign banks whose U.S. operations consist largely of trade financing, money-market operations, and wholesale banking. New York permits formation of investment companies by foreign banks; these function much as agencies do.

The geographic pattern of foreign banking activity in the United States has been determined largely by the particular types of activity in which the foreign banks have wished to engage and by the regulatory climate, both national and within individual states. Foreign banks wishing primarily to finance foreign trade or to participate in the U.S. money and capital markets have located in New York City and in some other major money centers, including other East Coast cities, Chicago, and San Francisco. New York City has been the chief site of foreign banking activity in the United States because of its central role in the U.S. money and capital markets. In addition, East Coast cities have traditionally provided international services more extensively than inland banks, and thus have attracted more foreign banks.

The regulatory climate also has played a significant role in the growth of foreign banks in the United States. Chartering of foreign banking institutions prior to the enactment of the International Banking Act of 1978 (IBA) was the sole prerogative of individual states. Although since enactment of the IBA foreign banks can operate under a national charter, state laws still determine the scope and organizational form of operation. Thus, some states allow no foreign bank operations (for instance, Texas), and others do not permit extensive operations (for instance, Florida, which prohibits establishment of foreign branches). The principal states with foreign banks are New York and California. The laws of the state of New York allow foreign banks from reciprocating countries to accept both domestic and foreign-owned deposits and to make the same types of loans that domestic banks make. Since 1973 Illinois has allowed full-service branches of foreign banks in downtown Chicago if reciprocity is granted.

The absence of any federal legislation prior to 1978 contributed significantly to the growth in the number of foreign banks and in their assets in the United States. Only two aspects of federal law then affected foreign banks. If they controlled a subsidiary, they fell under the Bank Holding Company Act; if this subsidiary was a member of the Federal Reserve System, it had to comply with Federal Reserve requirements. Otherwise foreign banks were free from the federal legal restrictions and regulations that domestic banks had to observe. Thus, by default, foreign banks enjoyed a competitive advantage over domestic banks. While the McFadden Act of 1927 did not allow domestic banks to engage in interstate banking, foreign banks were able to establish banking facilities across state lines. Moreover, they were permitted to underwrite and sell stocks in the United States, an activity prohibited to domestic banks by the Banking Act of 1933. Last, foreign banks were not required to join the Federal Reserve System. As a result their reserve costs were much lower than those of domestic banks.

Armed with these competitive advantages, foreign banks have flourished in some areas, competing successfully for domestic customers for such services as deposit holding and loan making. The International Banking Act of 1978 established specific federal regulation of foreign banks and attempted to limit inequities with domestic banks. According to this legislation, each foreign bank must now select one state as its "home state" of operation, and it can establish a new branch or agency outside the home state only with permission of the state in which it will operate. New branches and agencies outside the home state are now permitted to accept deposits only from nonresidents or from activities related to international trade financing. Foreign banks still have an advantage because of a grandfather provision that exempted foreign banks' existing out-of-state operations from the new legal restrictions. A further effort provide equal treatment of domestic and foreign banks came in 1980 with the DIDMCA, which subjected all branches and agencies of foreign banks to Federal Reserve requirements.

SUGGESTED REFERENCES

Boczar, Gregory E. "The Growth of Multibank Holding Companies: 1956-73." *Federal Reserve Bulletin*, April 1976, pp. 300-01.

Commission on Financial Structure and Regulation. *The Report of the President's Commission on Financial Structure and Regulations*. Washington, D.C.: U.S. Government Printing Office, 1971.

Commission on Money and Credit. *Money and Credit*. Englewood Cliffs, N.J.: Prentice-Hall, 1961.

Federal Reserve Bank of Atlanta. "Line of Commerce." *Economic Review*, Federal Reserve Bank of Atlanta, April 1982, pp. 4-65.

Federal Reserve Bank of Chicago. *Proceedings of the Conference on Banking Structure and Competition*. Chicago: Federal Reserve Bank, 1972, 1975, 1976, 1977.

Frodin, Joanna H. "Electronics: The Key to Breaking the Interstate Banking Barrier." *Business Review*, Federal Reserve Bank of Philadelphia, September/October 1982, pp. 3-11.

Gamble, Richard H. "Merger Prospecting." *Southern Banker*, September 1982, pp. 26-28.

Garcia, José, and Carl Mueller. "To Be or Not to Be-Acquired." *Florida Banker*, September 1982, pp. 30-33.

Gup, Benton E. *Financial Intermediaries*. 2nd ed. Boston: Houghton Mifflin, 1980.

Horvitz, Paul. "Consolidation of the Regulatory Agency Structure: Has the Time for It Come?" *Economic Review*, Federal Reserve Bank of Atlanta, December 1982, pp. 43-52.

_____, and Richard A. Ward. *Monetary Policy and the Financial System*. 5th ed. Englewood Cliffs, N.J.: Prentice-Hall, 1983.

King, Frank B. "Deregulation, Innovation, and New Competition in Financial Services Markets: An Overview." *Economic Review*, Federal Reserve Bank of Atlanta, August 1981, pp. 8-10.

Koch, Donald L., and Delores W. Steinhauser. "Challenges for Retail Banking in the 80s." *Economic Review*, Federal Reserve Bank of Atlanta, May 1982, pp. 13-19.

Schonk, Robert M. "Merger: Assessing the Prospect." *Southern Banker*, June 1981, pp. 18-19, 69.

Thompson, Thomas W. "The New Competition: 'Near-Banks' Close in." *Directors Digest*, February 1980, pp. 2-5.

U.S. Congress, House of Representatives, Subcommittee on Financial Institutions Supervision, Regulation and Insurance of the Committee on Banking, Currency and Housing. *Financial Institutions and the Nation's Economy (FINE): "Discussion Principles."* Hearings, vols. I-III. 94th Cong., 1st sess. Washington, D.C.: U.S. Government Printing Office, December 1975-January 1976.

Waite, Donald C., III. "Deregulation and the Banking Industry." *Bankers Magazine* 165, no. 1 (January-February 1982): 26-35.

Wooden, James H. "A Perspective on Financial Structural Change." *Bankers Magazine* 165, no. 5 (September-October 1982): 32-36.

Woolridge, Randall J., and Klaus D. Wiegel. "Foreign Banking Growth in the United States." *Bankers Magazine* 164, no. 1 (January-February 1981): 30-38.

PART II

FORMATION OF
A BANK AND FUNDS
GATHERING

4

ESTABLISHMENT AND
MANAGEMENT OF A BANK

A bank's subjection to regulatory control actually begins before its formal establishment and commencement of operations. The chartering process, whether at the state or the federal level, requires bank organizers to comply with legal and regulatory prescriptions. This chapter will review the process of forming a bank and describe the key characteristics of a bank's organizational structure. As a quasi-public institution, a bank must function within the constraints set by the many regulations affecting the banking industry. The organizational structure of a bank is in part affected by this regulatory environment. However, within these constraints there is considerable room for diversity of organization and of management policy that reflects the differing personalities and objectives of individual management teams.

ESTABLISHING A COMMERCIAL BANK

Establishing a commercial bank is a process that is considerably more involved than establishing any other type of business. Because of the serious effects attendant on bank failure, bank charter applications undergo close scrutiny to prevent the establishment of potentially weak or poorly managed banks. Bank failures not only injure individual depositors; they also affect the economic climate of their respective communities. One failure may spark a panic, spurring customers of other banks to withdraw their deposits. Under the fractional reserve system, in which total deposits exceed available reserves, excessive withdrawals can exert undue pressure on a bank having immediately to convert all its deposits into cash. In addition, large-scale withdrawal of deposits from banks reduces the nation's money supply, and this may retard economic activity.

A variety of motives may explain the interest in starting a new bank. The settlement of new territories has historically accounted for much bank formation in the United States and population growth and shifts continue to create a need for new banks in individual communities. In addition, there may be dissatisfaction with existing bank services or the desire for more sources of loans to promote real estate and business development. More personal motives for wishing to be involved in the founding of a bank include desire to share in expected earnings and the prestige associated with bank ownership. Bank organizers are usually businessmen interested in their community's economic development and possessing considerable financial and personal standing.

Filing of the Application and Preliminary Approval

Since the procedures for organizing banks under national laws are uniform throughout the United States, they can serve as the basis for a discussion of bank chartering in general. The National Bank Act stipulates that five or more individuals may apply for a national bank charter. The application must be submitted to the Regional Administrator of National Banks, the officer in charge of the field office of the Comptroller of the Currency in the region where the bank is to be established. The form is entitled "Application to Charter a National Bank." It must indicate the proposed name of the bank, which should not duplicate that of another bank in the community and, moreover, should include the word "national" or the initials N.A. (for national association). Other information requested includes the location of the bank and its market area; existence of competing banks and financial institutions in that area; initial equity capital funds, which must be in excess of $1 million, net of organizational expenses; pro forma financial statements for the first few years of operation; experience and integrity of the proposed directors and executive management; and other details, such as whether the bank will be operating out of rented or owned premises, and the expenditures for furniture, fixtures, and equipment. In order to supply this information, the bank organizers must make an economic or market survey of the area, estimate costs involved in securing and equipping a bank site, and obtain legal advice on a variety of matters.

The information requested serves to assure the Comptroller of the Currency that the applicants possess adequate capital, experience, and managerial ability to conduct banking operations safely and profitably. However, another factor enters into the chartering decision. The applicants must demonstrate that their community needs a new bank and that its entry into the area will not pose a threat to existing banks. This process ensures not only the viability of the individual bank but also the preservation of a climate of stability for the banking industry as a whole.

Upon receipt of the application, the Regional Administrator's office—through a national bank examiner—will conduct a thorough field investigation to verify and/or supplement the material submitted by the organizers and proposed directors (the organizing group). The resulting field investigation report, the application, and all supporting data become part of a public file (except for material deemed confidential). Members of the public have an opportunity to comment on the application during the 21 days following the publication by the organizers of the Regional Administrator's notice that their application has been accepted for filing. Besides making written comments, individuals may challenge the legality of an application by requesting a hearing, which may be granted by the Regional Administrator if it is determined that such a hearing would be beneficial to the decision-making process.

After review of all materials submitted by the applicants, interested members of the public, and office staff, the Regional Administrator may—under delegated authority—act on the case and grant preliminary approval for the proposed bank. It is important to note that occasionally the regional administrator's office may grant a preliminary approval and yet disapprove the participation of certain individuals (among those who submitted the application) as directors, officers, or shareholders of the bank, or altogether bar any affiliation of such individuals with the bank. A preliminary approval in essence authorizes the organizing group to take certain procedural actions that will lead, within 18 months, to final approval of the bank (a charter) and commencement of operations. These actions include establishing the bank as a body corporate with directors, articles of association, and bylaws.

Establishing the Bank as a Body Corporate and Securing a Charter

The process of establishing the bank as a body corporate is initiated through the filing with the Regional Administrator of two forms, the articles of association and the organization certificate. The articles of association contain information on the organization of the bank, largely drawn from the preliminary application papers. The organization certificate states the purpose of the organization; lists particulars regarding the bank's name, location, and capital stock; and states the net worth of shareholders and number of shares held by each. Acceptance of the articles of association and organization certificate by the Regional Administrator establishes the bank's corporate existence for the purpose of entering into contracts and performing all necessary actions other than the business of banking. The organizing group then meets to fix the number of interim directors and to elect to these positions the individuals approved by the Regional Administrator in the letter of preliminary approval. These interim directors are to serve until the bank's stock is sold and the stockholders are convened to elect the bank's board. In their first meeting the interim directors appoint the board's interim chairman, adopt bylaws, adopt a form of stock certificate, authorize the solicitation of stock subscriptions, designate an insured bank as depository of stock subscription funds, and authorize the purchase of fidelity insurance to cover the funds that will be raised from the sale of capital stock. Documents covering these items and the minutes of the meetings of the organizers and the interim board are forwarded to the Regional Administrator, in compliance with procedural requirements.

If they were not approved in the letter of preliminary approval, the interim board proceeds at this time to select the bank's executive officers: president, cashier, and senior officers. Their appointment must be approved by the office of the Regional Administrator after proper inquiry into the professional histories and backgrounds of these individuals. With at least the president in place, and an offering circular approved by the Regional Administrator, the organizing bank may proceed to solicit subscription offers for stock in the bank (see Figure 4.1). The selling price of the stock will be above its par value, so as to provide the bank with the necessary capital and an amount of surplus out of which organizational expenses are paid, even though, for regulatory purposes, they appear as charges to the undivided profits account (see Table 4.1). As the stock is being sold, the proceeds are deposited in an escrow account with a previously designated bank, to the credit of the organizing bank. The bank serving as an escrow agent will inform the Regional Administrator of the amount of money received and, under the provisions of the escrow agreement, will purchase government securities and indicate their maturities. The funds in escrow can be released to the interim board only after authorization of the Regional Administrator to the escrow bank. Some of the reasons for which releases can be made include the purchasing of fixed assets, payment of salaries, and other expenses necessary for preparing the organizing bank to conduct business.

Once the sale of capital stock has been completed and a list of shareholders has been submitted to—and approved by—the Regional

Figure 4.1. Sample Cover of Offering Circular

OFFERING CIRCULAR

FIRST BANK OF HIALEAH GARDENS, NATIONAL ASSOCIATION
(In Organization)

8200 N.W. 103rd Street
Hialeah Gardens, Florida 33016
(305) 558-2800

$2,600,000
COMMON STOCK

260,000 Shares

$5 Per Share — Par Value
$10 Per Share — Offering Price

THE MERITS OF THESE SECURITIES HAVE NOT BEEN PASSED UPON BY THE COMPTROLLER OF THE CURRENCY NOR HAS THE COMPTROLLER OF THE CURRENCY PASSED UPON THE ACCURACY OR ADEQUACY OF THE OFFERING CIRCULAR.

NO AGENT OR OFFICER OF THE BANK OR ANY OTHER PERSON HAS BEEN AUTHORIZED TO GIVE ANY INFORMATION OR TO MAKE ANY REPRESENTATIONS OTHER THAN THOSE CONTAINED IN THE OFFERING CIRCULAR, AND IF GIVEN OR MADE, SUCH INFORMATION AND REPRESENTATIONS SHOULD NOT BE RELIED UPON AS HAVING BEEN AUTHORIZED BY THE BANK.

THE ISSUANCE OF THE STOCK OFFERED HEREBY IS SUBJECT TO THE APPROVAL OF THE COMPTROLLER OF THE CURRENCY. THE BANK RESERVES THE RIGHT TO CANCEL ACCEPTED SUBSCRIPTION OFFERS AT THE DIRECTION OF THE COMPTROLLER OF THE CURRENCY UNTIL THE DATE THE BANK COMMENCES OPERATIONS. IF, FOR ANY REASON, THE BANK DOES NOT OPEN FOR BUSINESS OR IF FUNDS ARE RETURNED TO SUBSCRIBERS, ALL OF THE CASH PAID BY THE SUBSCRIBERS FOR THEIR SHARES WILL BE RETURNED, PLUS OR MINUS ANY PROFITS OR LOSSES INCURRED THROUGH INVESTMENT OF SUCH FUNDS IN UNITED STATES GOVERNMENT SECURITIES. ANY OTHER COSTS OR EXPENSES WILL BE BORNE BY THE ORGANIZERS.

	Price to Public	(1) Underwriting Commissions	(2) Expenses of the Offering	(3) Proceeds to Bank
Per Unit	$ 10.00	$-0-	$ .04	$ 9.96
Total	$2,600,000.00	$-0-	$10,400.00	$2,589,600.00

(1) These securities will be sold by the Organizers and Directors of the Bank, who will receive no commission in connection with such sales, but who will be reimbursed for expenses, if any, in connection with such sales. The Bank has not employed, nor does it intend to employ, any professional underwriters, brokers or salespersons in connection with this Offering.

(2) All expenses consist solely of legal, accounting, printing, mailing, filing and similar expenses. Expenses of the Offering Circular are subject to approval by the Comptroller of the Currency before they are reimbursed to the Organizers.

(3) Does not take into account expenses incurred by the Organizers in obtaining the charter ("Organizational Expenses"), which Organizational Expenses will be reimbursed to the Organizers, subject to approval by the Comptroller of the Currency.

The Effective Date of this Offering Circular is February 9, 1983.

Source: Reprinted by permission of First Bank of Hialeah Gardens, N.A.

Administrator, the first shareholders meeting will be called. The agenda of this meeting will include the election of a board of directors consisting of the individuals set out in the offering circular and approved by the Regional Administrator; approval of all organizational expenses and commitments made, which are to be reimbursed or paid from the capital funds; and ratification of the articles of association, the organization certificate, and all the official acts of the organizers, interim directors, and officers. Following the shareholders meeting, the Board will convene to take such actions as executing the oath of

Table 4.1. Sample Pro Forma Statement of Capitalization, First Bank of Hialeah Gardens, N.A. (in organization; February 25, 1983)

Equity Capital		Pro Forma Capitalization
Common stock (par value $5.00 per share)		
260,000 shares authorized		
260,000 shares issued and outstanding		$1,300,000
Surplus[a]		$1,289,600
Deficit accumulated during developmental stage[b]		
Organizational and preoperating expenses	($209,000)	
Less: Estimated investment income[c]	$ 25,000	($ 184,000)
TOTAL EQUITY CAPITAL		$2,405,600

[a]Expenses of the offering circular are charged to surplus.

[b]Organizational and preoperating expenses, if approved by the Comptroller of the Currency, are charged to undivided profits when the bank opens for business.

[c]Subscription funds are held in escrow and invested in U.S. government securities. Income from these investments is estimated to be $25,000.

Source: Offering Circular, First Bank of Hialeah Gardens, N.A. (February 25, 1983), p. 5. Reprinted by permission of First Bank of Hialeah Gardens.

national bank directors (that they will "diligently and honestly administer the affairs" of the bank), appointing all executive officers (who must have been approved by the Regional Administrator), and ratifying the bylaws. Once documents of the above actions and minutes of meetings are submitted to the Regional Administrator, the board and executive management should draft and adopt the policies of the bank (on loans, investments, and funds management), its organizational chart and job descriptions, internal control safeguards, and security devices.

When all preparations for opening are complete, a national bank examiner will be scheduled to visit the bank to conduct a preopening audit and to ascertain whether satisfactory operational procedures and policies have been established. Upon completion of this visit, the examiner will meet with the management to apprise it of his findings and the need for any corrective action. If the results of the examination are satisfactory, the bank must proceed to subscribe to stock of the district Federal Reserve bank and submit evidence that it has paid an amount equal to 3 percent of its capital stock and surplus. This and other information, including the definite date for opening the bank, constitute the final preopening documentation submitted to the Regional Administrator.

Once all the required steps of the organizational phase have been completed, the Regional Administrator will submit to the Comptroller of the Currency the bank's complete file with a recommendation that a "certificate of authority to commence business" be issued (banks commonly refer to it as the "charter"). The Comptroller of the Currency will notify the bank accordingly, and mail the charter. At the time the bank commences business, FDIC insurance is immediately in effect, as is Federal Reserve membership.

After the bank opens for business, it is required to advise the Comptroller of the Currency of the date it commenced business as a national bank and of the amount of total deposits it took that first day. It is also required to issue its stockholders stock certificates. Another postcommencement requirement for the bank is to publish its new charter in a local newspaper at least once each week for nine consecutive weeks and return to the Comptroller of the Currency an affidavit to this effect, signed by the newpaper's publisher. Once issued, a charter is perpetual unless it is terminated by action of the bank's owners (dissolution) or a regulatory body (as in cases of insolvency or violation of law).

Proposed charters may be rejected, usually because the community need is not considered great enough, the capital base is deemed inadequate, or the applicants are judged unsatisfactory with respect to financial standing or character. In addition, many prospective bank organizers are discouraged at an early stage from pursuing their application. Applications unsuccessful at the national level may be submitted to state chartering bodies, but the latter use virtually identical criteria in judging the proposed new bank.

ORGANIZATIONAL STRUCTURE OF A BANK

A bank, like any institution, mobilizes human resources for a defined purpose. The organizational structure of a bank reflects the specific arrangements that have been devised to accomplish desired goals. This structure consists of three main elements: the shareholders, who have invested their capital in the bank in hopes of realizing a profitable return; the board of directors, which is responsible for setting bank policy and bears ultimate responsibility for the bank's performance; and management, which carries out the policies set by the board and conducts actual bank operations. The roles of each of these groups will be discussed in the following sections.

Shareholders

A bank's stock may be distributed in a number of ways. It may be owned by a single individual or it may be a closely held corporation with a small number of shareholders. In the latter case the shareholders may consist solely of the board of directors as a matter of policy. Other banks seek broad-based ownership through public sale of stock in small lots. The distribution of a bank's stock is one aspect of a bank's character. Closely held corporations are more directly related to the interests of a small group of people. Banks with large and diverse groups of shareholders are more independent in character, and change of ownership occurs as a matter of course. When directors must answer to large numbers of shareholders, they are more likely to be responsive to community needs and to adopt a public service stance. The bank issues annual reports to its shareholders to inform them of the scope and profitability of bank activities.

Board of Directors

At the top of the bank's organizational chart is the board of directors. As noted above, this group sets policy for the bank, oversees its management, and is liable for the bank's activities and performance.

By law, national banks and state banks that are members of the Federal Reserve System must have at least five, and no more than twenty-five, board members. At least two-thirds of them must have resided for at least a year in the state in which the bank is located or within 100 miles of its main office, and must continue such residence during their term of office. These directors are elected to one-year terms by the shareholders. A majority of the directors must be U.S. citizens. Each director is required to own at least $1,000 worth of capital stock in the bank. Requirements for directors of state nonmember banks vary somewhat, but for the most part are similar to the federal requirements.

Although federal laws prohibit interlocking directorates among banks, the same individual may be a director of a bank and of another type of business as long as no conflict of interest occurs. Such a conflict would exist, for instance, if the other business is a competing financial institution. Thus the same individual would not be expected to serve as director of a bank and of a savings and loan association.

Duties and Responsibilities

The duties and responsibilities of the directors are many. They are in part determined by the directors' fiduciary responsibility to the bank's shareholders and customers and by banking statutes. Broadly speaking, they may be categorized as follows: setting bank objectives, formulating bank policies, selecting management, creating committees, providing supervision and counsel, and developing business for the bank.

Setting Bank Objectives. One function of the board of directors is to chart the bank's course, and this is generally done by setting goals and objectives toward which bank activities are directed. Goals and objectives are an integral part of any successful planning effort. They may be of several types. It is useful for an organization to have an overall goal that can be communicated, briefly and specifically, to the bank's entire staff. Such a goal might be to capture a certain share of the local market (for instance, to hold 8 percent of a community's deposits) or to attain a designated level of deposits (for instance, $5 million) by a certain time. Besides building morale and a sense of teamwork among bank employees, such goals improve coordination and efficiency of bank activity because all bank operations are directed toward this goal.

More specific objectives are formulated to provide targets for particular areas of bank activity. Thus the board might decide that certain types of loans are in the bank's best interest, and set objectives in this regard that become the basis for the loan department's planning. Progress toward these objectives is continually monitored. In addition, such objectives are adjusted or revised as changing economic or market conditions warrant. Many boards set short-, intermediate-, and long-term profit objectives. Setting these objectives involves the formulation of a detailed plan that sets targets for each type of activity in which the bank engages. The board receives regular reports on the profit performance of all bank activities and uses them to monitor progress toward the bank's overall goals.

Formulating Policies. To guide management in its progress toward defined goals and objectives, the board of directors formulates bank policies. These provide the framework for the specific types of activity that are to be undertaken. Liquidity and reserve levels, types of investment to pursue, kinds of loans to solicit, the establishment of branches, and the introduction of automation are matters of policy that allow managers to direct their efforts in coordinated fashion toward the stated objectives. Policies are also set regarding public relations, customer relations, and marketing strategies. In order not to straitjacket management, policies must be flexible and subject to periodic review and adjustment. Personnel policies represent a specific category of policy issues governing salaries and benefits, vacations and leaves, and other matters relating to bank staff.

Selecting Management. Although one or a few board members may wear the dual hats of board member and senior bank officer, the directors do not run the bank. They recruit and hire officers and managers who are skilled in bank operations. Competition for managerial talent in banking is keen, and the board must keep salaries and benefits competitive in order to attract high-caliber management personnel.

Creating Committees. Most boards create committees that are charged with overseeing specific areas of bank operations. Committees serve several purposes. By focusing the ongoing attention of a few directors on a specific area of concern, they allow the board to stay in closer touch with a bank's diverse activities. They provide an excellent means of tapping the specialized skills and experience of individual directors. In larger banks, committees help coordinate the activities of the different bank departments. Committees also serve the public interest because they provide the safety of group decision making in the handling of the deposits entrusted to the bank.

The most common standing committees are listed below. In addition, ad hoc committees may be formed to oversee specific, short-term matters, such as moving to a new building.

—Executive Committee. Decides on issues requiring action between board meetings; conducts studies and reports findings to the board

—Loan Committee. Ensures that the bank's loan policies are being carried out appropriately. Reviews interest rates, types, and amounts of loans to be made; passes on individual loans above a specified amount

—Investment Committee. Ensures that the bank's investment policies are being complied with; decides on types of investments and amounts to be placed in each

—Trust Committee. Oversees administration of the trust department and investment of trust funds. Large banks may have a separate committee for each of these functions

—Audit Committee. Conducts periodic unannounced audits similar to bank examinations. These may be conducted either by the members of this committee or by a hired accounting firm

—Salary and Employee Relations Committee. Reviews salaries and employee benefits, ensuring that they are competitive and otherwise appropriate.

Providing Supervision and Counsel. Although boards of directors vary considerably in terms of their direct involvement in bank activities, all are responsible for seeing that their bank is run in a sound and profitable manner, and is in compliance with the many regulatory requirements to which banks are subject. This supervisory function may be carried out, for instance, through periodic review of the loan and investment portfolios to ensure that they conform to bank policies in these areas. In addition, the directors stand ready to provide counsel to the bank's managers in many areas. Since bank directors are usually individuals with substantial business interests or high professional standing, and possess wide community contacts, they have many kinds of knowledge that will be valuable to the bank's managers. For example, a director's extensive knowledge of a particular industry may be useful to loan officers in the extension of credit to companies in that industry.

Developing Business. Again, because of their community contacts and standing, a board of directors drawn from a cross section of business and professional fields is in a good position to attract deposits and loan customers to the bank. Some boards set specific objectives in this regard for each member. In addition, directors are expected, in their other activities, to act as public relations agents for the bank.

Having reviewed the duties and responsibilities of bank directors, we may now look into their legal liabilities.

Liabilities

Bank directors are personally liable for a bank's operations under both criminal and common law. Thus, they may face prosecution under criminal law for participation in, assent to, or knowledge of bank activities that violate statutory requirements and prohibitions. Such legal restrictions include bans on falsification of records and entries, on loans to bank examiners or loans of trust funds to directors, and on political contributions. Theft or fraud by bank employees and misrepresentation of FDIC coverage are among criminal violations for which directors may be held liable. In addition, under common law they are liable for negligence if they fail to exercise ordinary care and prudence in overseeing the bank's activities.

Clearly, bank directorship is not a role to be undertaken lightly. In order to function adequately, a director must learn the rules and regulations under which banks operate, and must participate actively, so as to be aware of actual bank procedures and operations. Ignorance of bank activities is not accepted as a defence against a charge of negligence. Once one has decided to accept the challenge of bank directorship, with its responsibilities and liabilities, specific steps can be taken to minimize the risk involved. First, the directors establish procedures to ensure that they are receiving adequate information about bank activities. This is one purpose of internal auditing and ongoing supervision. Second, the risk can be transferred through the purchase of liability insurance to cover losses from criminal acts, burglary, theft, forgery, and errors. Because of its coverage of these and other risks involved in bank activity, this type of policy is frequently referred to as a blanket bond.

Management

The third component of a bank's organizational structure is the management team headed by the bank's senior executive officers. It is the job of management to carry out the policies set by the board of directors and to conduct the bank's day-to-day operations. However, policy is not simply handed down by the board of directors. In most banks management proposes policy. These recommendations are discussed, perhaps modified, and ratified by the board. Thus policy emerges from a dynamic interaction between senior management and the board of directors.

The management team of a bank is usually headed by the chairman of the board of directors, the president, and other officers. This group is the primary liaison between the bank's employees and the board. These individuals provide executive leadership for the bank. The chairman of the board is often the chief executive officer of the bank. Through this combined position he is responsible for harnessing the energies of the board of directors in the best interests of the bank. He is active in civic affairs and his stature in the community builds goodwill for the bank.

The president is the administrative head of the bank. In cases where the board chairman is not also a bank officer, he is the bank's chief executive officer. His duties are of two basic types: representing the bank in the community and overseeing bank operations. Usually one or the other of these roles is emphasized. Thus one bank president may spend much time developing business and goodwill for the bank, while another may devote most of his time to internal operations and planning. The latter case is more typical of smaller banks.

In the performance of his tasks the president is assisted by a number of officers. One of these, the cashier, is a traditional bank officer who, in small banks, works directly under the president and oversees the bank's internal operations. Once the board and the president have set bank policy, the cashier assumes responsibility for the actual transactions that implement it. His many functions include overseeing bank funds and investments; signing certificates of stock, cashier's checks, and bank drafts; endorsing notes and drafts to be submitted to other banks for collection; hiring junior staff members; and purchasing.

All banks except very small ones have a comptroller, who oversees the accounting department and makes statistical reports on bank activities to senior management and the board. These reports enable the board to gauge the profitability of bank activities and the soundness of current policies. In addition, the comptroller is responsible for seeing to it that bank operations are conducted as efficiently as possible. For instance, he might recommend increased automation or the elimination of unnecessary procedures. Finally, the comptroller drafts proposed budgets that serve as the basis for final budget adoption by the board.

The auditor has ongoing responsibility for assuring that bank operations are conducted in a manner that is consistent with generally accepted accounting practices, the policies of the bank, and the rules and regulations of supervisory agencies. To prevent or control fraud, the audit staff frequently verifies the bank's cash accounts and security holdings. In addition, it scrutinizes operating procedures to identify inherent weaknesses and enhance internal security. The auditor has the authority to examine every aspect of a bank's operations. This vigilance is designed to protect the bank against waste, misappropriation of funds, and unauthorized manipulation of bank assets. The activities of the auditor are independent of outside audits conducted by supervisory agencies and contracted accounting firms. The auditor reports directly to the board of directors.

In branch banking each branch has an administrative head whose title may be manager or vice-president. This individual reports to the branch supervisor at the bank's administrative headquarters.

Determinants of Bank Internal Structure

Although all banks possess shareholders, board of directors, and management, there is important variation among banks in the extent of departmentalization. Organizing managerial functions by departments occurs in all but the smallest banks and serves several functions. Departmentalization means that individuals with particular talents or specialized knowledge can concentrate their efforts in areas where they have the most to offer. It allows banks to provide more complex services and thus to draw customers they could not otherwise attract. It promotes efficiency and growth.

As mentioned, many small banks do not have departments. Larger banks may have separate departments for one or a few major functions while grouping other functions in the hands of a single officer. In other words, departments tend to emerge as a given area of functioning outgrows one individual's capacity to manage it. Since banks range in size from those with less than five employees to those with several thousand, there is room for considerable variety in organizational arrangements. In addition, bank organization is affected by such factors as the personalities and abilities of individual managers and the relative scope of various bank activities.

Bank departments may also be organized along line and staff functions. Line functions are the bank's activities that are integral to attaining its objectives, such as lending, investing, accepting deposits, managing trusts, and issuing credit. Staff functions are the activities that support the performance of line functions, such as accounting, control, training, marketing, personnal functions, and building maintenance. In small or medium-size banks there may be a clear-cut division between line and staff activities, while in larger banks, with their more elaborate organizational structures, they may be somewhat intertwined.

The specific nature of a bank's organizational structure is largely determined by three factors: the kinds of markets the bank serves, the bank's size, and the prevailing statutes regarding branching.

The markets in which banks operate vary according to the types of economic activity prevalent in the community the bank serves and the geographic scope of the bank's operations (local, regional, national, or international). Thus, banks in the Detroit area may have departments that specialize in financing the automobile industry, while banks in rural areas may have departments focusing on agribusiness. Such specialized departments accumulate the knowledge to make wiser lending decisions in these areas; they also attract customers who will benefit from such specialization. In addition, banks may create departments according to types of service offered, thus having a trust department, an international department, or a leasing department. Finally, banks that offer specialized financial services on a nationwide basis may divide these departments according to geographic markets.

Size is another important determinant of a bank's organizational structure. As a bank grows, the number of people needed to do its work grows, and the job of coordinating its activities becomes more complex. At some point in a bank's expansion, growth and specialization feed each other. Growth creates the need and the capacity for greater specialization; the creation of specialized departments, in turn, promotes further growth in several ways. Highly talented and specialized managers increase bank productivity and efficiency. Service departments with in-depth knowledge of certain areas of investment or service attract customers whose needs could not be met by a smaller bank with less specialized knowledge. Meanwhile, growth affects the overall organizational structure of a bank. Whereas in a medium-size bank all departments may report directly to the president, in larger banks there may be several levels of administrative officers with broader authority to oversee the diverse areas of the bank's activity.

If the state in which a bank is located is a unit banking state, branches are prohibited, and are therefore of no consequence to a bank's organizational structure. However, if a bank operates in a branching state, there is a need for some type of control and coordination of the individual branches from the head office. Several reporting methods are practiced. In some cases all branches in a particular geographic area report to a single officer at the bank's headquarters. In other cases the bank's smaller branches (as measured by deposits held and loans issued) report to one officer and larger branches report to another. A third reporting mechanism does not involve a single branch coming under the authority of a single individual at the head office. Rather, the branch's loan department reports to the main office's senior loan officer; the branch's deposit officer reports to his or her counterpart at the head office; and so on. In small branch banks each branch manager typically reports directly to the bank president.

A bank's organizational chart identifies the channels of administrative responsibility of the principal officers, the degree and kinds of departmentalization, the bank's committees, and the use of line and staff functions. Figure 4.2 shows the organizational chart of a medium-size bank, the Republic National Bank of Miami, the sixth largest bank in Dade County, Florida, with total assets in excess of $628 million as of December 31, 1982. The bank is composed of two main divisions, the Banking Division and the Financial and Investment Division. Each is headed by an executive vice-president reporting to the president and chief executive officer of the bank. Each division consists of two clusters of departments. In the Banking Division there are three customer-related departments (commercial and construction loans, international banking, and installment loans) and three internal operations departments (comptroller and operations, personnel management, and branch administration, which is responsible for efficient operation and administration). Each of these departments is headed by a vice-president, who reports to the division's executive vice-president. Similarly, the Financial and Investment Division includes two clusters of departments, the asset and liability management group and the corporate management group. Under the former are the money market,

Figure 4.2. Organization Chart, Republic National Bank of Miami (April 15, 1983)

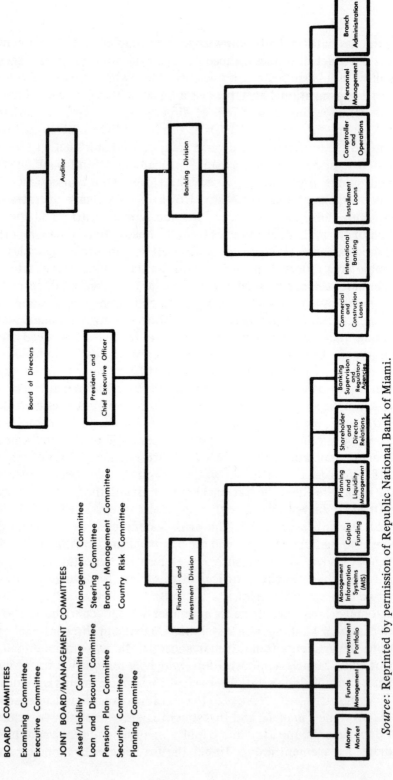

BOARD COMMITTEES

Examining Committee
Executive Committee

JOINT BOARD/MANAGEMENT COMMITTEES

Asset/Liability Committee   Management Committee
Loan and Discount Committee   Steering Committee
Pension Plan Committee   Branch Management Committee
Security Committee   Country Risk Committee
Planning Committee

Board of Directors

Auditor

President and Chief Executive Officer

Financial and Investment Division

Banking Division

Money Market

Funds Management

Investment Portfolio

Management Information Systems (MIS)

Capital Funding

Planning and Liquidity Management

Shareholder and Director Relations

Banking Supervision and Regulatory Agencies

Commercial and Construction Loans

International Banking

Installment Loans

Comptroller and Operations

Personnel Management

Branch Administration

Source: Reprinted by permission of Republic National Bank of Miami.

funds management, and investment portfolio departments. The corporate management group includes management information systems, captial funding, planning and liquidity management, shareholder and director relations, and banking supervision and regulatory agencies.

The bank is headed by the president, who is both the chief executive officer and a director. As officer-director the president is the liaison between the management and the board. His main task is to present to the board the various problems that confront the institution, so that it may determine the appropriate course of action and formulate policy.

Figure 4.3. Organization Chart, All American National Bank of Miami (June 15, 1982)

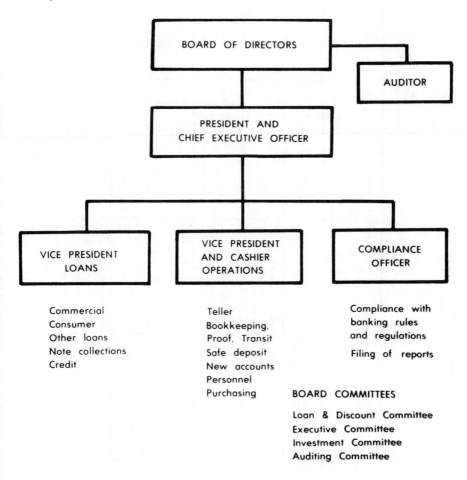

Source: Reprinted by permission of All American National Bank.

Figure 4.4. Organization Chart, Flagship National Bank of Miami (December 15, 1982)

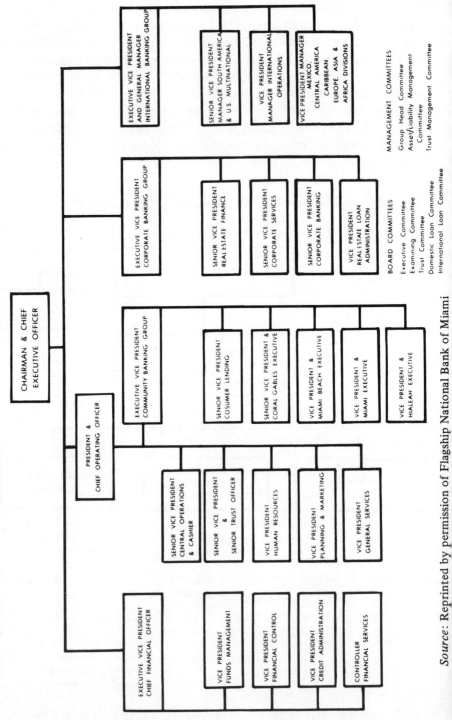

Source: Reprinted by permission of Flagship National Bank of Miami

Another important feature in the organization of Republic National is its reliance on committees. This feature, typical of many banks, had its origin in the depression years and the need for sound judgment in a period of increased bank failures. As shown in Figure 4.2, the bank has a number of joint board/management committees. In addition there are two committees consisting of board members only. The duties of these committees are similar to those described earlier in this chapter.

Clearly, the organizational structure of a bank may be simpler or more elaborate than that of Republic National, depending upon individual circumstances. Figure 4.3 presents the organizational structure of a small unit bank, the All American National Bank of Miami. Figure 4.4 is the chart of a large bank, the Flagship National Bank of Miami. The differences are quite striking. Since there is more to manage in a bank the size of Flagship, there is a wider range of titles and increased delegation of authority to the lower levels of management.

All related functions are grouped together under four individuals who make up the bank's top management and report to the chairman of the board in his additional capacity as the bank's chief executive officer. One of these four individuals is the president, who oversees such basic aspects of the bank as branch banking, operations, marketing, human resources, consumer lending, trust, and general services (such as purchasing and telecommunications). Branch banking is identified by region and the branch executive in charge of it. Each branch executive is responsible for the branches in his region. Flagship's other major activities are headed by three executive vice-presidents: the chief financial officer, who covers such aspects as investments, asset/liability management and accounting; an executive vice-president covering corporate banking; and one in charge of international banking. In the latter instance the bank's international interests are readily identifiable by the regions covered and also by the seniority of the officers in charge of these regions.

SUGGESTED REFERENCES

Baughn, William H., and Charles E. Walker, eds. *The Banker's Handbook*. Rev.ed. Homewood, Ill.: Dow Jones-Irwin, 1978.

Burke, Ronald G. "Bank Directors Face Stronger Role." *Magazine of Bank Administration*, September 1978, pp. 28-31.

Chaps, B. D. "If I Were a Bank Director . . . ." *Magazine of Bank Administration*, September 1977, pp. 18-21.

Comptroller of the Currency. *Duties and Liabilities of Directors of National Banks*. Rev. ed. Washington, D.C.: Comptroller of the Currency, 1972.

Comptroller of the Currency. *Comptroller's Manual for National Banks*. Pt. 5, pp. 2.23-2.30.2. Washington, D.C.: Comptroller of the Currency, November 1980.

Rubin, Harvey W. "A Banker's Guide to Directors' and Officers' Liability." *Bankers Magazine*, May-June 1978, pp. 27-31.

As Chapter 4 indicates, there is considerable variation in bank organizational structure. However diverse their structures may be, however, all banks have two basic objectives: acquiring funds and utilizing them. Utilization of funds is the subject of Part IV; acquisition of funds is examined here and in Chapter 6.

A commercial bank has access to three sources of funds: capital, deposits, and borrowing. Specifically, when a bank sells stock, accepts deposits, or borrows, it is thereby provided with funds that enable it to acquire earning assets—that is, to grant loans and make investments. Interest earned on these loans and investments provides the principal source of earnings out of which the bank meets the operating expenses involved in attracting and servicing deposit accounts and in managing its loans and investments. Residual earnings accrue to the bank's owners.

The sources of bank funds constitute the right-hand side of a bank's balance sheet (the left-hand side shows the assets that a bank owns—that is, the uses to which a bank puts available funds). Unlike other businesses, however, the right-hand side of a bank's balance sheet is made up overwhelmingly of liabilities, and only to a much lesser extent of capital. Indeed, a closer look at the funds sources reveals that banks rely heavily on debt to finance the acquisition of assets, which in fact are the debts of others—the federal government, state and local governments, businesses, and individuals. This situation has earned banks the reputation of being dealers in debts.

Bank reliance upon each of the sources of funds and the extent of such reliance are neither incidental nor a matter of an attitude, such as "the more funds, the better." Instead, it is a matter of policy, developed by the board of directors of each individual bank. Indeed, it is the responsibility of the board to develop policies regarding amounts and types of funds to be acquired.

The nature and characteristics of each of the sources of bank funds, as well as the extent of bank reliance upon each source, are covered here and in chapters 6 and 7. Deposits and borrowing are discussed in chapters 6 and 7, while this chapter concentrates on a bank's capital structure, describing the different types of bank capital, their cost, and their functions.

TYPES OF BANK CAPITAL

Bank capital cannot be treated as a single and homogeneous item. Such consideration might have been possible earlier in the twentieth century, but it is no longer. Management is now confronted with different forms of bank capital and even different ways of raising a given form of it. Choice of the form of capital, of the amounts needed in each form, and of the way of raising it have important implications for bank profitability. It is in this regard that the term "capital management" is often used today. It means concern with the way in which capital, like other bank funds, can best be acquired and managed.

The different types of capital available to banks are generally classified into two broad categories, equity capital and debt capital (capital notes and debentures). Capital notes and debentures, though they are instruments of indebtedness, are frequently used by banks as a permanent part of their capital structure. Many banks with continuing needs for long-term funds follow the practice of re-funding a maturing issue of such debt with the proceeds of a new issue. Such a practice makes capital notes and debentures a permanent addition to a bank's capital structure. From a regulatory perspective, too, debt instruments can qualify as part of a bank's capital base. Most regulatory agencies have criteria that these instruments must meet to qualify as bank capital.

To the two sources of capital mentioned above, bankers add a third, reserves on loans and securities. These accounts represent funds earmarked from current earnings to absorb possible loan and security losses. Thus, although explicitly reported on the asset side of the balance sheet as offsets to a bank's loan and investment portfolios (technically referred to as asset valuation reserves), in practice these accounts are viewed as another source of capital funds. Of these two accounts the more important is the loan-loss reserve account. Since loans constitute the largest single component of bank assets, proportionally more funds are set aside for loan losses than for security losses. Moreover, because the large majority of security holdings of many banks consists of risk-free federal issues and/or high-grade municipals, the size of reserves for security losses has been relatively insignificant. Thus, our discussion, in addition to equity and debt capital, will include reserves for loan losses.

Table 5.1. Capital Accounts and Reserves for Loan Losses, All Insured Commercial Banks, 1961-81 (millions of dollars)

Year	Total Capital and Reserves	Equity Capital	Capital Notes and Debentures	Reserves for Loan Losses
1961	24,729	22,101	22	2,606
1965	33,916	28,252	1,653	4,011
1966	36,030	29,963	1,730	4,337
1967	38,738	32,021	1,984	4,733
1968	41,844	34,518	2,110	5,216
1969	45,462	37,578	1,998	5,886
1970	48,566	40,475	2,092	5,999
1971	53,056	43,949	2,956	6,151
1972	58,992	48,275	4,093	6,624
1973	65,365	53,721	4,117	7,527
1974	71,665	59,028	4,260	8,377
1975	77,372	64,309	4,408	8,655
1976	83,567	72,249	5,123	6,195
1977	91,714	79,280	5,739	6,695
1978	100,998	87,418	5,865	7,715
1979	112,156	97,241	5,956	8,959
1980	123,684	107,599	6,267	9,818
1981	135,646	118,306	6,222	11,118

Source: Federal Deposit Insurance Corp., *Assets and Liabilities* (Washington, D.C.: FDIC, 1965-76); and *Statistics on Banking* (Washington, D.C.: FDIC, 1981), p. 43.

The relative importance of each of these sources of bank capital in 1961-81, for all insured commercial banks, is shown in Table 5.1. Banks have depended overwhelmingly on equity capital, which between 1961 and 1981 increased from $22.1 billion to $118.3 billion. Its dominance over the other two sources is to be expected, since traditionally equity capital has been the major component of commercial banks' capital accounts. Following in importance, by a significant margin, were reserves for loan losses, which at the end of 1981 amounted to $11.1 billion. Last, debt capital—in the form of capital notes and debentures—stood at $6.2 billion at year-end 1981. This item reached this level from a mere $22 million in 1961. Each of these sources of bank capital and the factors responsible for its pattern of growth are reviewed in the following sections.

Equity Capital

Equity capital identifies the value of the stockholders' investment in the business. Traditionally equity capital has been decisive in the establishment of a bank and in its functioning as a going concern. It is not a single account but a composite of the following types of accounts: common stock, surplus, undivided profits, and contingency reserves. To the extent that a bank has issued preferred stock, that account, too, would be part of its equity capital. Historically, issuance of common stock has been the dominant method of raising long-term capital. As we saw in Chapter 4, banks sell common stock when they are chartered in order to raise part of the funds needed for operation. After a bank is in operation, it can raise additional capital by issuing more shares of common stock. The total number of shares outstanding, valued at par, determines the value of the capital stock of a bank as listed on its balance sheet. This item, however, must not be interpreted as representing the total amount of capital raised by a bank through sale of its common stock. First, it may include the par value of stock distributed to stockholders in the form of stock dividends. Like other corporations, banks can declare dividends payable in stock, which adds to the total par value of the shares outstanding. Second, bank stock is customarily sold to the public—both at the time of organization and later—at a price in excess of par value, with such excess allocated to the paid-in surplus account.

The surplus account is a permanent part of a bank's equity. What this means is that a bank cannot reduce its surplus account by, for example, making dividend payments or by charging (unless in the process of liquidation) operating losses. Balances in the surplus account are derived from premiums on stock sold over par to the public and from transfers of earnings from the undivided profits account. These transfers are made upon decision of a bank's board of directors and are intended to augment the surplus account. In fact, since 1935 national banks have been required by federal law to make such transfers until their surplus account is at least equal to the value of the bank's capital stock. This requirement came to replace the double-liability clause carried by all national-bank stock. Prior to 1935, if the capital of a national bank was depleted by losses, each stockholder was personally liable for an amount equal to the par value of the stock he or she held in that bank. Shareholder assessments were thus relied upon to restore the capital of a bank. The purpose of this double-liability clause was to ensure a double margin of safety for depositors. During the depression years this provision proved unworkable, and was therefore abandoned. The requirement that national banks maintain a surplus account that is at least equal to their common-stock capital was then substituted. This parity is also required by some states.

Apart from its functioning as a buffer against losses, the paid-in surplus account played an important role in determining legal lending capacity. Until the early 1970s the legal lending limit for all national banks and most state banks was a set percentage of the combined total of common-stock capital and surplus accounts. An increased surplus account thus enhanced the ability of banks to meet the credit needs of their larger customers. However, redefinition of the lending base by the Comptroller of the Currency to include total capital (both debt and equity capital and 50 percent of the loan loss reserve account) has reduced the significance of the paid-in surplus as a determinant of lending limits. Since few states have followed suit, the size of the paid-in surplus account continues to be an important consideration for many state banks.

"Undivided profits" is the equivalent of the retained earnings account of nonbank businesses. This is an operating account that includes current as well as accumulated earnings that have not been paid out as dividends, transferred to surplus, or placed in any of the reserve accounts that banks keep for specific purposes. Management has much greater flexibility with the undivided profits account than with the surplus account. When a national bank is established, it can charge its organizational costs and other expenses approved by the Regional Administrator to undivided profits (see Table 4.1). Since profits do not yet exist, this technically results in a negative undivided-profits account balance, which will be adjusted as earnings develop. Also, management has the freedom to charge losses against the undivided profits account when the balances of loss-reserve accounts are insufficient to absorb them.

Subject to regulatory guidelines, management can allocate funds from undivided profits to one or more reserve accounts to take care of some contingency or expected event. Amounts so allocated are reported in equity capital either as "reserves for contingencies" or as "other capital reserves." Funds set aside because of a pending lawsuit are an example of a contingency reserve; funds set aside for dividend payments or for the anticipated retirement of preferred stock are examples of capital reserves. The amounts allocated to these and other capital-reserve accounts are not deductible from income taxes.

Some banks raise capital funds through the sale of preferred stock. These stocks are called preferred because they give investors contractual rights that precede those of common stock. A preferred stock gives a prior claim—relative to a common stock—to a bank's earnings and, in the event of liquidation, to its assets. However, since a preferred stock is part of equity capital, its claims with regard to earnings and assets are subordinate to deposits and all other indebtedness of the bank. Except on matters involving their own rights and privileges, preferred stockholders have no voting rights. This feature of preferred stock has rendered it especially appealing to banks that are closely held. When ownership of a bank is concentrated in a relatively small group of common stockholders, issuance of preferred stock permits this group to raise the necessary capital while maintaining close control of the bank.

Preferred stock dividends are generally stated as a percentage of par; for instance, a dividend of 9 percent of par on a preferred stock with a par of $50 would be $4.50 ($50 × .09). A bank need not pay dividends on preferred stock if it so chooses, so long as it does not pay common stock dividends. Therefore, nonpayment of the preferred dividend does not increase the probability of default, as is the case if interest on debt is not paid. Preferred stocks have no maturity, but many issues contain call provisions that permit a bank to reduce the amount of preferred stock outstanding by purchasing it at a predetermined price.

Until quite recently commercial banks have been reluctant to issue preferred stock because during the depression, distressed banks used this method of raising capital to such an extent that issuance of preferred stock came to be associated with banks in trouble. In the 1930s the Reconstruction Finance Corporation made many purchases of preferred stock in order to bail out banks experiencing financial difficulties. Following economic recovery, much of the preferred stock issued by banks in the 1930s was retired through call or open-market purchase. During the growth period of the 1950s and 1960s, when many banks increased their range of activities to national or international dimensions, they needed to raise additional outside capital to carry out these expansions. Thus there was growing pressure from the banking industry for permission to issue senior capital (debt instruments and preferred stocks). The breakthrough came in the form of a December 1962 ruling from Comptroller of the Currency James J. Saxon that gave national banks more flexibility in the management of their capital account. National banks were allowed to issue preferred stock as part of their capital structure.

Each of the equity capital accounts discussed above and its dollar balances for the period 1961-81 is shown in Table 5.2. The largest single account is undivided profits, which at year-end 1981 amounted to nearly $53 billion. This amount is net of dividend payments and all transfers of funds to surplus and reserve accounts. In this respect, that amount is an understatement of the true magnitude and importance of undivided profits as a source of equity capital. Even so, however, a close look at the evolution of undivided profits vis-à-vis that of total equity capital during 1961-81 reveals that the former has been responsible for most of the growth of the latter. This means that the banking industry's equity growth came essentially from internally generated funds—a product of profitable bank operations and a high earnings retention rate for the period under consideration.*

Two other sources of equity capital shown in Table 5.2 are preferred and common stocks. As indicated in the table, the contribution of preferred stocks in the equity capital structures of commercial banks has been insignificant. To some extent this has been due to the continued association of preferred stocks, by both present-day bankers and investors, with distress financing. Another reason is the hybrid character of preferred stocks in relation to bonds and common stocks. Thus, unlike bond interest, preferred-stock fixed-dividend payments are not tax-deductible, which makes the cost of such funds equal to the full precentage amount of the preferred dividend. On the other hand, unlike common-stock dividends, preferred-stock dividends are most frequently of a cumulative nature—that is, all past preferred dividends must be paid before any payment of common dividends. These disadvantages may, of course, be lessened through a convertibility feature that permits conversion into common stock at a predetermined price, at the option of the preferred stockholder. Last, preferred stocks

---

*Available data indicate that from 1969 to 1981, the average earnings retention rate for all FDIC-insured banks was 61.85 percent of net income.[1]

Table 5.2. Equity Capital Accounts, All Insured Commercial Banks, 1961-81 (millions of dollars)

Year	Total Equity Capital	Preferred Stock	Common Stock	Surplus	Undivided Profits	Equity Reserves
1961	22,101	15	6,585	10,798	4,157	546
1965	28,252	40	8,508	13,465	5,438	802
1966	29,963	62	8,857	13,999	6,166	880
1967	32,021	87	9,254	14,983	6,611	1,087
1968	34,518	91	9,773	16,174	7,420	1,061
1969	37,578	103	10,529	17,461	8,427	1,058
1970	40,475	107	11,138	18,073	10,146	1,011
1971	43,949	92	11,811	19,896	11,135	1,015
1972	48,275	69	12,854	21,528	13,012	812
1973	53,721	66	13,846	23,593	15,362	854
1974	59,028	43	14,789	25,313	17,970	912
1975	64,309	48	15,565	26,713	21,182	800
1976	72,261	67	16,219	28,894	25,252	1,829
1977	79,280	99	17,265	31,085	29,085	1,746
1978	87,418	114	18,158	33,203	34,536[a]	1,407[a]
1979	97,241	126	20,274	35,329	40,168[a]	1,345[a]
1980	107,599	135	21,677	37,776	46,649[a]	1,362[a]
1981	118,306	171	23,588	40,302	52,985[a]	1,290[a]

[a]Estimated by author.

Note: Details may not add to totals because of rounding.

Source: Federal Deposit Insurance Corp., *Assets and Liabilities* (Washington, D.C.: FDIC, 1965-76); *Statistics on Banking* (Washington, D.C.: FDIC, 1981), p. 43.

have been less appealing to investors because of their limited appreciation potential.

Unlike preferred stock, common stock has been the most sizable, and definitely the most traditional, source of external capital generation for commercial banks, including issuance of capital notes and debentures (see Table 5.1). Despite its dominance as a source of external capital, common-stock issuance has trailed in importance, by a wide margin, behind use of undivided profits. A number of reasons are likely to have been responsible for this development. For some banks it may have been the cost involved in marketing new issues of common stock; for others, the earnings dilution or control dilution of such issues.

Marketing new issues generally involves certain costs, usually referred to as flotation costs. These include commissions to those selling the new issue, printing expenses, advertising costs, and registration fees with the SEC. Flotation costs are generally higher for the issues of smaller and less-known businesses because of the greater risk involved in marketing them. Since these expenses are relatively large and fixed, the cost percentage runs higher on small issues. Clearly, then, for most small banks—and for small businesses in general—sale of common stock entails a disproportionate cost compared with the retention of earnings, which is the most convenient and least expensive way to provide additional equity capital. And if the sale of additional common stock is essential, a small group of interested local investors usually provides a ready outlet. This helps explain why the common shares of most U.S. banks are held by a relatively small number of stockholders, and hence the absence of an active market for these shares. Consequently, only a limited number of banks would be in a position to have their stocks traded on the over-the-counter market or a national stock exchange.* In fact, this is encountered only among the large banks.

---

*The banking industry has a tradition of not listing its stocks. The reason given for this was that banks were afraid that a falling market price of their stocks would lead depositors to think that a bank itself was in danger, and thus would cause a run on the bank. Some basis for such fears may have existed before the creation of the Federal Deposit Insurance Corporation (FDIC), but the fear is no longer justified. The other reason for banks not listing has to do with reporting financial information. The exchanges require that quarterly financial statements be sent to all stockholders; banks have been reluctant to provide financial information. With bank regulatory agencies requiring public disclosure of additional financial information, it is expected that banks will increasingly seek to list their securities on exchanges. A notable first in this respect occurred when the Chase Manhattan Bank was listed on the New York Stock Exchange in 1965.

Some banks avoid equity financing because of the dilution of earnings that it entails. For a small bank whose stock is closely held, issuing new shares of stock to outsiders means giving more owners the right to share income. In other words, new stockholders acquire equal rights with existing stockholders to share in the net profits of the bank.

In other instances equity financing is avoided because it would involve dilution of control, since the sale of common stock extends voting rights or control to the additional stockholders. In closely held banks existing stockholders are unwilling to share control of the bank's operations with outsiders. Thus, the potential dilution of earnings and/ or control has in many cases caused existing stockholders to veto the sale of new shares of common stock.

Debt Capital

Another important source of funds for commercial banks has been debt capital. Since the early 1960s banks have been increasingly relying on capital notes and debentures to provide for the growth of bank capital funds. The extent of bank reliance on this source is shown in Table 5.1. As indicated, between 1961 and 1981 the value of capital notes and debentures outstanding increased from a mere $22 million to $6.2 billion. This increase is quite impressive and creates new perspectives on the growth of bank capital.

Capital notes and debentures are fixed-claim, interest-bearing obligations that enable banks to raise capital. They are unsecured and are subordinate to the claims of depositors and other creditors. Whatever the original intention of the regulators may have been with respect to the specific features of each of these instruments, supervisory agencies use the terms "capital notes" and "debentures" interchangeably, with no apparent practical distinction between them.

Bank issuance of long-term debt first occurred during the Great Depression as a means of easing financial difficulties. When issuing additional common stock was not possible, banks turned to capital notes and debentures. Because this form of capital raising was thus associated with troubled banks, many banks were reluctant to use it in the 1950s and early 1960s. However, in 1961 the Commission on Money and Credit, in its comprehensive study of the U.S. banking and financial system, recommended that banks consider the issuance of subordinated debt as a means of raising capital. Soon thereafter the Advisory Committee on Banking to the Comptroller of the Currency echoed this recommendation: "There is no sound reason why national banks should be deprived of any legitimate capital-raising method that is available to corporations generally." In December 1962 the Comptroller of the Currency issued a ruling that permitted banks to issue capital notes and debentures as part of their ordinary raising of capital. The funds thus obtained were to be viewed as part of a bank's capital for the purpose of calculating lending limits on unsecured loans to any one borrower. Certain limitations were imposed in the ruling, notably that a national bank's capital notes and debentures were not to exceed 100 percent of the bank's capital stock plus 50 percent of surplus. Most states have since enacted similar legislation.

Although bank issuance of capital notes and debentures was associated with the distress financing of the early 1930s, the present-day attitudes of bankers and investors have changed significantly enough to make such debt instruments more acceptable in bank capital structures. Thus, throughout the 1960s and in the 1970s, a great many banks sold capital notes and debentures to raise additional capital. These instruments offered banks important advantages vis-à-vis long-term deposits as a source of funds. One major advantage to the issuing bank is that notes and debentures do not require reserve backing or FDIC insurance assessments, as deposits do. Moreover, the long-term maturity of these obligations minimizes a bank's need to maintain liquidity reserves against them. As a result, most of the proceeds from the sale of these instruments can be placed in longer-term, higher-yielding assets. Also, the administrative costs associated with these instruments are much less than for large time deposits attracted from national money markets.

Similarly, capital notes and debentures compare favorably with equity capital. The flotation costs of debt instruments are usually less than those for a similar dollar amount of common or preferred stock because the latter involve a higher degree of risk. Also, unlike dividends on common or preferred stock, which are paid from after-tax income, interest on capital notes and debentures is paid before taxes. This feature significantly reduces the after-tax cost of these instruments to a bank.

Common stockholders generally view favorably issuance of capital notes and debentures by their bank. Although these instruments increase a bank's leverage, their issuance is associated with important benefits for the common stockholders. Thus, assuming that the issuing bank is in a position to service the debt, issuance of capital notes and debentures does not cause dilution of control, since the holders of these instruments have no voting rights. Also, the holders of such debt do not participate in earnings beyond the stated interest rate on these instruments. Thus, the equity position of common stockholders in the bank is not diluted, but the bank has obtained additional capital for profitable expansion of its operations.*

Banks may raise, and often have raised, capital with issues of convertible subordinated debentures. These securities are like the subordinated debentures except that they give the holder the opportunity to trade the debenture for stock at some time in the future at a specified price. Because such issues offer the investor the attractive feature or interest payment protection plus the opportunity to convert to common stock, and thus participate in all future earnings, the interest rate on such debentures is generally lower than for those without a conversion feature. That makes convertible security issues desirable from the bank's point of view. Moreover, since they offer a bank the opportunity to obtain permanent capital with less dilution than if stock were issued immediately, convertible issues have been used extensively, and will continue to be employed. One disadvantage of convertible, compared with nonconvertible, debt instruments is that the underwriting fees are generally higher because of the risk that the price of the stock might drop before the convertible securities are issued.

Reserves for Loan Losses

As indicated earlier, loan-loss reserves represent earnings earmarked to cover possible loan losses. Over the years banks have accumulated substantial loan-loss reserves. At the end of 1981, reserves for losses on loans, for all insured commercial banks, had risen to $11.1 billion (see Table 5.1). In 1951 these reserves amounted to only $814 million, so in the span of 31 years they increased 13.6 times.

In their practice of maintaining loan-loss reserves, banks have been encouraged by both supervisory authorities and the Internal Revenue Service. Until 1969 banks were allowed to make additions to the reserve for loan losses out of pretax earnings until these reserves amounted to 2.4 percent of the eligible loans. As a result of this stipulation, loan-loss reserves grew significantly and were far in excess of actual losses (between 1950 and 1968, out of $8.8 billion placed in reserves, net loan charge-offs amounted to only $3.2 billion). In 1969, however,

---

*In the mid-1960s several of the large New York City banks sold millions of dollars' worth of subordinated debentures at an interest cost of 5 percent—at that time a very high rate of interest—and prompted widespread predictions by financial commentators of subsequent regret by the bankers. In retrospect, such sales were extremely wise moves that permitted expansion with safety at an interest cost that was modest in comparison with the 8.5 percent prime rate of the late 1960s or the 12 percent that prevailed in July 1974.[2]

the Tax Reform Act reduced this allowance to 1.8 percent of eligible loans and indicated that after succeeding adjustments through 1987, such reserves would be justified only up to the average of actual losses sustained over the most recent six-year period.[3] Clearly, the legislative reduction of the amount of pretax earnings permitted to be transferred to the reserves for loan losses will adversely affect the importance of this source of capital. Barring any legislative changes in this respect, banks will have to rely increasingly on some of the other sources of capital.

COST OF CAPITAL

As indicated in the preceding section, a bank can raise capital funds in a variety of ways. Debt can be issued in the form of subordinated notes and debentures. Earnings can be retained rather than paid as dividends. Preferred stock may be issued or additional common stock may be sold. Capital funds, however, are only one of the sources of funds available to a bank. A more sizable source, and one that banks use on a regular basis to finance asset growth, is deposits. Larger banks also make use of such nondeposit sources of funds as Eurodollars and federal funds. Management needs to know the cost of bank funds in order to make profitable decisions.

A simple, often-used approach to calculating a bank's cost of funds is based on the interest rate of negotiable 90-day CDs, on the premise that the CD rate is a reliable indicator of the "free-market cost of money," as long as an active secondary market exists. This cost proxy is the basis for deciding interest rates to charge borrowers and yields to seek in making investments. Although this method does not consider the cost of all available bank funds, the importance of CDs as a source of bank funds makes this approximation useful. For example, Citibank bases its floating prime-rate formula on the 90-day CDs rate as follows:

$$PR = \bar{R}_{cd} + M$$

where $\bar{R}_{cd}$ stands for the three-week average rate on 90-day CDs in the secondary market and M is the percent markup, which has been amounting to 1.25 percent. Thus, when the three-week average CD yield is 12 percent, Citibank's prime rate is 13.25 percent.

A more thorough method of computing the cost of capital, and one more suitable for planning purposes, involves computing the cost of each separate type of funds as well as the overall cost of the bank's aggregate pool of funds. This concept is known in banking as the weighted-average cost of funds, sometimes simply called the cost of funds. To determine this cost, one must take into account the different dollar amounts of funds from different sources, their proportion of total funds, and the respective cost of each type of funds. The resulting figure can be used as a standard in evaluating alternative uses of funds. In other words, this cost functions as the baseline for determining allocation of funds among alternative earning assets. Thus, earning assets will not be acquired unless their projected return exceeds the weighted-average cost of funds.

An example of the computations involved in developing a bank's weighted-average cost of funds is shown in Table 5.3. This table summarizes the different sources of funds of a hypothetical community bank, the First Hellenic Bank of Tarpon Springs. The financial structure of First Hellenic is made up of deposit funds (demand, time, and savings) and funds obtained through subordinated debt and equity capital. Also shown is the proportion, or weight, of total funds represented by each source, and the individual cost per type of funds. The product of these two items represents the weighted cost of each individual type of funds (WACF). As indicated in Table 5.3, the WACF for First Hellenic is 4.4 percent. Since cost data were computed on an after-tax basis, the bank can undertake only those loans and investments that have a pretax rate of return in excess of 8.5 percent. For example, a loan or investment with a pretax yield of 8.5 percent (net of service costs) would produce an after-tax rate of return of .085 $(1-.48)=.044$, or 4.4 percent.

As implied by the data of Table 5.3, the cost of each type of funds has an important bearing upon a bank's WACF. For example, funds obtained from deposit sources and subordinated debt have a lower cost than equity capital because of the tax deductibility of interest. Computing the cost of each individual type of funds exhibits important variation. Although this material is traditionally covered in financial management textbooks, the effort will be made here to summarize, and where necessary adapt, the relevant concepts as they apply to bank funds. The following sections deal with the methods of determining the costs of individual sources of funds.

Cost of Deposits

The principal source of bank funds is deposits. Traditionally deposits have been classified into demand, time, and savings. Demand deposits were noninterest-bearing deposits, while time and savings paid interest in accordance with the provisions of Regulation Q. In recent years, as interest rate restrictions began to break down, banks began to offer new types of accounts—NOW accounts, automatic

Table 5.3. Weighted-average Cost of Funds, First Hellenic Bank

Source of Funds	Amount (in millions)	Percent of Total	Cost Rate	Pct. × Cost
Noninterest-bearing demand deposits	$14[a]	.32	.020[c]	.006
Interest-bearing demand deposits, time and savings deposits	18[a]	.41	.037[c]	.015
Debentures	3.5[b]	.08	.057[c]	.005
Preferred stock	1.5[b]	.03	.090	.003
Common stock	2[b]	.05	.091	.005
Paid-in surplus	1	.02	.091	.002
Undivided profits	4	.09	.090	.008
Total	$44.0	1.00		.044

Weighted-average cost of funds=4.4%

[a]Net of legal reserves.

[b]It is a more realistic approach to report the amounts of these instruments on the basis of their current value in the marketplace. Historical values are not relevant to current decisions.

[c]Adjusted for tax purposes on the basis of the bank's tax rate of 48%. That is, initial costs were multiplied in each case by (1-t) to obtain the after-tax cost. This adjustment is necessary because the other cost items of this column are by definition on an after-tax basis.

Source: Prepared by author.

transfer services (ATS), and money-market deposit accounts—that blur traditional differences between demand and time and savings deposits. For the purpose of our analysis we will group deposits into two categories: interest-bearing and noninterest-bearing. In the former category belong the time and savings deposits and those demand deposits that earn interest, while in the latter category are the noninterest-bearing demand deposits.

Interest-bearing deposits entail both direct and indirect costs for a bank. Direct cost is the amount of interest that banks pay depositors for use of their funds. The indirect cost is a composite of the following items: cost of attracting deposits, cost of servicing deposits, and deposit insurance premiums. Both direct and indirect costs must be considered in determining the effective cost of interest-bearing deposits. Any charges or fees earned by the bank in the servicing of deposits are treated as offsets to these costs. Cost computations should be based on the average interest-bearing deposits for any given period of time. These deposits should be adjusted for the amount of funds set aside for legal reserves. The rationale for this adjustment is that since reserve requirements limit the amount of deposit funds available for loans and investments, they must be deducted from available deposits in determining the cost of these funds. Take, for example, the First Hellenic Bank. Assume that its average time and savings deposits for the year were $18.2 million and required reserves were $200,000. If the total annual interest paid to depositors was $1.115 million, the cost of attracting and servicing these deposits was $170,000, and deposit insurance premiums were $18,200, the effective cost of these funds would be

$$K_{ids} = \frac{1.115 + .170 + .018}{18.2 - .2} = .072 \ (7.2 \text{ percent}).$$

On an after-tax basis this would be equal to

$$K_{ids} = .072 \ (1 - .48) = .037 \ (3.7 \text{ percent}).$$

The same process would be followed in computing the cost of First Hellenic's interest-bearing demand deposits. Differences in the reserve requirements and/or the cost of acquiring and servicing these deposits may warrant separate cost computations for this group of deposits. The next step would be to develop an average-cost figure for the combined amount of interest-bearing deposits, using the weighting process shown in Table 5.3.

The formula for determining the after-tax cost of interest-bearing deposits can therefore be expressed as follows:

$$K_{id\,s} = \frac{IE + ASE + DI}{AD - R} \quad (1\text{-}t)$$

where:

IE = interest expense for the period under consideration

ASE = expenses of attracting and servicing deposits for this period

DI = deposit insurance premiums for this period

AD = average value of interest-bearing deposits for this period

R = dollar amount of legally required reserves for these deposits.

The above formula can also be used to determine the cost of non-interest-bearing deposits. The only adjustment needed regards interest cost, since these deposits bear no interest, the bank's direct interest cost would be zero. Using this formula, we can therefore develop the cost of noninterest-bearing demand deposits for the period under consideration. Assume that First Hellenic's noninterest-bearing demand deposits for the year were $14.4 million and required reserves were $400,000. Also assume that its costs of attracting and servicing these deposits were $532,000 and its deposit insurance premiums $14,400. In that case, the after-tax cost of these funds would be

$$K_{d\,s} = \frac{.532 + .014}{14.4 - .4} \quad (1\text{-}.48) = .020 \ (2 \text{ percent}).$$

Cost of Capital Notes and Debentures

The cost of debt capital to a bank is equal to the rate of return earned by investors in the bank's outstanding debt instruments or the interest rate that the bank must pay to sell new securities of this kind. The best measure of the rate of return on fixed income instruments is the yield to maturity. This is defined as the rate of return that is expected if a debt instrument is held to its maturity (for the yield-to maturity formula see Chapter 9). Thus, the yield to maturity of an outstanding debt issue is ordinarily used as the cost of a bank's debt capital. However, since the interest payments on debt instruments are tax-deductible, the yield-to-maturity figure must be converted to an after-tax basis by multiplying it by a tax factor. The equation for computing the after-tax cost of debt financing is

$$K_d = (1\text{-}t) \ YTM$$

where K_d is the after-tax cost of debt capital, t is the bank's marginal tax rate, and YTM is the yield to maturity of the outstanding debt instruments or the rate of interest that would be acceptable to investors in new issues of this type. If we were to replace the elements of this equation with the corresponding data of First Hellenic Bank, we would obtain an after-tax cost of 5.7 percent. Assuming that the market value of the outstanding debentures of First Hellenic is \$3.5 million and their yield to maturity is 10.9 percent, the bank's after-tax cost is

$$K_d = (1 - .48)(.109) = .057 \ (5.7 \text{ percent}).$$

If First Hellenic were a larger institution, it is likely that it would have made use of some borrowed funds. In other words, its liabilities would have included such items as federal funds purchased and securities sold under repurchase agreements (RPs). Since the maturity of these transactions varies from overnight to very short periods of time, and the rate charged fluctuates according to market conditions, the before-tax cost of these liabilities for the period under consideration would be equal to the geometric average of the short-term rates paid during this period. This is expressed by the equation

$$K_{bf} = [(1 + k_{1bf})(1 + k_{2bf}) \cdots (1 + k_{m\,bf})]^{\,1/m} - 1$$

where k_{tbf} is the cost of the borrowed funds in period $t = 1, 2, \ldots m$. For example, the cost of successive overnight borrowings of federal funds over a 20-day period, at going market rates (7%, 10%, 12%), would be

$$K_{bf} = [(1 + \frac{.07}{360})(1 + \frac{.10}{360}) \cdots (1 + \frac{.12}{360})]^{\,1/20} - 1.$$

Cost of Preferred Stock

As with capital notes and debentures, the cost of preferred stock to a bank is equal to the rate of return earned by investors in the bank's outstanding preferred issue. Unlike capital notes and debentures, however, most preferred issues have no maturity—that is, they are of perpetual nature. The holders of preferred stock thus expect to receive a fixed (stipulated) amount of dividends indefinitely. This fact, plus the absence of tax deductibility (since dividends are paid out of profits), means that the cost of a preferred issue is in essence the effective yield of the stock. This can be found by dividing the annual preferred dividend (D_p) by the price of the stock (P_p). In equation form the cost of preferred stock is

$$K_p = \frac{D_p}{P_p}.$$

If the preferred stock is newly issued, this formula can be adjusted to reflect the net price received by the bank because of flotation costs (f). These costs, expressed as a percentage of the selling price, will be incorporated in the above formula as follows:

$$K_p = \frac{D_p}{P_p(1-f)}.$$

For example, if buyers of the preferred stock of First Hellenic Bank paid $50 a share and brokers charged a commission of $5 a share, the cost of the preferred stock to the bank—assuming an annual dividend of $4—would be

$$K_p = \frac{4}{50(1-.10)} = .09 \text{ (9 percent)}.$$

Cost of Equity

Unlike debt issues and preferred stock, which call for fixed contractual payments, common stock has no explicit interest cost. To determine the cost of common stock, we need to compute the rate of return required by stockholders. This rate is a function of investors' perception of risk associated with the bank in question as well as the returns on alternative investment opportunities.

Issuance of common stock is but one source of equity capital. Another source is the retention of earnings. Retaining earnings has a cost that is equal to the rate of return stockholders require on the bank's common stock. The reasoning behind this is that if earnings were not retained but were paid out to stockholders, one investment option they would have would be to buy more of the bank's common stock. It is assumed that they would require a return equal to what they are earning on their present equity position. Thus the cost of retained earnings, though an opportunity cost, must equal the cost of existing common stock.

Several approaches have been put forward in financial literature to compute the cost of equity. The three standard ways to estimate it are summarized below.

Dividend Growth Model

According to this model, the cost of common equity, K_s, is given by the equation

$$K_s = \frac{D_1}{P_o} + g_s \qquad (5.1)$$

where D_1 is the dividend expected to be received in the next period, P_o is the current market price of common stock, and g_s is the growth rate of earnings or dividends. As a practical matter g_s is estimated from the past earnings, because dividends do not usually increase (or decrease) in proportion to the earnings, even though the model assumes that they do. This model has many assumptions that must be satisfied. Two of the most important are that K_s is always greater than g_s, and that there is no debt in the capital structure and none will be added in the future. This last assumption restricts the application of the model, yet the model is simple to understand and compute, and as a result it is widely used.

If no new common stock is issued, this model provides the cost of equity as well as the cost of retained earnings. If new stock is issued, the formula can be adjusted to reflect flotation costs (f). Thus, adjusting equation 5.1 for flotation costs, we have

$$K_s = \frac{D_1}{P_0 (1-f)} + g_s. \tag{5.2}$$

Furthermore, every bank experiences a period of abnormal growth —that is, when $K_s < g_s$. If this happens for a time period (t) and then the bank's growth rate reverts back to $K_s > g_s$, the cost of equity can be computed indirectly from the following formula:

$$P_0 = D_1 \frac{\frac{(1+g_n)^t}{(1+K_s)^t} - 1}{g_n - K_s} + \frac{D_1(1+g_n)^{t-1}(1+g_s)}{K_s - g_s} \frac{1}{(1+K_s)^t} \tag{5.3}$$

where g_n is the abnormal growth ($g_n > K_s$) up to time period t. It should be noted that K_s cannot be explicitly represented in terms of D_1, g_n, g_s, and t. Thus it can be obtained only implicitly. The examples below illustrate the application of this and the preceding two formulas.

Let us consider the case of First Hellenic Bank, whose structure of equity capital as depicted in Table 5.3, includes the following items:

Common stock	$2 million
Paid-in capital	$1 million
Undivided profits	$4 million

The bank is expected to pay a dividend of $0.50 next year. The current market price of its common stock is $50, and the growth rate of dividends has been estimated to be 8 percent. In this particular case, no matter what the composition of the bank's equity-capital structure, the cost of equity will not be affected. The cost will depend only on the growth rate of dividends, the expected dividend payment, and the common stock's current market price. The cost of equity (per equation 5.1) would be

$$K_s = \frac{0.50}{50} + .08 = .09 \text{ (9 percent)}. \tag{5.4}$$

Assume that the First Hellenic Bank sustained flotation costs for issuing its stock. If it received only $45 instead of $50 for each share of common stock it issued, its flotation cost (f) is $5 (50-45) per share, 10 percent of the selling price. Thus, the cost of its common stock (according to equation 5.2) would be

$$K_s = \frac{0.50}{50 (1-.10)} + .08 = .091 \text{ (9.1 percent)}. \tag{5.5}$$

As is apparent, flotation charges push the cost of the common equity above the cost of retained earnings.

In the preceding examples we assumed a constant annual growth rate (g_s) smaller than the required rate on (cost of) equity (K_s). Let us assume instead an abnormal growth pattern in determining the cost of equity. Thus, assume that the current selling price (P_o) of the stock of First Hellenic is $20.25. Moreover, the bank is expected to grow at the astronomical rate (g_n) of 15 percent for 10 years, its rate of growth leveling off after that (g_s) at 8 percent. If the expected dividend for the next year (D_1) is $0.50, what is the cost of equity?

Using equation 5.3, K_s will be the amount that satisfies

$$20.25 = 0.50 \; \frac{\frac{(1+.15)^{10}}{(1+K_s}-1}{.15-K_s} + \frac{(.50)(1+.15)^9(1+.08)}{K_s-.08} \; \frac{1}{(1+K_s)^{10}}. \tag{5.6}$$

By trial and error we find

$$K_s = .12 \text{ (12 percent)}.$$

CAPM Method

With the advent of the capital-asset pricing model (CAPM), an alternative approach to estimating the cost of equity was introduced. It is based upon the risk-return trade-off. The formulation is

$$K_s = R_f + [R_m - R_f] \; \beta \tag{5.7}$$

where R_f is the risk-free rate of return estimated by the return on U.S. Treasury securities (such as Treasury bills), R_m is the expected return on the market portfolio, and β (beta) is the index of the sensitivity of the rate of return on equity to the market rate of return, popularly known as systematic risk.* This model provides the risk-

---

*The concept of systematic risk as used in the portfolio theory is that part of a security's risk cannot be diversified away. Examples of systematic risk are *(Continued on page 128)* adjusted cost of equity capital of a bank. The value of R_f can be obtained from the *Wall Street Journal* or similar sources on any weekday. The value of β is published by *The Value Line Investment Survey* or *Moody's*, and usually does not change very often. The value of R_m can be obtained from the Center for Research in Security Market Prices (CRSP) of the University of Chicago.

Markup-on-Debt Approach

This method is ad hoc. The presumption is that owners (the holders of common stock) will require an appreciably higher rate of return than that earned by the institution's debt holders. Thus, the cost of equity capital is

$$K_s = \text{ROR to bondholders} + \text{markup}. \tag{5.8}$$

The rate of return to bondholders is usually taken as the average return on bonds of similar risk. For example, if a bank's bonds have been classified as AAA by *Moody's* and the average rate of return on AAA bonds is 11 percent, this will be taken as the rate of return to bondholders. The amount of markup is determined by management. For example, if management, on the basis of historical patterns, decides that the rate of return on the bank's common stock should run four percentage points over the yield on debt, this would imply a cost of equity (K_s) of 15 percent.

FUNCTIONS OF BANK CAPITAL

Equity capital performs a variety of functions. These may be classified into the following four categories: to provide for the necessary physical facilities through which the bank will become operational, to protect the creditors, to generate a competitive rate of return to bank shareholders, and to comply with the requirements of supervisory agencies.

Providing Start-up Funds

As we saw in Chapter 4, before a bank begins operations, its organizers sell stock to raise the capital to finance (provide funds for) fixed

---

(Continued from page 127)

inflation, recession, political unrest, and general conditions that affect all stocks in the same manner. Systematic risk is distinguished in portfolio theory from unsystematic risk, which refers to conditions unique to a company (such as a strike or a lawsuit) and their effect on an individual stock. Unsystematic risk can be eliminated by diversification.

investments, such as land, building, furniture, machinery, equipment, and supplies necessary to establish the bank as a going concern. This function of capital is typical of any new business. As the bank grows, additional capital funds are used to build and equip branches, introduce improved technology, and finance other fixed assets needed to sustain growth momentum. The high rates of interest experienced in the late 1970s have affected traditional practices in the financing of fixed assets. Since market returns have generally exceeded the relatively modest yields of fixed assets, many banks have sold their buildings and equipment to insurance companies or specially formed subsidiaries, which lease these assets back to the bank. This practice has released frozen funds to be invested or loaned more profitably.

Protecting Creditors

At year-end 1981 nearly 76 percent of the total assets of all insured commercial banks were financed by deposits. If one adds the portion of assets financed by nondeposit liabilities (both short-term and long-term), then 93 percent of bank assets were financed by debt. By contrast, only 7 percent of bank assets were financed by equity capital. What this means is that banks utilize a high degree of financial leverage (a high debt/assets ratio) in the financing of their assets. This degree of leverage is uncommon among nonfinancial businesses, whose margins of leverage are generally more conservative.

This high ratio of debt to assets, so typical of the banking industry, places great importance on the function of capital to protect the interests of the bank's creditors. From the depositors' and other creditors' point of view, capital's function is to provide a margin of protection for their claims in the event of liquidation. Capital plays an even more important role in the daily operations of a bank. Its capacity to generate earnings is important in absorbing losses as they occur and in spreading their impact over time. Thus, in the broadest sense, it protects the depositors and any other creditors by providing the security with which to take sensible business risks and maintain the institution as a going concern. In other words, capital performs the function of a guarantee or safety fund against any losses arising from the lending, investing, and all other activities incidental to commercial banking.

Since the advent of the FDIC, depositors with accounts of up to $100,000 have not had to be concerned with losses in the event of bank failure; their deposits are fully insured. Those with larger deposits assume a greater risk. If a bank fails, FDIC reimburses them up to the legal limit. Beyond this they face a loss if the failing bank liquidates. This risk to large depositors is highlighted by the liquidation of the

Penn Square Bank in Oklahoma in mid-1982. However, if the failing bank is acquired by another bank, they usually suffer no loss. Banks also acquire funds from short-term lenders in such forms as federal funds and commercial paper. Holders of these liabilities are noninsured creditors of the bank. Because of the risk they assume, they have the greatest interest in carefully evaluating the bank's capital adequacy. A primary consideration for these creditors will be the existence of debt capital, which, as was stated earlier, is contractually subordinate to all bank liabilities. The existence of subordinated notes and debentures provides these creditors an extra margin of safety, since debt capital is second in line after equity capital to absorb losses if the bank has to be closed and liquidated. As for the holders of subordinated notes and debentures (though they, too, are liability holders of the bank), their only margin of safety if the bank fails is equity capital. Indeed, since their claims precede the residual claims of stockholders, capital note and debenture holders must rely solely on equity capital to protect against losses.

Generating a Return to Shareholders

Profits in banking, just as in other businesses, have been an important determinant of investors' interest in bank stock. Thus, from the stockholders' point of view, the function of bank capital is to achieve a sufficient yield to meet operating costs and net a fair return to its owners. With possible rare exceptions, the suppliers of bank capital are motivated solely by the desire to own a good investment. They realize, of course, that the nature of the business entails special obligations essential to the public welfare, and are in sympathy with the conduct of the business in a manner compatible with the bank's obligations to its customers, the community, and the nation. They are, nevertheless, properly insistent upon the protection of their investment (through sound planning and administration) and upon a rate of return that is as great as that which they could obtain from comparable investment elsewhere. They invest in the stock of a bank for the same reasons that they invest in the shares of any other business enterprise: to obtain a competitive return on their funds, with the hope of appreciation in the value of their stock. Unless this return is obtained, they have no reason for wishing to continue to supply capital to the bank. An unprofitable bank is, after all, an unhealthy bank, and cannot survive. The profit motive of bank shareholders is, therefore, both proper and unavoidable so long as banking is supported by private means.

Complying with Laws and Regulations

The myriad regulations that govern bank activity include stipulations regarding capital that are designed to ensure the safety and soundness of bank operations. These requirements extend from the chartering of a bank through its operations and growth. As we have seen in Chapter 4, the Comptroller of the Currency prescribes minimum capital requirements for the establishment of national banks; state chartering agencies have similar requirements. Most states permitting some form of branching set minimum capital requirements for the opening of branches. Acquisitions by banks or bank holding companies are also subject to capital requirements.

Of special importance to banks are lending limits, inasmuch as they are determined by a bank's capital base. At present national banks are allowed to loan to any single borrower, on an unsecured basis, amounts up to 15 percent of their total capital (debt and equity capital plus 50 percent of reserves for loan losses). This lending limit is extended to 25 percent of capital if loans are secured by a readily marketable collateral. These higher limits became effective in 1983, replacing an earlier limit of 10 percent. Given these restrictions, banks wishing to attract large borrowers must ensure that their capital base is adequate to accommodate their loan requests. The size of a bank's capital thus affects the type of clientele it can ordinarily serve.

CAPITAL ADEQUACY

Although equity capital is a prerequisite for the establishment of a bank, its most important function is to protect depositors and other creditors. If a bank is to continue as a going concern, its capital must inspire sufficient confidence among depositors and other creditors. For unless such confidence exists, a bank will not be able to retain existing deposit and nondeposit liabilities and to attract new ones.

Such has traditionally been the role of bank capital. Throughout banking history bank capital has had almost no other purpose than the protection of depositors.* Since 1962 this function of equity capital has been shared by debt capital. With debt securities subordinated to the claims of depositors, debt capital actually serves the same protective function as equity capital.

---

*More than a century ago Walter Bagehot wrote: "The main source of the profitableness of established banking is the smallness of the requisite capital. Being only wanted as a 'moral influence,' it need not be more than is necessary to secure that influence."[4]

The adequacy of bank capital, and hence the safety of commercial banks, has been the concern of state and federal regulatory authorities throughout U.S. banking history. U.S. financial history is characterized by a number of periods of unrestrained bank expansion and individual bank abuses, which led to bank failures, with resulting losses to depositors and holders of bank notes. In order to avoid the destabilizing effects of bank failures, the need became apparent for regulatory intervention to supplant the judgment of the individual bank in matters relating to capital adequacy. This intervention has taken the form of laws and regulations, at both the federal and the state levels, that prescribe minimum capital requirements for the organization of a new bank and set norms to ensure the adequacy of bank capital thereafter.

With the general public basically unversed in this field, supervisory judgment has become especially decisive for a bank's continued existence over the years. Thus, today it is among supervisory authorities that a bank must inspire sufficient confidence as to its adequacy to withstand whatever strains may be placed upon it. In a closely supervised private banking system, it is the supervisory appraisal of capital adequacy that determines whether and under what conditions a bank may continue to exist. If capital is considered adequate by the examining supervisory authorities, it will be satisfactory for the general public.

Measures of Capital Adequacy

Over the years several standards or ratios have been developed for the amount of capital considered necessary for the safe and efficient operation of a bank. They related capital to a key magnitude in the balance sheet of commercial banks. Each of these ratios, introduced at a different phase of U.S. banking history, was projected as the best index for measuring a bank's capital adequacy.

The first measure of capital adequacy to be introduced by U.S. banking authorities was the capital:total deposits ratio—a ratio that seemed quite natural, since it readily identified the extent of capital protection enjoyed by depositors. Introduced in 1909 by a California banking law, this measure also appeared in the Comptroller of the Currency's annual report of 1914. The report strongly recommended use of this ratio for national banks, stipulating a minimum relationship of capital funds to total deposits of 1:20—that is, capital should account for at least 10 percent of total deposits. Until World War II this ratio was considered satisfactory for the safety of depositors. During the war years, however, supervisory authorities realized that the 10 percent ratio was seriously hampering bank financing of the war. Bank purchases of government securities, through deposit creation, had led to a rapid increase in bank deposits, which threatened significant narrowing of safety margins. This led supervisory authorities to abandon this traditional rule. The ratio of capital accounts to deposits had the virtue of simplicity, and for this reason it has been extensively used by commercial banks and is frequently mentioned as a satisfactory measure of the adequacy of bank capital.

In 1947 the FDIC, joined by the Federal Reserve System, began using the ratio of capital to total assets. This ratio identifies the extent to which a bank's assets are financed by its capital. A minimum capital: total assets ratio of 7 percent was suggested by the Federal Reserve as indication of adequate capitalization.

A refined approach to the measurement of capital adequacy was introduced in 1948 by the Comptroller of the Currency and came to be known as the risk-asset ratio. This ratio sought to measure capital adequacy by relating capital only to those assets in a bank's balance sheet that are subject to losses. The basic premise of this approach was that all bank assets are not of the same quality—some are risky and others are not. Thus, for any measure of capital adequacy to be valid, it had to relate capital to the risk factors involved in a bank's assets. The risk-asset ratio was conceived as the ratio of capital funds to risk assets, the latter being defined as all bank assets minus cash and U.S. government securities. A 20 percent risk-asset ratio was originally considered satisfactory by the office of the Comptroller of the Treasury.

In the years that followed, several variants of the risk-asset ratio were put forward. Some students of the subject, for example, defined risk assets as all assets less cash and U.S. government securities due in five years or less. The obvious reason for this definition was that although government securities are free of the risk of default (the risk that interest and/or principal will be defaulted as they come due), their prices are nevertheless subject to fluctuations as a result of changes in the market rate of interest. In other words, these assets are not free of the interest-rate risk (the risk that interest rates will change, causing the market values of securities to change). However, issues maturing in five years or less are considered to be relatively short-term and, therefore, as being close to riskless. This definition of risk assets underlies the capital-to-the nonliquid-asset ratio.

Another definition of risk assets, one that was heavily relied upon by supervisory authorities, was total assets less cash, U.S. government securities, and loans insured and guaranteed by the federal government and its agencies. This approach, known as the adjusted-risk-asset ratio,

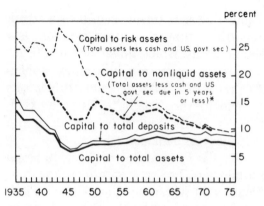

percent

Figure 5.1. Trends in Capital Adequacy Ratios for All Insured Commercial Banks, 1935-75

*Available only from 1940 through 1972.

Source: Federal Deposit Insurance Corp., *Annual Reports* (Washington, D.C.: FDIC, 1935-75). Data based on June 30 figures.

included in the riskless asset category all loans insured and guaranteed by government agencies, since these are virtually free of risk.* In other words, if the debtors experience financial difficulty, the government agencies—and behind them the government itself—would be liable for the repayment of the loans. A 1:6 relationship between capital and adjusted-risk assets was considered satisfactory by examining authorities.

Figure 5.1 shows the trends in four of the conventional capital ratios discussed above, for all insured commercial banks, from 1935 through 1975. These ratios have declined considerably from their prewar levels. In the 1950s and 1960s the relationship of capital to either total assets or total deposits increased modestly, then declined slightly in the early 1970s. By contrast, the ratios of capital to risk assets and to nonliquid assets continued their downward trend through most of the postwar years as both the risk assets and the nonliquid assets of commercial banks grew faster than capital. This development was widespread among banks of different sizes and reflected the increased amounts of loans and municipal securities held by banks.

In the 1950s efforts were directed to developing refined methods of measuring capital adequacy. Of these methods, two deserve consi-

---

*The intent of the government insurance and guarantee programs is not to displace banks as lenders, but to make private debts more attractive to them by virtue of government backing of these debts. Of the governmental agencies that insure and guarantee loans made by banks and other financial institutions to private borrowers, the most widely known are the Federal Housing Administration (FHA), which insures selected mortgage loans; the Veterans Administration, which guarantees mortgage loans for veterans; the Small Business Administration (SBA), which guarantees loans to small businesses; and the Farmer's Home Administration (FmHA), which guarantees farm-housing mortgage loans and rural industry financing.

deration and comment because of their contribution to the problem of measuring capital adequacy. These techniques were that of the Federal Reserve Bank of New York (1952) and that of the Board of Governors of the Federal Reserve System (1956). Unlike the previous approaches, which considered all risk assets as possessing the same degree of risk, these new formulas assumed that the exposure of bank assets to risk shades all the way from a considerable loss potential to virtually no risk. To develop a realistic appraisal of an individual bank's capital adequacy, these formulas therefore allowed for varying capital requirements against a bank's different assets.

The formula of the Federal Reserve Bank of New York segregated bank assets into six categories, according to the amount of risk involved. It then allocated to each category a specified percentage that, on the basis of the given dollar value of each category, determined the capital needed to support the risk inherent in that category. The sum of the individual capital allocations against risk assets represented a bank's total capital requirements. These, compared against the actual capital position of the bank, determined whether the bank had a deficiency or excess of capital. If the bank was deficient, it had the choice of eliminating some of its more risky assets or acquiring more capital.

The capital analysis formula of the Board of Governors (formally referred to as "Form for Analyzing Bank Capital" or ABC form) was somewhat more complex. In addition to computations of capital requirements, which were based on the classification of assets into ten categories, this formula included a liquidity test. The purpose of this test was to require more capital for banks that had a lower level of liquidity. In 1972 the Board of Governors introduced a revised version of this formula that called for separate capital computations for 29 different categories of assets, total assets, and trust department gross earnings. Capital requirements were determined after assessment of the credit risk and market risk of each category of assets and the amount of liquidity available. Again, if a bank's capital position was found deficient, its management was directed either to sell some of its riskier assets or to raise additional capital. This formula was used by the Federal Reserve until 1978.

In regard to the various standards of capital adequacy described, no uniformity existed among federal banking supervisory authorities. In fact, national bank examiners, on the basis of guidelines issued by the Office of the Comptroller of the Currency in 1971, moved away from formal analysis and reliance on capital ratios, and toward qualitative factors. In other words, the capital adequacy of a national bank was determined by analyzing and appraising its capital position in relation to such factors as character of its management, quality and character of its ownership, quality of operating procedures, and capacity to provide the broadest service to the public.

Current Trends in the Regulation of Bank Capital

In December 1981 the federal supervisory agencies adopted new capital-adequacy guidelines. The Federal Reserve and the Comptroller of the Currency, in a joint policy statement, set forth uniform guidelines for banks under their supervision, and the FDIC introduced its own approach to capital adequacy for insured state nonmember banks.

The capital policy developed by the Federal Reserve and the Comptroller of the Currency has three basic features: it bases capital guidelines on bank size; it gives the agencies significant flexibility to recognize the unique qualitative characteristics of sound and well-managed banks; and it measures adequacy through two principal ratios—primary capital:total assets and total capital:total assets. Primary capital consists of funds that have no due dates—common and perpetual preferred stocks, debt instruments with mandatory convertibility into stock, surplus undivided profits, equity reserves, and allowance for possible loan losses. Total capital includes, in addition, funds with due dates: limited-life preferred stock and subordinated notes and debentures.* These instruments constitute what is known as secondary capital. In order to qualify as secondary capital, they must have an original maturity of more than seven years and be phased out of the bank's capital as they approach maturity. The Federal Reserve-Comptroller of the Currency guidelines limit secondary capital to no more than 50 percent of the amount of primary capital.

The Federal Reserve-Comptroller of the Currency approach, taking asset size into consideration, divides all banks into two categories: multinational-regional banks and community banks. In the first category are large multinational and regional banks with assets in excess of $1 billion; in the second, community banks with assets under $1 billion. Banks in the former category are subject to formal capital requirements that are somewhat lower than those for community banks. Within the multinational-regional and community categories, the federal agencies established three capital-adequacy zones. Banking institutions with a ratio equal to or exceeding the percentage stipulated in zone 1 are considered to have adequate capitalization, and therefore

---

*In the case of bank holding companies, total capital also includes the unsecured long-term debt of the parent company and its nonbank subsidiaries.

receive no special supervision. Institutions with a ratio in the range of the percentages stipulated in zone 2 are viewed as possibly undercapitalized. The supervisory response for these institutions will consist of more-than-routine analysis, monitoring, and supervision. The federal agency will engage in extensive contact and discussion with the bank's management and will require the submission of comprehensive capital plans. Banks with a ratio below the percentage of zone 3 will be presumed undercapitalized and will be subject to continuous supervision. The regulator may require additonal capital to ensure the institution's safe and sound operation.

The capital-adequacy guidelines of the Federal Reserve-Comptroller of the Currency for commercial banks are shown in Table 5.4. Also included in this table are the FDIC's guidelines for banks under its supervision. As indicated by the FDIC data, this agency, too, sets forth three tiers of capital ratios that, although not formally referred to as zones, serve essentially the same function: to monitor the capital adequacy of insured state nonmember banks. FDIC capital requirements are independent of bank size; that is, they apply to all insured banks under its supervision. This, however, is of little consequence, since all insured state nonmember banks are basically below the $1 billion asset figure. One important difference in FDIC capital guidelines, compared

Table 5.4. Capital:Asset Ratios Recommended by Federal Supervisory Authorities (in percent)

Zone	*Federal Reserve-Comptroller*[a]		*FDIC*[b]
	Multinational and Regional Banks	*Community Banks*	*All Banks*
1. Aceptable	6.5 or more[c]	7.0 or more[d]	6.0 or more
2. Possibly under-capitalized	5.5 to 6.5	6.0 to 7.0	5.0 to 6.0
3. Undercapitalized	Less than 5.5	Less than 6.0	Less than 5.0

[a]May include debentures and limited-life preferred stock.
[b]May not include debentures or limited-life preferred stock.
[c]Primary capital must be greater than 5.0 percent of assets.
[d]Primary capital must be greater than 6.0 percent of assets.
Sources: Comptroller of the Currency, *Capital Adequacy Guidelines*, Examining Circular, no. 206 (December 18, 1981); Comptroller of the Currency and Federal Reserve Board, joint press release, June 13, 1983; Federal Deposit Insurance Corporation, *Capital Adequacy*, News Release PR-86-81 (December 21, 1981).

with those of the Federal Reserve-Comptroller of the Currency, is the definition of capital. The FDIC does not count limited-life preferred stock and subordinated debt as capital because they lack permanence.

As implied by their official statements and policy actions, federal regulatory agencies expect banks to comply with the recommended capital-adequacy ratios. Bankers generally favor lower capital requirements and less supervisory control. If a bank can operate with a minimal capital:asset ratio, it can boost its rate of return to shareholders. However, the intention of federal agencies is to ensure that asset growth does not exceed bank capital growth, thus leading to further declines in bank capital ratios similar to those experienced in the 1960s and 1970s (see Figure 5.1). The regulators' concern is that excessively low ratios will undermine the safety and soundness of individual banks and the public confidence in the banking system.

Federal regulatory agencies have various powers to enforce a bank's compliance with the stated guidelines. These range from moral suasion to extreme action. For example, if verbal communication fails to jar bank management into remedying the situation, bank regulators may impose a variety of sanctions. Milder sanctions include denying a bank's application to merge or to open branches. More severe actions include charter revocation by the Comptroller of the Currency, membership termination by the Federal Reserve System, and insurance suspension by the FDIC. Also, the Federal Reserve, by virtue of its authority over bank holding companies and its power to approve or deny applications for expansion of their activities, can induce them to augment the capital of their affiliated banks.

Looking back over the past decades, we see that there have been continued adjustments in the capital policy of federal regulators as the banking industry has responded to changes in the needs of the economy. However, these adjustments in capital policy also reflected the regulators' quest for a precise method of measuring capital adequacy. It should be evident from our discussion that the regulators' concern for such a method stems essentially from their need to develop an indicator that would identify institutions vulnerable to financial deterioration and possible failure. As we have seen, these methods ranged from a simple ratio to elaborate formulas, and from quantitative to qualitative considerations. Current capital standards are size-oriented, on the premise that larger banks, because of their potential for greater diversification, have lower risk exposure and are therefore safer than smaller institutions.

Although this approach adds a new dimension to the capital adequacy issue, indications are that keener competition in the financial services industry will make maintenance of these standards difficult in the years ahead. Increased competition from thrifts and nonbank institutions in the 1980s will force banks to accept lower profit margins in several product markets, which will mean a smaller amount of generated funds, and therefore limited ability to increase bank capital. Slower internal capital formation will force banks to rely increasingly on external sources to maintain capital ratios. Even if a bank is willing to ignore the dilutive effects of new equity financing, a new stock issue may not be practical if existing stock is selling below book value. A bank's only other alternative, and one subject to stringent regulatory requirements, would be to issue debt capital. However, in periods of high interest rates, the cost of debt may be so high as to virtually exclude it as a viable alternative. Thus banks may be forced to accept slower asset growth in order to maintain capital requirements. This would pose undue hardship for commercial banks in competing effectively with the new entrants in the financial services market.

Several recommendations have been put forward. One is to subject all banks to identical marginal capital requirements, in order to eliminate the competitive advantage enjoyed by banks that are able to leverage to a greater degree than are others. Critics argue that uniform requirements would be too arbitrary and would risk the failure, with all its adverse consequences, of banks disadvantaged by such a measure. A second proposal is to deregulate capital adequacy altogether and allow market forces alone to exert pressure on banks to keep capital at adequate levels. In other words, if a bank became overleveraged, the market forces would drive up its cost of funds—that is, investors would demand a higher rate of return to supply capital, and uninsured creditors would charge higher rates for certain liabilities. This proposal, too, has opponents, who argue that the market for stocks and uninsured liabilities is not active enough to provide the ongoing feedback that would keep banks sufficiently cautious about their capital position. Moreover, past market activity, except for large, publicly traded bank holding companies, has not indicated that investors shy away from banks with weak capital positions. Whatever the merits of these arguments, it is clear that regulatory bodies must address the impact of emerging competition on banks through review of their capital-adequacy guidelines.

NOTES

1. Robert M. Baker, "Sources of Bank Capital: An Issue for the 80s," *Economic Review*, Federal Reserve Bank of Atlanta, December 1982, p. 69.

2. George W. McKinney, Jr., "New Sources of Bank Funds: Certificates of Deposit and Debt Securities," *Law and Contemporary Problems* 32 (Winter 1967): 85-86.

3. *Standard Federal Tax Reporter*, 9 vols. (Chicago: Commerce Clearing House, 1967), vol. IV, para. 3458.01.

4. Walter Bagehot, *Lombard Street: A Description of the Money Market*. 8th ed. (London: Kegan Paul, Trench, and Co., 1882), p. 245.

SUGGESTED REFERENCES

American Bankers Association. *Use of Senior Capital by Commercial Banks*. Washington, D.C.: American Bankers Association, 1967.

Austin, Douglas V. "Senior Debt and Equity Securities." *Bankers Magazine*, Winter 1974, pp. 73-84.

Beranek, William. "The Weighted Average Cost of Capital and Shareholder Wealth Maximization." *Journal of Financial and Quantitative Analysis* 12 (March 1977):17-39.

Golembe, Carter H. "Capital Adequacy and Bank Losses." *Journal of Commercial Bank Lending*, August 1975, pp. 23-40.

Heggestad, Arnold A., and B. Frank King. "Regulation of Bank Capital: An Evaluation." *Economic Review*, Federal Reserve Bank of Atlanta, March 1982, pp. 35-43.

Hempel, George H. "Bank Capital Needs in the Coming Decade." *Journal of Contemporary Business*, University of Washington, Summer 1977, pp. 77-93.

Johnson, Thomas S. "Capital Planning." *Journal of Commercial Bank Lending*, July 1976, pp. 24-31.

Orgler, Y. E., and B. Wolkowitz. *Bank Capital*. New York: Van Nostrand Reinhold, 1976.

Pike, William E. "Loan Loss Reserves." *Journal of Commercial Bank Lending*, June 1977, pp. 3-10.

Pringle, John. "The Capital Decision in Commercial Banks." *Journal of Finance* 29 (June 1974):779-95.

Robinson, Roland I., and Richard H. Pettway. *Policies for Optimum Bank Capital*. Chicago: Association of Reserve City Bankers, 1967.

Taggart, Robert A., Jr. "Regulatory Influences on Bank Capital." *New England Economic Review*, Federal Reserve Bank of Boston, September-October 1977, pp. 37-46.

Vojta, George J. *Bank Capital Adequacy*. New York: Citicorp, 1973.

6
DEPOSITS

In every study on money and banking, it is expounded that in the commercial banking system as a whole, the volume of deposits depends essentially upon the amount of credit extended by banks. When banks extend loans or make investments, they do so by granting their customers deposit credits against which they can, and usually do, write checks. Through its lending and investing activities the banking system thus affects the volume of demand deposits in the economy and, consequently, the total stock of money. The deposit-creating powers of commercial banks are subject to one important limitation: the legal requirement of maintaining reserves equal, at the minimum, to a certain percentage of their deposit liabilities. Thus, depending upon what the legal reserve ratio may be, the banking system as a whole can lend and create demand deposits equal to a multiple of its excess reserves.

What follows from the deposit-expansion process of the banking system is that the line of causation runs from the assets side to the liabilities side of the balance sheet. In other words, assets give rise to liabilities. For the individual bank, however, the line of causation is reversed. That is, liabilities give rise to assets. An individual bank first must attract deposits, and then put them to work. Since Part II is examining the sources of funds available to an individual bank, in this chapter deposits will be studied from that perspective.

As we saw in Chapter 5, in connection with capital adequacy, banks have been relying extensively on deposits in the financing of their assets. At year-end 1981 deposits accounted for 76 percent of the total assets of all insured commercial banks; non-deposit liabilities and capital accounted, respectively, for 17 and 7 percent of bank assets. Deposits have always been the principal source of bank funds. Recognizing their importance in the financing of assets, banks have always been pleased to receive deposits, and most banks have made a continuing effort to solicit them from various sources.

Traditionally the deposit structure of a commercial bank was thought to be determined primarily by the depositors, and not by bank management. This view has been undergoing important changes. With the introduction of negotiable CDs in the early 1960s and the subsequent liberalization of regulatory controls, banks have become increasingly effective in influencing the volume and types of deposits they receive and, hence, in bringing about desired shifts in their deposit structure. Thus banks have evolved from relatively passive acceptors of deposits to active bidders for funds. Deposits, however, are but one aspect of the bank liabilities that management has been influencing through deliberate policy actions. The other aspect is nondeposit liabilities, the diverse channels through which banks borrow funds to relend to their customers or to meet unexpected deposit outflows. Most of these borrowing channels, developed first by large money-center banks, have evolved into important devices for attracting interest-sensitive funds. Eurodollar borrowings, RPs, and federal funds are only a few of the nondeposit sources of funds developed by commercial banks.

This new approach of influencing liabilities through management policy actions, generally called liability management, is an important aspect of the funds management of a commercial bank. As such, it is complementary to capital management. Liability management involves selecting the source of financing to be used (that is, choosing among alternative deposit and nondeposit sources) and determining the amounts needed from each source. In a stricter sense, however, liability management implies obtaining interest-sensitive funds when they are needed to supplement a bank's liquidity requirements.

This chapter considers the various factors that affect a bank's ability to attract deposits, describes the main deposit classifications, traces the effects of Regulation Q on deposits, and reviews the changing nature of the payments mechanism.

ATTRACTING DEPOSITS

It is apparent that a commercial bank's deposit policy is the most essential policy for its existence. Put another way, the growth of a bank depends primarily upon the growth of its deposits. The volume of funds that management will use for creating income, through loans and investments, is determined largely by the bank's policy governing deposits. When that policy is unduly restrictive, growth is retarded; when it is liberalized, growth is accelerated.

Factors affecting the ability to attract deposits include the following:

Types of customers

Physical facilities

Management accessibility to customers

Participation in community activities

Types and range of services offered

Rate of interest paid on deposits.

In addition to these factors, which are largely under the bank's control, the prevailing economic conditions exert a decisive influence on the amount of deposits the bank receives. Moreover, characteristics of the local economy, such as dependence on one or a few agricultural or industrial products, have a bearing upon the volume of bank deposits. These factors are discussed below.

Bank policy in respect to deposits is clearly reflected in the option exercised by customers in using retail or wholesale banks, a choice limited mainly to banks located in large urban financial centers. Retail banks cater to large numbers of customers who have small means, as well as to business interests; the wholesale banks have as customers major corporations possessing large means and often having large sums on deposit. One is catholic in its approach to attracting clientele; the other selective.

Retail banks, more than wholesale banks, serve the needs of the mass market, which today, with constantly rising standards of living, tends to demand increasingly varied banking services. Retail banks experience a growth syndrome: new depositors, swelling the ranks, demand a wider variety of services; the banks expand their services, and thus accelerate their growth. Profits and growth are more likely to ensue from wider circles of depositors and from meeting their demands for services. A concomitant development also occurs: by serving the maximum number of persons, retail banks have closer ties with the communities in which they are located, and are recognized as contributors to the development of their communities. The rewards of a bank's community service are great.

Bank policy regarding deposits may be shaped by factors other than whether the bank serves a select or a mass clientele. Most banks today, whatever their type, sense the importance of creating attractive and inviting surroundings. The mausoleum atmosphere that formerly marked the interiors of banks has given way to bright appointments and an air of cheerfulness. An attendant development has been that bank employees have dropped their old airs of reserve and today appear warm and friendly. Pleasant surroundings and cheerful employees tend to attract new depositors without impairing the bank's efficiency.

Closely allied to attractive surroundings and friendly employees as influences on bank deposits is easy accessibility of the bank and of its services. Sharp increases in urban population and accelerated movements of population from inner-city to surburban areas have combined to lead large urban banks to open growing numbers of branches in neighborhood and surburban shopping centers. This diffusion of banking services has made banking transactions both simpler and more inviting for customers; branch banking enables customers to escape many of the tensions born of inner-city traffic congestion, paucity of parking facilities, and the general headlong tempo of doing business in a city's downtown financial area. The branch bank in a neighborhood or surburban plaza will have ample parking space, and customers can transact their business in a much more relaxed environment. Customers at the branch bank have easier access to officials for transactions requiring consultation, usually spend less time in lines at tellers' windows, and, if they are motorists, find drive-in banking facilities more readily available than at an inner-city bank.

New bank deposits often derive from public attitudes toward bank officials. Where a bank's officials are thought to be indifferent to, or aloof from, a community's problems, the public tends to shun that bank. Recognition of this fact has caused bankers to identify themselves and their institutions more closely with the concerns of the communities they serve; bank officials serve on boards and committees of community organizations, encourage new industries to locate in their community, stimulate the growth of small businesses, and through all such activities evince the bank's interest in the well-being of individuals and of the corporate community of which it is a part. In short, civic consciousness among bankers, the understanding that what is good for the community is also good for the bank, tends to attract new accounts and the utilization of banking services through loans and investments.

It is no overstatement to say that new deposit accounts are frequently the result of the types of services offered by banks. Banking is highly competitive; banks offering better and more diversified services have advantages over those whose services are limited. Nowhere is this more true than in the United States. Commercial banks have been advertising extensively in all media, emphasizing the range of services available to the public. Calling themselves full-service banks, they offer the widest range of banking services available anywhere under a single roof. This multiplicity of services is made available through specialists who can give maximum aid to clients who seek counsel and loans. Banks still perform the roles that they carried out a century ago: they are today, as then, safe depositories for customers' funds, they continue to provide for the transfer of funds, and they maintain credit facilities for their clients. But today's bank offers services hardly dreamed of by bankers half a century ago. Hence, it is not surprising to discover a bank dispensing information to clients on domestic or foreign markets, on acquisitions, or on tax matters, as well as handling the clients' personal affairs through trust and fiduciary arrangements. Services vary, of course, from bank to bank, one institution serving special needs of its community that may differ markedly from the needs of another community. But one thing seems to determine what specific services a given bank may make available to its customers: the needs vocalized by customers, on the one hand, or sensed and provided for by bankers, on the other hand. This had led some banks to become known as oil banks, textile banks, electronics banks, and the like. Eventually companies in an industry seek a relationship with these specialized banks because they know that the intricacies of their particular business will be understood and their needs will be adequately served.

The interest rate that a bank pays on time and savings accounts is another factor influencing the size and growth of these deposits. As Regulation Q is gradually being phased out, interest-rate considerations are becoming a major determinant of a bank's ability to attract deposits. In no other type of deposit is this more apparent than in large CDs, whose exemption from Regulation Q dates back to the early 1970s. The funds tapped through large CDs are so interest-sensitive that some prefer to call them "purchased monies." Large certificates of deposit—especially of money-center banks—are purchased and sold in active, well-developed, and impersonal financial markets largely on the basis of interest rate. Sizable investors (businesses, pension funds, and mutual funds) interested in purchasing large CDs ordinarily call various recognized banks to inquire about their issuing rates and buy the CD of the bank paying the highest rate. If rates are comparable, they are likely to acquire the certificate of the bank with which they maintain an account.

The efficiency of bank policy in attracting new deposits depends to a large extent upon the level of economic activity. Bank deposits increase in periods of prosperity and decline in periods of recession. Individual banks may represent departures from aggregate experience, but most of them tend to feel the same effects. A period of prosperity is characterized by relatively high levels of employment, rising consumer spending on durable goods and houses, and a strong demand for credit by businesses and individuals. Banks are generally more liberal in their lending activities when a feeling of optimism prevails in the economy. On the other hand, during periods of adverse economic conditions, bank deposits fall to a level lower than that of a period of prosperity. A period of recession is characterized by rising unemployment, a cutback in consumer spending, and a slackening business demand for credit, which makes banks seek investment outlets.

Although a local economy tends to reflect the total economy of which it forms a part, it may have some characteristics that cause sharp fluctuations in a bank's deposits. Any two given types of economy—for example, an industrial and an agricultural—will have within themselves differences in the factors that govern bank deposits. In fact, even economies of one type are bound to have such differences within themselves. In general, in an agricultural economy with a single cash crop, deposit declines will be greater during the spring months, when money must be spent for seeds, fertilizers, and other production factors. By contrast, deposit buildups will be greater when crops are harvested and sold. If crops are harvested twice a year (in the spring and in the fall), deposits show less fluctuation, and instead of one high point during the year, there will be two. An economy that depends on the raising of cattle for market will cause bank deposits to rise chiefly when cattle are sold, whereas one that depends on dairying will tend to have much steadier deposits throughout the year.

Industrial communities, too, experience deposit fluctuations, some more than others. Deposits will fluctuate less in a community that has diverse industries than in one that has a single industry or several industries of the same kind. In the latter case there is the danger that a falling demand for that particular product, or a shortage in raw materials originating outside the community will have effects upon local bank deposits. In such an instance the industry and its employees, local merchants, and the population of the community will generally suffer, and deposits in the community's banks will correspondingly slacken. Similarly, if the industry is cyclical in nature or likely to suffer frequent fluctuations in its tempo of activity, there will be ups and downs in the local banks' deposit patterns.

NATURE AND CLASSES OF BANK DEPOSITS

Bank deposits are subject to various forms of classification. The most common are according to ownership, to security, and to availability of funds. On the basis of these criteria, deposits may be distinguished into public, private, and interbank; secured and unsecured; and demand and time. Each of these types is examined below.

Public, Private, and Interbank Deposits

Public deposits are those owned by all levels of government: federal, state, and subdivisions of states. The deposits of the federal government at commercial banks have been known as tax and loan (T&L) accounts. First established in 1917 in banks throughout the country, these accounts are maintained for the deposit of income tax receipts, Social Security taxes, proceeds from the sale of securities, and other types of government receipts. Treasury's T&L accounts have generally been used as feeder accounts for Treasury's "general accounts" at Federal Reserve banks, against which all payments are made. Transfers made several times each week out of T&L accounts enable the Treasury to draw on its general accounts to make payments to the public.

Banks formerly paid no interest on government balances in T&L accounts but provided various services for the U.S. Treasury at little or no cost. The high rates of interest experienced since the 1960s led the Treasury to sponsor legislation in 1977 that allowed it to earn interest on its temporary cash balances. Under the new rules a depository bank no longer has free use of balances in T&L accounts. Generally such a bank has a twofold option in processing T&L receipts. It may transfer them, within one day, to the Treasury's general account at the Federal Reserve bank or to an interest-bearing demand note issued by the bank. The funds invested in these notes are made available to the Treasury upon request. Since these notes do not constitute a deposit account, no reserve requirements are held against them and they are not subject to Regulation Q interest-rate ceilings. The rate of interest paid by banks is determined by the federal government. It has been set at 25 basis points below the going federal funds rate. Banks are compensated for the services they perform for the Treasury by payment of set fees (for instance, they earn 50 cents for each tax deposit form forwarded to the Treasury).

For a bank to become a qualified depository for U.S. government funds, it must pledge qualified securities for the unsecured portion of those deposits. Requirements for becoming a state or municipal depository vary from locale to locale, but they frequently require bidding on the interest rate the bank is to offer. An additional consideration may be the bank's willingness to underwrite or purchase the state's or municipality's securities. Competition for these deposits is often intense.

Interbank deposits are owned by other commercial banks—domestic and foreign—as well as mutual savings banks. The bulk of deposits in this category is correspondent bank balances.

Private deposits are those owned by individuals, partnerships, corporations, and other private institutions. As might be expected, most of the deposits in the United States are owned by individuals and businesses. At the close of 1982, business and personal deposits at large commercial banks accounted for 87 percent of total deposits; interbank deposits accounted for 7 percent; and public deposits for 6 percent.

Secured and Unsecured Deposits

Secured deposits are those that require the pledging of security. Public deposits—those of federal, state, city, county, and other subdivisions of the state—are the most common type of secured deposits. The bank has to guarantee the safety of these deposits by pledging securities as collateral. For example, commercial banks that accept federal government deposits greater than the amount insured by the FDIC must pledge U.S. government securities or other form of collateral approved by the Secretary of the Treasury to cover the uninsured excess.

Most private deposits are unsecured, in that the bank pledges no specific assets to guarantee their safety. However, all accounts in banks insured by the FDIC are automatically covered up to a maximum of $100,000. Deposits with balances exceeding this amount stand to lose if a bank liquidates. Large deposits have been always the losers in recent bank liquidations.

Demand and Time Deposits

Deposit arrangements permitting funds to be withdrawn by the depositor, or to be transferred by the depositor to a third party, at any time, without prior notice to the bank, have come to be known as demand deposits. Arrangements permitting withdrawal of funds after the elapse of a stated period of time are known as time deposits. Time deposits may take any one of three forms: savings deposits, time certificates of deposit, or time deposits, open accounts. Demand deposits are of special importance because they are the dominant medium of exchange in the U.S. economy. Time deposits, on the other hand, have grown to the point where they constitute the principal source of funds for commercial banks. The size and importance of demand and time deposits is shown in Table 6.1.

Table 6.1. Size and Importance of Demand and Time Deposits of Insured Commercial Banks, 1965-81 (in billions of dollars)

		Time Deposits			
Year	Demand Deposits	Savings	Other Time	Total	Total Deposits
1965	183.8	92.6	55.1	147.7	331.5
1970	246.2	98.2	134.8	233.0	479.2
1971	262.3	112.2	164.7	276.9	539.2
1972	296.4	124.2	196.3	320.5	616.9
1973	309.1	127.8	244.7	372.5	681.6
1974	314.4	136.3	295.7	432.0	746.4
1975	321.4	160.7	298.6	459.3	780.7
1976	334.0	203.9	293.1	497.0	830.9
1977	378.8	220.1	330.4	550.5	929.3
1978	400.3	220.9	395.2	616.1	1,016.4
1979	431.6	207.1	456.0	663.1	1,094.6
1980	432.3	201.2	558.7	759.9	1,192.2
1981	385.0	223.7	667.8	891.5	1,276.5

Note: Details may not add to totals due to rounding.

Source: Federal Deposit Insurance Corporation, *Annual Report* (various issues); and *Statistics on Banking* (Washington, D.C.: FDIC, 1981), p. 42.

Demand Deposits

Checking accounts provide the most common form of demand deposits. They are highly liquid; they provide a mechanism for the safe transfer of money; they are relatively immune to financial loss due to robbery or forgery, since the bank is at fault if a forged check is paid; and they serve as receipts for payments made.

The safety and convenience of making payments by writing checks and the ability to withdraw cash on demand have made demand deposits useful to a variety of groups, especially to individuals and businesses. This group is not only the most numerous class of demand depositors but also the largest holder of such deposits. Federal Reserve figures on IPC (individuals, partnerships, and corporations) ownership of demand deposits are shown in Table 6.2. The bulk of IPC demand deposits in commercial banks, as of September 1982, was owned by nonfinancial businesses, which held half of the total amount. Individuals owned 30 percent of the total deposits; financial business, about 12 percent, foreign holders, 1 percent; and others, the remainder.

Table 6.2. Gross Demand Deposits of Individuals, Partnerships, and Corporations, All Commercial Banks: September 1982

Type of Holder	Amount (billions of dollars)	Percent of Total
Financial businesses	$ 31.9	11.5
Nonfinancial businesses	142.9	51.6
Consumer	83.3	30.1
Foreign	2.9	1.0
All other	15.7	5.7
Total	276.7	100.0

Note: Details may not add to totals due to rounding.
Source: *Federal Reserve Bulletin*, February 1983, p. A 25.

Prior to 1933 banks typically paid interest on demand deposits, but in subsequent decades that practice was rendered illegal by the Federal Reserve System's Regulation Q. In 1976, however, in the New England states savings and loan associations, mutual savings banks, and commercial banks were authorized to introduce negotiable orders of withdrawal, commonly known as NOW accounts. The NOW accounts broke tradition in two ways. They not only permitted interest to be paid on demand deposits, but also broke the monopoly on demand deposits that the commercial banks had enjoyed. In 1980 enactment of DIDMCA extended the authority to offer NOW accounts to every state.

Automatic transfer services (ATS), which were introduced in 1978, provide a function similar to that of the NOW account. Although they usually involve service charges, often in the form of monthly maintenance fees, ATS accounts automatically transfer funds from a savings account to a checking account in order to cover overdrafts and to maintain a minimum balance in the checking account. It thereby allows the customer to keep in an interest-earning savings account funds that otherwise would be tied up in a checking account that pays no interest. The DIDMCA classified ATS accounts, NOW accounts, and telephone and preauthorized transfers as transaction accounts and, effective 1981, they were subject to the reserve requirements for transaction accounts rather than to those for savings deposits.

In the fall of 1982, the Garn-St. Germain Act, in an attempt to enhance the competitiveness of banks and thrifts vis-à-vis mutual funds, authorized regulators to offer a deposit instrument that would be directly equivalent to and competitive with private funds. In response to this mandate, the Depository Institutions Deregulation Committee (DIDC), which was established by the DIDMCA to handle the gradual phaseout through 1986 of Regulation Q ceiling rates on deposits in all depository institutions—created the money-market deposit account. Through this account banks and thrifts were freed to pay their customers ceiling-free interest rates and to offer them limited checking privileges. Since this account is a savings instrument, the DIDC authorized banks and thrifts to offer another high-interest-paying account, this one for checking. Dubbed "Super NOW" account, the new deposit instrument allows customers to write an unlimited number of checks, just like regular checking accounts, yet offers them a rate of interest higher than the 5.25 percent that regular NOW accounts pay. Eligibility requirements for the Super NOW account are the same as for the original NOW account: only natural persons, government bodies, and nonprofit organizations may open such an account. Requiring a minimum balance of $2,500, the Super NOW was first offered to the public in early January 1983, with many banks and savings and loan associations advertising a bewildering array of double-digit interest rates, bonuses, and prizes to attract customers.

Super NOW accounts are generally a costlier source of funds than money-market deposits. By being considered a transaction account, the Super NOW is subject to reserve requirements from which money-market accounts are exempted because of their savings-deposit character. In addition, the unlimited checking and transfer privileges offered by this account make its cost to a bank quite high. For this reason banks are paying somewhat lower rates of interest on Super NOWs than they do on money-market accounts. Moreover, they have imposed stiff requirements on these accounts. Many institutions require higher than the minimum balance of $2,500, with monthly service charges and check fees for accounts that fall below certain levels. The Chemical Bank of New York, for example, when it introduced its Super NOW account, paid only 6.75 percent interest—when other banks were paying between 9 and 11 percent—and levied a $ .20-per-check fee on all balances below $20,000 and an additional $6 per month service charge on accounts of less than $10,000.[1] Regulatory stipulations also provide that if balances fall below the minimum amount of $2,500, deposits will earn only the 5.25 percent rate paid on regular NOW accounts.

Savings Deposits

Unlike demand deposits, which can be withdrawn or transferred without prior notice, a bank reserves the right to require a 14-day advance notice before funds can be withdrawn from savings deposits. Since banks rarely exercise this authority, depositors can withdraw their funds immediately. Savings deposits have indefinite maturity, receive interest, and can be withdrawn only by being converted into currency or demand deposits. Until 1975 only individuals and certain nonprofit organizations could hold savings deposits, but now partnerships and corporations can have savings deposits of up to $150,000.

The passbook savings account, so named because at each transaction the customer must present a passbook that records the transaction and contains the rules and regulations governing the account, has been the traditional form of savings deposit. Recently, though, banks have been offering "statement savings" instead of passbook accounts. With statement savings the depositor maintains the transaction records, which are confirmed by a bank statement mailed quarterly or more frequently. The statements include the amount of interest earned. With the advent of computerization, banks can credit interest from date of deposit to date of withdrawal, and they can compound interest daily, a practice that costs little but is a good advertisement.

Until the enactment in 1980 of the DIDMCA, which provided for the six-year phaseout of ceiling interest rates on savings and time deposits, the passbook and statement savings market was not a major source of bank funds. Convenience was all that banks could offer their customers in the light of a Regulation Q ceiling-rate differential favoring thrifts over banks (in the interest of channeling funds in the housing industry), and the higher returns offered investors by money-market mutual funds. Thus commercial banks began to stress the greater convenience they could offer savers, and the image of "one-stop" and "full-service" banking became part of their advertising campaign.

As part of the gradual phaseout of interest ceiling rates, in the fall of 1982 Congress, through the DIDC, authorized banks and thrifts to offer money-market deposit accounts in order to recover part of the $232 billion that had been diverted over the years to mutual funds. Although—as anticipated—some funds were shifted into money-market deposits from lower-interest-paying savings accounts, significant amounts of new money came to banks and thrifts from outside sources. A week after their introduction, the new accounts took their toll on money-market funds, whose assets plunged by $6.5 billion.

The principal characteristics of the money-market deposit account, as provided for in the Garn-St. Germain Act, are as follows. A money-market deposit account may be established with a minimum of $2,500.* Banks and thrifts may pay any interest rate they want and can afford. Deposits of as much as $100,000 are insured by the FDIC (the shares of money-market funds enjoy no such coverage). Additional deposits need not be in any minimum amount and need not be made at any specific time. Each deposit earns interest immediately on the basis of the daily rate posted by the institution. Transfers to a third party—whether preauthorized through a telephone call or by check—are limited to six per month. No more than three of these six transfers may be made by check.

No minimum amount requirements are imposed on withdrawals or transfers from a money-market deposit account. However, if the account's average monthly balance falls below $2,500, the interest rate paid will revert back to the 5.25 percent ceiling that applies to ordinary NOW accounts. The institution reserves the right to require at least seven days' notice before funds are withdrawn from the money-market account, though it may seldom insist on such a notice. The depositor receives a monthly record of the interest earned and of the amounts deposited, withdrawn, or transferred.

Shortly before the introduction of money-market deposit accounts (December 14, 1982), banks and savings and loan associations were outbidding money-market mutual funds and each other to attract funds with their savings accounts. Although short-term money market rates at the time were between 8 and 9 percent, in Atlanta the First National Bank of DeKalb County, by offering 25 percent interest and an E.T. doll, took in $7 million the first day, increasing its total deposits by 17 percent.[2] On the West Coast, Bank of America and Security Pacific Bank started a bonus war—through newspaper coupons—by offering individuals opening money-market deposit accounts between $25 and $100, depending upon the amount of initial deposit. In Dallas, First Texas Savings, two weeks prior to the introduction of money-market deposits, began paying 20 percent on funds deposited immediately for conversion to this account on December 14.[3]

Time Certificates of Deposit

The certificate of deposit (CD) is an interest-earning deposit of funds left with the bank for a fixed, stated time period. The bank

---

*In the fall of 1983, the DIDC provided for the gradual phaseout of all minimum-balance requirements on deposit accounts and for their complete elimination by January 1, 1986.

knows exactly how long it will have these funds available for lending or investing, and so it rewards the customer for providing it a greater level of certainty by offering higher interests rates then those given to savings accounts. CDs are the major form of time deposit. They may be purchased at any time and begin earning interest on the date of purchase. Introduced in February 1961 by First National City Bank of New York, CDs were conceived as a means to retain and attract interest-sensitive deposit funds. Prior to 1961, a few large CDs had been issued, but the total dollar value was unimportant because they were not negotiable; thus they did not offer corporate treasurers the same options as other money-market instruments. When First National City Bank announced the acceptance of term deposits in the form of large CDs, it provided for the full negotiability of this instrument. A government securities dealer had agreed to make a secondary market for these new instruments by matching buyers and sellers.

Since their inception negotiable CDs have become a convenient source of deposit funds, and many banks issue them. By the end of 1982, the volume of outstanding CDs issued by large commercial banks amounted to $132 billion, with about $1 billion in 1961. Because CDs are negotiable, a significant number of securities houses provide an active secondary market in these instruments. This fact has enabled banks to attract funds from large investors who otherwise might place their funds in Treasury bills or other money-market instruments. Negotiable CDs are generally short-term, with maturities of one year or less, and are most commonly sold to corporations, pension funds, and government bodies in denominations of $100,000 to $1 million.

In recent years bankers have sought to increase the appeal of negotiable CDs to investors by introducing variations in the terms under which CDs are offered. One such variant is the rollover CD, informally referred to as the roly-poly CD, which was introduced in 1976 by Morgan Guaranty Trust. Since in the secondary market CD maturities do not usually exceed six months, the bank offered a contract whereby the investor would purchase a longer-term CD (for instance, five years' maturity) composed of a series of automatically renewable six-month CDs, issued with a fixed interest rate. This arrangement offered investors the advantage of higher interest rates along with the flexibility to sell CDs in the package ahead of the contractual maturity to meet cash needs. The bank benefited from the longer-term use of these funds, which were associated with a declining marginal reserve requirement over the life of the contract. For example, on a five-year CD reserve requirements were set at 6 percent for the first six months, from then through the fourth year dropped to 2.5 percent, and finally declined to 1 percent in the fifth year. Another CD innovation is the variable-rate CD. It draws its name from the periodic (every 30 to 90 days) adjustment of its rate on the basis of the secondary market rate for major bank CDs.

Banks have also gone beyond the domestic market in their efforts to purchase funds by offering Eurodollar CDs. These are negotiable, dollar-denominated deposits that, by virtue of being issued abroad, are exempt from reserve requirements and FDIC insurance assessments. First offered by Citibank in 1966, Eurodollar CDs are now offered by foreign branches of many U.S. banks and by some foreign-owned banks.

Prompted by the success of the large CDs, banks began to offer consumer CDs in smaller denominations. These are usually not negotiable, though depositors can recover their funds prior to the certificate's maturity by paying a penalty. Since July 1, 1979, the penalty for early redemption of certificates issued after that date is loss of six months' interest if the certificate matures in more than one year, and loss of three months' interest if it matures in less than one year.

Consumer CDs, which also pay higher interest rates than savings deposits, vary from six months to eight years in maturity. Although the rate of interest tends to increase with the duration of the certificate, the most popular consumer CDs are the six-month money-market certificates, first offered in June 1978. The rates on these CDs vary from week to week, depending on the auction rates on six-month Treasury bills. However, once a depositor purchases a money-market certificate, the rate becomes fixed until the CD has matured. Six-month money-market CDs are sold only in denominations of $10,000 or more.

Recently other changes in regulation have made CDs more competitive. In August 1981 the ceiling rate was removed from the two-and-one-half year certificate, and in May 1982 ceilings on three-and-one-half-year or longer certificates were removed. Also in May 1982 banks were permitted to offer three-month savings certificates similar to the six-month certificate, but tied to the rate on three-month Treasury bills.

In 1974 banks began offering to individuals not covered by employer pension plans special time deposit accounts called Individual Retirement Accounts (IRAs), pursuant to the Employee Retirement Income Security Act (ERISA) of that year. More recent legislation (1981) qualified nearly all U.S. wage earners to establish individual tax-sheltered retirement accounts, limiting annual contributions to $2,000. The tax-sheltered nature of these deposits and their exemption from Regulation Q ceilings will contribute to their development into a relatively permanent source of funds for banks.

Time Deposits, Open Accounts

Compared with the other types of time deposits, open-account time deposits are generally a minor source of bank funds. These are short-term deposit plans offered by banks to induce savers to make regular deposits of a stated amount of money. The understanding is that within a specified period of time there will be a large enough balance to enable the depositor to meet bills (for instance, at Christmas or for a vacation). In accordance with the nature of the anticipated expenditure, these plans have been known as Christmas Club, Vacation Club, Tax Club, and so on. They are covered by written contracts that do not permit their owners to withdraw all or any part of the funds deposited prior to maturity of the accounts or without giving written notice not less than 14 days in advance of withdrawal. If funds are withdrawn prior to maturity, the depositor incurs an interest penalty. The maximum rate payable on these deposits depends upon the maturity of the account and the amount involved. Retail banks find these plans beneficial because they help increase their deposit holdings and induce customers to save money. Without the incentives offered by these programs, many people would probably forgo savings altogether.

THE REGULATION Q ISSUE

Regulation Q had its origin in the Banking Act of 1933, which prohibited the payment of interest on demand deposits and authorized the Federal Reserve to set maximum rates on time deposits. The authority of the Federal Reserve to regulate interest payments on deposits by member banks was extended two years later to insured nonmember banks, when the Banking Act of 1935 gave the FDIC similar powers. Since then, both federal agencies have coordinated their rulings on the maximum interest rates that can be paid by banks on time and savings deposits. The Temporary Interest Rate Control Act of 1966 (Public Law 89-597) extended Regulation Q to mutual savings banks and savings and loan associations.

Regulation Q reflects much of the determination so characteristic of the Great Depression to establish a sound banking structure. The wave of bank failures that occurred in the early 1930s led many to believe that it was essentially a product of deposit competition among banks and the payment of excessive rates, which in turn encouraged unsafe lending and investing practices in the effort to earn enough to cover the cost of higher rates. Hence the reasoning that by regulating interest payments on deposits, price competition among banks would be eliminated, thereby producing a safer banking system. Another argument in favor of interest regulation was the concern that the payment of higher interest rates by larger banks would attract funds from rural areas and lessen the availability of credit in those areas. However plausible these arguments may have appeared at the time, Regulation Q had important implications not only for banks but also for the entire financial system. By prohibiting banks from paying interest on demand deposits and by imposing ceiling rates on time and savings accounts, Regulation Q was instrumental in controlling the lending ability of banks and, consequently, their role in the process of allocating credit among the various sectors of the economy. In other words, Regulation Q evolved into an active tool of monetary policy through which the Federal Reserve sought to constrain credit and influence its allocation within financial markets. The following sections trace the effects of Regulation Q upon commercial banks and, through them, upon financial activity. In this respect we shall review first the effect of Regulation Q on banks' demand deposits, and subsequently on time and savings deposits.

Demand Deposits

The immediate effect of the prohibition of interest payments on demand deposits was to limit the importance of these deposits as a source of loanable funds. This led banks to develop methods of offering a yield to demand deposit holders as a means of attracting such deposits. In other words, they engaged in nonprice competition. This yield has taken many forms. It has been a common practice, for example, to charge lower loan rates to corporate borrowers maintaining large balances in their checking account. In other instances reduced service charges are applied to accounts with large balances, and some banks have gone so far as to waive service charges entirely to attract demand deposits. Still others have introduced premiums in an effort to boost their new accounts. A few large banks have made it a practice to assist corporate treasurers in investing corporate funds in the money market.

Higher interest rates over the years have made demand depositors more conscious of the advantages of careful cash management. With many large depositors, especially business firms, increasingly concerned with conserving their use of demand deposits, some large banks have been stressing prompt collection and payment services to lure them. Such services are made possible in a number of ways: through direct arrangements with the Federal Reserve banks in other districts or with major-city correspondent banks, altogether bypassing the Federal Reserve System; through use of special carrier services to major cities to ensure faster collection than can be afforded by mail; through wire transfer of funds; and through locked-box arrangements.* Through these and other cash management techniques banks sought to lure corporate demand deposits. The more economical use of demand deposits made possible by these banks, however, affected the velocity or turnover of demand deposits. With demand deposits used more actively, the level of such deposits fluctuated more rapidly and widely. As a result, banks have found it difficult to use these funds for very short-term loans or investments. At best they can be used in the federal funds market, where transactions are typically for one day or for a weekend.

The economic effects of the prohibition of interest payments on demand deposits and the gradual adjustments, and eventual liberalization, of the ceilings applicable to time deposits—particularly large CDs—were decisive for the direction and level of bank deposit growth in the 1970s.

Time Deposits

In the years that followed its introduction, Regulation Q had little impact on bank time deposits because market rates of interest were much lower than established ceiling rates. The excessive liquidity of the economy and the lack of adequate demand for bank loans in the 1930s and 1940s led many banks to discourage deposit growth by paying minimum rates on time and savings deposits.† From 1935 through the early 1950s, Regulation Q ceiling rates—2.5 percent on savings deposits and 1-2.5 percent for time deposits, depending upon maturity—were, for all practical purposes, ineffective.

---

*Under a locked-box plan, local and regional payments on company billings are sent directly to a post office box under the control of the collection bank, thereby saving time in the collection and clearing of these items. If the billing company is located in another city, once the checks are cleared, the local bank remits the funds by wire to the company's bank of deposit. Through such a method collection time can be reduced by one to five days. Examples of freeing funds in the amount of $5 billion or more by this method have been cited by firms.

†It has been estimated that from 1929 through the early 1950s, time and savings deposits grew at only half the rate of demand deposits, with consequent implications for the share of commercial banks in the assets of all financial institutions.[4]

By the mid-1950s, however, this situation had changed significantly. Much of the change was brought about by many new savings and
loan associations, which, established in the immediate postwar years
in response to the rising demand for mortgage credit, began to bid
actively for household savings by offering rates that exceeded those
commercial banks were willing or able to pay. As the economy expanded and the demand for credit increased, many banks found themselves in great need of loanable funds. Requests for larger commercial
loans by corporate borrowers, combined with an inadequate growth
in demand deposits during the 1950s, made apparent to banks the
need to actively seek time and savings accounts. Since the rates paid
for such funds by competing deposit institutions (savings and loan associations, mutual savings banks, and credit unions) were free from
regulation, banks soon found themselves at a competitive disadvantage
in attracting time and savings deposits. After due consideration of the
situation, in mid-1957 the Federal Reserve System revised upward the
interest rate ceiling on bank time and savings deposits. Ceiling levels
changed on several occasions in the 1960s and early 1970s. In these
and in other instances the symptoms were the same: during periods
of high business activity and interest rates, the banking industry was
experiencing shortages of funds as a result of the "price control" imposed by Regulation Q.

Although the Board of Governors of the Federal Reserve System
made frequent adjustments of Regulation Q ceilings to improve the
competitive position of commercial banks, there were times (for instance, in 1966, 1969, and 1973) when its action came after significant
delay. While market rates of interest had risen above Regulation Q ceilings, the Federal Reserve, pursuing a tight money policy, delayed upward adjustment of bank interest-rate ceilings. This delay led depositors to withdraw their funds from (or deposit less funds in) commercial
banks and place them instead in higher-yielding marketable securities.
These massive withdrawals of funds—known as disintermediation—
deprived banks of time and demand deposits at the very time when
the most profitable opportunities were available for their employment.
Disintermediation thus forced banks to reduce their loan commitments
and generally to slow their lending activity. The Federal Reserve appeared to view Regulation Q as a monetary instrument, and welcomed
the limitation that it indirectly imposed on the expansion of bank
loans.

As indicated earlier, savings and loan associations and mutual savings banks were subjected to Regulation Q through the Temporary

Interest Rate Control Act of 1966. However, since these institutions provided the bulk of the permanent financing for the home mortgage market, the Federal Home Loan Bank Board saw to it that they enjoyed slightly higher Regulation Q ceilings than commercial banks, even though federal law did not require it. In 1970 Federal Reserve revision of interest-rate ceilings standardized a deposit-rate differential favoring thrifts over banks by 50 basis points for most deposit classes. The changes in 1973 reduced this differential to 25 basis points for most deposit classes. Formal recognition of an interest rate differential in favor of thrift institutions came with the passage of the Home Mortgage Disclosure Act of 1975 (Public Law 94-200), which stipulated that the differential in effect on December 10, 1975, could not be eliminated or reduced unless notice was given to Congress by the Federal Reserve. Thus the 25 basis points' differential in effect at the time of this enactment was thereafter maintained, providing an incentive for savers to keep their deposits at thrifts. The Garn-St. Germain Act of 1982 provided for the elimination of this differential by December 31, 1983, if not removed sooner by the DIDC.

June 1970 was a turning point in the development of time deposits, and particularly large CDs, as a major source of bank funds. In that month the Penn Central Railroad, the sixth largest corporation in the country, defaulted on $82 million of maturing commercial paper. This default undermined investor confidence in commercial paper and threatened corporations facing cash-flow problems with a severe shortage of funds. To prevent a liquidity crisis, the Federal Reserve encouraged banks to suspend Regulation Q ceilings on large CDs with maturities of less than 90 days. Because this measure was thought to be a temporary one, the suspension of ceiling rates for large CDs did not apply to maturities longer than 90 days. In mid-1973, as the business cycle was reaching the peak of its expansion, the Federal Reserve chose to extend the suspension of Regulation Q ceilings to all maturities of large CDs. The ability of large banks to innovate by developing new nondeposit sources of funds convinced the Federal Reserve of the need to reduce its reliance on Regulation Q in favor of additional reserve requirements, which affected the cost rather than the availability of additional liabilities. The 1973 suspension of Regulation Q ceilings on all maturities of large CDs was accompanied by the imposition of an 8 percent reserve requirement on any further increases in large CDs.

Removal of interest-rate ceilings on large CDs left banks free to compete for funds in the money markets in order to supply the credit needs of their corporate clients. Thus, though market rates of interest reached record levels in 1974, banks were in a position to compete effectively for funds. In the years that followed, reliance on large CDs increased further as banks sought to meet the enormous credit demands of the late 1970s and early 1980s. At the same time the Federal Reserve began to shift away from Regulation Q, relying instead upon reserve requirements and the market rates of interest for the allocation of funds among borrowers.

Since removal of Regulation Q ceilings on large CDs, banks have made increasingly frequent use of CDs in financing their activities. Banks typically post the rates they are offering for negotiable CDs of various maturities, and may adjust these rates daily or even hourly. Whenever a bank needs or desires funds with a particular maturity, it raises the rate to make it competitive with rates of comparable money-market instruments, including the CDs of other large banks. When the bank has obtained sufficient funds, it lowers the rate and keeps it noncompetitive until it desires to obtain additional funds. The negotiable CD is thus an excellent example of liability management referred to earlier. By varying the interest rates offered on CDs, a bank is in a position to purchase interest-sensitive funds every time loan demand outstrips the size of its regular deposit base. CD issuance therefore offers a significant degree of liquidity for a commercial bank. Instead of liquidating assets to obtain funds, a bank now has an alternative; it can elect to use CD financing.

The increased vigilance necessitated by the general relaxation and gradual phaseout of Regulation Q ceilings has brought an end to the day when bankers could rely on the simple 3-6-3 management concept. Pay 3 percent interest on time deposits, lend them out at 6 percent, and adjourn to the golf course at 3 p.m.[5]

Changing Composition of Deposits

Within a decade and half, the large CD emerged as a dominant source of bank funds. From 1961, when it was first introduced to retain interest-sensitive funds, to 1973, when ceiling rates were suspended for all large CD maturities, this instrument grew into the largest single source of funds for banks. The high rates of interest experienced during this period made depositors, both small and large, increasingly sophisticated in their approach to cash management. The forgone income inherent in demand deposits when interest rates were high led depositors to shift more and more of their demand-deposit balances into time and savings deposits. Thus in retail banks, the real growth in deposits came from consumer time and savings deposits, while in wholesale banks it came from large negotiable CDs. The

Figure 6.1. Growth and Changing Composition of Deposits, All Commercial Banks: 1959-82 (seasonally adjusted, quarterly averages)

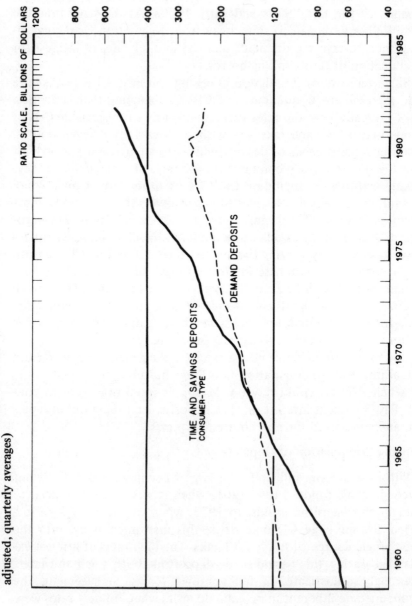

Source: Board of Governors of the Federal Reserve System, *Historical Chartbook* (Washington, D.C.: FDIC, 1982), p. 79.

growth pattern of consumer time and savings deposits for all commercial banks from 1959 to 1982 is shown in Figure 6.1. From the late 1960s on, the dominant role as a source of funds that demand deposits had enjoyed was assumed by the faster-growing (consumer) time and savings deposits.

Figure 6.2 shows the growth of large-denomination time deposits ($100,000 and over) for all commercial banks from 1959 to 1982. They have shown a steady increase except in 1969, which saw a dip due to the delayed action of the Federal Reserve in adjusting ceiling rates on time deposits.

The change in the banks' deposit mix led to their evolution from demand-deposit-oriented to time-deposit-oriented institutions. One result of this development was the introduction of a new pricing policy by large banks. They started charging fees for services with which they used to compensate demand depositors for their inability to pay interest on their accounts. Thus, depositors earn explicit interest rates and customers are charged explicit fees for various services. However, a more important effect of the change in banks' deposit mix has been a shift in the management of bank funds. As long as demand deposits dominated their sources of funds, banks sought to match the very short-term nature of these liabilities with short-term assets: highly liquid investments and short-term loans. With the lengthening of their deposit maturity, however, banks have extended the maturities of their earning assets. Many banks have expanded their

Figure 6.2. Growth in Large-Denomination Time Deposits, All Commercial Banks: 1959-82 (seasonally adjusted, quarterly averages)

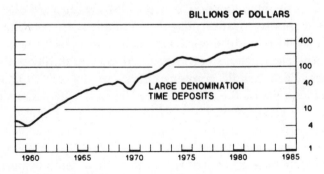

Note: Effective September 1, 1982, the Federal Reserve amended Regulation Q so that time deposits no longer had to be evidenced by a certificate or other negotiable or nonnegotiable instrument.

Source: Board of Governors of the Federal Reserve System, *Historical Chartbook* (Washington, D.C.: FDIC, 1982), p. 79.

holdings of higher-yielding intermediate- and longer-term government securities, and have increased their mortgage loans to individuals and term loans to businesses. Whether because of the longer-term nature of their liabilities or because of the need to cover the higher rate of interest paid on time deposits, the increase in the maturity of their asset portfolios is transforming commercial banks into more effective competitors of life insurance companies and other institutions engaged in long-term financing.

THE PAYMENTS MECHANISM

The writing of checks represents the chief means of exchange of funds in the United States. The routing of these checks to the banks on which they are drawn and the return flow of funds to the depositor's account is referred to as check clearing. Millions of checks are written every day, many of them originating at points a great distance from the banks on which they are drawn. Since the convenience of being able to pay for things with checks is a major reason people put money in banks as demand deposits, it is in the interest of banks to accomplish check clearing as smoothly and expeditiously as possible.

Check clearing methods vary, depending primarily on the geographical proximity of the banks involved. In small towns or rural areas where communities are served by only a few banks, bilateral transfers of funds between banks may be arranged by messenger every day. The amounts drawn on each bank by the other are compared and the difference is credited appropriately, usually by adjusting each bank's balance at the regional Federal Reserve bank. In larger towns and cities, representatives of all the banks in the community meet daily at a designated location, called a clearinghouse, to clear checks. The clearinghouse location may be permanent or rotating (such as the back room of a different bank each week). Each bank sends its clerk to the clearinghouse at a specified time each day with bundles of checks. Each bundle contains checks of one of the other banks and includes a list of the amounts due the clerk's bank from the other bank. At the clearinghouse the clerks hand over the checks drawn on the other banks, receive the checks drawn on their banks, and settle net differences among themselves.

A hypothetical record of a net settlement among participating banks is reproduced in Table 6.3. Total credits equal total debits. The difference between the total credits and total debits for any bank determines the net position of the bank. Net settlement is effected by notifying the Federal Reserve bank which bank accounts are to be credited and which are to be debited. In Table 6.3 the accounts of

Table 6.3. Clearinghouse Transactions

	Checks Received by			Total	Net
Checks Drawn on	Bank A	Bank B	Bank C	Debits	Debits
Bank A	–	300	100	400	
Bank B	$400	–	700	1,100	300
Bank C	200	500	–	700	
Total Credits	600	800	800	2,200	
Net Credits	200		100		

Source: Prepared by author.

Banks A and C at the Federal Reserve are credited $200 and $100, respectively, while the account of Bank B is debited $300. The reserve accounts of banks are then adjusted according to the net result of the day's check clearing process.

When the banks involved are located at some distance, collection may be effected through the correspondent banking system or through the Federal Reserve System. In cases where banks choose to collect items through their correspondents, they will send these items to their correspondent banks, without having to sort them (as they must if they clear through the Federal Reserve). For banks located in the same federal reserve district, collection through the Federal Reserve is quite simple. The reporting bank receives credit to its account at the Federal Reserve bank, while the bank on which the check is drawn will have its account debited a like amount. If the banks are located in different districts, the bank receiving the check sends it to its district Federal Reserve bank, which in turn sends it for collection to its counterpart in the district in which the drawee's bank is located. Settlement between the two Federal Reserve banks is effected through the Interdistrict Settlement Fund, which is a sort of clearinghouse for the Federal Reserve banks. The fund, in which each Federal Reserve bank maintains a balance, settles net amounts due between Federal Reserve banks daily.

To make the payments system more efficient, the Federal Reserve operates 46 regional check-processing centers throughout the nation, thus cutting down on both cost and time to process checks. During 1980 the Federal Reserve System handled 15.7 billion checks with a total value of $8 trillion. Of course, that was only part of the nation's total check volume. Other checks were collected by correspondent banks, local clearinghouses, or directly between banks. Projections for 1990 estimate that 40 billion checks will flow through the commercial banking system.

In recent years growing concern over the rising volume of checks and its effects upon the check-clearing and collection mechanism has led to the increased mechanization of funds transfers. The actual transfer of paper is being replaced by the transmission of electronic impulses in systems known generically as electronic funds transfer systems (EFTS). Several types of EFTS are currently in various stages of experimentation and implementation.

The Fed Wire, as the Federal Reserve Communications System is known, represents the first U.S. experience with electronic funds transfer. Although established in the 1910s, it has become a significant means of funds transfer only with the advent, in the 1970s, of high-speed computers and sophisticated corporate cash-management techniques. The Fed Wire connects all of the Federal Reserve banks and their branches, the Treasury and other government agencies, and member banks. By this means funds can be transferred from one bank's reserve account to another; transactions can be conducted in the Federal funds market; funds can be transferred for bank customers; and transfer book entries representing U.S. government and federal agency securities can be made. In 1950 a group of 14 banks established a similar communication system among themselves, and since that time Bank Wire has grown to link hundreds of banks across the country.

Another way the Federal Reserve contributes to the payments mechanism is through the automated clearinghouses (ACHs), operated for the most part at the Federal Reserve banks. ACHs effect transfers of information among accounts and banks by means of computer tape. There are at present over 35 ACHs in the United States, serving financial institutions of all types: savings and loan associations, credit unions, and mutual savings banks as well as commercial banks. They are used primarily to process payrolls, welfare payments, and federal government transactions. For instance, Social Security payments are routed into the accounts of recipients who have authorized direct deposit of their payments. Many businesses make payroll disbursements via ACHs, submitting a computer tape that calls for transfers of funds from the employer's account directly to the accounts of individual employees. This method of transferring funds realizes a substantial savings through reduced paperwork, and for this reason ACH activities are expected to expand and proliferate. The Federal Reserve's fees for use of ACH services are below cost in order to foster greater use of this method of conducting bank-related transactions.

Increasing deployment of EFTS at the consumer level, such as automatic teller machines, is also affecting the nature of the payments mechanism, reducing both payroll and paperwork costs for banks. The more recent introduction of point-of-scale (POS) systems suggests the possibility of even greater savings in transaction costs as well as increased customer convenience. By this means the customer not only can pay for purchases by means of a direct transfer of funds from his or her account to that of the merchant through a debit card; he or she can also use the POS terminal to withdraw cash from an account or can charge the purchase to a credit card. An advantage for the store is that this method of payment, in which the POS terminal verifies the transfer of funds from the customer's account as payment for the goods purchased, eliminates the possibility of a bad check being written. Finally, the bank realizes savings because less paperwork is needed to document the various funds transfers. The customer obtains a receipt from the merchant and, each month, a bank statement listing all transactions in and out of the account. A bulky bundle of checks no longer need be processed and mailed. An important development in this direction is Visa's "electron" card, which has been designed to function as both a debit card and a cash dispensing card. Visa is in the process of developing a "smart" card that will add the credit card function to these functions. In the international arena the "electron" card is already functioning as a cash dispensing card through the cooperation of many Western European and Latin American banks, and is just one step away from functioning as a debit card as well.

In-home banking, whereby a customer communicates with the bank via a push-button telephone or a computer terminal linked to the bank's computer, represents another dimension of paperless banking. These systems can also effect transfers of payment, as the customer's instructions to debit his or her account and to credit another's are routed among the banks involved. Finally, linking POS systems with home terminal banking will allow individuals to make retail purchases without leaving home. In addition, customers will be able to request a display on the television screen showing the status of their accounts at any time. Other kinds of information can be requested as well, such as current interest rates on different forms of investments and even investment advice. The desired investment transactions can also be conducted via the home terminal. Expanded telephone bill-paying services will further facilitate electronic funds transfers. The day may soon come when an individual can conduct all financial affairs without ever having to leave home.

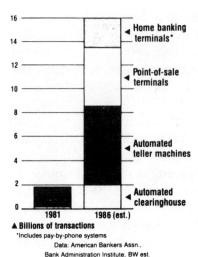

Figure 6.3. Growth of Electronic payments, 1981-86

Source: Reprinted from the January 18, 1982, issue of *Business Week* by special permission, (c) 1982 by McGraw-Hill, Inc., New York, N.Y. 10020. All rights reserved.

In the meantime, many banks are achieving significant savings in the processing of payments by retaining the checks drawn on their customers' accounts rather than returning them with the monthly statement. This process, known as truncation, reduces both postage costs and the costs of sorting the checks by customer account at the bank. Should a customer require a particular canceled check—to verify, for example, payment of a bill—it can be obtained from the bank.

Banks have been pressed to achieve savings in the processing of payments by increased competition and by the advent of interest-bearing checking accounts. In the coming years we can expect to see extensive deployment of the cost-saving electronic means of conducting banking transactions as well as the development of yet more advanced technology to realize even more kinds of savings. Figure 6.3, which shows expected growth in EFTS by 1986, is an indication of the accelerating pace of the electronic revolution in funds transfers.

NOTES

1. "A Big Brawl in Banking," *Time*, January 17, 1983, p. 34.
2. Ibid.
3. G. Christian Hill, "Banks, S&Ls Gear up New Savings Accounts That Will Stir Rivalry," *Wall Street Journal*, December 10, 1982, p. 18.
4. For the trend in the growth of bank time and savings deposits vis-à-vis that of other financial institutions since the turn of the century, see Raymond W. Goldsmith, *Financial Intermediaries in the American Economy Since 1900* (Princeton: Princeton University Press, 1958).
5. John Helyar and Julie Salamon, "Big Banks Set Agenda for the Entire Industry as Regulation Loosens," *Wall Street Journal*, November 18, 1982, p. 1.

SUGGESTED REFERENCES

Crosse, Howard D., and George H. Hempel. *Management Policies for Commercial Banks*. 3rd ed. Englewood Cliffs, N.J.: Prentice-Hall, 1980.

"Electronic Banking." *Business Week*, January 18, 1982, pp. 70-74, 76, 80.

Friedman, Benjamin M. "Regulation Q and the Commercial Loan Market in the 1960s." *Journal of Money, Credit and Banking* no. 3 (1976):277-96.

Gilbert, R. Alton, and Jean M. Lovati. "Disintermediation: An Old Disorder with a New Remedy." *Review*, Federal Reserve Bank of St. Louis, January 1979, pp. 10-15.

Godfrey, John M., and B. Frank King. "Money Market Certificates: An Innovation in Consumer Deposits." *Economic Review*, Federal Reserve Bank of Atlanta, May-June 1979, pp. 59-64.

Higgins, Bryon. "Interest Payments on Demand Deposits: Historical Evolution and the Current Controversy." *Monthly Review*, Federal Reserve Bank of Kansas City, July-August 1977, pp. 3-11.

"Home Banking Moves off the Drawing Board." *Business Week*, September 20, 1982, p. 39.

Kimball, Ralph C. "The Maturing of the NOW Account in New England." *New England Economic Review*, Federal Reserve Bank of Boston, July-August 1978, pp. 27-42.

Marbacher, Josef. "Characteristics and Problems of Modern Payment Systems." *Journal of Bank Research*, Winter 1981, pp. 206-13.

Melton, William C. "The Market for Large Negotiable CDs." *Quarterly Review*, Federal Reserve Bank of New York, Winter 1977-78, pp. 22-34.

Metzker, Paul F. "The Debit Card at the Crossroads." *Economic Review*, Federal Reserve Bank of Atlanta, March 1983, pp. 33-45.

Pyle, David H. "The Losses on Savings Deposits from Interest Rate Regulation." *Bell Journal of Economics and Management Science*, Autumn 1974, pp. 614-22.

Sinkey, Joseph F., Jr. *Commercial Bank Financial Management*. New York: Macmillan, 1983.

Wolkowitz, Benjamin. "The Case for the Federal Reserve System Actively Participating in Electronic Funds Transfer." *Journal of Bank Research*, Spring 1978, pp. 15-25.

7
NONDEPOSIT LIABILITIES

Nondeposit liabilities, the second largest source of bank funds, are not a homogeneous category of accounts. Instead, they represent a broad concept encompassing a variety of items, such as liabilities for borrowed money, capitalized leases, expenses accrued and unpaid, deferred income taxes, mortgage indebtedness, subordinated notes and debentures, and minority interests in subsidiaries. Dominant are liabilities for borrowed money, accounting, at year-end 1982, for two-thirds of all banks' nondeposit liabilities. Since the rest of nondeposit liabilities are either of limited importance (such as accrued and deferred items) or have been previously discussed (such as subordinated notes and debentures), we shall focus our attention in this chapter on borrowed liabilities and their development as sources of bank liquidity in satisfying loan demands. Moreover, we will discuss the considerations that determine bank reliance on one or more sources of borrowed funds at any particular time, and review trends in interest rates in the money market.

BORROWING

The increasing importance of borrowed funds for commercial banks in recent years is depicted in Table 7.1. Total borrowings increased from $163 million in 1960 to $19.4 billion in 1970, more than a hundredfold increase in a decade. By December 1982 aggregate bank borrowings had risen to $215.1 billion. As follows from these data, the 1960s were benchmark years in the growth of bank borrowings. This decade saw an unprecedented expansion in economic activity and a concomitant growth in the financing needs of corporations and the private sector in general.

Much of this demand for credit was directed to money-center banks in the form of requests for short-term loans. During the early phases of the 1966 and 1969 expansions, banks responded to the rising loan demand by increasing their reliance upon negotiable CDs

Table 7.1. Borrowings of Domestically Chartered Commercial Banks, Selected Years

Year	Amount (billions of dollars)	Year	Amount (billions of dollars)
1960	$ .1	1976	$ 80.2
1970	19.4	1977	96.2
1971	25.9	1978	136.8
1972	38.1	1979	140.5
1973	59.0	1980	156.8
1974	58.4	1981	190.4
1975	60.2	1982	215.1

Source: *Federal Reserve Bulletin*, selected issues.

to raise the necessary funds. However, as the loan demand intensified and inflation began to increase, rates on competitive money-market instruments rose through Regulation Q ceilings, undermining the ability of banks to compete for interest-sensitive funds. When the Federal Reserve—in its effort to control the pace of economic activity—did not adjust, or delayed adjusting, bank interest-rate ceilings upward, maturing CDs were not renewed by depositors. In addition, banks began experiencing large outflows of funds, which placed them in an awkward and precarious situation. Disintermediation was making it difficult for commercial banks to honor their loan commitments to traditional customers and to maintain adequate liquidity levels. It was under these pressures that banks began to develop new sources of loanable funds by incurring, at their own initiative, liabilities for borrowed money. To offset their shortages of loanable funds and reduced liquidity, they started bidding for interest-sensitive funds in such markets as the commercial paper market and the overseas dollar-denominated markets (Eurodollar markets).

Bank reliance on interest-sensitive deposits and borrowed funds during the credit crunches of 1966 and 1969 gave prominence to liability management. Bank reliance on liability management as a liquidity management technique represented an important departure from earlier practices. In preceding tight money periods, when demands for credit outstripped deposit growth, banks usually sold off large amounts of U.S. Treasury bills or other marketable securities accumulated during the war years to accommodate their customers' credit needs. Banks thus relied heavily on asset management and paid little attention to the management of liabilities. However, during the tight money period of 1966, though banks again liquidated significant amounts of securities from their investment portfolios, reliance on borrowed funds became increasingly important in cushioning the effects of a contracting deposit volume. Especially aggressive in their bidding for such funds, and hence effective in the development of these sources, were the larger banks, which, despite the prevailing tightness, were able to provide for the short-term finance needs of their corporate clients. From then on, liability management took on—for a great many banks—an importance comparable with that of asset management.

Liabilities for borrowed money include a variety of interest-sensitive sources of loanable funds. One such source—interest-bearing demand notes issued to the U.S. Treasury—was discussed in Chapter 6 in connection with public deposits. Our discussion here will therefore concentrate on the other sources of loanable funds that constitute the thrust of bank borrowing.

Depending upon prevailing financial and economic circumstances, banks may acquire funds through one or more of the following arrangements: purchase of federal funds, sale of securities and loans under agreement to repurchase, sale of bankers' acceptances, sale of commercial paper, borrowing of Eurodollars, and borrowing from the Federal Reserve bank. Liabilities of this type, with one exception (Federal Reserve credit), are known as money-market liabilities because they are generally purchased or acquired by paying a competitive price for them in the money market. Each of these liabilities is discussed below.

Federal Funds

"Federal funds" refers to banks' deposit balances at Federal Reserve banks. Since enactment of the DIDMCA in 1980, all banks have been required to maintain reserves against their deposit liabilities in the form of vault cash and balances with their district Federal Reserve bank. Because these reserves yield no income, and any deficiency is penalized by the Federal Reserve, well-managed banks try to avoid more of them than is necessary. The federal funds market thus provides the vehicle for the efficient management of a bank's reserve position.

If a bank has excess reserves on deposit with a Federal Reserve bank on a particular day, it can sell them to a bank with a shortage in its legal reserve position. If the banks involved are located in the same area, the transaction is effected through a telephone call. The lending institution authorizes the Federal Reserve bank to transfer from its reserve account to that of the borrowing bank the agreed amount of reserve funds. Accordingly, the Federal Reserve bank debits the reserve account of the lending institution and credits the reserve account of the borrowing institution. Since these transactions are usually for overnight, the bookkeeping entry will be reversed the following day. If the banks are located in different parts of the country, the transfer of funds will be accomplished through the Fed Wire and will involve a series of instantaneous accounting entries to reflect the interdistrict nature of the transaction.

In terms of maturity, more than 90 percent of the transactions in this market are overnight (one-day) or continuing contracts. Continuing-contract federal funds consist of a series of overnight transactions that are automatically renewed each day unless terminated by either party. A typical example of such a contract is the purchase by a correspondent bank of the federal funds that a respondent bank has available for sale. The automatic rollover of overnight funds represents, in essence, an arrangement of open maturity. The interest payment, though it varies from contract to contract, is computed on the basis of the daily rate quotation.

A limited number of transactions take the form of term federal funds. Banks anticipating a need for borrowed funds over a period of time or a trend of a higher federal funds rate in the months ahead, may contract for term federal funds (for 30 days, 90 days, or occasionally 180 days). Since federal funds transactions are exempt from reserve requirements, this alternative would be preferred, for example, to the issuance of comparable maturity CDs as a means of securing funds for loan commitments. Many large banks use this market to fund their entire reserve requirements on a rather permanent basis.

The rate charged on federal funds purchases has never been subject to Regulation Q ceilings, and the transaction is not subject to reserve requirements. However, from October 1979 to July 1980, the Federal Reserve imposed a marginal reserve requirement of 8 percent (later during this period it was raised to 10 percent) on member banks' federal funds purchases, security repurchase agreements, and other managed liabilities (large negotiable CDs and borrowings of Eurodollars). The requirement applied only to borrowings that were over $100 million or in excess of a certain amount in a base period. By raising the effective cost of federal funds and security repurchase agreements, the Federal Reserve sought to slow bank borrowing and, hence, continuation of inflationary pressures in the economy. The practical implication of this move is that the Federal Reserve will not hesitate to impose reserve requirements on banks' managed liabilities in order to prevent excessive and reckless borrowing by individual institutions.

Federal Funds Rate

The rate charged on federal funds transactions is called the federal funds rate. Although expressed on an annual basis, the federal funds rate is computed to reflect the daily nature of the transaction. For example, assuming a federal funds transaction for $2 million at a going rate of 15 percent, the bank selling federal funds would earn for one day $833.30 ($2,000,000 × .15 × $\frac{1}{360}$). If the transaction was effected on a Friday, the selling bank would earn $2,500, since it would take three days (until the next clearing on Monday) to get its funds back. The purchasing bank's reserve balances would be adjusted to reflect access to these funds over the weekend. The amount of interest earned would be added to the value of the loan at the time of its repayment. However, it may also be paid by separate check or by adjusting correspondent bank balances through bookkeeping entries.

The rate of interest paid on federal funds on any particular day or at a specific time of day is a function of demand and supply conditions in the marketplace. Since the purchase of federal funds is primarily induced by the need to offset a reserve deficiency, heavy trading is frequently encountered on the last day of the reserve settlement period (Wednesday). This fact, along with time differences across the nation, has been responsible for significant volatility in the federal funds rate during a single trading day. Similar volatility is frequently encountered on the last day of the year, which constitutes the closing date for banks' financial statements. The need for "window dressing" by certain banks helps, for example, to explain why on December 31, 1982, the federal funds rate fluctuated between 3 and 20 percent.

Apart from demand and supply conditions, the rate is affected by monetary policy. When monetary policy is restrictive and money-market conditions are tight, the federal funds rate will remain high. In the summer of 1981, for example, the rate fluctuated around the 20 percent mark. When conditions eased in the spring of 1983, the rate hovered around 8 percent.

The rate on federal funds is an indicator of major significance. By representing a key marginal cost of bank funds, it affects the market rates of interest, including the prime rate. The federal funds rate is so sensitive that the Federal Reserve looks to it to identify the degree of tightness or ease of the money market. Moreover, it uses this rate as a target of monetary policy—that is, it buys or sells securities in the open market to affect the rate and bring it to the desired level. Table 7.2 shows the effective federal funds rates from 1967 through 1982. Since

Table 7.2. Effective Federal Funds Rate, 1967-82 (percent per annum)

Year	Average Daily Rate	Year	Average Daily Rate
1967	4.22	1975	5.82
1968	5.66	1976	5.05
1969	8.21	1977	5.54
1970	7.17	1978	7.94
1971	4.66	1979	11.20
1972	4.44	1980	13.36
1973	8.74	1981	16.38
1974	10.51	1982	12.26

Note: Figures are averages of daily effective rates for the week ending Wednesday. Since July 1973 the daily effective federal funds rate is an average of the rates on a given day weighted by the volume of transactions at these rates. Prior to this date the daily effective rate was the rate considered most representative of the day's transactions, usually the one at which most transactions occurred.

Source: *Federal Reserve Bulletin*, selected issues.

these rates are averages of daily effective rates for each week during the indicated year, the magnitude of the rate's day-to-day or week-to-week volatility is not identified.

Development of the Federal Funds Market

Trading federal funds is not a recent development. Although the federal funds market has been in existence since the 1920s, it was not until the 1960s that its growth and development began in earnest. Before the early 1960s federal funds were viewed as an alternative mode of reserve adjustment to borrowing from the Federal Reserve discount window. In other words, banks needing reserves borrowed federal funds only if their cost was lower than the discount rate. By late 1964, however, the character of this market started to change as the practice of liability management gained momentum. Confronted with a growing demand for loans and a tight monetary policy, major money-market banks—located principally in New York City—began to bid for federal funds at rates above the discount rate. To them, paying a premium rate for federal funds was justified in the light of the higher rates at which they could profitably lend these funds. As more and more banks realized the potential of the federal funds market as a source of purchased liabilities, their participation in this market and the volume of trading expanded rapidly. The phenomenal growth experienced by the federal funds market during this period can be sensed from the trading activity of 46 large money-market banks, whose daily average purchases of federal funds between 1960 and 1970 jumped from $1.1 billion to $8.3 billion.

In recent years the federal funds market has expanded even further with the entry of other participants as sellers of funds. The U.S. offices of foreign banks, thrift institutions, businesses, and even the International Bank for Reconstruction and Development (IBRD or World Bank) have been feeding the market with their temporarily surplus funds. For the former two types of institutions, their participation in the federal funds market does not change the process of transferring funds, since the DIDMCA, enacted in 1980, requires them to maintain reserve accounts at Federal Reserve banks. However, even if the participants maintain no reserve account, the transfer of funds is, in the final analysis, effected through a bank or other depository institution that maintains balances with a Federal Reserve bank.

The developments described above were instrumental in transforming the federal funds market from a negotiated market into an impersonal open market with a standardized commodity and rates that respond rapidly to changing market conditions. Many banks prefer to borrow in this market rather than subject themselves to the scrutiny of the Federal Reserve bank when requesting a loan. Commercial banks purchase billions of dollars of federal funds each business day. Table 7.3 shows the year-end volume of federal funds sold and purchased (including security resale agreements) by all insured commercial banks from 1976 through 1981. The excess of the funds purchased over those sold reflects the increased participation in this market of foreign banks, thrifts, and other suppliers of temporarily available funds.

Table 7.3. Federal Funds Sold and Purchased by All Insured Commercial Banks, 1976-81 (billions of dollars)

Item	1976	1977	1978	1979	1980	1981
Federal funds sold and securities purchased under agreements to resell	45.9	49.9	48.8	61.1	70.1	90.7
Federal funds purchased and securities sold under agreements to repurchase	70.3	83.0	91.3	112.1	132.5	163.5

Note: Since separate reporting of federal funds transactions has been discontinued, the above data include security resale agreements.

Source: Federal Deposit Insurance Corporation, *Statistics on Banking* (Washinton, D.C.: FDIC, 1981), pp. 41-42.

Correspondent Banks and the Integration of the Federal Funds Market

A bank wishing to purchase or sell federal funds has three options: it may approach and deal directly with another bank, go through a federal funds broker, or contact its correspondent bank. Stock brokerage firms in New York City may function as federal funds brokers by bringing together, at a commission, institutions buying and selling federal funds. Correspondent banks often make a market for federal funds to accommodate respondent banks—because they realize that if they do not do so, competing institutions will. The process is initiated when the respondent bank, through a telephone call, informs the correspondent bank of its intention to sell funds. This call solicits the purchase of funds by the correspondent bank. If the latter has more funds than it needs, it will sell some of its excess federal funds to other banks. Thus, many money-center banks and regional banks are both purchasers and sellers of federal funds.

This activity of correspondent banks opened the federal funds market to banks of all sizes, a development that has a number of effects. First, transactions of less than $1 million have become more common than in the past. Second, small banks, because of limited loan opportunities in their markets, have become—through their correspondent banks—net suppliers of federal funds while large banks have become net borrowers of these funds. In essence, the federal funds market has been functioning as a conduit for the excess funds of smaller banks to support the lending activity of larger banks. A third effect, and a direct result of the preceding development, is that by converting excess funds into loanable, and hence profitable, funds, the federal funds market has enabled the banking system to make more efficient use of its reserves. A fourth and more important effect is that the federal funds market has joined banks of disparate size and thrift institutions into an integrated banking system. This integration process has enhanced the effectiveness of Federal Reserve action in pursuit of tight monetary policy. The federal funds market transmits the effects of Federal Reserve action nationwide and, in turn, makes the commercial banking system more responsive to the tightening actions of the Federal Reserve.

The growing presence of foreign banks in the United States and their participation in the federal funds market are linking the domestic interbank market with foreign financial markets. As a direct consequence trends in the domestic interbank market are transmitted to the international financial markets and vice versa, thus integrating financial markets across national boundaries.

Repurchase Agreements

In recent years repurchase agreements (RPs) have become a major source of money-market funds, rivaling more familiar financial instruments such as negotiable CDs or commercial paper. Under a repurchase agreement a bank can obtain supplementary funds by selling securities from its portfolio with a simultaneous agreement to repurchase at a later date. In essence RPs are a secured and liquid means of borrowing and lending funds for short periods; the securities involved in the transaction are usually obligations of the federal government or its agencies; and most transactions take place between large, prime credit institutions. In addition, the securities serve as collateral against the loan, and the lender (buyer) is assured a repurchase price that equals the original sale price plus earned interest. As a further protection to the lender against adverse conditions in the marketplace, the securities pledged are valued at a discount from their current market prices.

From the lender's perspective the RP transaction is termed a reverse repurchase agreement; the lender buys a security and resells it upon maturity. Reverse RPs are often arranged by large commercial banks and government securities dealers in order to acquire government securities with which to engage in repurchase agreements.

In order to engage in an RP transaction, the lender must have the necessary funds readily available the same business day the transaction takes place. Whether in the form of deposit balances with the district Federal Reserve bank or with a local commercial bank, these funds can be made immediately available to the borrowing bank through the Fed Wire. RP negotiations are handled directly between the borrower and lender, or through a small group of U.S. government securities dealers who are market specialists. Large banks and businesses usually employ traders who negotiate interest rates with potential participants. Since there is no central marketplace for arranging RPs, all transactions are negotiated on the telephone. Interest rates are usually comparable with the federal funds rate, but are often slightly lower because RPs are collateralized and federal funds are not.

Most RPs are in sums of $1 million or more, although they can be for less than $100,000. The time of maturity is either fixed (from overnight to several days) or negotiated under a continuing contract agreement, which automatically renews the RP daily until terminated by either party.

Market Participants

Some of the more important participants in the RP market are commercial banks, government securities dealers, insurance companies, businesses, foreign financial institutions, state and local governments, and the Federal Reserve System. RPs offer holders of sizable cash balances a means of converting their demand deposit accounts into interest-earning assets, with funds committed for very short periods and thus readily available. Larger commercial banks are usually borrowers in the RP market. Funds so obtained are not subject to interest-rate ceilings or reserve requirements (provided the transaction exceeds $100,000 and matures within 90 days). Effective October 11, 1979, managed liabilities of member banks (including RPs issued against U.S. government and federal agency securities) were subject to an 8 percent marginal reserve requirement. On April 3, 1980, Regulation D was amended to increase marginal reserve requirements to 10 percent, then reduced to 5 percent in June 1980, and finally to zero beginning July 24, 1980.

The use of RPs as a source of funds for commercial banks increased significantly in the early 1980s, in response to rising short-term interest rates. During 1981 bankers used RPs as a means of attracting consumer funds in retaliation against money-market mutual funds. In an effort to tap small investors as a source of financing, the parent companies of large banks offered small-denomination "repurchase agreement certificates" that could be cashed in prematurely without penalty. As implied by their name, these certificates were issued against securities that were sold by these institutions to savers' pools under agreements to repurchase.

Other important participants in the RP market are government securities dealers, who borrow RP funds to finance their inventories of government securities. They have also become lenders in this market, through reverse RPs. As a result, dealers have emerged as important intermediaries in the RP market for borrowers and lenders of funds. Large, well-known dealers obtain more competitive rates than smaller dealers and corporations, thus generating their profits through arbitrage (matching an RP transaction with a reverse RP at a higher rate but of equal maturity).

The RP market has grown considerably in the last few years for several reasons. The prohibition of interest payments on demand deposits and rising market interest rates have induced many state and local governments, as well as businesses, to enter the RP market to lend their temporarily idle funds. In the case of businesses, the increasing use of computers and more sophisticated cash management techniques have played an important role in the extent of their participation in this market. The end result has been that both businesses and municipalities have come to view RPs as an income-earning substitute for their demand deposit balances. RPs are also a more attractive alternative to commercial paper and newly issued negotiable CDs. It is very rare for commercial paper to be issued for a period as short as a day or two, and Regulation Q requires a minimum maturity of at least 14 days for large CDs. For these reasons substantial funds have been channeled daily into the RP market, contributing to its further development. The growth of RP transactions has also improved the liquidity of the securities used as collateral, since they may generate funds on short notice, without incurring the possible losses resulting from an outright sale. In effect, RPs offer investors and borrowers an instrument with flexibility, liquidity, short-term maturity, and low-risk factors unsurpassed by other money-market instruments.

Role of the Federal Reserve in the RP Market

Large banks have traditionally sold loans to smaller correspondents as a way of increasing their own loanable funds while providing the smaller bank with a return exceeding security investments. To maintain satisfactory correspondent relations, these loans were usually sold with the understanding that the selling bank would buy back any of the loans that experienced difficulty in repayment. Since the selling bank generally continued servicing the loan, the original borrower would probably never become aware of the sale of the loan.

A technique was developed early in 1969 by which money-market banks needing to improve the liquidity of their portfolios could do so by selling loans, or participation in pools of loans, to nonbank customers under agreement to repurchase. As banks realized the potential for acquiring loanable funds through use of this type of agreement, RPs became increasingly widespread. In the early months of 1969, banks began to extend this practice to customers holding maturing CDs at interest rates comparable with the money-market rates. It is estimated that during the summer of 1969, RPs involving loans or participations in pools of loans doubled, with most of these transactions directed to unaffiliated bank customers.

The Board of Governors finally interceded, concluding that banks were using RPs in much the same way as deposit transactions, but not conforming to the purposes and policies of regulations D and Q. Consequently, these regulations were amended to state that after July 25, 1969, any RPs entered into with a nonbank institution or customer, using any asset other than U.S. government or agency obligations, would be subject to reserve requirements and interest-rate ceilings. This made the sale of loans under RPs too costly for banks and contributed to its gradual loss of appeal.

The Federal Reserve System plays a dual role in the RP market. It regulates the market by limiting the types of transactions undertaken by member banks, and largely affects interest rates available daily on the RP market by influencing the federal funds rate. The Federal Reserve is also a significant direct participant in the RP market, temporarily absorbing or supplying reserves to commercial banks through RPs or reverse RPs.

Bankers' Acceptances

A banker's acceptance is a short-term time draft drawn by an individual or business concern upon a bank. ordering it to pay a stipulated amount of money at a specified date in the future. When the bank accepts the draft, it guarantees its redemption at maturity. This guarantee raises the credit quality of the draft and makes it negotiable. In return for this guarantee, the party on whose behalf the bank accepts the draft agrees to provide the bank with the necessary funds prior to maturity and pays a nominal charge. The customer's outstanding debt to the bank is noted on the bank's books as an asset, while the bank's guarantee to the customer is shown as a liability.

Although bankers' acceptances have for centuries been an important instrument in international commerce, this market has only recently grown in the United States. The amount of bankers' acceptances outstanding have risen from less than $400 million in 1950 to approximately $80 billion at the close of 1982. Most of this growth took place in the 1970s, when acceptances outstanding exceeded $54 billion—a sevenfold increase in a decade. The factor responsible for this impressive growth in acceptances outstanding was the spectacular increase in foreign trade. While the volume of acceptances created to finance U.S. foreign trade increased rapidly, most of the growth in acceptances came from the expansion in the foreign-trade transactions between foreign countries, such as Japan and Middle East countries. The latter type of acceptances are generally referred to as "third-country bills." These acceptances represented, at year-end 1982, a little over half of the total acceptances outstanding.

Despite the sizable development of this market, bankers' acceptances continue to be one of the least familiar of all money-market instruments. A banker's acceptance may arise out of import or export transactions, commodity warehousing, or domestic shipping. The banker's acceptance market consists of three major participants: the accepting banks, the dealers, and the investors. Since an accepting bank simply guarantees payment upon maturity, bankers' acceptances offer banks the advantage of financing their customers' credit demands without reducing their own loanable funds. Thus, during periods of restrictive credit, when liquidating or rediscounting conventional loans can be inconvenient and costly or poor customer relations, bankers' acceptances become an attractive option in funding customer needs, since they can easily be sold in the money market to generate the necessary funds.

The great majority of bankers' acceptances are issued by large banks with specialized staffs, good foreign connections, and an established name. Increasingly in recent years smaller regional banks have become important issuers of bankers' acceptances. In order to sell their paper, however, they must locate dealers interested in making a market in their acceptances. The rates on such acceptances are slightly higher than those of the large, established banks.

The trading activity of about 15 dealers determines the marketability of bankers' acceptances. Although some dealers post bid and asked prices, trading is mostly done on a negotiated basis. Dealer profits result from selling acceptances at a fractional percentage above their buying price.

An increasing number of money-market investors have begun buying bankers' acceptances because they recognize the safe and liquid nature of this type of investment; banks themselves had holdings at year-end 1982 that amounted to $10.9 billion. Table 7.4 shows the volume of acceptances outstanding between 1976 and 1982, and the different holders. Holdings of the Federal Reserve were essentially for the accounts of foreign central banks, while 83 percent of the total market was held by other financial and nonfinancial corporations.

Because of the rapid expansion of the bankers' acceptance market in the 1970s, the Federal Reserve has reduced its own market participation. In March 1977 the Federal Open Market Committee decided that the Federal Reserve would no longer buy acceptances in the open market, except under two specific circumstances: at the request of its foreign correspondents (such as foreign central banks) and under the repurchase agreements in order to increase bank reserves. This decision of the Federal Reserve did not extend to its accepting them as collateral from member banks borrowing from the discount window.

Even though the Federal Reserve no longer buys acceptances for its own account, it still specifies the conditions that make acceptances eligible for discount and purchase. The implication of this regulation is that bank proceeds from the sale of eligible acceptances are not subject to reserve requirements. By contrast, the proceeds from the

Table 7.4. Bankers' Acceptances Outstanding, 1976-82 (millions of dollars)

Holders	1976	1977	1978	1979	1980	1981	1982
Accepting banks	$10,442	$10,434	$ 8,579	$ 9,865	$10,564	$10,857	$10,910
Federal Reserve banks	1,366	1,316	665	2,086	2,567	1,442	2,429
Others	10,715	13,700	24,456	33,370	41,614	56,926	66,204
Total	$22,523	$25,450	$33,700	$45,321	$54,744	$69,226	$79,543

Note: Details may not add to totals due to rounding.
Source: *Federal Reserve Bulletin*, selected issues.

sale of ineligible acceptances are subject to reserve requirements, which raises the cost of acceptance financing.

During 1969 several large banks sought to obtain market funds to meet their customers' credit needs through the creation and sale of acceptances that were not eligible for discount at the Federal Reserve bank because they did not arise from foreign trade-related transactions or the storage or shipment of readily marketable staples. Reflecting the original purpose of these acceptances, they were often referred to as "working capital acceptances" or "finance bills."

During the credit crunch of 1969, and more significantly during that of 1973-74, the creation of ineligible acceptances reached such proportions as to warrant the intervention of the Federal Reserve. On June 18, 1973, the Board of Governors extended reserve requirements to funds raised by member banks through the sale of finance bills. It applied a basic 5 percent reserve requirement to all outstanding bills. An additional 3 percent requirement was imposed on all funds raised by banks through finance bills, large CDs, and commercial paper issued by affiliates, to the extent that such funds exceeded $10 million or a base-period amount, whichever was larger. At the time of these measures, $1.6 billion in finance bills was outstanding.

Commercial Paper

Commercial paper is an unsecured promissory note that provides creditworthy corporations with short-term funds without the intermediary services of commercial banks. It is sold to money-market investors as unsecured obligations bearing only the name of the issuer. For that reason companies successfully issuing commercial paper are nationally known, prime credit corporations that inspire investor confidence and have minimum risk of default. Denominations of commercial paper are usually in multiples of $100,000, with an average purchase of $2 million. The exact time of maturity is determined by individual requirements and investor preference; it usually averages 20-45 days and has a mandatory 270-day ceiling.

A company issuing commercial paper may choose to sell directly to money-market investors through its own sales force, or contract one of the ten or so investment banking or brokerage houses specializing in the marketing of commercial paper. Dealer-placed issuers usually have limited, very specific borrowing needs, whereas large companies with continuous, sizable funding requirements will place paper directly through their permanent, in-house sales staff. At year-end 1982 the volume of commercial paper outstanding amounted to about $167 billion, with bank-related commercial paper accounting for approximately 21 percent of the total market. Table 7.5. identifies the volume of bank-related paper outstanding between 1976 and 1982. Direct paper has enjoyed significant growth over the years as a greater number of large bank holding companies opt for direct placement. Although there is no secondary market for commercial paper, investors facing an urgent need for cash prior to the maturity date may redeem their notes from the issuer on a rate-adjusted basis or arrange a resale through the dealer originally contracted, who often maintains a limited secondary market for such resale transactions.

The Federal Reserve and the Commercial Paper Market

One of the provisions of the 1962 ruling by the Comptroller of the Currency with respect to bank debt capital provided that it was within the corporate powers of a national bank to borrow for general banking purposes by issuing commercial paper. Immediately after this

Table 7.5. Volume of Bank-Related Paper Outstanding, 1976-82 (billions of dollars)

Type	1976	1977	1978	1979	1980	1981	1982
Dealer-placed	$1.9	$2.1	$ 3.5	$ 2.8	$ 3.6	$ 6.0	$ 2.0
Directly placed	6.0	7.1	12.3	17.6	22.4	26.9	31.4
Total	$7.9	$9.2	$15.8	$20.4	$26.0	$32.9	$33.4

Source: Federal Reserve Bulletin, selected issues.

ruling was made, several large-city banks began to offer such notes to tap short-term funds. Bank interest in the issuance of these notes stemmed basically from the fact that they were looked upon as nondeposit obligations. As such, they were exempt from a number of supervisory regulations: they were not subject to interest-rate ceilings (Regulation Q); no reserves were required against them; and they were not part of the deposit base upon which FDIC assessments were calculated for deposit-insurance premium payments.

Commercial paper, however, was rendered uneconomical for banks in 1966. During that year Federal Reserve authorities ruled that these note issues constituted time deposits and therefore were subject to all the provisions applicable to such deposits.

Banks were then able to circumvent existing regulations and obtain the necessary funds from the open market through bank holding companies. In other words, a bank could tap market funds by having its holding company issue its own commercial paper. Typically the funds acquired through the issuance of commercial paper to the public by the holding company were used to acquire loans and investments from the subsidiary bank. So far as the banking organization as a whole (holding company plus bank subsidiary) was concerned, the result of commercial paper issuance was the same as in the case of direct bank-issued obligations. As far as the investors were concerned, the holding company's paper was of a quality at least equal to that of issues of promissory notes by the bank itself. The holding company's physical assets may be virtually nil, but it owns the stock of the commercial bank.

In other cases, banks formed independent companies, not holding companies, that sold paper in the market, then bought loans and investments from the commercial bank. The two techniques were analogous, although the legal aspects differed.

The Board of Governors finally concluded that restrictions applying to interest payments on deposits were being circumvented through these practices; effective September 17, 1970, commercial paper sales by bank holding companies or their nonbank affiliates were subject to marginal reserve requirements and Regulation Q, if the proceeds of the issue were being channeled to the bank's funds. As a result the sale of commercial paper by bank holding companies or their affiliates declined sharply. By mid-1970, however, holding companies had acquired a record number of nonbanking firms, and growth in bank-related commercial paper resumed. The primary activities of these nonbank firms include commercial finance, factoring, and leasing.

Recent Developments in the Commercial Paper Market

Besides bank holding companies, finance companies have been important participants in the commercial paper market. These companies rely heavily on the sale of their paper to finance consumer purchases and to extend credit to businesses in the form of receivables financing, inventory financing, and leasing financing. Since the mid-1960s nonfinancial corporations have also increased their reliance on the commercial paper market, in order to offset seasonal variations or meet short-term operating needs. The high credit rating of these corporations has enabled them to tap this market directly and enjoy significant savings compared with the cost of bank credit. This differential is understandable, since CDs—banks' primary source of financing loans—are subject to reserve requirements. In addition, since bank loans are negotiated on a personal basis and banks often extend concessions that are unobtainable in the open market, there is a significant spread between the prime rate and the commercial paper rate. Consequently, the number of businesses issuing commercial paper as a means of acquiring operating funds increased considerably in the 1970s. Although the Penn Central Railroad defaulted on $82 million worth of commercial paper in 1970, the market did not suffer any serious long-term difficulties. The default did, however, encourage lenders to analyze carefully the risks involved by considering the availability of backup lines of credit at commercial banks and the credit rating of the specific issue. The growth in the commercial paper market in the late 1970s and early 1980s indicates that investor confidence in this market has been restored.

Banks' response to their loss of market share in 1978-80 was a more aggressive lending policy. Many large banks sought to lure back large corporations by extending them loans of maturity comparable with the average maturity for commercial paper and pricing such loans below the prime rate. In addition, banks introduced more flexible borrowing arrangements to accommodate issuers of commercial paper. An example of such service is Morgan Guaranty Trust Company's "commercial paper adjustment facility," an open line of credit that is priced below the prime rate and allows commercial paper issuers flexibility in the timing of their paper sales. Both of the arrangements discussed above have been provided by banks in addition to the availability of backup lines of credit and banks' functioning as issuing and paying agents for the commercial paper issuers.

Still another service extended by banks is guaranteeing customers' paper issued in the money market. Smaller firms can now enter the commercial paper market by obtaining a letter of credit from a commercial bank, thereby substituting the credit of a strong institution for theirs and reducing issuance costs. This arrangement is often referred to as a "documented discount note," since the letter of credit is appended to the commercial paper. Although there is no actual shipment of goods, commercial paper supported by a letter of credit works in much the same way as bankers' acceptance financing. It is valid for a specific length of time, or can be made subject to termination upon the written request of either party. In order to have a commercial bank support the issue of a firm's paper, the firm must pay a fee to the bank. The issuers of commercial paper supported by a letter of credit are usually subsidiaries of larger corporations, including firms involved in auto leasing, power plant construction, and nuclear fuel supply. By mid-1980 documented discount notes reached a volume of approximately $2 billion, still comprising a relatively small segment of the market.

Two recent participants in the commercial paper market have been foreign banks and thrifts. Foreign banks have become participants in the U.S. commercial paper market in a dual capacity—funding their own activities and guaranteeing, through a letter of credit, their clients' commercial paper. In the former instance foreign banks were able to acquire operating funds at 0.25 percent or more below the London Interbank Offered Rate (LIBOR). To these banks the U.S. market has been a more economical source of dollar borrowing than the Eurodollar market. As guarantors of commercial paper, foreign banks have been extending their clients the same kind of support arrangement offered by their U.S. counterparts. As a result foreign firms have access to one of the cheapest dollar sources currently available. In either case the selling of paper within the commercial paper market serves to expand the foreign issuers' investor base and to facilitate their entry into, and acceptance by, the U.S. capital markets.

The first applications allowing savings and loan associations (S&Ls) to issue commercial paper and short-term notes secured by mortgage loans were approved by the Federal Home Loan Bank Board in January 1979. Commercial paper provides flexibility in liquidity management to S&Ls needing substantial sums to finance their secondary mortgage market operations or to offset seasonal increases in loan demand. Mutual savings banks (MSBs) entered the commercial paper market in March 1980, after removal of regulatory restrictions that prevented them from issuing commercial paper. Despite the removal of restrictions, however, these institutions are still not active in the commercial paper market because of their impaired earnings, which prevent them from obtaining the necessary high credit rating.

Borrowing of Eurodollars

The vast need for funds denominated in dollars, pounds, marks, yen, and other fairly stable currencies after World War II gave rise to the emergence of a worldwide network of international financial centers trading in the world's most convertible currencies. These centers make up the Eurocurrency market. A Eurocurrency is simply a deposit account in a bank denominated in a currency other than that of the host country. A deposit account denominated in dollars, marks, or yen in a London-based bank is a Eurocurrency. Since the dollar is the main international currency in use today, Eurodollars occupy a dominant position in the Eurocurrency market. Eurodollars are deposits denominated in U.S. dollars and held by banks located outside the United States, including foreign branches of U.S. banks. These deposits may be owned by corporations, governments, or individuals.

Development of the Eurodollar Market

The term "Eurodollars" originated during a time when the market was almost exclusively located in principal European financial centers.* Although the major portion of Eurodollar deposits are still held in Western Europe, they are also held in Japan, Hong Kong, the Cayman Islands, the Bahamas, Canada, Panama, Singapore, and Bahrain, countries that attract Eurodollar business by offering low taxes, few regulations, and other incentives.

The development of the Eurodollar market was made possible by the free convertibility of the major currencies at the end of 1958 and the emergence of the dollar as a medium of exchange for international transactions. But its phenomenal growth is primarily attributable to

---

*The beginnings of the Eurodollar market are usually traced to two Russian-owned banks in Western Europe, the Banque Commerciale pour l'Europe du Nord in Paris and the Moscow Narodny Bank in London. These banks actively solicited dollars and other foreign-currency deposits for use as working balances and to supply funds for investment. As the cold war heightened, however, fear of expropriation of their dollar deposits at U.S. banks led these institutions to disguise their dollar balances by placing them with Western European banks in exchange for dollar claims on these banks—hence the reference to these dollars as Eurodollars.

Mendelsohn indicates that it was actually the Chinese Communist government that initiated this practice in 1949, a year before the outbreak of the Korean war and the blocking of Peking's identifiable dollar balances in the United States under legislation forbidding trade with the enemy.[1]

the immense balance-of-payments deficits the United States has experienced since the late 1950s. The expansion of U.S. firms abroad and the establishment of multinational operations led to the transfer of dollar-deposit ownership to foreign companies, banks, and governments. The extensive borrowing in the United States by foreign-based firms, in the form of bank loans or issuance of securities, had similar effects. Since the U.S. financial markets were cheaper and more convenient sources of long-term funds than foreign financial markets, substantial sums were borrowed in the domestic markets by nonresidents. Then came the Vietnam war, which required large expenditures abroad. All these developments increased the U.S. balance-of-payments deficits and added significantly to the size of the Eurodollar market. In the 1970s a huge outflow of dollars resulted from domestic oil and natural gas shortages that forced the United States to import up to 40 percent of its petroleum needs. The OPEC countries accept payment for oil in dollars and use this currency as a standard for their oil pricing. A sizable portion of the OPEC financial assets are thus in the form of bank deposits in the Eurodollar market. The freezing of Iranian assets in the United States in the late 1970s led foreign investors—including OPEC countries—to prefer deposits in the Eurodollar market rather than the head offices of U.S. banks, which are subject to the jurisdiction of U.S. authorities.

Banks can avoid many U.S. banking regulations by accepting dollar deposits and making loans outside the United States. Banks outside the United States are not required to maintain reserves against their Eurodollar deposits. In addition, there is no FDIC insurance assessment associated with Eurodollar deposits; virtually no restrictions are in effect concerning maximum interest rates (Regulation Q) payable on Eurodollar deposits or charged on Eurodollar loans (usury laws); few restrictions govern the types of assets allowed in portfolio; and banks can effect Eurodollar transactions anywhere that tax rates are low, such as Nassau or the Cayman Islands.

Foreign monetary authorities do not impose limiting regulations on the Eurodollar market for two reasons: that a host country would lose income, tax revenue, and jobs; and that it would be virtually impossible to enforce regulations unless every country would agree not to host unregulated Eurodollar business—an unlikely consensus in a business with fierce competition.

Since the Eurodollar market thrives in areas having minimal or no controls (no disclosure requirements exist for international banks), estimates on the size of the Eurodollar market are derived from aggregate Eurocurrency data. Figures compiled by Morgan Guaranty Trust

Company in New York estimate the gross size of the Eurocurrency liabilities outstanding in September 1982 at $2 trillion. Netting out interbank transactions, the net size of this market was determined at that date as $940 billion. With Eurodollar liabilities reportedly accounting for 81 percent of all Eurocurrency liabilities, the gross size of the Eurodollar market was estimated at about $1.6 trillion and its net size at close to $761 billion.

Eurodollar Instruments

The bulk of the Eurodollar market consists of fixed-rate time deposits (TDs), with maturities ranging from one day to several years. However, most of these deposits mature in anywhere from one week to six months. An important difference between Eurodollar TDs and their domestic counterparts is that the former are to a large extent interbank liabilities. Eurodollar TDs are nonnegotiable and pay a fixed rate of return for the term of the deposit. Quoted rates for TDs are determined competitively.

Eurodollar certificates of deposit (CDs), introduced in 1966, are negotiable receipts for dollars deposited in a bank located outside the United States. Eurodollar CDs can be sold prior to their maturity through an active secondary market. Banks issue Eurodollar CDs in order to tap the market for funds. As a result these CDs are known as Tap CDs; their denominations usually range from $250,000 to $5 million. Tranche CDs (from the French *tranche*) are sizable Eurodollar CD issues—in amounts of $10 million to $30 million—marketed in several smaller portions to appeal to investors with a need for smaller instruments. Tranche CDs are usually offered in $10,000 certificates, each bearing the same interest rate, issue date, interest payment dates, and maturity.

In order to minimize interest-rate risks for both the borrower and the lender, Eurodollar floating-rate CDs (FRCDs) and Eurodollar floating-rate notes (FRNs) have recently come into use. FRCDs serve as an alternative to short-term money-market instruments; FRNs, to straight fixed-interest bonds. Both shift the risk from the principal value of the issue to its coupon. They are negotiable bearer paper, with the interest rate reset at a marginal spread above the LIBOR approximately every three to six months. FRCDs are normally issued in maturities ranging from one and a half to five years, whereas FRNs can mature in anywhere from four to twenty years, but averaging five to seven years.

American banks have often adjusted their domestic reserves by borrowing from Eurodollar deposits. Thus, a large U.S. bank foreseeing a need for additional funds may contact its foreign correspondents holding dollar deposits in order to arrange a Eurodollar loan. Alternatively, it may go through brokers and dealers or contact another U.S. bank with branches abroad. If the borrowing bank operates a foreign branch that accepts dollar deposits, the head office may acquire these funds from its branch.

Role of Eurodollars in Domestic Banking Activity

During periods of rising interest rates in the United States, Eurodollar borrowing increases significantly. Between January and December 1966, liabilities of U.S. banks to foreign branches (a measure often used to indicate Eurodollar borrowings) rose sharply, from $1.7 billion to $4.0 billion. Banks with foreign branches were able to offset approximately 80 percent of their CD losses with borrowings from these branches. In 1969, when demand for credit far outdistanced the ability of banks to supply it, borrowings by U.S. banks from their foreign branches rose throughout the year from $6 billion to nearly $15 billion. With Eurodollar borrowings more than doubled, as banks sought to profit from the record-high domestic interest rates, the Board of Governors became convinced that banks were using this market to circumvent monetary restraints. Thus, effective September 4, 1969, the Federal Reserve imposed a 10 percent reserve requirement against any additional borrowings from overseas branches, in an effort to raise the cost and curtail the additional use of these funds. In the years that followed, this requirement was adjusted by the Federal Reserve Board, as warranted by prevailing conditions. The imposition of reserve requirements on such borrowings did not stop banks from relying on them. In fact, as the 1970s drew to a close, the Eurodollar borrowings of U.S. banks reached a record high level, totaling nearly $35 billion in 1979.

Past experience indicates that borrowings fluctuate significantly and are extremely sensitive to changing interest rates. In 1980, for example, when U.S. money-market rates plummeted from all-time highs and domestic reserves became much less costly to acquire, U.S. banks almost immediately repaid their Eurodollar borrowings. U.S. bank net Eurodollar borrowings from foreign-related institutions, which stood at $28 billion in December 1979, had dwindled to about $8 billion by late 1980. During 1981 and 1982 the trend was reversed, with U.S. banks making net advances to foreign-related institutions in the magnitude of $48.3 billion at year-end 1982 (see Table 7.6). Clearly, foreign markets offered greater opportunities for the placement of funds than the domestic market, which was experiencing a slackening in economic activity.

Table 7.6. Eurodollar Borrowings by Banks in the United States, 1976-82 (billions of dollars)

Item	1976	1977	1978	1979	1980	1981	1982
Net balances due to foreign-related institutions	$ 3.7	−$ 1.3	$ 6.8	$28.1	$ 8.2	−$18.6	−$48.3
Domestically chartered banks' net positions with (their) own foreign branches	−6.0	−12.5	−10.2	6.4	−14.7	−22.5	−39.5
Gross due from balances	12.8	21.1	24.9	22.9	37.5	54.9	72.2
Gross due to balances	6.8	8.6	14.7	29.3	22.8	32.4	32.7

Source: *Federal Reserve Bulletin*, selected issues.

Borrowing from the Federal Reserve's Discount Window

Commercial banks and other depository institutions have an extra source of borrowing in their regional Federal Reserve bank. This source of funds has been available to commercial banks, particularly member banks, since the inception of the Federal Reserve System. Federal Reserve loans take the form of discounts (often called rediscounts) and advances. If the borrowing institution resorts to a rediscounting transaction, it offers for discount at the Federal Reserve bank eligible paper: notes, drafts, and bills of exchange arising out of commercial transactions. In effect, the borrowing institution sells its customers' paper to the Federal Reserve bank, and by endorsing them becomes liable to the Federal Reserve bank if the original maker defaults at the maturity date of the instrument. But the institution may elect to obtain a direct advance from the Federal Reserve bank on its own promissory note, pledging as collateral some acceptable asset, such as U.S. government securities. Both transactions have the effect of increasing the commercial bank's reserve balances at the Federal Reserve bank.

Most borrowing from the Federal Reserve banks takes the form of advances. Securing funds by means of an advance is generally believed to be a simpler and more flexible tool than discounting in correcting imbalances in the reserve position. By keeping government securities in the vaults of the district Federal Reserve bank, and having signed in advance loan authorization agreements ("continuing lending agreements") with its discount department, it takes only a telephone call for a bank to borrow. In contrast, by discounting customer paper the bank has to provide financial statements and other information routinely required by the Federal Reserve bank about the individuals or companies liable for paying the discounted instrument on maturity. More important, banks frequently want to borrow for only a limited number of days, and eligible paper of the right amount and maturity may not be readily available.

Types of Credit

Regardless of the method of borrowing, Federal Reserve credit is generally granted as a privilege rather than a right. In other words, extension of credit by the Federal Reserve is never assured. Federal Reserve banks observe certain guiding principles in the administration of credit. Regulation A provides for Federal Reserve lending to eligible depository institutions under two programs: the adjustment credit and the extended credit. Each of these is described below.

Adjustment Credit. The primary form of Federal Reserve lending is adjustment credit. It is advanced to banks for brief periods to help them meet their short-term needs when funds are not readily available from other sources. Enactment of the DIDMCA in 1980 directed the Federal Reserve to open its discount window to nonmember banks and thrift institutions. As a result these institutions may now apply for adjustment credit when experiencing great short-run volatility in their deposit and reserve positions. Thrift institutions, however, should depend primarily on their usual sources (the Federal Home Loan Bank Board, the National Credit Union Administration's Central Liquidity Facility, and corporate central credit unions) before applying to the discount window for funds. Prior to extending credit, the Federal Reserve banks will consult with the borrowing institution's supervising agency to determine whether alternative sources of funds are in fact unavailable.

At the time of each request, the borrowing institution must provide information regarding liquidity needs and proposed use of funds obtained. The discount officers will monitor an institution's borrowing record by noting fluctuations in its key weekly financial statement items and federal funds transactions, as well as reviewing its past and current use of the discount window, often maintaining periodic personal and telephone contact with bank officials.

The largest institutions are expected to borrow only to the next business day, since they have access to money-market funds and their reserve positions change daily. Other large institutions, which may have somewhat more limited market access, should not borrow past the current reserve period. Medium-size and smaller institutions may extend advances beyond the current reserve period, however, and slightly longer maturities are permitted for small institutions. The borrowing institution should demonstrate in its overall performance its ability to operate within the limits of its own resources, and continuous borrowing may indicate that the borrowing bank has permanent reserve problems that require basic portfolio adjustments. Borrowing to support increases in loan or investment portfolios, to profit from interest-rate differentials, or when other short-term, interest-sensitive funds are available, is deemed inappropriate by the Federal Reserve.

Extended Credit. Extended credit is provided through three programs that meet the longer-term needs of depository institutions. Like adjustment credit, extended credit has been accessible to nonmember banks and thrifts since 1980. Here, too, thrifts' access to the discount window is limited to instances when credit is not available through their supervisory agencies. The different types of extended credit are outlined below.

Before 1970 many small banks were unable to provide full service to customers in their local communities because of inadequate access to national money-market funds. This lack of funds led small institutions to accumulate excess liquid asset positions throughout the year that would allow them to meet peak seasonal demands. In the early 1970s the Federal Reserve seasonal credit program was initiated, enabling these smaller banks to maintain fewer liquid assets during regular periods, thus releasing additional funds for local lending. Small institutions showing a recurrence of intrayearly need are extended advances for up to nine months. A seasonal line must be established with their Federal Reserve bank in order for them to become eligible for such credit.

Institutions experiencing difficulties arising from exceptional circumstances involving only that institution may be allotted what is called extended credit in exceptional circumstances. In 1974 Franklin National Bank experienced massive deposit withdrawals and deteriorating earnings, which prompted the Federal Reserve, in its capacity as a lender of last resort, to advance funds to this bank. These funds peaked at $1.75 billion before Franklin's assets and deposits were finally taken over by the European American Bank. More recently, First Pennsylvania Bank underwent significant liquidity problems that necessitated large discount window borrowings. Regulation A authorizes emergency credit to nondepository institutions when other sources are not available and the failure to obtain such credit would have adverse effects on the economy. However, such credit will ordinarily be extended at interest rates above those applicable to depository institutions.

Other Extended Credit. This form of extended credit was established as a result of the DIDMCA and the ensuing revision, in September 1980, of Regulation A to implement the provisions of the act. Other extended credit can now be arranged in cases where more general liquidity problems are affecting a diverse range of depository institutions. In other words, depository institutions having portfolios composed primarily of longer-term assets and experiencing difficulties adjusting to changing money-market conditions—particularly during periods of deposit disintermediation—may borrow under this provision.

Borrowing Levels

Member bank borrowings from the Federal Reserve System have fluctuated over the years. Table 7.7 shows the aggregate amounts borrowed by banks and other depository institutions from the discount window, from 1970 to 1982. Recessionary years (such as 1971 and 1975-76) are characterized by a low volume of borrowings; periods of economic expansion (such as 1972-73 and 1978-80), by a high volume of borrowings. The extent of such borrowings during boom periods is significantly affected by the magnitude of the differential between the federal funds rate and the discount rate (the rate charged by the Federal Reserve on loans to banks). Rapidly rising money-market rates and infrequent changes in the discount rate can significantly increase the (federal funds-discount rate) differential and, consequently, demands on the discount window. In other words, in periods of economic expansion, lag of the discount rate behind money-market rates

Table 7.7. Volume of Borrowings from Federal Reserve Banks, 1970-82 (monthly averages of daily figures)

Year	Amount (millions of dollars)	Year	Amount (millions of dollars)
1970	$ 335	1976	$ 25
1971	39	1977	265
1972	1,981	1978	1,174
1973	1,258	1979	1,454
1974	299	1980	1,617
1975	211	1981	642
		1982	697

Source: Federal Reserve Bulletin, selected issues.

renders the cost of borrowing at the discount window significantly more economical. Such was the case in 1979, when increases in the discount rate lagged behind open market rates, resulting in a general increase in banks' borrowing levels. In October 1979 bank borrowings grew quite rapidly, reaching a level of $3 billion.

In recent years the Federal Reserve has sought to refine its administration of the discount window. Instead of the infrequent and sharp changes in the discount rate of the past, current changes in the discount rate have been more frequent and of a relatively smaller magnitude. This practice, though reducing the announcement effect that a change in the discount rate traditionally had for financial markets, enables better control of the spread between money-market rates and the discount rate, and affects banks' incentive to borrow accordingly.

The spread between the discount rate and the cost of alternative reserve-adjustment media is not the sole determinant of the volume of commercial bank borrowing from the Federal Reserve. Traditional dislike for operating on borrowed funds is also an important element. As might be expected, sensitivity to indebtedness varies from bank to bank. Certain banks may consider borrowing from the Federal Reserve as a last resort, while for others it may be a matter of managerial policy to avoid such borrowing altogether. The latter attitude holds especially true among small banks, which are very sensitive about listing borrowings in their published statements.

The Discount Rate

As indicated above, the rate of interest that depository institutions are charged for borrowing reserves from the discount window is known as the discount rate. In principle, discount rates are set by each individual Federal Reserve bank, subject to the approval of the Board of Governors of the Federal Reserve System. When the Federal Reserve System was established, it was felt that discount rates should be set in the light of prevailing conditions in each Federal Reserve district. As a result, during the 1920s there was significant variation from one district to another in prevailing discount rates. Over the years, however, the emergence of a national money market has contributed to uniform discount rates.

A closer look at the discount rate reveals that in reality there is not one single rate but a variety of rates, depending upon the type of credit involved. The base rate (or discount rate proper) is the lowest one and applies to advances for short-term liquidity adjustment or seasonal credit needs, secured by eligible commercial paper, bankers' acceptances, or U.S. government securities. On loans to institutions in exceptional circumstances and on other extended credit, the base rate is adjusted upward if the maturity of the loan is in excess of 60 days.

In September 1980 a revision of Regulation A authorized the Federal Reserve to add, at its discretion, a surcharge on the discount rate charged to borrowing institutions. This authorization covered both adjustment and extended credit. On the basis of this authorization, in March 1980 the Federal Reserve briefly imposed—as part of its credit restraint program—a 3 percent surcharge on any adjustment credit to large depository institutions (with deposits in excess of $500 million). This penalty rate applied when these institutions attempted to borrow from the discount window in two or more successive weeks or in more than four weeks in a calendar quarter. Its purpose was to bring the cost of Federal Reserve credit closer to open-market rates, and thus discourage frequent use of the discount window by the nation's largest depository institutions. The surcharge proved quite effective and was eliminated in May of the same year. Thereafter it was reinstated as dictated by circumstances.

The discount rate has been an important tool of monetary policy. In fact, the founders of the Federal Reserve System envisaged the discount policy as the main monetary policy tool. For many decades the discount mechanism has been used in a manner consistent with the objectives of the monetary policy—that is, to influence economic conditions in a manner conducive to economic growth, price stability, and a high level of employment. Thus, when the Federal Reserve pursued a policy of tightening credit, the discount rate was raised to discourage bank borrowing and curb inflationary pressures; when monetary authorities pursued a policy of easing credit, the discount rate was lowered. Discount rate changes were used by the Federal Reserve to signal its intentions in monetary policy. Indeed, announcing discount rate changes signaled to the financial markets the intention of the Federal Reserve to tighten or ease money and credit (announcement effect). Increasingly in recent years, however, use of the discount rates to signal policy changes has become incompatible with the need for more effective coordination of those rates with open-market operations.

To coordinate these two instruments effectively, the Federal Reserve must make frequent, small adjustments in the discount rate to keep it in line with money-market rates if banks' incentive to borrow is to be controlled. Although discount rate adjustments by the Federal Reserve are discretionary, the fact remains that this rate has been trailing, rather than leading, other rates in the money markets. These and other related issues have led academicians and financial experts to propose changes in the administration of the discount window. Some of these proposals (for instance, those of the Nobel Prize winner Milton Friedman) take the extreme position of recommending the abolition of the discount mechanism. Banks would still have access to money markets to tap reserve adjustment funds or even could maintain higher-than-necessary excess reserves. As for emergency credit, the existence of the FDIC—according to Friedman—reduces the need for the Fed to function as a lender of last resort for the banking system in the event of runs on banks.

Despite the various proposals advanced since the 1960s, no consensus has been reached with respect to the role of the discount mechanism. The debate continues.

MONEY-MARKET STRATEGY

The 1970s saw a growing dependence of banks upon money markets to meet their seasonal and other needs for funds. While before this period it was only the larger U.S. banks that generally relied upon liability management strategies, recent years have seen expanded use of these strategies as medium-size banks have increased their reliance on money markets. Four basic concerns determine policy in managing money-market liabilities: projected interest rate, considered in conjunction with maturity dates; liquidity needs; diversification of the liability portfolio; comparative interest rates of different forms of liabilities.

The overriding goal in liability management is to obtain funds at the least interest cost, given maturity requirements. To do this, the bank must consider not only the current level of interest rates but also project their likely changes in the period ahead. For instance, although on a given day federal funds may cost less than a three-month CD, the decision on which source to tap must take into account whether the federal funds are likely to become more costly in the near future and thus, over the three-month period, cost more than the CD. Thus, in managing money-market liabilities, maturity dates and the cost certainty provided by the CD must be balanced against the risk of escalating costs for federal funds.

Liquidity constraints also come into play in managing liabilities. Short-term liabilities must be balanced against short-term assets in order to assure liquidity as maturity dates arrive. In practice, banks try to match terms and amounts of funds raised in the money market to the terms and amounts of loans made. At times, however, there may be a deliberate mismatching in maturities—that is, purchasing short-term funds for longer-term loans, in hopes of rolling them over under more advantageous terms.

The bank distributes its liabilities across several sources in order to avoid excessive reliance on any single source of purchased funds. Depending too heavily on one source of funds increases bank vulnerability to changing conditions in that segment of the market. In addition, banks wish to stay active in a variety of markets in order to keep trading channels open for each type of funds. Finally, banks maintain diversification within each type of funds so as not to become overly dependent on any single supplier. For instance, some CDs may be sold through brokers while others are issued directly to a variety of corporate buyers.

The fourth consideration, lowest comparative cost of funds, dominates the actual practice of purchasing funds. As will be seen below, trading activity occurs briskly throughout the banking day, in response to ever-fluctuating rates for different types of funds. The traders seek those funds available at least cost. Only when one of the other factors, such as market diversification, is out of kilter are the traders instructed to diverge from the practice of following lowest interest cost in making their purchases.

Thus, the day-to-day purchase of funds is not conducted as a careful orchestration of all four of these considerations, but is based on the feel of the market at any given time. The analogy of strategy versus tactics is useful for understanding the implementation of money-market funds policy. Strategy is the overall game plan intended to achieve a goal, while tactics are the small-scale or daily decisions that constitute the real action in the field. Maturity needs, interest forecasts, and diversification are strategic concerns, and are gauged periodically—for example, once a month or once a quarter. Liquidity and current interest rates, on the other hand, are concerns of a more tactical nature. Liquidity checks are made on a weekly basis, so that quick adjustments can be made. On a daily basis, prevailing interest rates govern trading activity.

On a typical business day the money-market team—consisting of specialists in federal funds, CDs, Eurodollars, RPs, and government securities trading—exchanges information on market rates at the day's opening. As the day progresses, the members stay in constant touch, trading information and identifying the most advantageous rates and terms for meeting their daily needs for funds. For example, the rate for a 90-day domestic CD would be compared with those for a Eurodollar CD and for term federal funds of corresponding maturity. Or, for overnight money, the rate of federal funds would be compared with that of one-day RPs.

Despite the growing importance of liability management for liquidity, bank reliance on this strategy should not be absolute. Reliance upon purchased funds has to be carefully controlled and managed because of its effects upon the total cost of funds and the rates of return that can be earned from the employment of these funds. These factors emphasize the close relationship between asset and liability management in determining bank profitability.

Furthermore, in periods of inflation, Federal Reserve System concern over the growth of the aggregate amount of bank credit may lead to regulatory controls limiting banks' access to these sources of funds. In other words, the ability of banks to purchase interest-sensitive funds is conditional upon support of regulators. Past experience indicates that when they are faced with unusual financial and economic circumstances, regulators' attitudes and objectives can change quickly.

INTEREST RATES IN THE MONEY MARKET

Banks borrow huge amounts of money every day from the money market that they, in turn, use to accommodate other borrowers in that market. Through their extensive borrowing and lending activities, banks have come to dominate the money market. The rates at which they purchase funds, although they vary from time to time and from source to source, are fundamentally determined by the prevailing yield of U.S. Treasury bills. Because these are the lowest-risk instruments in the market, they carry the lowest yield. Table 7.8, which shows interest rates for different instruments on February 25, 1983, illustrates the relationship between Treasury bill yields and those of other money-market instruments.

As the table indicates, the three-month yields of the various money-market instruments were paying premium rates over the Treasury bill. One factor responsible for this spread is the perceived risk of these instruments. In other words, since Treasury bills are default-free, spreads offered by the other instruments are higher to compensate money-market investors for the higher element of risk. Another factor determining the size of the spreads is demand and supply forces in the market place. Since the U.S. economy was going through a process of slow recovery at this time, it is not surprising that spreads over the Treasury bill rate were generally of small magnitude. In the case of Eurodollar deposits, the higher yield also reflected the lower cost of these funds due to the absence of reserve requirements and deposit insurance fees.

Table 7.8 includes the prime rate for business loans and the commercial paper rate. Large corporations, because of their prime credit

Table 7.8. Money Market Rates, February 25, 1983

Instrument	Yield Rate (percent per annum)	Spreads over U.S. Treasury Bills Rate (basis points)
Federal funds rate	8.47	+56
Bankers' acceptance, 3-month	8.16	+25
Certificate of deposit (large), 3-month[a]	8.34	+43
Eurodollar deposits, 3-month	9.01	+110
U.S. Treasury bills, 3-month[b]	7.91	–
Commercial paper, 3-month	8.16	+25
Prime rate on business loans[c]	10.98	+307
Federal Reserve discount rate	8.50	+59

[a] Secondary market.
[b] Average of closing bid rates in the secondary market.
[c] Average for February 1983.
Source: *Federal Reserve Bulletin*, February and March 1983.

standing, can go directly into the market and issue their own commercial paper at a cost lower than the prime rate charged by commercial banks. The cost savings to corporations is greater than the differential between the prime rate and the commercial paper rate, since banks ordinarily require corporate customers to maintain large minimum balances (compensating balances) amounting to a specified percentage of the loan amount (15 to 20 percent).

The last item shown in Table 7.8 is the discount rate, which reflects at any moment in time the Federal Reserve System's assessment of credit conditions in the market and the state of the economy. The level of this rate can either attract bank borrowing to the Federal Reserve or drive it into the open market.

An overview of the money market is shown in Figure 7.1, which displays interest-rate fluctuations for key instruments since 1930. The tightness in the credit markets, and its effect on interest rates during 1969, 1973-74 and 1979-80, are readily identified. Interest rates, reflecting the prevailing money-market conditions, rose substantially during these years, surpassing all previous levels. A closer look at this figure shows the relatively lower level of the discount rate during these years. Of course, the discount rate is not a natural market rate, but an administered rate altered by Federal Reserve authorities to conform to prevailing money market rates. The other rates illustrated are market-determined and, as can be seen, have been highly volatile. This is especially true for the federal funds rate. As stated earlier, federal

Figure 7.1. Short-Term Interest Rates, Money Market: 1929-82 (discount rate, effective date of change; all others, quarterly averages)

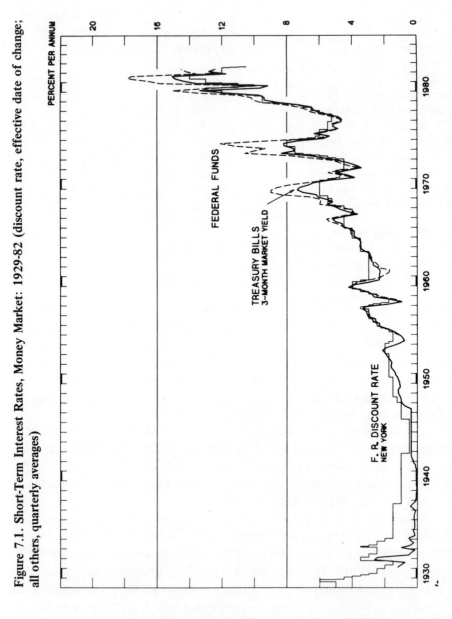

Source: Board of Governors of the Federal Reserve System, *Historical Chartbook* (Washington, D.C.: Federal Reserve, 1982), p. 98.

funds transactions are affected by the reserve position of individual banks. Since most banks wait to adjust their reserve positions with the Federal Reserve bank until the reserve settlement period is drawing to a close, the federal funds rate often exhibits important volatility on the last day of this period. In other words, banks that did not adjust their reserve positions earlier in the period are actively in the market so as to avoid any deficiency in their reserves with the Federal Reserve bank (and, consequently, the penalties involved).

The rate of U.S. Treasury bills is included in the figure because Treasury bills are the dominant money-market instrument. At the end of 1982, $312 billion in Treasury bills were outstanding, with maturities stretching up to one year. Since they constitute short-term debt obligations of the U.S. government, they are a popular money-market instrument among U.S. government agencies, Federal Reserve banks, and such private investors as thrift institutions, insurance companies, commercial banks, and state and local governments. Commercial banks rank at the top of the private investors' list because of the high degree of liquidity that the Treasury bill possesses.

Although all three instruments illustrated in Figure 7.1 are key magnitudes, the best single indicator of conditions in the money market is frequently regarded to be the going rate on federal funds. Since federal funds represent monies available for immediate payment in the money market, the federal funds rate identifies the cost of the principal means of payment in this market.

NOTE

M. S. Mendelsohn, *Money on the Move* (New York: McGraw-Hill, 1980), pp. 18-19.

SUGGESTED REFERENCES

Beebe, Jack. "A Perspective of Liability Management and Bank Risk." *Economic Review*, Federal Reserve Bank of San Francisco, Winter 1977, pp. 12-25.

Bowsher, Norman H. "Repurchase Agreements." *Review*, Federal Reserve Bank of St. Louis, September 1979, pp. 17-22.

Cook, Timothy Q., and Bruce J. Summers, eds. *Instruments of the Money Market*. Richmond, Va.: Federal Reserve Bank of Richmond, 1981.

Darst, D. M. *Handbook of the Bond and Money Markets*. New York: McGraw-Hill, 1981.

Dufey, Gunter, and Ian H. Giddy. *The International Money Market*. Englewood Cliffs, N.J.: Prentice-Hall, 1978.

Gabel, Philip M. "Nondeposit Liability Management . . . . in a Pressure-Laden Financial Environment." *Savings Bank Journal*, February 1980, pp. 24-33.

Hurley, Evelyn M. "The Commercial Paper Market." *Federal Reserve Bulletin*, June 1977, pp. 525-36.

Knight, Robert E. "An Alternative Approach to Liquidity: Part I." *Monthly Review*, Federal Reserve Bank of Kansas City, December 1969, pp. 11-21.

_____. "An Alternative Approach to Liquidity: Part II." *Monthly Review*, Federal Reserve Bank of Kansas City, February 1970, pp. 11-22.

_____. "An Alternative Approach to Liquidity: Part III." *Monthly Review*, Federal Reserve Bank of Kansas City, April 1970, pp. 3-12.

_____. "An Alternative Approach to Liquidity: Part IV." *Monthly Review*, Federal Reserve Bank of Kansas City, May 1970, pp. 10-18.

Lucas, Charles M. "Federal Funds and Repurchase Agreements." *Quarterly Review*, Federal Reserve Bank of New York, Summer 1977, pp. 33-48.

Morgan Guaranty Trust Company of New York. *World Financial Markets*. New York: Morgan Guaranty, 1983.

Rose, Peter S. *Money and Capital Markets: The Financial System in the Economy*. Plano, Tex.: Business Publications, 1983.

Silber, William L. *Commercial Bank Liability Management*. Study prepared for the trustees of the Banking Research Fund, Association of Reserve City Bankers. Chicago: Association of Reserve City Bankers, 1977.

Stigum, Marcia. *The Money Market: Myth, Reality, and Practice*. Homewood, Ill.: Dow Jones-Irwin, 1978.

PART III

8
LIQUIDITY

The nature of a bank's liabilities, together with the thin layer of equity on which it operates, renders the employment of bank funds a factor of primary significance. Available resources must be used in a manner that will permit the bank to attain a number of objectives. This fact leads naturally to a discussion of the basic objectives of bank portfolio management and, hence, the factors that affect the general character and composition of commercial bank assets.

First, a bank's portfolio policies should be designed to enable the bank to meet liquidity requirements without exposing itself either to embarrassment or to unusual pressure—in other words, to maintain the degree of liquidity necessary to meet deposit withdrawals and increased requests for loans.

Another consideration that must govern portfolio policies is that the greatest part of a bank's liabilities is subject to withdrawal either on demand or on very short notice. Bank portfolio policies must therefore be guided by prudence; that is, lending and investing are meaningful only when undertaken with almost complete assurance that the principal will be returned. Another way of stating this objective is that the bank has specific liabilities, and the bulk of its assets must take the form of specific claims that are reasonably protected against risk. Clearly, asset quality, and hence solvency, considerations are in the foreground of this objective.

In addition to the maintenance of liquidity and solvency, bank policies should be geared toward achieving sufficient income on bank portfolio so that operating costs can be met and the bank can continue profitably as a going concern.

To attain these objectives, bankers must achieve a certain pattern and distribution of bank assets. In other words, the bank's asset structure must strike a delicate balance among liquidity, solvency, and income. Here lies the difficult task of asset management. If one considers income to be complementary to quality, attaining these ends means solving the basic conflict between liquidity and income. This conflict arises from the inverse relationship of liquidity to income. The nearer an asset is to cash, the more remote is the possibility of potential loss to the bank. Such a highly liquid asset, however, would yield a relatively lower income over time than a less liquid, and riskier, asset. In other words, the rate of return on assets tends to vary inversely with their degree of liquidity. This trade-off between liquidity and profitability constitutes the core of asset management. "The art of commercial banking," wrote Roland I. Robinson, "is solving this basically conflicting requirement: that of being safe and yet profitable."[1]

As might be expected, solving this conflict rests entirely upon each bank's management. It is a matter of individual judgment based upon experience and knowledge. Hence, no two banks would solve this conflict in the same way, and the composition of their portfolios would vary accordingly. This chapter examines how banks attempt to resolve the liquidity-profitability conflict and concentrates on the liquidity issue: identifying, estimating, and providing for bank liquidity needs.

ALTERNATIVE APPROACHES TO THE LIQUIDITY-PROFITABILITY DILEMMA

Within the constraints established by law and regulation, three different approaches are open to banks in allocating funds among various classes of assets: pool of funds, asset allocation, and management science. They enjoy varying degrees of acceptability and are used singly or in combination in bank asset management. Each of these strategies is discussed below.

Pool-of-Funds Approach

This approach derives its name from the fact that it views the right-hand side of a bank's balance sheet as a pool of funds that a bank has available to use. Considering this pool as given, it emphasizes the allocation of funds among various classes of assets on the basis of certain priorities. It suggests that bank management must be guided by some sort of order of priorities in the use of bank funds. That is, if a bank is to discharge its community obligations in a satisfactory manner and continue as a going concern, available funds must be allocated on the basis of anticipated requirements of differing degrees of urgency. Such allocation is implicit in any attempt to provide a rational solution to the fundamental banking problem. The "schedule of priorities" indicates that bank funds are used in four basic ways: to maintain primary reserves, to provide secondary reserves, to meet customer credit demands, and to make purchases of investment securities for income.

Of top priority in a bank's employment of its funds, under the pool-of-funds approach, is the maintenance of adequate primary reserves. The term is an economic rather than an accounting concept, coined to designate a bank's cash assets. Hence it is not found in a bank's statement of condition, but it is a key part of the functional balance sheet that stresses the uses of the bank's resources.

The assets generally designated as primary reserves are the non-earning assets of commercial banks that are in the form of cash or are convertible into it on demand. Nothing else can provide the immediate liquidity of cash holdings, which are immediately available with no risk of loss whatsoever. But cash holdings generate no income. Primary reserves constitute a bank's source of pledgeable assets. They enable commercial banks to fulfill the requirement of the law that they maintain cash reserves against their deposits. Another function of primary reserves is to serve as the first line of defense in meeting the withdrawals of depositors. Depositors can draw against their deposit accounts either by demanding hand-to-hand money or by writing checks payable to others. If they demand hand-to-hand money, the bank must pay out of its cash holdings carried in the vault. If they write checks, the bank must use its balances with other banking institutions (the Federal Reserve bank and correspondent banks) to meet them as they come in for payment through clearing channels (provided that the clearing balance is "adverse"—that is, that the amount of incoming checks on any day exceeds the amount of checks upon which the bank obtains payment from other banks on that day). These different functions of primary reserves led to the distinction between legal reserves (the cash reserves that the law requires a bank to maintain with the Federal Reserve bank) and working reserves, which are held in the form of vault currency, cash in process of collection, and deposits at other banks, including deposits at the Federal Reserve bank over and above the amount required by law (excess reserves).

The second priority in the allocation process is to provide for secondary reserves. The origin of this term is traced back to the late 1920s. It was then that, for the first time, bankers and prominent students of banking began to realize the significance of the subject and to discuss it. Like the primary reserves, secondary reserves represent an economic rather than an accounting concept, and hence they do not appear in commercial bank balance sheets as a separate category. However, this item constitutes a key part of a bank's functional balance sheet that stresses the uses of the bank's resources. Secondary reserves, or protective investments, perform precisely the role suggested by their name. They are assets that yield some income to the bank but, more important, can be converted from earning assets into cash with little or no delay or loss of principal. Secondary reserves are thus the principal source of bank liquidity. They constitute a reservoir of near-cash assets that is drawn upon to replenish the primary reserves when they become depleted.

The first two priorities serve to ensure the bank's ability to continue in business by meeting the claims presented to it for payment. After providing for these the bank is able to consider its third priority item in the funds allocation process, customers' credit needs. A basic function of the commercial bank is making funds available to the local community. Traditionally banks have been primarily direct lenders to their customers. Business firms have demanded credit to finance their productive and distributive processes; consumers, to finance the acquisition of goods and services for which they will pay at a later date. Through extending credit to customers whose operations and needs are intimately known and understood, commercial banks tend to have a thorough knowledge of the local market. This advantage of banks over other financial institutions does not, however, extend to transactions in the open market for investments. In this market financial institutions (that is, insurance companies and trust funds) play a more important role because of the more stable nature of their liabilities and the large investment research staffs they maintain.

The last priority in the allocation process of bank funds is the purchase of investment securities for income. If the first three use priorities have not exhausted bank funds, then, to maximize income, the otherwise idle funds are used in the open market for the purchase of long-term securities. The investment portfolio, under the pool-of-funds approach, is thus viewed as residual in character, although this should not be taken to imply any inferiority in the quality of assets of which it is composed. As a matter of fact, the quality of these assets is thought of as being as important for the bank as that of the loan portfolio assets.

The pool-of-funds approach does not include in these priorities investment in fixed assets such as land and buildings. These are treated separately.

The pool-of-funds model for asset management has both advantages and disadvantages. The advantages include its simplicity, which makes it easy to learn, and its low administrative costs, which can increase profitability. The drawbacks are more numerous, although they are neither serious enough nor numerous enough to rule out use of this approach. The pool-of-funds approach to asset management is essentially a rigid model that concentrates on protection of assets. It fails to take account of future conditions or of the interaction among balance-sheet items. Its conservative stance may result in loss of potential income and, thus, diminished profitability.

Asset Allocation

One of the criticisms advanced against the pool-of-funds approach is that by failing to distinguish among the differing liquidity requirements of the various funds that are pooled, it overestimates overall liquidity needs at the expense of profitability. During the 1950s and 1960s prosperity and economic growth led to increases in time and savings deposits compared with demand deposits. Since the former require less liquidity than the latter, this development in essence reduced banks' aggregate liquidity requirements; however, the pool-of-funds method failed to account for this change and thus sacrificed potential profits by calling for higher-than-necessary liquidity reserves. To correct this situation, the asset-allocation or conversion-of-funds approach was developed. This method, recognizing the differing liquidity requirements of the various sources of funds, divides these sources into categories according to their legal reserve requirements and velocity, or turnover, rate. Then it provides guidelines for the percentage of each source of funds to be allocated among the different classes of assets. For example, for demand deposits—which have a high legal reserve requirement and a high velocity rate—a larger share of each dollar is allocated to primary and secondary reserves and a smaller share to loans, mainly short-term commercial loans. Savings and time deposits, on the other hand, are subject to lower legal reserve requirements and exhibit a lower degree of volatility; therefore, greater proportions of these funds can be devoted to loans and investments. Capital funds require the least liquidity, and thus can be used to finance fixed assets (such as land and buildings), with any excess funds allocated to long-term loans and less liquid securities investments.

This method's advantages lie in its relative simplicity and ease of mastery, which make it relatively inexpensive to implement, and in its ability to increase profits by eliminating excess liquidity provisions against the different forms of bank funds. However, it has limitations.

Although velocity is a basic criterion in distinguishing among deposit categories, there may not be a strong relationship between the velocity of a group of accounts and the variability of the total deposits in that category. For example, while a bank's demand deposits may, in the aggregate, turn over 30 times per year, a group of accounts within this category may exhibit a significantly lower degree of volatility that would justify the allocation of these funds in longer-term, higher-yielding securities than would otherwise seem appropriate. Another limitation of the asset-allocation approach is that it assumes that sources of funds are not related to their uses. This is unrealistic, for as deposits in a particular category grow, they represent a growing group of customers who expect other forms of service from the bank, such as commercial loans. Allocations must be made to allow for these increased service demands. A more important limitation of the asset-allocation approach, however, is that it is essentially a rigid model that does not allow for any seasonal movements in deposit flows and loan demands. In other words, it ignores the ongoing changes in a bank's economic environment or any new developments that would have important bearing upon asset management. The model implicitly assumes that the future will be identical to the present.

There are other disadvantages of asset allocation that also apply to the pool-of-funds approach. First, both approaches stress the need for liquidity to provide for legal reserves and deposit withdrawal demands, but give less attention to the equally important requirement of meeting customers' loan requests. In periods of economic expansion, both deposits and loans tend to increase as the pace of business activity gains momentum. During such periods liquidity is needed mainly to meet the loan demands of businesses and individuals, which tend to outstrip deposit growth. Second, both asset-management models emphasize average, rather than marginal, liquidity requirements. Actual liquidity needs for any individual bank can be determined only through examination of its deposit structure, individual customer accounts, and the general business climate within which it operates.

Management Science

A more sophisticated approach to asset management lies in the use of elaborate mathematical models and statistical techniques to analyze—with the aid of computers—the complicated relationships among the components of the balance sheet and the income statement. These methods are basic tools of management science or operations research. Three common bank applications of these methods are the determination of the optimal number of teller lines by the use of queuing theory; the use of simulation to replicate financial statements of a bank (playing "what if" games) or operations (to determine the best number of computer centers or proof machines); and the use of linear programming to solve the allocation-of-funds problem in asset management and portfolio selection. (For more information on management science applied to portfolio selection and planning, see the appendix to this chapter.)

In order to use management-science techniques on asset management, there must be a statement of objectives, identification of the relationships among the elements of the problem and of the variables that are—and are not—controlled by management, an estimate of the behavioral pattern of the uncontrolled variables, and identification of (internal or external) management constraints. Once these parameters have been drawn up, the program can address specific problems, generate alternative solutions, and identify the best alternative.

Linear programming is a mathematical model that shows the relationships among decision elements. Various computational methods are used to determine the best combination of elements that can be controlled by the decision maker. Standard computer programs have been developed to perform the complex computations. Nevertheless, in order to be able to interpret and evaluate the results of the analysis, bank management must know the kinds of problems that can be solved by linear programming and be aware of the implications of the model's assumptions regarding economic developments and banking activity.

Linear programming models are characterized by an objective function specified by the decision maker and a set of variables subject to constraints. Since the linear program has only one optimum solution, the constraints must be specified or approximated.

Every linear programming model is developed around an explicit objective to be optimized. This objective must be continuous (the coefficients of the decision variables must be able to assume any value), and it must be stated in linear form (each variable must contribute proportionally to the value of the objective function). Optimization may be defined as minimal costs or maximal profits. If the objective is to maximize profits, a bank's management naturally would be interested in the combination of investments and loans that generates the most profits. A simplified example may illustrate this point. If the alternatives (decision variables) available to a bank are a Treasury bill, an AAA corporate bond, a consumer loan, a commercial loan, and a term loan with net yields (after expenses of administering and servicing these assets) of 5.5, 6, 7.5, 9, and 10.5 percent, respectively, we would have a hypothetical equation of the following form:

$$P = .055x_1 + .06x_2 + .075x_3 + .09x_4 + .105x_5$$

where P stands for profits and x for the amounts to be loaned or invested among the alternative types of assets considered. In this case, maximizing the objective function P maximizes profits. If there was no concern for risk or for liquidity, then all available funds would be placed in term loans (x_5), which offer the highest yield (10.5 percent). Obviously this is impossible, since bank customers demand diverse services, and both common sense and government regulations forbid such a concentration of funds.

Constraints are another characteristic of linear programming models. They are based on both law and common sense; some are matters of management judgment, while others, such as reserve requirements, are stated specifically. In addition, some, such as reserves, are easily computed as the sums of percentages applied to various deposit categories, while others, such as commitments to mortgages and other loans, cannot be predicted or estimated with great certainty. One can sometimes estimate the demand for loans of various types. If, for instance, the demand for auto loans with a net yield of 7.5 percent is estimated at $3.5 million, then its maximum value in the objective function above would be x_3-3.5 million. The principle of formulation is the same, regardless of the complexity of the constraints.

Additional constraints that may be part of a linear program are liquidity, risk, and legal limitations. The liquidity constraint might include a requirement that specific types of investments be related to total deposits, with minimums and maximums specified. Such a stipulation must be based upon predicted withdrawals, loan requests, and consumer perceptions of the bank's position. The risk constraint might include a requirement that the total volume of risk assets must be a set percentage of the value of capital funds. Management may also incorporate into the model those legal restrictions that it deems appropriate.

Restrictions play an important role in multiperiod models, which link one period to the next. For instance, they can limit the available funds in a given period to sums generated in the preceding period: loan repayments, securities matured or sold off, new deposits, and net profits. Multiperiod models also allow decision makers to incorporate their own views about future trends, thus yielding, for instance, a decision to invest so as to take advantage of predicted changes in interest rates.

The solution obtained by the use of linear programming reveals the investment in each category that will yield maximum profits under the specific conditions in the model. The program may have to be run several times for several sets of assumptions, in order to test their sensitivity. For instance, a range of interest rates may be considered in order to see their effect on optimal allocation of funds. Moreover, the linear programming solution would also show the opportunity costs of the constraints in the model. These opportunity costs can be used to increase profits, for example, by relaxing liquidity requirements or by raising funds through issuing capital notes.

The linear programming model offers flexibility through the use of shadow prices associated with constraints and affecting profits or the value of the objective function. (A shadow price is the amount by which the objective function would increase if the constraint were decreased by one unit.) For instance, if the solution indicated that profit could be maximized by lending as much as possible in term loans, this could be accomplished through increased demand for such loans. If the maximum that could be invested were $10 million and the shadow price were .05, then each additional dollar of loan demand up to $10 million would generate $.05 of additional profit.

Shadow prices can be used in making policy decisions, especially when they show that profitable activities can be undertaken at less than shadow prices, or that the cost of additional activities is justifiable. In the latter case the information could, for instance, lead to a decision to increase bank funds by issuing notes with a net cost not exceeding the shadow price.

For banks that have computers and properly trained staff, the linear programming model has several advantages. First, it helps to reveal the implications of decisions. Second, it can be used to test the sensitivity of decisions to errors or changes in economic conditions. Third, it can be used in summarizing the interactions of variables that affect the allocation of funds. Fourth, it helps to formulate bank objectives and have a clear statement of constraints. Fifth, it forces the examination of loan and investment portfolios in terms of types of investment, expected return, and costs.

The only serious disadvantage of using management science, especially the linear programming model, is experienced by small banks, for which computers and trained personnel may be too costly in relation to the expected benefits. This problem is lessening as more bankers are receiving training in the use of the computer and as more banks install their own computer systems, join computer time-sharing networks, and provide personal computers to individual staff members.

IDENTIFYING LIQUIDITY NEEDS AND
DETERMINING REQUIREMENTS

In its quest for an optimal allocation of bank funds, management is constantly confronted with the issue of making adequate liquidity provisions to meet customer demands for funds. A bank must maintain sufficient amounts of highly liquid assets and/or be able to raise funds quickly from money-market sources to meet deposit withdrawals and legitimate loan requests. Liability management for liquidity is generally relied upon by large money-market banks and some aggressive regional banks, while the vast majority of U.S. banks have traditionally relied upon liquid assets to provide for the varied demands for funds. The maintenance of liquid assets against deposit demands has been termed by some analysts "deposit liquidity" or "protective liquidity," as distinguished from "lending liquidity" or "portfolio liquidity," which applies to the maintenance of liquid assets for meeting the community's additional loan demands. Before discussing the nature of the assets that meet these liquidity needs, we will examine how banks go about establishing their liquidity requirements. This is all the more important because an excessive or deficient liquidity position can result in an unprofitable operation. Thus, for a bank to develop a comprehensive liquidity policy, it is first necessary to forecast the size and timing of its liquidity needs.

Analysts have developed various approaches to liquidity planning. Although there are differences among these approaches, they all consider liquidity in the context of prevailing economic conditions and their projected effects on deposit withdrawals and loan demands. Forces at work in the economy (local, regional, or national) impact the customer demand for funds (deposit withdrawals and loans), which directly affects a bank's liquidity position. These forces may be random, seasonal, cyclical, or secular.

Random forces are unexpected and unpredictable developments that affect the economy. They include natural disasters (such as earthquakes and hurricanes) and unanticipated human actions (such as widespread labor strikes or a sudden threat of war). Because of their unpredictable nature, random forces are difficult to take into account in liquidity planning. Seasonal forces recur in a regular pattern every year. They are therefore more predictable and are determined by such developments as planting and harvesting of crops, retail activity during holiday seasons, and stockpiling of inventory to take advantage of weather conditions (for instance, the accumulation of iron ore by Midwest steel mills during the summer months, when the Great Lakes are navigable). The great predictability of seasonal forces allows bankers to use them more effectively in liquidity planning. Cyclical movements are less predictable, and hence less useful for liquidity planning. They are, in simplest terms, alternations of expansive and contractive phases of economic activity. Since cycles do not occur at regular intervals, cyclical liquidity needs are difficult to predict. Past experience indicates that cycles are of unequal duration, and each has its own distinguishing features. Just as individual people differ even though they are members of the same family, so do business cycles. Nonetheless, there are some common repeating features: at the beginning of each cycle, economic growth rates and credit flows increase significantly, later they peak, and subsequently they fall quite rapidly. Thus, comparison with previous cyclical booms may, to some extent, provide helpful indications about the magnitude of a bank's cyclical liquidity needs.

Forces that influence the economy over a longer period than a business cycle constitute a secular trend. Changes in such magnitudes as savings, consumption, investment, technological developments, and population are examples of secular forces. Clearly these forces affect a bank's liquidity. However, though significant for long-range financial planning, they are of limited importance for shorter-run liquidity management. Thus, from a planning perspective, a bank's need for defensive liquidity stems basically from the seasonal and cyclical movements of the economy.

Since the outcome of future events cannot be predicted with complete certainty, no commonly agreed-upon forecasting technique exists for liquidity planning. Some banks, especially the larger ones that possess greater resources and expertise, have turned to computer models to develop quantitative forecasting techniques. The majority of banks, however, rely on a more judgmental approach, based on the experience of their bank officers. This is especially the case with smaller, community banks, in which bank officers have an intimate knowledge of the local market and the developments that may be shaping up. Nevertheless, one method, trend analysis, is widely used to forecast liquidity needs. Trend analysis is a valuable analytical tool well suited to smaller banks that have limited resources, but it is also used by larger banks with access to computers in order to generate more elaborate calculations and trace more detailed data.

The sections that follow describe the use of the trend-analysis technique in establishing a bank's deposit and loan liquidity requirements. Having separately identified the loan and deposit requirements, the bank can then determine aggregate liquidity needs and formulate policy for meeting them.

Determining Deposit Liquidity Requirements

As stated in Chapter 6, the bulk of bank liabilities consists of deposits. The fact that a bank must honor its depositors' withdrawal requests as efficiently as possible dictates a certain type of liquidity policy in the employment of these funds. In other words, the nature of bank liabilities makes it essential that bank resources be managed in such a way as to provide the means for meeting demands for funds as they are made. This obligation constitutes the most immediate and compelling necessity confronting the management of a bank. Indeed, failure to remain in a position to meet such demands as they are presented leaves management with no alternative but to close the bank. The maximum of liquidity would, of course, be attained through the maintenance of all bank assets in the form of cash. However, the impracticability of such a measure is obvious. Even with its assets entirely in cash, a bank would still incur major costs of operation. For, however liquid and safe cash may be, its profitability is nil. Under the circumstances the service charges for maintaining deposit accounts would be so high as to discourage customers from placing their funds with the bank.

In determining a bank's policy toward maintaining liquidity, management must consider the behavioral pattern of deposit accounts. As might be expected, deposit accounts do not all exhibit the same behavioral pattern. Indeed, due to a number of factors and differing situations, deposit accounts do not move in the same direction and at the same time or with the same velocity. It may be argued, of course, that fluctuations of individual accounts or groups of accounts may be offset by changes in other accounts or groups of accounts. Yet a bank cannot depend on that possibility. For example, for banks located in communities subject to the economic effects of one industry, such as resort and agricultural areas, deposit accounts would not produce their own offsetting changes or even nominal changes. And rightly so, since changes in deposit accounts would move in the same direction and at about the same time. If the industry suffers, so will its workers and local merchants—all undoubtedly bank customers—and bank deposits will decline. Conversely, if the industry prospers, bank deposits will build up.

It follows that whatever the type or classification of deposits—whether they are demand or time, whether they are of private or public ownership—what matters for the bank is the likelihood that any specific deposit, or group of deposits, may be drawn down within a relatively short period of time. Some deposit withdrawals, and hence demands for funds, may be predicted with a high degree of certainty;

some are likely but not certain; and some could possibly occur under certain conditions. Taking into account the likelihood of deposit withdrawals enables a bank to determine the types of assets it needs to maintain adequate liquidity.

Rather than undertaking a detailed examination of each deposit account, trend analysis permits management to group accounts and identify their overall behavioral pattern. In this case the criterion for such groupings would be the degree of volatility of deposit accounts. It will usually be found that the major portion of a bank's deposit volatility is due to the behavior of the larger accounts, the unexpected or sudden withdrawal of which would cause relatively heavy pressures upon the liquidity position of a bank. In the demand deposit area, large deposit accounts are more susceptible to wide fluctuations than all other demand deposit accounts because their holders do not usually leave them idle for long periods of time. In the time and savings deposit category, too, large accounts are responsible for most fluctuations. With the exception of large CDs, whose liquidity requirements are predictable because of their specified maturity dates, other large time and savings accounts call for protective liquidity provisions. Indeed, there are instances when the vulnerability of these accounts may match, if not surpass, that of large demand deposits. This certainly held true in the 1960s and 1970s during periods of economic expansion and higher interest rates. It was during these periods that holders of large savings accounts, and of CDs mostly of less than $100,000 denominations, generally sought outlets offering more return on their funds than banks were willing or permitted to pay.

In computing liquidity requirements against large deposit accounts, bank management must first separate the large accounts from all other accounts in each class of deposits. What constitutes a large account is, of course, a relative matter, which can be determined only by each individual bank's management. As a rule of thumb, any account equal to 0.50 percent of a bank's total deposits is considered a large account. Once the large accounts are determined, a semimonthly figure may be established for the aggregate of the large accounts category in each class of deposits. Management may then proceed to chart separately the aggregates established for each category in each class of deposits. These aggregates, carried back over a number of years, provide management with a historical pattern of deposit behavior by groups of deposits in the demand, time, and savings areas. An example is illustrated in Figure 8.1 which shows a hypothetical pattern of deposit volatility for the aggregate of large accounts in demand deposits, passbook savings, and time deposits. Parallel trend lines may

Millions of dollars

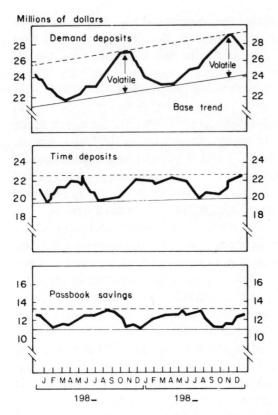

Figure 8.1. Deposit Volatility

Source: Compiled by author.

be drawn through or near the high and low points of these plots. The spread between the lines indicates the maximum liquidity required against these deposits at any given time. The trend line drawn through or near the low points designates the base level of nonvolatile deposits. Where a clearly rising or falling trend manifests itself, allowance can be made for increasing or decreasing the base level. The amount by which deposits exceed this baseline represents deposit volatility and is a statistical measure of the amount of liquidity required against them. Thus, at any given time in the year, bank management may relate the actual deposit position of the bank to these plots in order to determine the amount of liquidity required. By relating the bank's deposit position to historical patterns, management may also determine the approximate timing of liquidity requirements.

The amount of liquidity established on the basis of large deposit volatility constitutes a bank's first line of liquidity defense. Adjustment to this amount may be made only to the corresponding percentage of required reserves maintained against such deposits. The reasoning behind this adjustment lies in the fact that deposit withdrawals release amounts equal to the required reserves maintained against them.

The second line of liquidity defense is related to the withdrawal vulnerability of specific deposit accounts. There will be times when a careful examination of certain large or special accounts on an individual basis may require providing a larger degree of liquidity protection than that suggested by the analysis. In such instances detailed knowledge of the specific accounts and their prospective use would greatly aid bank management in determining the liquidity coverage required. A 20 percent liquidity reserve, for example, may be considered satisfactory on the assumption that a bank may be losing one out of five such accounts in the next few years. If warranted by circumstances, liquidity protection against these accounts may even extend to full coverage. These liquidity considerations may be applicable on demand and on time and savings deposits. A case of full liquidity protection may arise when, for example, the proceeds of a bond issue have been deposited at a bank and are held in demand or time deposits pending accurately timed payments for the financing of a specific project. In instances such as those described above, the culling of specific deposit accounts and a thorough knowledge of their prospective use would make possible the periodic projections of expected deposit fluctuations in the light of all known factors.

In the absence of exceptional circumstances (such as dependence on a single local industry), no specific provisions are necessary to ensure adequate liquidity to meet withdrawal demands for small accounts, since activity in these accounts is nominal and tends to average out. However, a conservative approach to meeting liquidity demands on these accounts calls for maintaining assets between 5 and 10 percent of the volume of these deposits as a residual liquidity reserve. Liability-management-oriented banks may rely on the lower percentage because of their ability to purchase funds from money markets if necessary. The assets that bank management may employ to cover this marginal area, however, can be in the form of slightly less liquid investments, though still readily convertible into cash (that is, securities of a one-to-five-year maturity range).

Determining Loan Liquidity Requirements

As stated earlier, bank liquidity serves two basic functions: meeting deposit demands and requests for funds arising from the community's needs for additional credit. Having examined the former, we may now turn to the latter.

In providing liquidity against potential loan requests, bank management is in a somewhat different position from that applying to deposit withdrawals. What must be observed here is that, unlike fluctuations in the deposit demand, increases in loan requests are subject to management control. In other words, it is incumbent upon a bank's management to tighten lending policies or to refuse to make some loans. The availability of funds exerts important influence upon the decision of bank management. Normally new loan requests should be met from the bank's largest source of loanable funds—the loan portfolio itself, through the turnover of loans.

The loan portfolio thus assures a bank's ability to make new loans. The degree of loan portfolio liquidity is, of course, affected by the length of loan maturities. Thus, the longer the maturities of a loan portfolio, the slower will be the loan turnover and, hence, the less its flexibility in meeting day-to-day requests for new loans. The opposite would hold true if a bank's loan portfolio contains short-maturity loans. Where the new loan demands exhibit a seasonal pattern, it is natural that the flow of loanable funds resulting from periodic loan repayments would at times be short of the loan demands and at other times in excess of them.

To determine the amount of liquidity required against such a seasonal, or normal, loan pattern, the same method as that employed for computing protective liquidity can be applied. The bank's loan pattern can be depicted by establishing total semimonthly loan portfolio aggregates, which can be charted over a period of time in the past. As was done with deposits, parallel lines may be drawn through the high and low points of these plots to indicate the overall loan trend and the range of liquidity required. Unlike deposit liquidity requirements, however, which are measured against the baseline, the amount of loan liquidity required at any time will be determined by the amount by which the graph falls below the upper trend line at any given point. In other words, with the upper trend line representing a maximum or ceiling to which loans may be expected to rise periodically or seasonally, the amount by which loans are below this maximum indicates a rough estimate of loan liquidity requirements at that time. The difference in the measurement of loan as against deposit liquidity requirements is a recognition of the fact that increases in loans make demands upon a bank's liquid position in the same way as decreases in deposits. A hypothetical pattern of loan demand variation, and hence loan liquidity requirements, is presented in Figure 8.2.

A bank's loan liquidity requirements, as determined above, may be supplemented by additional liquidity provisions as protection for

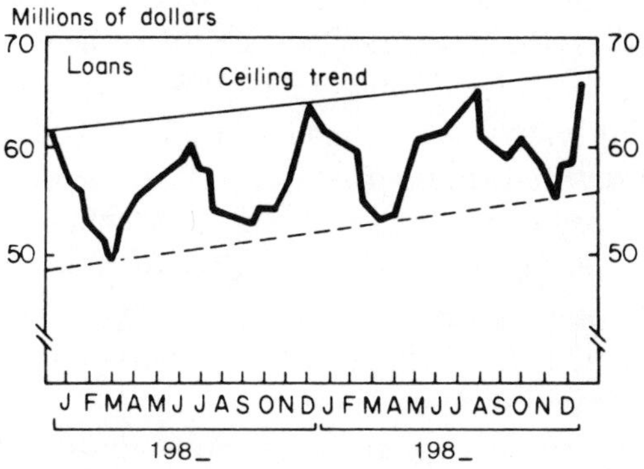

Millions of dollars

Figure 8.2. **Liquidity Needs for Loans**

Source: Compiled by author.

unforeseen loan developments. In other words, management may provide a margin of safety to meet unexpected loan demands. The amount arbitrarily suggested by some analysts is 20 percent of a bank's capital and surplus. In the final analysis, however, the amount that should be reserved as a margin of safety would be determined by bank management after careful appraisal of the composition of the loan portfolio. The loan portfolio of a bank actively engaged in commercial lending would require a relatively large margin of safety because the demand for business loans is usually more susceptible to fluctuations over the business cycle than is the demand for consumer or real estate loans.

If the demand for loans has been rising rapidly—as a result, for example, of a bank's aggressive lending policy or of a cyclical rise in business activity—and the management expects this rise to continue, provisions should be made for additional liquidity. In such instances bank judgment alone can determine how much additional liquidity should be reserved for the loan portfolio and what the degree of this liquidity should be. The rapidity of the anticipated loan growth will be a basic determinant of the liquidity of the assets employed. Funds reserved for such purposes are usually placed in slightly less liquid investments with their maturities arranged in a laddered form.

Aggregate Liquidity Requirements

The deposit and loan trends discussed above are a significant tool for management in determining the amount of combined liquidity cover that a bank should maintain. The graphic presentation of a bank's deposit and loan fluctuations will provide management with a picture of the similarity or dissimilarity of the two trends and enable it to determine the individual bank's protective and loan liquidity requirements at any particular time. Taken separately, a projected increase in deposits would call for increased protective liquidity, while a projected increase in loans would call for decreased loan liquidity. Combining or netting, whatever the case may call for, of projected changes in deposits and loans, in order to obtain a picture of the net liquidity requirements, would assume a direct relationship between the two trends—in other words, that a potential decrease in loan demand would, through loan repayments, release funds that could be used for protective liquidity, or that a potential increase in deposits would provide loan liquidity. Such an assumption would appear logical only if it were to be assumed that history repeats itself—that is, that historical trends will continue in the same pattern.

The practice of relying on loan portfolio to meet deposit liquidity is considered a questionable banking practice on other grounds. For one thing, during a period of depressed economic conditions, a bank's loan portfolio loses much of its liquidity through renewal of outstanding loans and forced loan liquidations. But under normal circumstances, too, it is not advisable that bank management looks to the loan portfolio as a source of protective liquidity. When a bank grants a loan, it is not possible to predict with absolute accuracy whether the loan will be repaid as agreed. The willingness and ability of the borrower to repay may change. Thus, loans that were considered good when they were made, could well become bad in a relatively short period of time. In some instances these loans—usually referred to as problem loans because of the problems they present as far as collections are concerned—may even require resort to the investment portfolio for additional liquidity so that they can be extended on the basis of a workout arrangement.* Hence the need for separate appraisals of the bank's protective and loan liquidity requirements.

It follows, then, that liquidity requirements must be established separately for deposits and loans. Once these are determined, the two amounts added together provide the bank's aggregate liquidity requirements. Such requirements will clearly be at a maximum if the bank's loans are down and the deposits are up. For it is at these times

---

*As implied by the term, a workout arrangement is a process in which the bank works with the borrower for the repayment of the loan instead of resorting to and exhausting every legal means to enforce collection. Such arrangement is not a legal device; it might be described as an austerity program imposed upon borrowers who have been desirable customers of the bank in the past, with their consent and cooperation. The steps may include bank advice on varied aspects of business policy to affect the borrower's earning capacity, the bank's active participation in the business, extending or redrawing the loan contract, and advancing additional funds to place the borrower in a stronger financial position.

that the future holds the greatest potential increase in loans or decline in deposits, and thus liquidity should be at a peak, so it can be used in meeting the loan increase in prospect, or the deposit decline that is coming up. On the other hand, requirements would be at a minimum if the position of loans and deposits is reversed. In any case, by allowing additional liquidity for a margin of error or for an extra margin of safety in liquidity estimates, the bank would be prepared for the unexpected in both loans and deposits. This kind of liquidity planning constitutes the foundation of a safe institution that can weather financial turbulence and prosper in the long run.

Table 8.1 provides a hypothetical computation of a bank's projected liquidity needs based on past experience. These computations do not include liquidity provisions for unusual or unforeseen circumstances, which would increase actual liquidity needs. As indicated earlier, providing for these unforeseen needs is a matter of bank management's judgment and intuition, based on the characteristics of the local market. As the table illustrates, once aggregate short-term liquidity requirements are established, they are stated as a percentage of total deposits. Actual liquidity reserves are created by setting aside the same percentage of current deposit volume each month.

Tempering Statistics with Judgment

Although a study of past experience yields a basic picture of a bank's aggregate liquidity requirements, considerable refinement of this picture is possible. Close monitoring of local economic conditions and consideration of larger-scale trends can provide the basis for sounder projections of liquidity needs than simple statistics do. Realistic forecasts of both deposits and loans are essential for efficient liquidity management, and such forecasts can be made only if the bank takes careful soundings of the activities and plans of major customers and follows local developments that may lead to such actions as bond issuance for community development, major construction projects, or the entry of new business into the local market. Bank officers directly involved in various market areas should gather this information and there should be a mechanism for pooling and analyzing it.

How is this information gathered? It should be an ongoing part of the bank's relations with its customers and with the community at large. Although some officers are reluctant to appear to interfere in their customers' planning endeavors, asking about future financing needs—regarding expansion, construction, capital acquisition, and so on—is in fact a part of the bank's service because it allows the bank

Table 8.1. Estimating Short-Term Liquidity Needs (millions of dollars)

	(1) Large Deposit Volatility				(2) Release of Reserves	(3) Liquidity for Large Accounts (1) - (2)	(4) Liquidity for Specific Individual Accounts	(5) Loan Liquidity	(6) Aggregate Short-Term Liquidity Requirements (3) + (4) + (5)	(7) Total Deposits	(8) Aggregate Short-Term Liquidity Requirements/Total Deposits (in percent) (6) ÷ (7)
	Demand	Time	Savings	Total							
January	4.0	1.5	2.0	7.5	.6	6.9	1.8	8.0	16.7	94	17.8
February	9.0	5.0	4.5	18.5	1.2	17.3	2.0	1.0	20.3	105	19.3
March	14.0	8.4	5.6	28.0	1.9	26.1	3.6	2.5	32.2	118	27.3
April	18.5	9.5	8.0	36.0	2.7	33.3	6.1	9.0	48.4	129	37.5
May	24.3	3.5	10.0	37.8	3.1	34.7	4.0	15.0	53.7	132	40.7
June	26.0	4.0	5.0	35.0	3.0	32.0	3.1	9.5	44.6	131	34.0
July	32.2	6.0	3.5	41.7	3.4	38.3	6.5	2.0	46.8	136	34.4
August	29.0	7.0	8.0	44.0	3.6	40.4	4.7	2.0	47.1	139	33.9
September	26.0	1.0	10.0	37.0	3.1	33.9	2.1	6.0	42.0	138	30.4
October	18.0	6.0	8.0	32.0	2.3	29.7	.2	14.0	43.9	137	32.0
November	10.0	10.0	4.0	24.0	1.7	22.3	2.9	10.0	35.2	127	27.7
December	3.5	4.0	3.0	10.5	.9	9.6	2.0	3.0	14.6	114	12.8

Source: Developed by author.

224

to stand readier to meet the customers' financing needs as they arise. A bank's active involvement in community affairs is also an important source of forecasting information. Chamber of commerce campaigns to attract business, municipal zoning hearings, and lobbying efforts for the building of a stadium are developments that the banker must take into consideration in order to be responsive to the community's borrowing needs.

In many cases bankers gather or are aware of information of this type but do not systematically use it to help forecast liquidity needs. One way to facilitate effective use of this information is to incorporate into each customer's credit file information on past borrowing and projected business activity, and tag it for easy retrieval for liquidity planning.

Funds management is an ongoing process and continual review is necessary, especially since cyclical and secular movements in the economy are largely unpredictable. Besides regular checks at least once a month to see that adequate liquid assets are available, an officer should keep an eye on the situation on a daily basis, so that quick adjustments can be made when necessary. Ideally, the level of liquid funds should match the bank's loan and withdrawal demands at any given moment. Excess liquid funds entail an opportunity cost because of forgone earnings. But if liquid reserves are too low to meet actual demand, the bank must engage in the costly process of purchasing funds immediately or converting assets to cash. In either case the bank is likely to sustain losses if adverse conditions prevail in the marketplace.

MANAGEMENT OF THE LIQUIDITY POSITION

A bank's overall need for liquidity may be classified into immediate, for day-to-day operations; seasonal, for deposit shifts and loan demands anticipated in the near future; cyclical or unforeseen, for longer-run deposit shifts and loan demands associated with the business cycle and/or extraordinary developments. Liquidity for a bank's immediate needs can be provided only in the form of cash. Primary reserves or cash assets are the most liquid form of assets and serve to meet a bank's day-to-day operational requirements. They include currency and coin to meet day-to-day transaction demands, cash items in process of collection, legally required reserves, and balances with correspondents as compensation for services rendered. To plan for all other needs, seasonal and cyclical, by means of adequate cash holdings would require the bank to forgo earnings needlessly. It can be just as safe for the bank to provide for its liquidity requirements by holding secondary reserves or by the technique of liability management.

Secondary Reserve Management

As indicated earlier in this chapter, secondary reserves is an analytical, rather than an accounting, concept used extensively by bankers in thinking about portfolio composition. The assets that make up these reserves are found in the investment and, to a certain extent, the loan portfolios of a bank. There is no hard-and-fast line of demarcation between a bank's secondary reserves and its investments and loans. What differentiates these reserves from a bank's other income-producing assets is that they are held primarily to meet its liquidity needs. A secondary reserve is one that may be drawn upon to replenish the primary reserve whenever the latter becomes depleted. Withdrawals of deposit first encroach upon the primary reserves, but a bank cannot afford to allow its primary reserves to be drawn down and remain below a desirable operating level. Withdrawal demands, therefore, require rapid replenishment of the primary reserves, and for this purpose the secondary reserves are used. Consequently, secondary reserves essentially constitute the real source of bank liquidity in meeting deposit and loan demands for funds.

Employment of funds within secondary reserves follows different patterns. Liquidity of the seasonal type can be provided by assets that possess certain important attributes: prime quality (minimum of default risk), less than a year's maturity (minimum of interest-rate risk), and in general a high degree of marketability (rapid and certain salability). Short-term, high-quality, but nonmarketable assets can also be considered in this class, with liquidity in this case based upon a flow of funds at maturity. In other words, the liquidity of these assets, and hence bank liquidity, would inevitably rely upon the flow of funds at a given maturity date rather than upon their flexibility as marketable instruments. Management should reduce the participation of these assets in the secondary reserves. Instead, it should place greater reliance upon readily marketable assets, so that if the demand for funds comes earlier than anticipated, the bank will not have to resort to substantial borrowing.

Obviously considered eligible as secondary reserves of the seasonal type are money-market instruments that have the characteristics mentioned above. Among the most widely accepted instruments in this category of secondary reserves are bankers' acceptances, commercial paper, short-term obligations of the U.S. Treasury and federal agencies, and in general any obligations of the Treasury or the federal agencies that are coming up for redemption in less than a year. Loans do not generally qualify, for they do not possess the aforementioned characteristics. In the first place, bank loans are not marketable. However self-liquidating a loan may be, it takes a relatively short period of time for a good loan to become a poor one and, therefore, to lose much of its liquidity value for the bank. This holds especially true during a period of adversity, when even short-term commercial loans may run into difficulties and require many renewals or extensions before final payment is made. Another reason for excluding loans from secondary reserves is that they do not possess any diversity, being concentrated geographically in the area or community that the bank serves. About the only loans that could be considered eligible would be those of a very short-term nature, such as the sale of federal funds (which are one-day loans to other banks) and call loans (which may be terminated at any time on very short notice, and are usually made to securities brokers and dealers for the purpose of purchasing or carrying highly marketable securities).

Secondary reserves of the nonseasonal or cyclical type are designed to supplement the secondary reserves of the seasonal type and facilitate the making of adjustments against cyclical or unforeseen demands; that is, they are designed to provide for a bank's protective and loan liquidity requirements that are of a cyclical or unforeseen nature.* To provide cyclical liquidity, management must be generally aware of the way in which the business cycle affects the local economy or market served. This holds especially true during the contraction phase of the business cycle, when deposit and loan declines are accentuated. During such periods, commercial bank activities are favorably affected by fiscal policy. The expansion of federal debt to finance deficit spending, which characterizes these periods, makes it possible for banks to partly offset declining loan outlets by placing idle funds into government securities. This acquisition of securities also partly offsets the declining deposits because it results in an overall deposit expansion for the banking system. Of course, the individual bank is not the banking system, and adequate liquidity provisions must still be made against cyclical demands. Here, again, management's past experience,

---

*Some writers, when discussing nonseasonal reserves, prefer to do so independently of the secondary reserve category. In other words, they present this type of reserve as a third category lying between the secondary reserves and the bank's bond portfolio. The term they use in identifying this tertiary reserve category is "investment reserves." [2]

coupled with knowledge of the bank's current deposit and loan make-up, are important determinants of the degree of cyclical liquidity needed.

The liquidity characteristics of the assets that may be included in this category fall short of the strict requirements placed upon the secondary reserve holdings of the seasonal type, but still exceed those of the assets included in the "bond portfolio," the latter term used hereafter to refer to that portion of the investment portfolio outside of both the seasonal and the nonseasonal classes of the secondary reserve category. In other words, with the potential need for liquidity further removed, a bank can accept somewhat greater interest-rate risk for income purposes. It follows, then, that secondary reserves of the nonseasonal type represent allocation of funds to high-grade marketable investments possessing a maturity of short-intermediate term (a maturity that ranges from one year, where the secondary reserves of the seasonal type leave off, to five years). Thus secondary reserves of the nonseasonal type may be selected from the promises to pay of the federal, state, and local governments and of corporations. In practice, many banks prefer to place the bulk of the funds available in this category in Treasury obligations maturing in from one to five years because of the high degree of marketability of these securities.

Each of the two distinct types of secondary reserves is designed, then, primarily to fulfill one function: to provide, respectively, short-range and longer-range liquidity. The basic asset characteristics of each of these two classes of secondary reserves should, therefore, be inviolate for all intents and purposes. There is, however, some ability to shift emphasis within their frameworks, and this pertains to the maturity pattern of the assets held in each class. There is some latitude for adjusting the maturity pattern of the assets held in each class of secondary reserves in accordance with the prevailing market climate (level of interest rates) and the monetary policy pursued. Potential market vulnerability and income considerations are the basic factors behind adjustments in the maturity pattern of secondary reserves. The latitude for such adjustments is somewhat greater for nonseasonal secondary reserves than for seasonal.

During periods of monetary ease, which coincide with economic contraction, interest rates are low and market prices of bonds are high. During such periods secondary reserves in general should be as short as possible. What this means is that as new or maturing funds become available for employment in the secondary reserve category, there should be an increasing emphasis on the shorter-end maturity pattern of this account. This shift in emphasis from the longer to the shorter end of the maturity pattern would have as a result the temporary ballooning of the shorter-term secondary reserves. This move would allow management to take advantage of the subsequent increase in business activity, which would entail higher interest rates and lower bond prices along with expanding loan demands. Conversely, during periods of tight money, which coincide with boom periods, interest rates are generally high and market prices of bonds low. In such periods secondary reserves should gradually shift in the direction of the longer-end maturity pattern, the five-year term. This move acts as a hedge against having to re-fund during the ensuing phase of the business cycle (recession) and consequently accepting lower-interest-rate instruments. As might be expected, this lengthening of maturities is possible only for secondary reserves of the nonseasonal type, the maximum maturity of which may normally extend to the five-year range. Secondary reserves of the seasonal type offer no latitude for maturity adjustments. Indeed, with these reserves generally geared toward a certain pattern of liquidity requirements, maturity lengthening would occur only for any excess or unassignable protective and loan liquidity, and then, perhaps, for not more than two years. It follows, therefore, that nonseasonal secondary reserves may be drawn down below the desirable level, provided the offset is found in the seasonal secondary reserves. The latter reserves, however, should never be drawn down below the desirable level, for with banks generally striving to keep no excess cash in their primary reserve account, the shorter-term secondary reserves constitute in essence the first line of a bank's defense.

Because of the importance of secondary reserves in meeting a bank's liquidity needs, tests have been developed to measure the degree of commercial bank liquidity. The two most commonly referred to in this respect are liquid assets to total assets and liquid assets to total deposits. Liquid assets may, of course, be interpreted in broad or narrow terms. In the former instance, for example, liquid assets would be considered a bank's cash assets and secondary reserves of both seasonal and nonseasonal nature; in the latter case, liquid assets would be considered a bank's cash assets minus required reserves plus seasonal secondary reserves. This latter definition of liquid assets appears to be conceptually preferable in measuring the degree of bank liquidity. In this context, then, the ratio of liquid assets to total assets would reflect the relative importance of a bank's liquid assets among its total assets. In other words, this ratio reveals the liquidity quotient of a bank's asset account. The ratio of liquid assets to total deposits shows what percentage of a bank's deposits is held in liquid form. Both ratios are significant because they reflect the ability of a bank (or of the banking system) to honor depositors' withdrawal demands and to grant loans.

Liability Management

Liability management also generates funds to meet liquidity needs. As we have seen in chapters 7 and 8, liability management involves acquiring funds by issuing CDs, purchasing federal funds, or borrowing from the Federal Reserve. Using funds acquired in this way to meet liquidity needs can allow a bank to reduce its holdings of secondary reserves. Liability-management-oriented banks generally rely upon money markets to provide for liquidity needs on a routine basis.

Liquidity Strategy

In determining liquidity policy, banks must decide to what extent they will rely on secondary reserves or liability management. The former focuses upon storing liquidity in assets; the latter on the acquisition of funds through a variety of borrowing arrangements that are unique in interest, maturity, and service characteristics. Degree of risk and return (cost) are important considerations in determining to what extent to rely on each strategy. Cost in liability management depends upon the specific borrowing arrangement employed and includes interest cost-adjusted, where applicable, for reserve requirements, processing costs, insurance fees, and other factors. If interest-rate forecasts are inaccurate, decreases in interest rates may leave the banks locked into high-cost funds, with a corresponding reduction in profits. Risk assessment must take into account the extent to which the bank may be able to roll over purchased funds to sustain expansion of its asset base. In periods of financial strain (such as during the failure of the Franklin National Bank in 1974), the availability of funds may be nil. In less extreme instances the quantity of funds available may be limited, thus creating a shortage. This risk and the constraints it imposes must be viewed in the context of the bank's overall risk exposure. On the secondary reserve side of the coin, the selling of assets to provide for liquidity needs has as its cost the amount of income that the bank would forgo during the life of these assets, adjusted for any gains or losses realized from the sale of these assets, tax effects, and brokerage fees.

Clearly, liquidity management does not have to be a choice between the secondary reserve approach and the liability-management approach, since a combination of both strategies is employed by many banks. The most common instrument used to raise funds for liability management is the large-denomination CD. Large, well-known banks are able to offer these on the open market in addition to selling them to customers or investment dealers. In addition, RPs and federal funds are widely used in liquidity planning. The most common assets sold by these banks to raise funds are short-term government securities.

In the final analysis, management philosophy determines the best course to follow. Generally, nonmoney-market banks maintain secondary reserves sufficient to meet projected liquidity needs for the next 12 months. If unexpected drains on liquidity occur and the bank does not wish to sell other assets to meet this need, it can turn to liability management on an ad hoc basis. Money-market banks and some other large banks are more likely to use liability management as an ongoing method of meeting liquidity needs. However, there is a limit on how much aggregate activity of this type can occur. If too many banks plan to purchase funds for liquidity at times when the Federal Reserve is tightening the money supply, some banks may get caught in the squeeze and experience liquidity problems.

APPENDIX: MANAGEMENT SCIENCE APPLIED TO PORTFOLIO SELECTION AND PLANNING

The objective of a flexible portolio policy is to provide an optimum portfolio balance: a portfolio containing those types and proportions of assets that represent, at any time, a most favorable balance of liquidity, safety, and profitability. An essential precondition for an optimum portfolio balance is, of course, that the bank's excess reserves be close to zero. Therefore, the issue that is presented to the bank's management is the familiar one of maximizing well-being subject to constraints. This means that within the framework that law and official regulation set, the marginal return per asset dollar must be equated in all directions. Stated differently, management must achieve such a distribution of portfolio assets that no further gain can be attained by shifting a dollar from one form of asset into another. When this is achieved, the distribution of assets is optimum.

Developing an optimum distribution of portfolio assets is not a new issue. Portfolio management has intrigued economists for a number of years. As early as 1888, F. Y. Edgeworth, a British economist, suggested that probability analysis could prove a useful device in portfolio planning. He postulated that portfolio management by a bank was analogous to a simple game:

> . . . [Imagine] a new game of chance, which is played in this manner:
> each player receives a disposable fund of 100 counters, part of which he
> may invest in securities not immediately realisable, bearing say 5 per cent
> per ten minutes; another portion of the 100 may be held at call, bearing

interest at 2 per cent per ten minutes; the remainder is kept in the hands of the player as a *reserve* against certain liabilities. [Twenty-two digits are randomly drawn every two minutes and the difference between their sum and their expected sum, 99, is obtained.] The special object of the reserve above mentioned is to provide against demands which exceed that average. If the player can meet this excess of demand with his funds in hand, well; but if not he must call in part, or all, of the sum placed at call, incurring a forfeit of 10 per cent on the amount called in. But if the demand is so great that he cannot even thus meet it, then he incurs an enormous forfeit, say 100£, or 1,000£.[3]

Unlike Edgeworth's game strategy, contemporary economists have attemped to present a more formalized approach to the issue of portfolio management. The various analyses that have been put forward since the 1950s fall into two broad categories: those that treat the three classes of bank assets (cash, loans, and securities) as homogeneous in themselves, and those that distinguish between the various assets in two of these classes (loans and securities) according to the degree of risk involved. In the discussion below, an attempt is made to provide a brief overview of the various formal techniques that have been put forward in this respect. In those cases where the literature available defies watertight classification, a classification is arbitrarily assigned.

Some of the models advanced view the problem as that of choosing a fraction of the total portfolio of assets to put into cash, loans, and securities. In these models the three classes of assets are believed to represent the range of liquidity and earnings. Although obviously cash is the most liquid of the assets, it yields no earnings. Conversely, loans are the least liquid but yield the highest returns. Investments are at the middle of the scale of both liquidity and earnings. These models, given the probability distribution of net deposit withdrawals and the anticipated yield on loans and investments, provide a portfolio mix that maximizes the expected value of the additions (profits) to the bank's net worth. The profits from a portfolio distributed among cash, loans, and securities are determined as follows: average loan return times the dollar amount of loans, plus the average securities return times the dollar amount of securities, minus average or expected loss on securities sold to meet unexpected cash needs.[4]

Attempts to refine this method have gradually led to the development of a dual criterion in evaluating different portfolio mixes. They suggest that consideration must be given to both the expected yield and the risk (that is, variance) of the portfolio. Stated differently, they advocate that the portfolio should be constructed by taking actions that maximize the expected return and minimize the variability of this return. This formula provides a trade-off between the advantages of higher returns and the disadvantages of greater variability in these returns. This dual criterion necessitates the use of a utility function to make possible the selection of an optimum portfolio in the case of more than one Pareto optimal alternative. In other words, a bank should select that portfolio whose expected return and variability have the highest utility, or that portfolio from among all possible portfolios for which the bank has the highest preference.[5]

Here portfolio management becomes basically a problem of concentrating on bank assets, determining the desirable asset structure, and treating liabilities as if they were determined entirely by forces outside bank control. New developments in financial markets, however, enable commercial banks to have some control over their liabilities—a fact that has significant effects on such a portfolio model. With banks allowed to vary the rates they pay on certain types of deposits (such as CDs) or to borrow the excess reserves of other banks, their portfolio choices now are quite different. Access to these forms of liquidity may allow for portfolios with much higher proportions of high-earning loans and investments, and much smaller amounts of liquid assets. Hence, portfolio management becomes a problem of determining a desired asset and liability structure rather than dealing solely with the asset structure.

The kinds of analyses referred to thus far treat all loans as equivalent to each other and all investments as equal to each other. Given these assumptions, a portfolio is then constructed that maximizes the expected return from the portfolio or an objective that explicitly recognizes both the return and its variability. Against this approach, other analysts have chosen to concentrate on the various types of assets within the different parts of the portfolio. One group believes that the main consideration in planning a bank portfolio is the determination of the maturity distribution within the different segments of the portfolio—for instance, taking loans as a class and investments as another. Much of the analytical material has, in fact, concentrated on only one of these portfolio classes: investment assets. There have been various attempts to construct mathematical models for the management of the government bond portfolio, which constitutes an important element of most commercial bank's assets. These models take into account estimates of net deposit withdrawals, expected future interest rates, and bond price movements, along with bank preferences for risk and return, to arrive at an optimal maturity distribution of government bonds. Considering probable cash needs and the possible losses on securities sold to meet these needs, a distribution by maturity of government securities is chosen. The distribution selected is that which best offsets the conflict between the higher expected yields from longer-term securities and the higher liquidity of shorter-term instruments.

Thus, the purpose of this approach is to determine a maturity distribution for the government security portfolio, considering possible changes in interest rates and liquidity requirements. Thus, the conflicts are resolved among the forces of liquidity, solvency, and yield, maximizing the bank's utility. Such a portfolio has just the right ingredients of risk and return, considering the bank's trade-off between the two.[6]

Another dimension of portfolio management for which analytical techniques have been developed is portfolio variability. The variability of a collection of assets is determined by the variability of each of the assets (variance) plus an amount related to whether the variations in the individual assets add to or subtract from each other (covariance). For instance, if a portfolio is composed of two assets whose fluctuations are likely to be in the same direction, its variability of return will be more than if it is composed of two equally variable assets whose fluctuations are likely to be in opposite directions.

Here the problem has frequently been viewed as that of choosing between alternative loans so as to select the combination that most enhances the utility of the portfolio in regard to maximizing return and minimizing risk. The loan alternatives are thought to be distinguished by their respective expected yield or return,* and by their expected variances and covariances. On this basis, selection from all possible combinations of loans is made with a view either to the highest return for given variance of risk, or to the lowest possible risk of variance for given return. Once one has determined several efficient portfolios, the problem is to choose the one that offers the combination of risk and return most fitting to the bank. Using this technique, one can split the problem of portfolio composition into two parts, the determination of combinations that are technically efficient and the selection of the single portfolio that best fits the particular bank.[7]

Several of the above approaches to bank portfolio planning are based on the assumption that the commercial banker is an investor seeking to allocate an investment fund among various investment opportunities and loan alternatives, so as to secure the highest expected earnings consistent with the degree of risk the bank is willing to accept.

---

*In determining the expected yield or return, allowance may be made for factors other than the loan rate of interest—that is, for bank benefits related to the attracting of new business or additional deposits.

This may, however, be a misleading guide for policy. The particular bank does not choose among all loans on the same basis; nondepositor borrowers will be distinguished from depositor borrowers. Moreover, a bank with many depositor borrowers will have preference for cash, loans, and investments different from that of a bank that makes more of its loans to nondepositors and therefore must anticipate larger cash withdrawals.

As progress is made toward a formal analysis of the problems of decision making under uncertainty, more quantitative aids will become available in the area of portfolio selection. Clearly, the techniques available today are much more practical and pertinent than the best efforts of only a few years back. However, the conceptual complexity of day-to-day funds' management and the difficulty of predicting with any degree of precision all the relevant variables involved render the construction of sophisticated models extremely difficult. The world in which the banker operates is an uncertain and complex one. An optimum portfolio policy will require the exercise of considerable judgment. The attainment of an optimum portfolio, then, will be a continuous process of adjustment carried on by each individual bank under conditions of economic change, uncertainty, and risk. The actual results are likely to be optimal only in a relative sense.

NOTES

1. Roland I. Robinson, *The Management of Bank Funds*, 2d ed. (New York: McGraw-Hill, 1962), p. 4.

2. See Robert G. Rodkey, *Sound Policies for Bank Management* (New York: Ronald Press, 1944), pp. 30-33. This approach is also followed in Roger A. Lyon, *Investment Portfolio Management in the Commercial Bank* (New Brunswick, N.J.: Rutgers University Press, 1960), pp. 26ff., 135ff.

3. F. Y. Edgeworth, "The Mathematical Theory of Banking," *Journal of the Royal Statistical Society* 51, pt. I (March 1888): 120.

4. On this approach see, for example, J. Duesenberry, "The Portfolio Approach to the Demand for Money and Other Assets," *Review of Economics and Statistics* 45, supp. (February 1963): 9-24; Donald D. Hester and John F. Zoellner, "The Relation Between Bank Portfolios and Earnings: An Econometric Analysis," *Review of Economics and Statistics* 48 (November 1966): 372-86; S. M. Besen, "An Empirical Analysis of Commercial Bank Lending Behavior," *Yale Economic Essays* 5 (Fall 1965): 283-315.

5. See, for example, James L. Pierce, "An Empirical Model of Commercial Bank Portfolio Management," in Donald D. Hester and James Tobin, eds., *Studies of Portfolio Behavior* (New York: John Wiley and Sons, 1967), pp. 171-90; James Tobin, "Liquidity Preference as Behavior Towards Risk," in Donald D.

Hester and James Tobin, eds., *Risk Aversion and Portfolio Choice* (New York: John Wiley and Sons, 1967), pp. 1-26.

6. See, for example, D. Chambers and A. Charnes, "Inter-Temporal Analysis and Optimization of Bank Portfolios," *Management Science*, July 1961, pp. 393-410; Harry M. Markowitz, *Portfolio Selection: Efficient Diversification of Investments* (New York: John Wiley and Sons, 1959); William Beazer, *Optimization of Bank Portfolios* (Lexington, Mass.: D. C. Heath and Co., 1975).

7. See, for example, W. R. Russell, "Commercial Bank Portfolio Adjustments," *American Economic Review* 54 (May 1964): 544-53; S. Royama and K. Hamada, "Substitution and Complementarity in the Choice of Risky Assets," in Hester and Tobin, *Risk Aversion and Portfolio Choice*, pp. 27-40; Donald D. Hester, "Efficient Portfolios with Short Sales and Margin Holdings," ibid., pp. 41-50.

SUGGESTED REFERENCES

Charnes, A., and S. Thore. "Planning for Liquidity in Financial Institutions." *Journal of Finance*, December 1966, pp. 649-74.

Crosse, Howard D. and George H. Hempel. *Management Policies for Commercial Banks*. 3rd ed. Englewood Cliffs, N.J.: Prentice-Hall, 1980.

Gup, Benton E. "Risk Management of Commercial Bank Portfolios." *Journal of Contemporary Business*, University of Washington, Summer 1977, pp. 15-29.

Hempel, George H., Alan B. Coleman, and Donald G. Simonson. *Bank Management, Text and Cases*. New York: John Wiley and Sons, 1983.

Kaufman, Daniel J., and David R. Lee. "Planning Liquidity: A Practical Approach." *Magazine of Bank Administration*, March 1977, pp. 55-63.

Luckett, Dudley G. "Approaches to Bank Liquidity Management." *Economic Review*, Federal Reserve Bank of Kansas City, March 1980, pp. 11-27.

Reed, Edward, Richard Cotter, Edward Gill, and Richard Smith. *Commercial Banking*. 2nd ed. Englewood Cliffs, N.J.: Prentice-Hall, 1980.

Sealy, Calvin W., Jr. "Commercial Bank Portfolio Management with Multiple Objectives." *Journal of Commercial Bank Lending*, February 1977, pp. 39-48.

Wood, Oliver G., Jr. *Commercial Banking*. New York: D. Van Nostrand, 1978.

9
SOLVENCY

Liquidity is one objective of portfolio management. Another is the maintenance of solvency—that is, ensuring that the value of assets is sufficient to cover liabilities. The former constitutes a short-run objective for bank management, while the latter is a long-run objective. Indeed, as we saw, the maintenance of a sufficiently liquid position constitutes the most immediate and compelling obligation of bank management, since failure to meet all claims as they come through would leave management with no alternative but to close the bank's doors. Solvency, on the other hand, ensures the safe, and hence continued, existence of the bank. Unless this objective is constantly considered, the day will come when the short-run objective of liquidity cannot be met. That is, the ability of the bank to remain open depends upon the fulfillment of the immediate objective of liquidity, but the attainment of that objective depends largely upon the achievement of the long-run objective of solvency.

The basis of an attack on the issue of solvency is suggested by the statement of the problem. The objective of bank management is to keep assets at least equal to liabilities, excluding subordinate notes and debentures plus capital stock. As long as such equality exists, a banking concern is solvent. Since bank liabilities are expressed in fixed amounts of money, it is evident that the causes of insolvency lie in changes in the value of bank assets. As losses occur, the value of assets declines, and such losses are customarily charged against the bank's capital account. If losses persist and the bank's capital falls below the par value of its outstanding shares, then capital is said to be impaired, yet the bank is still solvent. Should the assets decline in value by an amount in excess of the bank's capital, then insolvency exists—that is, the value of assets is less than the total amount of the bank's liabilities. It is possible for a bank or banks to be insolvent for a shorter or longer period and still remain in business. A number of banks, throughout their individual histories and in one or more instances, have been temporarily in a position where the current market value of their assets failed to cover liabilities. Yet many of them were able to overcome this situation and gradually restore full solvency. In connection with bank insolvency brought about through reductions in the value of assets, it is essential that we examine the causes of these losses and of the risk factors responsible for them.

RISKS IN THE BANKING BUSINESS

In the course of their operations, banks are exposed to risks. Some of these risks are specific to the banking business, while others are inherent in virtually any business activity. The former category includes the risks of default, bank runs, interest-rate risk, and unfavorable fluctuations in foreign-exchange rates. In addition, like other businesses, banks are exposed to the risks of defalcation (embezzlement) and theft. Each of these types of risk is discussed below.

Risk of Default

The most obvious hazard in banking is the risk of default, the possibility that the funds loaned or invested will not be repaid, with consequent loss to the bank. In their lending and investing operations few banks knowingly make poor loans and investments. It is what occurs after a loan or investment is made that will be decisive as to whether it will deteriorate in quality or go into default. Many unforeseeable developments can undermine a borrower's ability to meet contractual obligations as they come due. "Acts of God" (hurricanes, tornadoes, floods, and earthquakes) can lead to nonpayment of debt. And changes in consumer tastes can significantly affect the fortunes of companies. If consumers, for example, prefer soft drinks in bottles over those in cans, manufacturers of bottles would prosper at the expense of those producing cans. Boutiques and clothing manufacturers are affected by style changes. Technological advance can drastically alter the financial condition of a business firm. Mechanical calculators, for example, were rendered obsolete by electronic calculators. The swings of business cycles affect the profitability of businesses and influence their willingness to discharge their debt. Such diverse developments as prolonged strikes, construction of an expressway, loss of key management, entry of new competitors into the market, and additional future debt can lead to the nonpayment of debt.

The risk of default ranges from practically none, on instruments such as government obligations or the highest grade of corporate debt, through many gradations. Judging gradations of risk requires a considerable degree of skill. What may appear to be currently within a borrowing firm's ability to pay may, five years later, turn out not to be the case. The firm's prospects may have definitely turned for the worse because of developments such as the ones mentioned above. The further one looks into the future, the less certainty there is about the actual ability of the borrower to carry the debt. Even self-liquidating, short-term commercial loans get into difficulties during recession and may need many renewals or extensions before repayment is made.

Because of this uncertainty element the risk of default, and hence the risk to the quality of bank credit, is ever present. In the case of loans, this risk element is covered in the rate of interest charged, while in the case of securities it is reflected in their market value. In investing in securities, banks typically buy any debt that has only slight chance of default. Thus, the price differentials among various debt instruments, other factors being equal, presumably reflect the risk of default. This in itself presents the management of a bank with a problem. To maximize bank profits, the management needs high yields, but they are associated with the riskier opportunities. Thus, skill and judgment are required to evaluate the opportunities open to the bank, for if the loan or investment is defaulted, income suffers and solvency is impaired. To prevent and control losses resulting from default, banks seek to maintain high credit standards, diversify loan and investment portfolios, have a good knowledge of the borrower and understanding of his affairs, and pursue a vigorous collection policy. These are discussed in Part IV.

Bank Runs

Even if there is absolutely no question about repayment of principal and interest when due, a bank may be forced to sell or call in high-quality assets at a loss, thus undermining its ability to repay depositors and other creditors in full. Forced sale of securities or collection of loans occurs when customer demand for funds necessitates the liquidation of assets. A depositor's withdrawal demand is one that a bank must honor promptly; failure to do so would force the bank to go out of business. Demands for funds may occur at any phase of the business cycle—during recession or economic expansion. During periods of decline in economic activity, withdrawal demands originate mainly from depositors, who rush to convert their deposits into currency because of distrust of banks. In the depression of the 1930s, for example, hints or suspicions of bank losses and doubts about the ability of particular banks to meet withdrawal demands led depositors to converge on banks to obtain their funds before the bank ran short. There are many historical examples of bank runs (as this condition is called), and they often culminated in the downfall of the bank involved. As the depression intensified, the merest hint of a bank loss was enough to trigger a run on its assets. In both Nevada and Louisiana, state-declared bank holidays convinced depositors that the banks were on the verge of ruin. The governor of New York was forced to close New York banks statewide to prevent panicked withdrawals and the collapse of the state's banking system. By early 1933 commercial banking activity had virtually ground to a halt until President Roosevelt restored public confidence by declaring, on the morning of Inauguration Day, a national bank holiday.

The danger of such panics and the accompanying runs on banks have been greatly reduced, if not eliminated, by such banking reforms as the establishment of a deposit insurance system, stricter banking laws, and greatly improved bank supervision. These reforms have contributed to strengthening the banking structure and the confidence of the public in banks.

Interest-Rate Risk

Of more significance to banking policy, however, is the interest-rate risk, which is an outgrowth of depositor withdrawal demands during boom periods. Such was the case in 1966, 1969-70, and 1973-74, when depositors tended to draw down their deposit balances to take advantage of open-market instruments offering higher returns than banks were willing or permitted to pay. Along with depositor withdrawals, during these years banks experienced an even more significant demand for funds: a heavy demand for credit from their customers. This demand provided commercial banks with strong incentives to expand their loan portfolios, and hence to increase bank earnings. During these years, however, monetary authorities relied almost exclusively on bank credit restraint to promote a sustainable rate of economic growth and to counter inflationary pressures. Banks that could not obtain funds from other sources (that is, through liability management) because of limitations by Regulation Q and/or Regulation D had no alternative but to resort to their investment portfolios and liquidate securities to meet the extensive credit demands. Such a process of financing additional loan demands was a costly one for banks, especially if the securities liquidated were bonds of intermediate or longer-term maturity, the prices of which were generally affected by even moderate changes in the level of interest rates.

It may be argued, of course, that banks could have refused to grant additional credit. This, however, is not always possible. For example, a bank can hardly afford to refuse to accommodate the loan request of a depositor of long standing who has maintained large balances with the bank. The same would hold true for the loan request of a firm that plays an important role in the growth of the region, or for the request of the local municipality that is interested in financing a project that is essential to local welfare. Refusal by the bank to meet these and similar loan requests could lead to the closing of deposit accounts and the loss of valuable customers.

Any time a bank is forced to sell or liquidate long-term securities in periods of increased economic activity, it exposes itself to interest-rate risk—that is, the risk that the sale of these securities will be realized only at sizable discounts from their face value. The prevailing level of interest rates in the market at the time of the sale is thus a critical factor in the extent of bank losses. It is a basic principle in economics that the level of interest rates at any given time is the product of the interplay of the demand for and the supply of funds in the market. The demand for funds is affected by the level of business activity; it rises when business activity expands and declines when such activity slackens. The supply of funds, on the other hand, is affected by the monetary policy pursued: an easy money policy has an expansive effect upon the reserves of the banking system, and hence upon the extension of credit by commercial banks and—through them—by other lenders, while a tight money policy has a contractive effect upon the system's reserves, and therefore upon credit extension. During periods of monetary ease, market rates generally tend to decline, while in periods of restraint they increase.

The general level of interest rates, as it is affected by the market demand and supply forces, will determine, at the time of the liquidation, whether the market value of the securities owned declines, and hence whether capital losses will be sustained. The market value of securities moves inversely to changes in the current market rate of interest. Thus, if, as a result of market forces, the going rate of interest moves up, the market value of debt instruments calling for fixed payments over time (based on some previous lower rate) will fall. Let us assume that a bond bearing an interest rate of 6 percent and maturing in 20 years is purchased. If the bond is purchased at par (100 percent of face value), its market price would be $1,000. Suppose that, subsequent to this purchase, the market rate of interest for bonds of comparable quality rises to 8 percent. Clearly the market value of this bond will be affected. The extent of the effect can be determined through an equation that is based upon the concept of present value (worth today of funds to be received in the future), and is used to determine the yield to maturity of debt securities. This equation is

$$P = \frac{R_1}{(1+r)} + \frac{R_2}{(1+r)^2} + \frac{R_3}{(1+r)^3} + \cdots + \frac{R_n}{(1+r)^n} + \frac{M}{(1+r)^n}$$

Where P = current price of bond or present value of payments

R = annual interest revenue ($) from bond (coupon payments)

n = number of years to maturity

M = principal ($) payable at maturity

r = market rate of interest or yield to maturity.

Applying the information available, we would have

$$P = \frac{\$60}{(1+.08)} + \frac{\$60}{(1+.08)^2} + \frac{\$60}{(1+.08)^3} + \cdots + \frac{\$60}{(1+.08)^{20}} + \frac{\$1,000}{(1+.08)^{20}} = \$804.08.$$

Thus, as the result of an increase in the going rate of interest to 8 percent, the value of the bond will decline to yield a competitive rate of return. At the price of $804.08, this bond provides an annual rate of return of 8 percent. It follows that a change in interest rates inversely affects the value of a bond, with consequent effects upon its yield. A rise in interest rates depreciates the value of lower-interest-bearing bonds, causing their yield to decrease.

This fall in price will be similar for all bonds of similar risk and maturity. If coupon rates of interest differ, market prices will tend to fall accordingly, to keep the yields in line with one another. The longer the period that the instrument has before it matures, the greater will be the fall in its market price. This point can be illustrated by making reference to the above example. Suppose, for example, that the initial purchase included two additional bonds of the same quality and bearing the same interest as the one described above, but of longer maturities. Let us assume that one of these had a maturity of 25 years, and the other of 30 years. In such a case the rise in interest rates to 8 percent will cause the value of the 25-year-maturity bond to decline to $786.50 and the value of the 30-year-maturity bond to decline to $774.48. Clearly, the effect of this rise in interest rates is accentuated by the longer maturity of the debt instrument. By the same token, a decrease in interest rates would cause the value of the longer-maturity bonds to appreciate more than that of the shorter-maturity ones.

Clearly, then, the longer the maturity of the securities owned by the bank, the greater the decline in their market value, and hence the larger the capital losses to be sustained by the bank, which is forced to convert them into cash. But even if the bank may not have to sell the bonds that have declined in price because of the change in the rate of interest, the bank is not realizing the same amount of income it could be receiving at the higher rate if it had not invested in the bonds it now holds.

The interest-rate risk, is, therefore, inherent in all contracts calling for fixed payments over time. Consequently, bonds that are free of any default risk are still subject to the interest-rate risk, since the future level of interest rates is uncertain. This fact could make a case for loading up on short-term securities by the banks, since such securities are insulated from wide fluctuations in value. This is another aspect of liquidity. Even a long-term bond may become part of a bank's secondary reserves as it approaches maturity. This means that the realizable price in the event of its liquidation is more certain, and differs from its stated redemption value by only a small amount. But, of course, by loading up on short-term securities the bank precludes much chance of capital appreciation, should interest rates fall.

Managing Interest Sensitivity

Management concern over interest-rate fluctuations goes beyond their effect on individual securities. Since bank balance sheets are largely composed of financial assets and liabilities, bank earnings are, in varying degrees, sensitive to interest-rate fluctuations. Thus bank managers have sought to devise a policy for managing their asset/liability sensitivity. Efforts in this direction received prime attention in the late 1970s and early 1980s, as a result of both the intensified competition from "near banks"—which narrowed profit margins—and the wide swings in interest rates, which made bank earnings relatively more volatile.

An important tool through which banks have tried to manage their interest sensitivity is the net interest margin. This is the ratio of net interest revenue (interest revenues minus interest expenses) to earning assets. Before deregulation most bank liabilities consisted of noninterest-bearing demand deposits and fixed-rate time and savings deposits; consequently the net interest margin responded mostly to rates that banks could charge for loans and security investments. As those rates increased, banks were able to improve the rate spread between assets and liabilities. With the advent of deregulation, however, customers converted low-rate savings and time deposits to higher-rate CD liabilities. Also, banks began to bid aggressively for borrowed funds. These developments reduced the rate spread between the banks' assets and liabilities, and encouraged banks to emphasize variable-rate earnings in their loan and investment portfolios, in order to maintain adequate net interest margins.

While the net interest margin addresses the problem of interest-rate characteristics of financial assets and liabilities, a relatively new tool called gap management addresses the relation of interest rates to maturities. The first step in gap management is to divide balance sheet items by maturities (for instance, up to one month, one to three months, three to six months, six months to one year, one to two years). The next step is to calculate the difference, or gap, between the volume of assets and the volume of liabilities that will be repriced or are subject to interest-rate adjustment within each maturity frame. Assets and liabilities with matched maturities and rates of interest are excluded from this analysis. The predetermined maturities and rate spread of these accounts render their net interest margin immune to interest fluctuations and assure their profitability. Fixed-rate assets and liabilities of long-term maturity (such as mortgages and long-term debt) are also excluded, since they are relatively impervious to short-term fluctuations in interest rates. Their net interest margin will fluctuate slowly over time as individual items mature or are rolled over. Gap management comes into play with those remaining items that are subject to variable rates either because of their short maturity or because of the periodic adjustment in their rate of interest. Variable-rate assets include short-term loan and investments, variable-rate term loans, federal funds sold, and repurchase agreements subject to resale. Variable-rate liabilities include short-term CDs, federal funds purchased, repurchase agreements, and other short-term borrowings.

The sensitivity of these items to changes in interest rates from the present to some future time (such as two years ahead) can be gauged by looking at the cumulative gap up to that time and forecasting the direction of interest-rate fluctuations. When more assets than liabilities will be repriced within a given period, a positive gap exists; when liabilities to be repriced exceed assets, a negative gap exists. The bank will benefit from a positive gap when interest rates are rising because this means more assets than liabilities will be repriced at higher rates. Similarly, falling interest rates are beneficial when a negative gap exists. The following sections describe three different strategies for managing the funds gap: managing the gap over interest rate cycles, attaining gap targets using financial futures, and attaining gap targets by means of options.

Managing the Gap over the Interest Rate Cycle. This strategy emphasizes the maintenance of a positive gap, with the size of this gap subject to manipulation over the interest-rate cycle. In a period of rising interest rates, banks benefit from an increasing positive gap. However, during such periods banks cannot exercise much influence over their ability to attract fixed-rate, long-term funds; yet some adjustments may be made on the liability side of the balance sheet through sale of capital notes and debentures and/or common stock. On the asset side funds may be shifted to short-term investments and variable-rate term loans.

At the height of the interest-rate cycle, when the largest gap should occur, the bank should lock in high-yielding assets by shifting funds to long-term securities and fixed-rate loans. As rates fall, the gap should be gradually reduced until a minimum gap exists at the bottom of the rate cycle. In any event, a positive gap should always be retained. The size of the gap should be adjusted to enhance and stabilize the net interest rates peak and narrow when rates are low.

This strategy, like other methods of gap management, is generally practiced by large banks, which have the necessary talents to make realistic market predictions. However, even the most skilled forecasters cannot always make accurate predictions, and thus an element of risk is always present. In addition, some question the desirability of making rate structures for customers subservient to the bank's gap-management strategies.

Financial Futures and Gap Management. Increasingly in recent years large banks with sufficient resources in time and expertise have sought to limit their sensitivity to interest-rate fluctuations by trading in the financial futures market. Banks trading in the futures market can hedge either the complete asset/liability portfolio (macro hedging) or individual asset or liability items (micro hedging). Hedging is the process of controlling the risk of a position or transaction by engaging in an offsetting transaction. In the futures market buyers and sellers enter into contracts for the delivery of securities at a specified location and time and at a price that is set when the contract is made. The idea behind trading futures contracts is that buyers and sellers want protection against adverse movements in interest rates and prices. This protection is effected through investor adoption of equal and opposite positions in the spot (cash) market and in the forward (futures) market of the same or similar asset. By entering into such offsetting transactions, banks can effectively hedge their interest-rate exposure while transferring most of the risk of future changes in the prices of securities to another participant in the futures market who is willing to bear that risk.

Originally transactions in the futures markets covered only agricultural commodities, such as wheat and corn. Producers and users of farm products, to protect themselves from the wide price fluctuations that resulted from seasonal surpluses and shortages of these products, entered into forward contracts calling for the future delivery of such products at a specified location and time, and at a guaranteed price. Futures markets evolved from forward contracts, and generally allow greater liquidity—that is, transacting parties can buy and sell at will, while in forward contracts the parties involved are tied in for the duration of the contract. Eventually futures contracts evolved and futures markets expanded to include metals (such as gold and silver) and wood products and, since 1975, mortgage-backed Government National Mortgage Association (GNMA or Ginnie Mae) securities, U.S. Treasury securities, and CD contracts. The development of futures markets in these instruments was induced by deregulation as well as by the wide swings in interest rates and the value of securities that dominated the financial markets in the 1970s. Record high interest rates—under the pressure of tight money policies and inflation—drastically reduced the market values of securities and fixed-rate mortgages in the portfolios of financial institutions, threatening them with insolvency and ultimate failure. This was especially the case with savings and loan associations, whose assets consisted overwhelmingly of fixed-rate mortgage loans. Indeed, the rapid and sustained increases in interest rates in the late 1970s resulted in the decrease of the net worth of many associations to extremely low levels, which caused numerous failures or forced mergers with solvent institutions. This state of affairs elicited the favorable stance of some members of the regulatory community toward the growth of financial futures as a means of controlling the sensitivity of banks' and S&Ls' portfolios to interest-rate changes.

A transaction in the futures market can be in the form of a long hedge or a short hedge. A long hedge is the purchase of futures contracts today as a temporary substitute for the actual purchase of securities at a later date. Its purpose is to enable the transacting party to "lock in" a desired yield in the event that interest rates decline before the scheduled availability of funds and the actual purchase of securities in the cash market. Assume, for example, that today a bank purchases on margin Treasury bond futures contracts at their current market price, with cash payment on these contracts not due until the delivery date of the futures six months later. If later, as expected, interest rates fall and prices of securities increase, the gain realized in the futures markets from the sale of these contracts will help the bank offset the opportunity loss sustained in the cash market from the prevailing higher security prices at the time of the actual purchase (see Table 9.1).

Unlike a long hedge, which enables investors to benefit from falling interest rates (rising security prices), a short hedge guards investors against increasing interest rates (decreasing security prices). In other words, if a bank believes that interest rates are going to increase (security prices will decline) in the months ahead, it can protect itself against a reduction in the market value of its portfolio and the taking

Table 9.1. Long Hedge of U.S. Treasury Bond Futures

Consider a trust department officer who manages a pension fund for a client. On April 1, 1980, he expects that in three months he will receive $1 million—an amount he plans to invest in Treasury bonds. He suspects that interest rates will fall and bond prices will rise. The course of action he will pursue until cash is available on July 2 is outlined below. On April 1 he will go long (purchase) ten September bond futures contracts. Assume that by July 2 rates have fallen and bond prices have increased. He will then sell his futures contracts, realizing a gain of $119,062.50. This gain partially offsets the opportunity loss sustained by his late entry into the cash market.

Cash Market	*Futures Market*
April 1	April 1
Wants to take advantage of today's higher yield level on 20-year 8.25% Treasury bonds at 68-14	Buys 10 September bond futures contracts at 68-10
July 2	July 2
Buys $1 million of 20-year 8.25% Treasury bonds at 82-13 (yielding 10)	Sells 10 September bond futures contracts at 80-07
Loss: $139,687.50 (Given an opportunity loss per contract of 13-31/32, each 1/32 equal to $31.25, and the number of contracts bought amounting to 10, total loss = 447/32 x $31.25 x 10)	Gain: $119,062.50 (381/32 x $31.25 x 10)

Note: This illustration does not include commissions and Chicago Board of Trade service fees.

Source: Chicago Board of Trade, *A Guide to Financial Futures at the Chicago Board of Trade* (Chicago: Chicago Board of Trade, 1983), pp. 41-42. Reproduced by permission of the Chicago Board of Trade.

of losses upon the sale of securities by engaging in a short hedge. A short hedge involves the selling of futures contracts on selected securities until the actual sale is made at a later date in the cash market. Assume, for example, that in anticipation of higher interest rates (lower bond prices), a bank sells short Treasury bond futures contracts. Then, if interest rates do increase, the bank—to offset its short position—goes into the futures market and purchases, at the prevailing lower bond prices, an equal number of contracts to those sold short. The gain realized in the futures market would enable the bank to offset the capital loss from the actual sale of the securities in the cash market (see Table 9.2).

Table 9.2. Short Hedge of U.S. Treasury Bond Futures

Consider a trust officer who on October 1, 1979, manages a portfolio of $1 million, 20-year 8.75 percent Treasury bonds. He suspects that interest rates will rise and bond prices will fall. To protect the portfolio from a decline in value, he engages in a short hedge; that is, he sells U.S. Treasury bond futures contracts. Assume that by October 31, interest rates have risen and bond prices have declined. The officer offsets his previous futures sale by purchasing an equal number of contracts. Although his portfolio is worth $83,125 less as a result of the decline in bond prices, this loss is partially offset by the gain of $70,625 realized in the futures markets.

Cash Market	*Futures Market*
October 1	October 1
Holds $1 million, 20-year 8.75% Treasury bonds priced at 94-26 (yield 9.25%)	Sells 10 Treasury bond futures contracts at 86-28
October 31	October 31
Prices for bonds fall to 86-16 (yield 10.29%)	Buys 10 U.S. Treasury bond futures at 79-26
Loss: $83,125.00 (266/32 x $31.25 x 10)	Gain: $70,625.00 (226/32 x $31.25 x 10)

Note: This illustration does not include commissions and Chicago Board of Trade service fees.

Source: Chicago Board of Trade, *A Guide to Financial Futures at the Chicago Board of Trade* (Chicago: Chicago Board of Trade, 1983), p. 43. Reproduced by permission of the Chicago Board of Trade.

From the preceding it follows that a bank with a positive gap can hedge against an unexpected decline in interest rates by buying long 90-day T-bill futures. If such a decline materializes, the gains realized from the long position will offset some of the losses from the positive funds gap. If rates do not fall but continue to increase, the losses in the futures position will be offset by the gains from the positive funds gap. A negative gap is hedged by engaging in a short hedge. If rates increase, the gains realized in the futures market will offset some of the losses associated with the repricing of liabilities at higher rates. Of course, if interest rates decline, the losses in the futures position will be offset by the gains from the negative funds gap.

Although financial futures are an important tool of risk management, viable futures markets exist for only a limited number of financial instruments. If such a market for a particular security does not exist, a future for another security can be used (a technique referred to as cross-hedging), assuming that the price movements of the two securities are similar. The historical relationship between the price movements of the two securities must be derived mathematically in order to determine what amount of the existing future is needed to hedge the security for which there is no futures market. However, such indirect hedging does not guarantee complete insensitivity to changing interest rates, because interest rates for different financial instruments do not always move in the same manner relative to one another.

As of mid-1983, trading in financial futures was limited to the following high-quality financial instruments: 90-day Treasury bills, 90-day CDs, 90-day Eurodollar CDs, GNMAs, intermediate-term Treasury notes (maturing between 6.5 and 10 years), and long-term Treasury bonds (with maturities in excess of 15 years at delivery date). Futures for 1-year Treasury bills, 30-day and 90-day commercial paper, 2-year, 4-year, and 4-6 year Treasury notes, and 15-year Treasury bonds were started, but these markets did not survive because of lack of trading interest. Futures for other interest-rate instruments are in the planning stage. Three of the most active exchanges in futures trading in the United States are the Chicago Board of Trade (CBT); the International Monetary Market (IMM), a division of the Chicago Mercantile Exchange; and the New York Futures Exchange.

Thus far, commercial banks have engaged in futures trading only to a limited extent. Two factors have inhibited banks from plunging into this market. First, regulatory agencies have been reluctant to adopt specific guidelines to govern this practice. Second, the accounting profession has not yet agreed on procedures for recording hedged gains and losses realized through futures trading. For tax and public reporting purposes, losses are recognized immediately, while gains are deferred until the sale has been completed. These problems led the Financial Accounting Standards Board (FASB) to publish, in the summer of 1983, a draft proposal for industry comment. Effective resolution of these and related issues is expected to induce more active bank participation in the futures market.

Options and Gap Management. Options on debt instruments represent another important strategy for managing risk. Just as with futures, a bank may hedge individual securities or its overall balance sheet. Options give holders the right to buy or sell securities at predetermined prices on or before a specified date. A call option is an option to buy securities, and a put option is an option to sell securities. The values of puts and calls are determined by the volatility of the market value of the underlying securities as well as by other market considerations. The high interest rates that prevailed in the late 1970s and early 1980s make put options on debt instruments an important hedging tool because they can protect fixed-rate assets in bank portfolios against rising interest rates and lower security prices without limiting the potential to benefit from lower interest rates and rising prices.

A bank with long-term, fixed-rate assets funded by short-term liabilities may hedge against rising interest rates by buying a put option for these assets, or for securities of similar maturity and coupon in the absence of a market for the assets to be hedged. In the latter case such hedging can be effective only if the direction and size of price movements for both sets of assets are similar. The put option protects the bank against rising interest rates, and a corresponding drop in the price of the asset, by allowing the bank to sell it at a predetermined price by a predetermined date. If, as anticipated, interest rates increase and the market value of the asset goes down, the ensuing loss in the bank's actual debt instrument position will be offset by the gain in the price of the put. By the same token, if the price of the asset rises as a result of declining interest rates, the bank is free to sell it at the more advantageous price, losing only the cost of the put option.

On the other hand, if conditions in the marketplace indicate a trend toward lower interest rates and rising security prices, a bank with fixed-rate liabilities funding floating-rate assets may hedge its risk exposure through the purchase of debt call options. Assuming that this bank cannot buy back its fixed-rate liabilities, purchase of call options will help offset its losses from having to finance floating-rate assets in a falling-rate environment with high-cost, fixed-rate liabilities. The purchase of call options on the underlying securities, or on securities of similar maturity, protects the bank, in that if interest rates decrease, the value of the options will increase in response to increases in the market value of the underlying securities. While this hedge protects the bank if interest rates fall, it leaves it free to benefit from higher rates. This benefit would be reduced only by the cost of the call option.

It follows from the preceding that a negative gap can be hedged against interest-rate increases through the purchase of put options. If interest rates increase, the gains in the put options will offset some of the losses associated with the repricing of liabilities at a higher cost. By the same token, a positive gap can be hedged against a decrease in interest rates through the purchase of a call option. If rates fall, the gains in the call option will offset losses associated with the positive funds gap.

Investors hedging individual assets in the options market occasionally follow the practice of employing put and call options simultaneously for the same securities. This strategy can include one of two approaches: the selling of a call option and buying of a put option or vice versa. The former approach affords protection against the possibility of falling prices while reducing the cost of such protection by selling a call option. This strategy can be employed when the bank believes that the likelihood of declining security prices is greater than the likelihood of rising prices. In essence this practice allows the bank to protect itself against higher interest rates and covers the cost of this "insurance" through the sale of the call option on the same assets. On the other hand, a bank with fixed-rate liabilities can hedge itself by simultaneously buying a call and writing a put option against these liabilities. This practice can be employed when lower rates and rising prices are anticipated. In other words, if a bank believes that the likelihood of rising security prices is greater than the likelihood of declining security prices, it will sell a put option to cover the cost of purchasing a call option. The call option will increase in value as interest rates decline and security prices increase.

One important limitation on the implementation of an options strategy is that a viable options market exists only for a small number of debt instruments. As of mid-1983, a viable options market existed for 90-day Treasury bills, 10-year Treasury notes, 30-year Treasury bonds, and Treasury bond futures (futures on a basket of Treasury bonds maturing between 15 and 20 years). The first two instruments are traded on the American Stock Exchange; the third, on the Chicago Board Options Exchange; and, the fourth, on the Chicago Board of Trade. Among these instruments the most active options market exists for Treasury bond futures. Options on GNMAs have been scheduled for introduction pending court approval. Options for other instruments are still in the planning stage. Bank participation in the options market is inhibited by some of the accounting and regulatory problems mentioned in connection with activity in the futures market.

Foreign-Exchange Risk

Just as in the domestic payments system, banks are at the center of the international payments system. They are the channels through which money transactions flow, and claims are settled, across national boundaries. Transacting over national borders usually requires some kind of exchange of money. Thus, banks have come to play an important role in foreign-exchange markets, in which they may operate for their own accounts and for those of their customers.

Although many U.S. banks handle foreign-exchange transactions, only banks with strong international departments act as dealers. These banks make and maintain a market in a limited number of currencies, buying and selling them as warranted by market conditions. Transactions are carried out by specialized traders who use telephones, teletype equipment, and video display terminals to keep in touch with other foreign-exchange dealers and independent brokers. Each foreign currency is quoted in two prices. These prices, or foreign-exchange rates, are frequently referred to as "double-barreled." One quotation represents the "bid" (purchasing) price of the foreign currency, the other—which is slightly higher—the "offer" or "ask" (selling) price. Dealers and brokers in foreign exchange profit from the difference (spread) between the bid and ask prices.

To provide their clients with foreign-exchange services, U.S. banks maintain inventories of foreign currencies. These are held in the form of demand deposits, denominated in the currencies of other nations, in foreign banks. As might be expected, these inventories fluctuate. They are augmented as U.S. banks purchase from their customers credit instruments (drafts) denominated in foreign currencies. These instruments, once cleared abroad, are credited to their accounts in foreign banks. Their inventories decline when they sell to their customers credit instruments payable in foreign monies. Banks maintain large foreign-currency inventories in the currencies that are in greatest demand, such as the pound sterling, the German mark, the Swiss franc, and the Japanese yen.

U.S. banks' foreign-exchange transactions can be retail or wholesale. At the retail level they deal with individuals and businesses that use the market to effect a foreign commercial or investment transaction. This group includes tourists, importers and exporters, portfolio investors, and multinational corporations. At the wholesale level the foreign-exchange activity of U.S. banks is geared toward maintaining an interbank market. This market enables them to balance their positions in foreign currencies, depending upon their daily trading activity in these currencies. Based upon the daily volume of each kind of currency bought and sold, banks may experience shortages or overages in their inventories of individual currencies. To adjust their positions in particular currencies, banks use independent foreign-exchange brokers. These brokers, by operating among banks, play an important role in the negotiation of trades in the interbank market. For a fee they put a bank with a shortage in a specific foreign currency in contact with one experiencing a surplus. The brokers preserve the anonymity of the transacting parties until the deal is closed, to prevent any influence of their names upon price quotations.

Use of an independent broker is but one method of temporarily adjusting a bank's shortage in a particular currency. Other methods include borrowing from a foreign correspondent bank appropriate amounts of the currency in shortage; using a "swap" arrangement with a foreign correspondent, whereby each party credits equivalent amounts of local currency to the other's account; and purchasing the needed amounts from a foreign correspondent, or through it, and paying accordingly. The basic characteristic of all these methods of adjusting shortages is that foreign-currency inventory is replenished through bookkeeping entries that transfer deposits denominated in various currencies from one holder to another. No money leaves the country of its origin; only the ownership of deposit balances changes.

Making or maintaining a market in foreign exchange entails risk. In 1973 the countries of the world shifted their currencies from a fixed rate of exchange to a system of floating rates. As a result exchange rates fluctuate on a daily basis, according to the forces of supply and demand in the marketplace. Because the exchange rates of currencies fluctuate, banks incur a risk of loss in the value of foreign currencies they hold. The international stability and value of a currency depend on several factors. The economic and financial conditions of a country, as reflected in its balance of payments, have a direct bearing on the value of its currency. Political instability or drastic changes in a country's political condition may cause its currency's position in the marketplace to deteriorate. Another significant factor is activity by speculators, who constantly seek to acquire undervalued currencies and divest themselves of overvalued ones. Still another force impinging on foreign-exchange markets is the action of central banks, such as the Federal Reserve System or the Bank of England. These may intervene to stabilize the value of their country's currency by shoring it up when it is weak or slowing its appreciation when it becomes too strong.

Serious losses can be realized if a bank holds large inventories of a currency whose price drops significantly. Losses can also result from bank speculation in foreign exchange. In 1974 foreign-exchange losses precipated the closing of the Bankhaus Herstatt in West Germany and contributed significantly to the closing of the Franklin National Bank of New York. Sizable foreign-exchange losses have, at one time or another, created crises for banks in England and Switzerland.

Banks guard themselves against foreign-exchange loss in part by realizing a spread between the bid and ask prices of currencies. In addition, the bank must conduct a sufficient volume of foreign-exchange business to allow gains and losses to offset each other. Moreover, close monitoring of events likely to cause changes in the values of currencies can help banks avoid losses. Finally, banks can hedge their foreign-currency positions by engaging in forward transactions. Foreign currencies are traded on a spot basis (for immediate delivery) or on a forward basis (for delivery on a specified future date, usually within 30, 90, or 120 days). The spot rate and the forward rate for a given currency will differ to the extent that the currency is expected to rise or fall in value. When the forward rate exceeds the spot rate, the difference is referred to as a premium; when the spot rate is higher, the difference is referred to as a discount. When a bank must make a large purchase in a particular currency, it hedges this position by selling that amount of the same currency in the forward market. In this way the bank is assured of being able to divest itself of that currency at a specified future date without incurring loss. By the same token, if a bank sells a particular currency to be delivered on a specified date, it can hedge this position by buying a similar amount in the forward market to protect itself against appreciation of this currency. These measures protect the bank from price fluctuations in the currency market but sacrifice the opportunity of realizing gains from unforeseen favorable movements in the price of currencies.

Forward exchange contracts are briskly traded wherever spot currency markets exist. These are found in the major international money markets: Amsterdam, Brussels, New York, Paris, Zurich, and London. These markets all trade in the world's major currencies; however, forward trading in currencies of less important countries is sporadic. For highly unstable currencies forward contracts are costly because of the degree of risk involved.

Another form of hedging currency transactions is trading in foreign-currency futures contracts. These differ from forward contracts only in that the trading is done in organized exchanges instead of being negotiated directly between banks and their customers. As a result, in the former case the contracts are standardized, while in the latter terms are determined by the negotiating parties.

Foreign-currency futures contracts are traded on the International Monetary Market (IMM), a division of the Chicago Mercantile Exchange. On the IMM contracts are available for pounds sterling, Canadian dollars, Dutch guilders, German marks, Japanese yen, Mexican pesos, Swiss francs, and French francs. During 1983 the most actively traded among these were the pound, the mark, the yen, and the Swiss franc. Another important exchange is the London International Financial Futures Exchange. The Mid American Commodity Exchange in Chicago received approval to trade foreign-currency futures contracts, but by late 1983 it had not yet begun to do so.

Defalcation and Theft

Defalcation refers to the appropriation of bank funds by employees, while theft refers to such acts as forgery, burglary, and armed robbery performed by outsiders. Defalcation results from the continual exposure of bank employees and officials to large sums of money. It is a problem of surety. It is by no means unknown that bank employees and officials occasionally succumb to temptation and appropriate some of a bank's funds for themselves. As long as individuals are subjected to the financial, social, and moral pressures of our free society, the possibility of bank losses due to defalcation will be present. Yet it is in a bank's interest to take all necessary precautions to prevent, to the extent possible, the losses and embarrassment that result from the dishonest acts of its employees and officials.

A bank may protect itself against loss resulting from defalcation by adequate fidelity insurance. In fact, losses from defalcation may be covered through a blanket bond that insures, in addition, the directors and the bank against many of the statutory and common-law liabilities, and against the various risks associated with the nature of bank operations. A bank may also protect itself through improvements in administration, such as using better protective equipment, clarifying the duties of officers and employees, and improving auditing systems. In the latter instance continuous checking (preauditing), staff cooperation, and frequent postaudits can deter fraud or detect it at a fairly early stage. The best that can be done, therefore, is to control the opportunities and to shorten the time between commitment of an offense and exposure.

Losses from theft by outsiders are insignificant compared with the magnitude of internal crime. Although theft losses can be covered by a blanket bond, banks have taken a variety of measures to safeguard against this risk. Some of the more important measures include the posting of guards in bank lobbies, installation of television and alarm systems, monitors, and limiting the amount of cash to tellers. ATMs present an additional exposure to theft that is protected against by making the machines physically strong enough to withstand break-in attempts and by placing them in highly visible locations.

With the growing use of computers in day-to-day operations, defalcation and theft have become more sophisticated. Experts on the subject place banks among the top victims of computer crime. Disgruntled or dishonest employees represent the greatest threat. Tellers, computer data-entry technicians, and even computer consultants have, through their positions of trust, succeeded in obtaining bank funds through various methods of computer manipulation. These include embedding unauthorized commands in programs, altering data, and making direct commands to the computer to transfer funds to a designated account in the bank (or perhaps in another bank), from which the employee can later withdraw them. Generally, computer theft involves a depositor who can successfully manipulate ATM codes and passwords, or an outsider who through sheer ingenuity uses a computer terminal to gain access to the bank's computerized money-transfer mechanisms.

Computer crime is often difficult to detect, especially since the computer can be programmed to erase all evidence of the act. In a notorious case of embezzlement by a bank computer consultant, exposure of the criminal occurred only after he bragged of his exploit.

Although no security measures are foolproof against computer theft, many preventive steps can be taken. These include careful use of codes and passwords that are frequently changed. Of course, such measures depend on human cooperation—for instance not divulging passwords through carelessness. However, researchers are actively seeking additional safeguards. One possibility under review is a computer that memorizes the use routines of its authorized operators at each terminal and turns off if a user's behavior does not fit the established pattern.

REGULATING RISK EXPOSURE

Legal Prescription and Administrative Regulation

U.S. commercial banking activity has evolved from an atmosphere of considerable freedom to one of increased regulation. Because banks were the first of the financial intermediaries to appear on the U.S. financial scene—and, more important, because they were the only institutions that created money (first in the form of bank notes and later in the form of demand deposits)—they have been subjected to various forms of government control. As a result the judgment of the individual banks has been guided by both legal prescription and administrative regulation in achieving and maintaining solvency. In other words, laws and regulations provide the framework within which banks are free to operate. Regulatory authorities have sought to ensure bank safety through restrictions of different kinds. Although details differ between national banks and state banks, the general principles are similar. Some of the major rules covering national banks can be conveniently summarized under the following groupings.

One set of rules prohibits banks from holding certain kinds of assets either by explicitly proscribing them or by limiting bank acquisitions to certain expressly defined forms of assets. For example, national banks are forbidden to deal in real estate, commodities, and stocks. However, they are allowed to hold stocks if they have been acquired as collateral on defaulted loans, in which case they must be disposed of within a reasonable time (customarily interpreted as five years). Other exceptions are few. National, and member state, banks must own stock in the Federal Reserve bank of their respective district as a condition for membership in the Federal Reserve System. In addition, they may own stock in Fannie Mae, a U.S.-sponsored government agency that provides a secondary market for Federal Housing Administration (FHA), Veterans Administration (VA), and conventional mortgages; in corporations established to engage in foreign banking activity (such as Edge Act corporations); and in such subsidiaries as a safe-deposit company or a real estate concern that has been established to own the bank building. Furthermore, national banks are generally forbidden to grant loans on the security of their own stock, nor are they allowed to buy their own stock in the market, since this would, in effect, reduce the actual protection of the depositors. Moreover, national banks are prohibited from extending loans to their examiners—for obvious reasons.

A more moderate form of regulation does not prohibit, but sets ceilings on, certain types of assets. For example, a national bank may not extend personal loans to its directors and executive officers in excess of $10,000. Loans to affiliates require designated types of securities as collateral. The loan size is subject to ceilings based on the type and amount of security the borrower can pledge. If the securities pledged are obligations of the U.S. government, the amount of credit extended cannot exceed the par value of the securities. If the securities pledged are municipals, they must have a par value at least 10 percent more than the amount of credit extended, while for any other securities the margin is even higher (20 percent of their market value).

Another set of rules takes the form of quality standards. National banks may not acquire bonds that are regarded by the principal rating agencies as predominantly speculative, unless such bonds are acquired by way of settlement of a doubtful claim. Also, secured loans must meet various requirements to assure that the bank has a valid and enforceable claim. For example, loans on leaseholds can be made only if the lease has a stipulated maturity beyond the maturity of the credit. Real estate loans must be secured by a mortgage, a trust deed, or any other instrument that gives the bank an enforceable lien on the property. Loans on securities can be made only if the securities are assignable, and provided the borrower gives the bank a power of attorney authorizing it to sell the pledged securities in the event of default.

Still another set of rules aims at promoting diversification. Many banks have long applied this principle in the management of their loan and investment portfolios, in an effort to reduce their overall risk exposure with little impairment of expected return. Regulatory authorities promote bank asset diversification by specifying the proportion of assets that may be held in certain form. For instance, the amount that national banks may lend to any one borrower on an unsecured basis cannot exceed 15 percent of a bank's capital. For loans secured by a readily marketable collateral, this limit may rise to 25 percent of bank capital. Also, holdings of securities of any one obligor (with the exception of U.S. government issues and general obligations of state and local governments) are restricted to 10 percent of a bank's capital. These are only a few of the areas in which bank loan and investment activities are constrained by legal bounds. Most of these regulations are designed to ensure that banks do not take undue risks in the use of their depositors' funds. These restrictions encourage diversification—compel it, in fact—in order to reduce the risk of asset depreciation. The rules also serve to strengthen the bank's independence from any one extremely large borrower.

Regulatory authorities also stipulate capital requirements at the time of a bank's establishment and capital-adequacy criteria in the course of its operations as a means of securing safety. (See Chapters 4 and 5.)

Another important device for increasing bank safety is deposit insurance, available to commercial banks through the FDIC. Although this insurance coverage is available on a voluntary basis, it is mandatory for national banks and state banks that are members of the Federal Reserve System.

The Failure Record of U.S. Banks

For several reasons bank failure is considered more serious than the failure of most other kinds of businesses. As with any business, bank failure represents a loss of investment to stockholders. In addition, it means the loss of deposits to the bank's individual and business customers (although since the advent of the FDIC, deposits up to $100,000 are insured against such loss). These funds may constitute the bulk of a family's savings or a business's operating capital. Thus the loss of a bank's aggregate deposits can have a devastating impact on a substantial segment of a community. Finally, a bank failure erodes public confidence in the banking system and, in extreme cases, may trigger other failures.

In the twentieth century most bank failures have occurred in the 1920s and 1930s as a result of economic conditions. Sharp recessions in the 1920s hit rural districts especially hard, and weaker banks in small towns and farm communities were forced to close. The Great Depression caused bank failures throughout the United States and in every economic setting. However, since the end of the depression and the beginning of FDIC operations in 1934, there have been very few bank failures; and they have resulted from mismanagement and criminal actions rather than from economic conditions. Small banks have been especially vulnerable. They often lack the resources to attract highly skilled management and the resiliency to absorb losses. Such ill-advised practices as granting excessively high-risk loans, investing too heavily in promotion, jockeying for bank control, and operating with too low a capital base have contributed to their failures. Criminal actions leading to bank failure have included embezzlement and collusion with borrowers.

Large banks have not been immune to failure. Some of the factors that precipitated the closing of small banks were also responsible for the failure or forced merger of large banks. The collapse of the United States National Bank of San Diego on October 18, 1973, represented the then largest bank failure in U.S. history. The deposits of the failed institution amounted to $932 million. A year later, on October 8, 1974, the dubious record was assumed by Franklin National Bank of New York, with deposits—at the time of closure—of $1.4 billion. Concerned about the effects of this failure on the public, the FDIC published newspaper advertisements throughout the country to assure the coverage of possible losses. Franklin's assets and deposit liabilities (along with certain other liabilities) were bought from the FDIC by the European American Bank and Trust Company, a New York-chartered bank owned by six large European banks. Although the official transfer was effected in one day, the actual process stretched over five months and involved a variety of federal and state agencies. Other large bank failures included the Hamilton National Bank of Chattanooga, Tennessee, with deposits of $336.3 million (February 1976); the Penn Square Bank of Oklahoma City, with deposits of $465 million (July 1982); the United American Bank of Knoxville, Tennessee, with deposits of $794 million (February 1983); and the American City Bank of Los Angeles, with deposits of about $294 million (February 1983).

One major purpose of bank regulation is to prevent bank failure by assuring the soundness of banks. Regulatory examination is intended to assure the bank's health by providing an accurate picture of its activities and performance at all times. Thus, problems can be spotted at their inception and corrective steps taken before the problems grow large or serious enough to threaten the bank. The FDIC has recently become concerned that increased deregulation of banks will hurt earnings and thus may result in more bank failures. Increased reliance on various forms of purchased funds and the more recent advent of interest-bearing demand deposits have raised the cost of funds for banks. This trend has created especially acute problems for small banks, which lack the skill to manage interest margins effectively. Thus, cost problems, in addition to bad loans, have been blamed for the increasing rate of bank failures in recent years. Since 1975 several years have seen more bank failures than had occurred in any year since 1942, with an especially dramatic rise in 1982. Table 9.3 displays the number of bank closings because of financial difficulties for every year since 1934.

The FDIC takes both preventive and remedial action with respect to bank failure. Preventive steps are taken to avert the adverse effects of bank failure upon the community. To forestall such failures, the

Table 9.3. Number of Banks Closed Because of Financial Difficulties, 1934-82

Year	No.	Year	No.	Year	No.
1934	61	1950	5	1966	8
1935	32	1951	5	1967	4
1936	72	1952	4	1968	3
1937	84	1953	5	1969	9
1938	81	1954	4	1970	8
1939	72	1955	5	1971	6
1940	48	1956	3	1972	3
1941	17	1957	3	1973	6
1942	23	1958	9	1974	4
1943	5	1959	3	1975	14
1944	2	1960	2	1976	17
1945	1	1961	9	1977	6
1946	2	1962	3	1978	7
1947	6	1963	2	1979	10
1948	3	1964	8	1980	10
1949	9	1965	9	1981	10
				1982	42

Source: Federal Deposit Insurance Corporation, *Annual Report* (Washington, D.C.: FDIC, 1982), I, p. 31.

FDIC may extend loans to the weak bank, place deposits in it, or purchase assets from it. When First Pennsylvania Bank was hit by a huge depositor run in 1980, the FDIC loaned it $375 million; and a group of banks loaned First Penn $175 million and extended a $1 billion line of credit. The arrangement has kept First Penn operating, and it has begun repaying the loans extended to it.

In recent years the FDIC has urged and facilitated mergers between weak banks and sounder ones in order to avoid bank closure and direct FDIC action on behalf of depositors. When an insured bank does fail, the FDIC takes remedial steps, acting as a receiver and making direct payments to insured depositors.

Besides protecting depositors against actual losses, the FDIC has the positive psychological effect of lessening the likelihood of bank runs. Before its establishment rumors of bank difficulties often precipitated mass withdrawals by fearful customers. Besides exerting severe (and perhaps crippling) pressure on banks, such runs intensified the atmosphere of panic that prevailed during recessions. With their deposits insured, today's depositors are far less likely to make panicked withdrawals. Thus, by its mere presence the FDIC contributed significantly to the stability of the banking system.

Early in 1983 the FDIC proposed measures designed to increase pressure on banks to keep themselves healthy. The proposals call for allowing the FDIC to make public the condition of weak banks and to increase the risk to depositors of more than $100,000 of loss of funds in the event of bank failure. In this way it is hoped that consumer vigilance will supplement regulatory efforts to promote sound banking practices. "There is no good substitute for the market to make businesses behave,"[1] James L. Sexton, director of the FDIC Division of Bank Supervision, told Congress in support of these proposals. Specific proposed actions include making public information on a bank's bad loans, graduating insurance premiums according to risk, and making public which banks are charged higher premiums.

NOTE

1. Eleanor Levitt, "FDIC Wants to Change the Rules of the Bank-Failure Game," *Miami Herald*, February 22, 1983, p. 9D.

SUGGESTED REFERENCES

Beazley, J. Ernest. "United American Officials and Associates Held 40% of Bank's Loans Before Failure." *Wall Street Journal*, March 7, 1983, p. 2.

Chicago Mercantile Exchange. *Understanding Futures in Foreign Exchange*. Chicago: Chicago Mercantile Exchange, 1977.

Comptroller of the Currency. "National Bank Participation in the Financial Futures and Forward Placement Markets." *Banking Circular* (BC-79, 3rd rev.), April 19, 1983, pp. 1-7.

Crosse, Howard D. and George H. Hempel. *Management Policies for Commercial Banks*. 3rd ed. Englewood Cliffs, N.J.: Prentice-Hall, 1980.

Koch, Donald L., Delores, W. Steinhauser, and Pamela Whigham. "Financial Futures as a Risk Management Tool for Banks and S&Ls." *Economic Review*, September 1982, pp. 4-14.

Kubarych, Roger M. *Foreign Exchange Markets in the United States*. New York: Federal Reserve Bank of New York, 1978.

Levich, Richard M. *The International Money Market*. Greenwich, Conn.: JAI Press, 1979.

McMillan, L. G. *Options as a Strategic Investment*. New York: New York Institute of Finance, 1980.

Parker, Jack W., and Robert Daigler. "Hedging Money Market CDs with Treasury-Bill Futures." *Journal of Futures Markets* 1, no. 4 (1982): 597-606.

Powers, M. J., and D. J. Vogel. *Inside the Financial Futures*. New York: John Wiley and Sons, 1981.

Sinkey, Joseph F., Jr. "The Collapse of Franklin National Bank of New York." *Journal of Bank Research*, Summer 1976, pp. 113-22.

In addition to maintaining solvency and liquidity, a bank must achieve a sufficient income on its portfolio to pay operating costs and provide a competitive return on the capital ventured in the enterprise. In the quest for income, management must always keep in mind the need for maintaining liquidity and solvency. In fact, it should never subordinate the need for liquidity and solvency to the income function. While income is definitely important, and clearly essential for the successful performance of a continuing banking operation, the aggressive pursuit of income per se, without regard to these other factors, could rapidly precipitate the collapse of the bank. The employment of bank funds must, in the first place, be consistent with the bank's liquidity needs and, second, be within the limits of the amount of risk that capital available for the portfolio can bear. Within the confines of these two basic policy considerations, efforts may be directed toward the realization of adequate income. Management has some choice regarding the way in which income may be sought and the way in which profits are used.

The importance of profits to commercial banks is hard to exaggerate. They are a decisive factor for the continued existence of a bank and its success as a going concern. Profits represent the return on the capital funds invested in the bank. In fact, it is for this return that shareholders are willing to supply the capital that will enable the bank to fulfill its role as the chief credit-granting institution in the economy. If the return on existing capital is not comparable with the returns on other investments, capital will, in the long run, be attracted to other economic pursuits. Profits, moreover, constitute an important source of bank capital. It is a common practice of banks to retain a relatively large portion of their earnings for capital additions. To the extent that profits are used for the payment of dividends, they have favorable effects upon the marketability and value of bank shares, thereby rendering it possible for the bank to return to the market and raise additional capital to finance expansion and improvements in banking practices. Profits also make it possible to pay competitive salaries and attract competent management. But depositors, too, benefit from bank profits, since they result in a stronger and safer institution capable of absorbing losses and protecting against the risks inherent in the banking business. Borrowers also have interest, indirectly, in bank profits. Bank policy of plowing earnings back into equity capital results in a larger capital account, and therefore in an increased lending and investing ability. With an increase in the size of capital, banks can make larger loans to any single borrower and invest larger amounts in the securities of any single issuer. Even those economic groups that do not directly use commercial bank services benefit indirectly from adequate bank profits. The reason is that bank profits contribute to the strengthening of the banking structure, which results in the safety of deposits and the availability of credit to the economy, with consequences that are felt throughout it and are reflected in the nation's economic welfare. This chapter starts with a discussion of the profitability considerations at the level of the individual bank, then proceeds to review the performance record of the banking industry.

PROFITABILITY OF THE INDIVIDUAL BANK

Factors Affecting Bank Profitability

A number of studies have sought to identify the key elements in a bank's formula for profitability. They have selected groups of banks for examination and attempted to correlate degree of profitability with such factors as size, ownership, market concentration, bank structure, advertising expenditures, and management characteristics. In all cases the researchers concluded that the primary factor distinguishing successful or high-performance banks from the rest of the sample was effective management.

Although strong and able leadership is difficult to quantify, its effects are apparent in the composition of the balance sheet and the distribution of expenses in the income statement. These studies indicate that a bank's asset management and funding practices can contribute to superior balance sheet management. Balance sheet management, coupled with control of operating costs, has the most significant effect on bank profitability. A 1983 study[1] found that the asset portfolios of the most profitable banks were relatively inexpensive to service because they contained a high proportion of securities in relation to loans. On the liability side successful banks held large volumes of demand deposits, thus incurring lower interest expenses, and relied heavily on equity funds, which entail lower accounting costs. As deregulation progresses, interest paid on deposits may come to have a more significant impact on their profitability. Last, profitable banks had lower noninterest expenses than could be explained by differences in their asset and liability portfolios. This evidence suggested that the managers of these banks exercised more effective control over operating costs.

These findings have important implications for both regulators and managers. The weight of the management factor in determining bank profits raises important questions for public policy. As was mentioned in Chapter 3, since the early 1960s regulators—in deciding on bank merger cases—have relied on the concentration factor as a proxy for the degree of competition in a particular market. If concentration does not affect bank profits to any significant degree, as these studies imply, the use of this criterion in bank merger cases should be reconsidered.

The importance of these findings for bank managers is apparent. Although asset and liability mix is significant, the efficiency of bank operations is no less important. In other words, managers should pay close attention to bank control over operating expenses. This calls for a careful analysis of these expenses if great savings are to be effected.

Assessing Bank Performance

Benefiting from the findings discussed above requires a good knowledge of the factors that go into an individual bank's expenses and revenues. For any analysis of revenues and expenses to be effective, it must cover each and every area of bank activity. Current performance can be evaluated through comparison with the bank's past performance or with the record of other banks of comparable size and scope of activities. In the latter instance banks face a basic difficulty. Revenue and expense information, based on figures submitted to regulatory authorities, is routinely published; unfortunately it does not lend itself to the kind of analysis that allows banks to evaluate and compare the performance of individual services or departments. Operating costs vary widely from one bank to another, depending not only on the scope of bank activities but also on the proportional volume of business in each area of activity. This diversity can be highlighted, for example, by reference to the operating costs associated with the processing of demand and savings deposits. One cannot compare the operating costs of two banks of the same size if their deposit makeup is different. Demand deposits are relatively costly to process because of their volatility; thus a bank with large proportion of demand deposits as opposed to savings cannot fairly compare its operating costs with those of a bank whose deposited funds consist largely of savings. Similarly, salary figures must be viewed in the context of the services offered by the banks involved; otherwise they are meaningless. Comparing the salaries paid by two banks of the same size is meaningless when one has an international department while the other relies upon its correspondent bank to perform such services.

Despite the difficulty in obtaining suitable figures, banks must do the best they can to arrive at standards for evaluating the profitability of various activities. Deciding whether to extend a loan or make an investment cannot simply rest on the probability of a profitable return; the expected size of that return must be determined and a judgment must be made whether it makes a positive contribution to the bank's profits and stockholders' wealth. In other words, knowledge of the spread between the yield and the bank's cost-of-funds rate is decisive in determining whether a specific loan or investment should be undertaken. This type of judgment focuses upon the need for detailed analysis of bank revenues and expenses, a process usually called cost analysis.

Cost analysis yields standards for evaluating the performance of each function within the bank. In other words, it enables management to exercise better control over the costs associated with the different functions. Comparing expense with volume yields per-item costs, upon which service charges are often based. Department heads and supervisors are apprised of costs in their departments to enable them to assume greater responsibility for the profitability of their departments.

With departmental performance constantly evaluated and monitored, senior management can more effectively plan a bank's future course of action. Armed with knowledge of current performance, senior management is in a better position to decide on the expansion, or perhaps contraction, of specific activities within the bank. In recent years concern over the cost of retail business, and the large volume required to make such business profitable, has led some large banks to consolidate their retail services or to concentrate on their corporate customers. A case in point is Chase Manhattan Bank, which discontinued its MasterCard operations in 1979. Another case is that of Bankers Trust of New York, which between 1980 and 1983 sold most of its city branches (76) and four subsidiaries in upstate New York in order to minimize its retail business and build its wholesale banking activities.

Technical Considerations in Revenue-Expense Analysis

Revenue and expense analyses vary widely, and individual banks may use more than one approach, depending on the specific purpose of the analysis. In addition, there is a strong subjective element in any form of cost analysis because many cost items cannot be allocated with precision to the appropriate banking function.

Salaries of senior management, for example, cannot be attributed to their various activities with absolute accuracy. First, how a senior bank officer allocates his or her time varies from day to day and week to week. Second, the value of the officer's contributions is not a direct function of time devoted to a particular project. Because of his or her particular blend of aptitudes and experience, the officer deploys his or her talents in a unique fashion. An idea worth a great deal may suggest itself in a flash, while negotiating a single loan may take hours. The senior officer contributes to the bank outside of work hours as well, making social connections that may bring additional business to the bank: participating in chamber of commerce activities, helping raise funds for the United Way and other drives, accepting speaking invitations, taking a leading part in urban renewal, or serving on the board of the local hospital or that of some other civic operation. The activities of junior officers can also be sufficiently varied to defy easy allocation.

Nevertheless, such approximations as can be made through observation and educated guesswork can prove useful. When these approximations are kept consistent from year to year and are considered in conjunction with known cost categories, the banks can meaningfully compare present performance with its own track record. Comparison with other banks, however, cannot be effectively carried out by means of an in-house allocation system that may differ from those of other banks.

Until the late 1950s only large banks typically undertook the difficult job of cost analysis. Working from the general ledger, they allocated the various expenses and revenues to individual departments and to functions within those departments. These functions were generally categorized as either fund-using (lending and investing) or fund-supplying (acquiring deposits and capital funds).

In 1958 the Federal Reserve Bank of New York began the development of a cost-analysis system that was both feasible and affordable for small banks. Today an expanded version of that system, called the Functional Cost Analysis (FCA) program, is available to all Federal Reserve member banks. The program is designed to help banks assess overall profitability and the profitability and efficiency of each bank function.

Participating banks are given instruction manuals and worksheets on which they enter expenses and revenue information. For difficult-to-allocate items (primarily salaries and wages), guidelines on how to

Table 10.1. Functional Cost Analysis: Credit Card Function, 1982

	15 Banks Deposits up to $50M		63 Banks Deposits $50M-$200M		60 Banks Deposits over $200M	
1. Number of sales slips deposited	68,068		170,177		1,141,712	
Volume	Dollars	Percent	Dollars	Percent	Dollars	Percent
2. Outstandings	592,851	92.01	2,754,701	93.78	19,575,636	94.07
3. Cash advances	51,429	7.98	182,569	6.21	1,233,080	5.92
4. Total credit card outstandings	644,281	100.00	2,937,271	100.00	20,808,717	100.00
Income						
5. Merchant discount	56,273	8.734	154,335	5.254	1,216,282	5.845
6. Finance charge interest	85,975	13.344	429,602	14.626	3,456,240	16.610
7. Subtotal	142,248	22.079	583,937	19.880	4,672,523	22.455
8. Net interchange fees	3,626	.563	20,594	.701	-9,613	-.046
9. Other income	12,117	1.881	67,274	2.290	512,741	2.464
10. Total Income	157,992	24.522	671,806	22.872	5,175,651	24.873
Expense						
11. Officer salaries	12,875	1.998	43,550	1.483	172,572	.829
12. Employee salaries	17,487	2.714	62,987	2.144	474,169	2.279
13. Fringe benefits	6,612	1.026	22,878	.779	143,422	.689
14. Salaries and fringe, subtotal	36,975	5.739	129,417	4.406	790,164	3.797
15. Data service	27,515	4.271	32,570	1.109	240,728	1.157
16. Furniture and equipment	3,602	.559	11,735	.400	89,181	.429
17. Occupancy	5,290	.821	20,803	.708	127,083	.611
18. Publicity and advertising	1,898	.295	11,473	.391	70,010	.336
19. Credit card activity and franchise fees	21,847	3.391	82,695	2.815	388,409	1.867
20. Other operating expense	13,629	2.115	79,660	2.712	531,817	2.556
21. Total operating expense	110,758	17.191	368,356	12.541	2,237,395	10.752

Earnings	Dollars	Percent	Dollars	Percent	Dollars	Percent
22. Net earnings before losses	47,233	7.331	303,449	10.331	2,938,256	14.120
23. Net credit losses	8,931	1.386	49,256	1.677	358,451	1.723
24. Net fraud losses	300	.047	5,083	.173	45,497	.219
25. Net earnings	38,001	5.898	249,109	8.481	2,534,307	12.179
Memoranda						
26. Cost of money	51,692	8.023	270,437	9.207	1,932,062	9.285
27. Net earnings after cost of money	-13,690	-2.125	-21,327	-.726	602,245	2.894
Miscellaneous Data						
Number of credit card personnel per bank						
28. Officers		.56		1.66		6.65
29. Employees		1.83		6.09		43.23
30. Total personnel (average)		2.39		7.76		49.88
Other credit card data						
31. Number of credit card accounts		2.269		10.176		59.813
32. Active accounts / total accounts	1,840	81.11	7,513	73.83	43,417	72.58
33. Active Accounts Paying Interest / Active Accounts		57.87		65.25		69.06
34. Active account average size	1,065	350	4,903	390	29,987	479
35. Cash advance average size	322	159	844	216	3,065	402
36. Sales slip average size	2,542,614	37	7,128,597	41	51,234,880	44
37. Average volume per dealer	87	29,136	274	26,015	11,654	4,395
38. 3-yr. average loan losses/credit card volume	13,035	2.023	42,671	1.453	405,348	1.948

Note: Details may not add to totals due to rounding.

Source: Federal Reserve Bank of New York, *Functional Cost Analysis: Average Banks* (New York: Federal Reserve Bank of New York, 1982), p. 38. Based on data furnished by 608 participating banks in 12 Federal Reserve districts. Available from the Federal Reserve Bank of New York.

make the allocations are provided. The Federal Reserve will make the more difficult allocations if the bank does not wish to or cannot. For this purpose, the Federal Reserve has designed a computer program that allocates items based on "experience factors" formulated from the information provided by other participating banks. This technique has helped to minimize inconsistencies of interbank comparisons. The participating bank receives a report that summarizes and compares, in a standardized format, its current year's operations with those of the previous year. In addition, the report includes, for comparative purposes, average figures on overall profitability and on the profitability of specific functions for banks of similar deposit size and percent of time deposits to total deposits, and of similar functional activity (for instance, similar composition of the loan portfolio). Additional information is also provided, including per-item costs and break-even points in various service categories. These facts provide the judicious banker, who recognizes the limitations of this information's applicability to his or her own bank, with additional tools to measure performance.

Table 10.1 is an example of the kind of information provided by FCA. It refers to banks that administered their own credit card plans or were a primary regional agent of a national credit card plan in 1982. The data provided identify, for different groups of banks, the average assets generated in 1982 from credit card business; the amounts of income, expense, and earnings involved; the number of personnel employed; and related data.

Applications of Cost Analysis

Cost analysis does not by itself improve bank performance. It can identify those areas where performance lags behind management's objectives and expectations, but improving profitability in those areas requires further analysis to determine the causes of sluggish performance. Then changes must be instituted to correct those problems. When the volume of transactions is large, even a small increase in income per transaction can make a substantial difference. Certain factors affecting a bank's profitability may be out of its control—for instance, prevailing local conditions that would not affect similar banks in other areas. Others may be a product of legislative action (taxes) or of the general level of economic activity (interest expenses) affecting all banks, regardless of location. Although these forces are beyond a bank's control, management has significant room to maneuver in controlling cost and improving earnings performance. One way to accomplish this is by increasing the productivity and efficiency of the bank. This can be done through such measures as improving physical layout, increasing specialization of personnel, improving organizational structure, simplifying processes and procedures, and introducing automation. Another way to improve earnings performance is through effective profit planning, which combines a means of effective cost control with profit maximization. Profit planning can take the form of a budget or of a long-range plan.

Budgeting

A budget is a financial plan that forecasts the results of a bank's operations in the year ahead. It includes a bank's expected revenues, expenses, and profits, based on management's well-reasoned objectives for every item in the asset-and-liability statement. In other words, a budget is a reflection of management's expectations regarding the volume and character of bank assets and liabilities for the coming year.

Preparation of the budget must be a collaborative effort. A good budget system requires that those responsible for carrying out the budget be involved in its preparation. This approach contributes to better communication between top management and middle management, and helps guard against unrealistic targets and unattainable objectives. Participation of all the branch managers and department heads in the preparation of the budget has additional advantages. It increases managers' understanding of the complexity of today's economic environment and prepares them to react faster to developing events. It enables each departmental manager and unit supervisor to better comprehend the relation of his or her activities to the totality of the bank's operations and the extent to which he or she contributes to bank profits. It improves internal coordination and contributes to better cost control and increased operational efficiency.

For all of the above reasons, budget inputs must come from all the branches and departments of the bank, the units that are accountable for performance. These inputs usually reflect the previous year's experience, adjusted for anticipated changes in the year ahead. These initial budget data are then combined into an integrated forecast by the comptroller's department, which is customarily responsible for the formulation of the annual budget.

Once approved, the budget becomes an effective tool of control. Departmental and branch managers can be provided with budgets for their own areas of responsibility and can be asked to operate within the confines of their budget. This approach enhances the monitoring of the results of each department and makes it more likely that the bank's operations will approximate the overall plan. If actual results deviate appreciably from the budgeted targets, management investigates the reasons for the deviations. Depending upon the factors responsible for such deviation, management may either revise the budget to reflect changing circumstances or take action to bring operations into line with the plan.

Long-Range Planning

A growing number of banks, in addition to budgeting, have been making use of projections that cover periods longer than the next year. This kind of projection, commonly referred to as long-range planning, usually covers a five-year period. The planning process begins with a set of overall goals for the bank for the period under consideration. For example, a bank's long-range goals may include a combination of the following:

- —To expand the sale of its services over a wider geographic area
- —To increase its share of the market through improved services and more specialized, or perhaps a wider array of, banking products
- —To train and develop successor management to ensure continuity of policies and direction
- —To contribute as a responsible corporate citizen to its community's economic life and growth
- —To identify its position in the light of ongoing changes in the banking industry (for instance, to branch across state lines, acquire other banks, become part of a multibank holding company, form its own holding company, and/or establish a physical presence in foreign markets)
- —To increase annual profits by 10 percent a year over the next five years, or to set a profitability objective in terms of target rates of return (for instance, return on total assets in excess of 1 percent and on average equity capital in excess of 13.25 percent).

Once a bank's goals are defined, management must determine appropriate strategies to attain the set goals. The formulation of strategies or development of activities constitutes, in effect, the bank's long-range plan. In other words, this plan is a quantification of the ideas on how to get the bank where it wants to be five years later. The solicitation of business from local companies through personal calls (call program) or the introduction of credit cards, pay-by-phone services, bank-by-mail facilities, and preauthorized bill payments are only a few examples of goals. Whatever the recommended strategies may be, they must be realistic; that is, their formulation should be based upon such considerations as the bank's human and physical resources, the size of its market, economic conditions, competitive and technological changes, and legal and regulatory developments.

Just as in the preparation of the budget, so here the component units within the bank are expected to contribute their inputs for the realization of the set goals. If, for example, management's objective is to increase annual profits (or assets) by 10 percent a year over a five-year period, this objective provides guidelines for profit planning by the bank's component units. Their inputs would be integrated and result in a long-range projection of revenues, expenses, and earnings. These projections, however crude, are valuable in determining a bank's future course of action and in calling management's attention to the need for solutions to perceived problems ahead. Frequent comparisons of actual results with projections permit management to take corrective action promptly or to modify the plan to reflect changes in the economic environment. Clearly, the planning process must be a continuous activity and not an intermittent one. Recognizing the importance of this activity, many large banks have planning departments that engage in long-range planning. Other banks assign responsibility for this activity to a management committee, while in many small banks this function is nonexistent, at least in a formal sense. Today's deregulated banking environment makes some form of planning essential if a bank wishes to maintain efficient operations and sustain a pattern of growth. This growth will ultimately benefit stockholders by increasing the return on their investment.

PROFITABILITY OF THE BANKING INDUSTRY

The performance record of the banking industry at the close of the 1970s and the beginning of the 1980s is shown in Table 10.2. Substantial weakness in business activity and employment in the early 1980s, along with high interest rates, exerted considerable pressure on the profitability of commercial banks. In addition to these domestic pressures, world recession affected the profitability of the U.S. banking industry by undermining the ability of some major borrowing countries to meet their payment schedules on debt owed to U.S. banks. As a result reported earnings for 1982 continued to drop from their 1979 peak, and return on assets declined to the levels of the recovery period that followed the 1973-75 recession.

The remainder of this chapter is in three sections. The first considers the composition of bank revenues, the second deals with the expense

Table 10.2. Income and Expenses as Percent of Average Assets, All Insured Commercial Banks: 1975-82[a]

Item	1975	1976	1977	1978	1979	1980	1981	1982
Operating income	7.20	7.18	7.23	8.09	9.49	10.87	12.89	12.32
Operating expenses	6.23	6.30	6.30	7.02	8.36	9.76	11.84	11.40
Earnings before taxes	.97	.88	.93	1.08	1.13	1.11	1.05	.92
Net income	.78	.70	.71	.77	.81	.80	.77	.72

[a]From 1976 on, data reflect both domestic and foreign operations.

Note: Details may not add to totals due to rounding.

Source: Federal Deposit Insurance Corporation, *Annual Report* (Washington, D.C.: FDIC, 1979), p. 191; and *Statistics on Banking* (Washington, D.C.: FDIC, 1982), p. 74.

side, and the third with commercial bank profits. Each of these sections is presented in relation to the corresponding category of the income statement for all insured commercial banks found in Table 10.3.

Components of Bank Income

Table 10.3 identifies the operating income of all insured commercial banks for the period 1977-82. Operating income data may be conveniently grouped under three headings: income from loans, income from investments, and other income. The relative importance of each is discussed below.

Income from Loans

As Table 10.3 indicates, income from loans is the largest source of income for commercial banks, amounting at year-end 1982 to $167.2 billion. This source expanded significantly during the period under consideration, as a result of both the larger volume of loans outstanding and of the higher rates of interest experienced during this period.

The next two income items are, in reality, products of lending transactions, even though the Federal Reserve does not classify them as such. The first, interest earned on "balances with depository institutions," represents, to a large extent, income realized from the placement of interbank deposits in the Eurocurrency market. This source of income is especially important for the large money-center banks, which are very actively engaged in international lending. The second income item is a composite of income derived from two transactions: the sale of federal funds and the purchase of securities under agreements to resell. As indicated in Chapter 7, a bank can earn interest income by lending some of its excess reserves at the Federal Reserve bank to another bank or by purchasing securities from cash-strapped dealer houses and banks under agreements to resell. Technically, both of these transactions are loans, since neither is exposed to the risks associated with investments. Combining the income earned from all of these items with that of loans boosts the contribution of the latter to an impressive 78.5 percent of bank revenues.

Since one of the two factors responsible for the recent growth in loan income is a higher lending rate, it is useful to identify the forces that determine these rates. Unlike rates on money-market instruments (such as Treasury bills), which are determined by the competitive climate of public markets, interest rates on bank loans are a product of direct negotiation between borrower and bank. This negotiated method of pricing credit arrangements is responsible for significant interest variation from one loan to another. Other considerations contri-

Table 10.3. Income of Insured Commercial Banks, 1977-82[a] (amounts in millions of dollars)

Item	1977	1978	1979	1980	1981	1982
OPERATING INCOME, TOTAL	90,358	113,582	150,282	190,771	248,800	258,491
Interest and fees on loans	58,991	76,182	102,192	126,954	163,510	167,196
Interest on balances with depository institutions	4,888	6,713	10,670	16,258	24,297	24,270
Income on federal funds sold and securities purchased under agreements to resell in domestic offices	2,476	3,682	6,126	8,764	12,270	11,392
Interest on U.S. Treasury securities and on obligations of other U.S. government agencies and corporations	8,864	9,384	10,686	13,465	18,107	21,125
Interest on obligations of states and political subdivisions of the U.S.	5,365	6,039	6,955	8,172	9,704	10,661
Income from all other securities	969	1,095	1,198	1,438	1,639	1,727
Income from direct lease financing	699	862	1,073	1,371	1,746	1,943
Income from fiduciary activities	1,980	2,139	2,376	1,739	3,179	3,620
Service charges on deposit accounts in domestic offices	1,807	2,049	2,529	3,187	3,920	4,594
Other service charges, commissions, and fees	2,409	2,937	3,642	4,360	5,308	6,229
Other income	1,910	2,499	2,835	4,063	5,119	5,732
OPERATING EXPENSES, TOTAL	78,792	98,480	132,391	171,267	228,576	239,247
Salaries and employee benefits	16,346	18,744	21,562	24,675	28,044	31,424
Interest on time certificates of deposit of $100,000 or more issued by domestic offices	6,763	11,737	18,179	24,891	39,301	37,703
Interest on deposits in foreign offices	10,216	14,558	24,524	34,941	46,696	41,749
Interest on other deposits	21,833	23,918	29,185	38,588	53,450	62,288

Expense of federal funds purchased and securities sold under agreements to repurchase in domestic offices	4,543	7,264	12,356	16,770	23,879	20,724
Interest on demand notes issued to the U.S. Treasury and other borrowed money	818	1,458	3,167	4,387	5,904	6,218
Interest on subordinated notes and debentures	392	448	501	546	617	661
Occupancy expenses of bank premises, net and furniture and equipment expense	4,980	5,585	6,281	7,354	8,598	10,026
Provision for possible loan losses	3,301	3,525	3,786	4,479	5,069	8,343
Other operating expenses	9,599	11,244	12,849	14,635	17,018	20,112
INCOME BEFORE INCOME TAXES AND SECURITIES GAINS OR LOSSES	11,566	15,101	17,891	19,504	20,224	19,244
APPLICABLE INCOME TAXES	2,832	4,162	4,742	5,019	4,624	3,657
INCOME BEFORE SECURITIES GAINS OR LOSSES	8,734	10,939	13,149	14,485	15,600	15,587
SECURITIES GAINS OR LOSSES, GROSS	142	-447	-650	-855	-1,583	-1,280
Applicable income taxes	43	-222	-300	-362	-726	-621
Securities gains or losses, net	98	-225	-350	-492	-857	-659
INCOME BEFORE EXTRAORDINARY ITEMS	8,833	10,714	12,799	13,992	14,744	14,927
EXTRAORDINARY ITEMS, GROSS	55	44	40	3	68	68
Applicable income taxes	8	-1	1	-14	12	-1
Extraordinary items, net	47	45	39	17	55	68
NET INCOME	8,879	10,760	12,838	14,009	14,799	14,996

[a]Data are from fully consolidated reports of income, including domestic and foreign offices.

Note: Details may not add to totals due to rounding.

Source: Federal Deposit Insurance Corporation, Statistics on Banking (Washington, D.C.: FDIC, 1082), p. 72.

buting to interest-rate variations include the degree of risk of a particular loan, the length of its maturity, the size of the loan, the cost of originating and administering the loan, the size of borrower balances brought to or maintained with the bank (compensating balances), and the existence of collateral.

In addition, bankers' outlook on the state of the economy and the future course of interest rates can affect the rates charged on specific loans. This outlook is in part affected by the Federal Reserve's actions to expand or contract the money supply. Interest rates tend to be higher in periods of tight monetary policy and lower in periods of monetary ease.

Income from Investments

Interest from investments constitutes the second largest source of bank income. The relative importance of this source is a function of the amount and types of investment holdings and their yields. At year-end 1982, for example, most of the investment income of insured commercial banks came from their holdings of U.S. Treasury issues and obligations of government agencies; these securities dominated bank investment portfolios. Next in importance was interest from municipal securities, whose major attraction for commercial banks is that their interest is exempt from federal income tax. Overall, the security income of insured commercial banks experienced a significant decline in the six-year period under consideration. Between 1977 and 1982 interest on securities declined from 16.8 percent of operating income to 13 percent. This development primarily reflects a declining ratio of investments to total assets.

Yields on securities have increased substantially in recent years. Table 10.4 shows the effective gross yield on investment portfolios for all insured commercial banks. Loan yields dropped in 1982. This was due to a decline in market yields and to an increase in interest forgone because of problem loans. On the other hand, yields on bank securities increased in 1982 by 0.76 percent over their 1981 level because of fewer problem credits.

Qualitative considerations in choosing the short- and intermediate-term investment securities that make up a bank's secondary reserves were discussed in Chapter 8. The considerations that guide the selection of long-term securities in the bank's bond portfolio will be discussed in Chapter 15. The bond portfolio represents a means of employing residual funds once liquidity needs have been met. The income derived from the bond portfolio is of two types: interest income and capital gains. The interest income generated by the bond

Table 10.4. Rates of Return on the Consolidated Investment and
Loan Portfolios of All Insured Commercial Banks, 1980-82

Item	1980	1981	1982
Securities, total	7.88	9.27	9.96
U.S. Government	9.38	11.38	12.19
State and local	6.03	6.72	7.19
Other	10.55	11.54	11.64
Loans, gross	13.71	16.37	15.20
Net of loan-loss provision	13.19	15.83	14.39
Taxable equivalent			
Total securities	10.23	11.73	12.49
Total securities and gross loans	12.88	15.26	14.57

Source: Barbara Negri Opper, "Profitability of Insured Commercial Banks in 1983," *Federal Reserve Bulletin*, July 1983, p. 490.

portfolio was included in the general discussion of interest income above. Bonds may also generate income in the form of capital gains. This is considered a different form of income because it is a function of the bonds' value at the time of their sale. Since they do not represent operating income, gains (or losses) are reported after income taxes have been deducted. As seen in Table 10.3, in 1982 banks sustained gross losses amounting to approximately $1.3 billion.

Although these losses appear to be substantial, it must be recognized that in many cases they resulted from the sale of bonds in order to free funds for loans, which represent a more lucrative deployment of funds. Such losses, which occur during periods of tight economic conditions and high interest rates (as was the case in the late 1970s and early 1980s), are offset by loss write-offs and the higher yields of the loans.

Other Sources of Income

At year-end 1982 other sources of bank income accounted for 8.5 percent of total bank revenues, small compared with the sources already discussed. This category includes income from trust department activities, direct lease financing, service charges on deposit accounts, other charges and fees, and other operating income.

Trust departments have the advantage of generating income through the sale of services without utilizing bank funds. They can be highly profitable if they have a good list of profitable accounts—that is, accounts that produce high earnings relative to expenses. However, some trust departments, small ones in particular, lack enough profitable accounts to make the department as a whole profitable. The existence of these departments is justified by banks' desire to offer a full range of services in order to attract customers. Trust income amounted to $3.6 billion in 1982, an increase of 83 percent over the amount earned in 1977.

The growing popularity of lease financing has enticed banks into this field of activity. Since the early 1960s many banks have created departments or established subsidiaries for the purpose of leasing assets to businesses. Although in 1982 income accounted for only 0.8 percent of operating income, this source is expected to become increasingly important in the years ahead.

Service charges imposed on deposit accounts help defray the cost of processing checks. The relative importance of this income for banks has declined in recent years for two reasons. First, there has been a reduction in the percentage of demand deposits, the source of almost all service charges on deposit accounts. Second, as a means of competing for demand deposits, many banks have reduced or waived service charges for depositors with large balances, and in some instances they have done away with charges completely. Presumably the value of the deposits to these banks more than compensates for the cost of servicing them; that is, the income earned from these deposits covers the cost of servicing them and provides a profit margin. Income from service charges accounted for 3.4 percent of total income in 1970, 2.0 percent in 1977, and 1.8 percent in 1982. Further declines may be offset by the service charges on money-market deposit accounts introduced in late 1982.

The growing number of services that banks have been offering in recent years constitutes still another source of bank income. That income is reported under "other service charges, commissions, and fees." This account includes a great number of items, such as fees for the servicing of loans (such as mortgages) held by other institutional investors, charges for the sale of drafts and the issuance of commercial letters of credit, various renting and leasing fees, and many other payments made for bank services. This category accounted for 2.4 percent of operating income at year-end 1982.

The item "other income" is a miscellaneous income category that typically includes income not elsewhere classified, such as income from underwriting activities. At year-end 1982 this category accounted for 3 percent of operating income.

Distribution of Bank Expenses

Under the heading "operating expenses" Table 10.3 identifies the composition and trends of bank expenses. As this table illustrates, expenses rose faster than income during the time period under consideration. Between 1977 and 1982, while income increased by 186 percent, operating expenses rose by 204 percent. The reason for this drastic increase was the steep rise in the cost of funds. The interest on deposits and other liabilities has grown over the years to become the banks' greatest expense item. Between 1977 and 1982 these interests increased from $44.6 billion to $169 billion, a dramatic growth of 280 percent.

The paragraphs that follow examine the various types of bank expenses.

Salaries and Employee Benefits

There has been a decline in relative importance of salaries, wages, and fringe benefits since 1962, resulting principally from the much faster rise of the other expense items of commercial banks (such as interest expense). In 1982 this item constituted 13 percent of operating expenses, compared with 41 percent 21 years earlier.

Interest Expense

As already mentioned, this category is by far the banks' largest expense item, representing 71 percent of operating expenses in 1982. This figure can be broken down into interest on deposits (59 percent) and interest on nondeposit liabilities (12 percent). There are two reasons for the dominant role of interest on deposits among bank expenses. First, there has been a marked increase in the percentage of time and savings deposits relative to total deposits. They rose from 37 percent in 1962 to 73.5 percent in 1982. Second, there was a significant increase in interest rates during this period, as a result of the inflationary pressures of the late 1970s and of the deregulation of interest-rate ceilings on retail deposits. This deregulation was initiated, as discussed in Chapter 6, with the enactment of the DIDMCA in 1980 and accelerated rapidly in 1982. By the end of that year, deregulated accounts in commercial banks contained $82 billion in savings and small time deposits. An especially popular account was the money-market deposit account, which became possible with the passage of the Garn-St. Germain Depository Institutions Act in December 1982. Because high promotional interest rates enticed the public further, more than $60 billion had been placed in these accounts at commercial banks by the end of that year.

Nondeposit liabilities, the other type of interest expenses included in this category, increased from 7.3 percent of operating expenses in 1977 to about 12 percent in 1982. This increase reflects not only the higher interest rates experienced but also a growing tendency by banks to rely upon these nondeposit liabilities to meet expanded loan volume. This category includes interest on capital notes and debentures as well as other borrowed money, and the expense of purchasing federal funds and selling securities under repurchase agreements.

Other Operating Expenses

Along with interest expenses and salaries, banks incur a variety of other operating expenses. One is that of occupancy of bank premises and acquisition of furniture and equipment. This includes maintenance, insurance, depreciation, and taxes on bank premises, in addition to salaries of all employees connected with the operation and management of the property. This expense totaled approximately 4 percent of operating expenses in 1982.

Another expense is provision for loan losses, since there is always risk associated with lending. As discussed in Chapter 5, the amount of earnings that can be placed into reserve for this purpose is closely controlled by the Internal Revenue Service. Although the amount of loan loss provisions totaled 3.5 percent in 1982, it is expected to decrease in the years ahead.

There are also some operating expenses not previously discussed that are essential for the functioning of commercial banks. These expenses amounted to 8.4 percent in 1982 and include such outlays as fees for legal work and for directors, as well as expenses related to computer software, examination by regulatory agencies, and transportation for employees on bank business. One of the important expense items in this group is publicity and advertising. The competitive environment in which they operate has increased banks' awareness of the need for advertising. Competition for the public's business in general and, recently, for the business of the lower-income groups has produced a marked increase in outlays for advertising. Along with advertising expense is a more common expenditure of day-to-day business, office supplies and printing. Banks use enormous amounts of drafts, notes, deposit and withdrawal slips, loan applications, and other forms.

Since banks deal with a great amount of risk in the course of their operation, the assessment made by the Federal Deposit Insurance Corporation to insure deposits, as well as premiums paid to insure other aspects of the banking business, are significant expenses. Banks carry far greater risks than one might assume. The possibility of burglary, robbery, embezzlement, and defalcation is uppermost in people's minds. However, losses from forged checks, losses of important documents, and errors and omissions in various documents are also possibilities that require insurance protection.

Along with these expenses is that of income taxes. Since banks are subject to the standard corporate income tax rates, these taxes become a significant expense incurred by commercial banks, accounting overall (before any allowance for securities losses) for $3.7 billion in 1982.

Bank Profits

The opening paragraph of this chapter stressed the importance of bank profits for different parties: stockholders, borrowers, depositors, and the economy at large. In summing up this chapter, therefore, it is appropriate to look at the profitability record of banks and assess how it compares with other key sectors of the economy. Table 10.5 shows the trends in the postwar rates of return for commercial banks and manufacturing corporations. During 1965 and 1966 banks had lower returns, then narrowed the gap, and overtook manufacturing corpor-

Table 10.5. Rate of Return on Equity Capital of All Insured Commercial Banks and That of Manufacturing Corporations, 1965-82

Year	Banks	Manufacturing Corporations
1965	9.2	13.0
1966	9.2	13.4
1967	10.1	11.7
1968	10.3	12.1
1969	12.0	11.5
1970	12.4	9.3
1971	12.4	9.7
1972	12.3	10.6
1973	12.9	12.8
1974	12.5	14.9
1975	11.8	11.6
1976	11.4	13.9
1977	11.7	14.2
1978	12.8	15.0
1979	13.9	16.4
1980	13.7	13.9
1981	13.1	13.6
1982	12.1	9.9[a]

[a]Average rate for the first three quarters of the year.
Source: Federal Deposit Insurance Corporation, *Annual Reports*; *Economic Report of the President* (Washington, D.C.: U.S. Government Printing Office, 1983), p. 261.

ations by 1969. However, by 1974 bank returns again fell behind, much of the decline due to increased risk. This risk was caused in large part by the necessity to compete in providing services in a faster-paced economy, as well as the desire to increase earnings.

The high rates of return compiled by other industries in recent years have made clear the need for banks to earn competitive rates. High rates of return are their only means of maintaining investor confidence and sustaining an ongoing expansion of their capital base. With the unparalleled competition that banks are encountering from other financial institutions, and with their profit margins squeezed by deregulated interest rates, we ask ourselves whether increased earnings will continue to provide banks with the means for maintaining an adequate level of capital. If this is the case, commercial banks will be able to function more efficiently and effectively than at any time in U.S. history.

NOTES

1. Larry D. Wall, "Why Are Some Banks More Profitable?" *Economic Review*, Federal Reserve Bank of Atlanta, September 1983, pp. 42-48; and "Why Are Some Banks More Profitable? A Statistical Analysis," *Economic Review*, Federal Reserve Bank of Atlanta, October 1983, pp. 44-51.

SUGGESTED REFERENCES

Candilis, Wray O. *Long-Range Planning in Banking*. Washington, D.C.: American Bankers Association, 1968.

Crosse, Howard D., and George H. Hempel. *Management Policies for Commercial Banks*. 3rd ed. Englewood Cliffs, N.J.: Prentice-Hall, 1980.

Federal Reserve Bank of New York. *Functional Cost Analysis: Average Banks*. New York: Federal Reserve Bank of New York, 1982. Based on data furnished by 608 participating banks in 12 Federal Reserve districts.

Ford, William F. "Using 'High Performance' Data to Plan Your Bank's Future." *Banking*, October 1978, pp. 40-41, 43-44, 46, 48, 162.

Ford, William F., and Dennis A. Olson. "How 1,000 High-Performance Banks Weathered the Recent Recession." *Banking*, April 1978, pp. 36-38, 41-42, 45, 48.

Haslem, John A. "A Statistical Analysis of the Relative Profitability of Commercial Banks." *Journal of Finance* 23 (March 1968): 167-76.

————. "A Statistical Estimation of Commercial Bank Profitability." *Journal of Business* 42 (January 1969): 22-35.

Haslem, John A., and William A. Longbrake. "A Discriminant Analysis of Commercial Bank Profitability." *Quarterly Review of Economics and Business*, Autumn 1971, pp. 39-46.

Kwast, Myron L., and John T. Rose. *Profitability Differences Among Large Commercial Banks During the 1970s*. Research Papers in Banking and Financial Economics, Financial Studies Section, Division of Research and Statistics. Washington, D.C.: Board of Governors of the Federal Reserve System, 1981.

———. "Pricing, Operating Efficiency and Profitability Among Large Commercial Banks." *Journal of Banking and Finance* 6 (June 1982): 233-54.

Payne, C. Meyrick. "Profitability Management: Banking's New Generation." *Bankers Magazine*, Spring 1977, pp. 51-57.

Reed, Edward, Richard Cotter, Edward Gill, and Richard Smith. *Commercial Banking*. 2nd ed. Englewood Cliffs, N.J.: Prentice-Hall, 1980.

Rhoades, Steven A. "Structure-Performance Studies in Banking. An Updated Summary and Evaluation." Staff Studies 119. Washington, D.C.: Board of Governors of the Federal Reserve System, 1982.

Warberg, Carla M. "Functional Cost Analysis—A New System Approach to Gauging Profitability." *Business Review*, Federal Reserve Bank of Dallas, August 1971, pp. 7-11.

11
CASH ASSETS

Part III indicated that in the employment of bank funds, management must be guided by the objectives of liquidity, solvency, and profitability. If a bank is to discharge its community obligations in a satisfactory manner and to continue as a going concern, it must seek to provide a rational solution to the fundamental conflict between liquidity and profitability. The manner in which management goes about resolving this conflict is the ultimate test of its efficacy and success.

Whatever management's approach may be in each individual case, this liquidity-profitability conflict underlies the increased diversification of bank uses of funds. These uses are customarily grouped into the following categories: cash assets, investments, loans, and other assets (a category covering a variety of items including fixed assets, such as buildings and land). The first three are the object of asset management—the process of allocating funds among alternative uses —on an ongoing basis. The last category is not normally dealt with on a daily basis, although when expenditures are planned for fixed assets, adequate cash provisions must be made. Part IV thus focuses upon the first three asset categories. While chapters 12 through 15 cover a bank's loan and investment portfolios, this chapter deals with cash assets and their management.

Cash assets are the most liquid resources a bank holds; they are immediately available with no risk of loss whatsoever. Although these assets produce no income, they perform a basic function for commercial banks. They enable them to meet their legal and day-to-day operating requirements. In the latter instance, cash assets ensure the ability of commercial banks to meet their customers' liquidity needs and cope with a volatile financial environment. Because they function as the first line of liquidity defense, these assets (as stated in Chapter 8) are also referred to as a bank's primary reserves.

It follows that banks need to maintain adequate primary reserves. Clearly, it is not possible to lay down fixed rules regarding the size of a bank's primary reserve account. What would be desirable for one bank might not be for another. Moreover, what would be desirable under one set of circumstances may not be desirable under another. Obviously, then, individual bank requirements should determine the size of the primary reserves, which must be sufficiently large to meet legal reserve requirements. Moreover, banks must carry additional funds, working reserves, which must be sufficient to meet day-to-day operational needs. The size of working reserves thus depends primarily upon the bank's operational requirements.

Primary reserves, as determined by legal and operational requirements, must be managed as efficiently as possible. Banks are profit-seeking enterprises, and maximum utilization of their resources is naturally desirable. Carrying sizable amounts of primary reserves means sacrificing income for liquidity. Since liquidity needs cannot be forecast with absolute precision, the size of primary reserves is a matter of judgment. Banks do not want to sacrifice income unnecessarily by holding idle reserves against possible liquidity needs that might not arise. They therefore should keep these nonearning assets to a minimum. The maintenance of minimum primary reserves is generally thought of as a test of good management. A skilled management shifts the burden of meeting all possible demands for funds to the investment portfolio, which is used by many banks to provide backup liquidity against their short- and intermediate-term needs while also serving as a residual haven for longer-term employment of bank funds.

TYPES OF CASH ASSETS

Cash assets are made up of the following accounts: cash items in process of collection, balances with correspondent banks and other depository institutions, balances with Federal Reserve banks, and cash in vault. These accounts make up a bank's money position. Each of them, depicted in Table 11.1, is discussed below.

Cash Items in Process of Collection

Cash items in process of collection include checks, promissory notes, and other matured items deposited at the bank by its customers for collection. The widespread use of checks in the U.S. economy contributes to rendering this account the largest of all cash assets. As

Table 11.1. Cash Assets Held by All Insured Commercial Banks, 1982

Item	Amount (millions of dollars)	Percent of Total
Cash items in process of collection	$ 68,358	32.4
Demand balances with commercial banks in the United States	34,899	16.5
All other balances with depository institutions in the United States and with banks in foreign countries	61,449	29.1
Balances with Federal Reserve banks	26,665	12.6
Currency and coin	19,616	9.3
Total	$210,990	100.0

Note: Details may not add to totals due to rounding.
Source: Federal Deposit Insurance Corporation, *Statistics on Banking* (Washington, D.C.: FDIC, 1982), p. 41.

shown in Table 11.1, at year-end 1982 cash items in process of collection accounted for 32.4 percent of cash assets of all insured commercial banks.

The size of this account varies significantly from one bank to another, and reflects in each case the volume of checks received and the time it takes for them to clear. Because these items represent nonearning assets, banks make every effort to speed their collection, in order to benefit from their conversion from nonearning to earning assets. As stated in Chapter 6, checks drawn on local banks are customarily cleared through the local clearinghouse. Checks drawn on out-of-town banks may be sent for collection to a correspondent bank or the Federal Reserve bank. In the latter case the individual bank receives credit in its reserve account within the time frame provided for by the Federal Reserve System. For some items credit may be received immediately, while for others (such as checks drawn on banks in distant parts of the country) credit may be deferred for up to three full business days. For items cleared through a correspondent bank, credit is received after the correspondent bank has received credit for the item(s) in question. However, some arrangements with correspondent banks provide for the immediate credit of the remitting bank's account.

Balances with Correspondent Banks and Other Depository Institutions

As indicated in Chapter 2, banks maintain demand deposits with other banks for more efficient check clearing and to compensate correspondent banks for the provision of varied services (such as lines of credit, international banking services, loan participations, federal funds transactions, and investment counseling). The specialized talents of larger banks and the scope of their operations render correspondent banking a vehicle for substantial economies of scale for smaller banks. However, the correspondent relationship is profitable for the correspondent bank as well. Indeed, large banks in regional and national money centers compete actively for these deposits. Their attractiveness is obvious—they can amount to a substantial source of interest-free funds that can be loaned and invested for profit. Even though the profit realized is an implicit interest payment for services rendered to the respondent bank, the arrangement is still profitable, since correspondent balances subsidize activities that the correspondent would ordinarily have undertaken in the course of its operations.

The high rates of interest experienced in the late 1970s and early 1980s led many banks to review their correspondent relationships. The high opportunity cost of maintaining relationships with too many correspondents or of holding larger-than-necessary balances led to the streamlining of these relationships and the reduction of balances to more reasonable levels. At year-end 1982 correspondent balances accounted for 16.5 percent of cash assets (see Table 11.1).

Just as domestic banks carry deposits with larger city correspondents, so U.S. banks that engage in international banking maintain accounts with foreign banks. In Table 11.1 this item is reported in the "All other balances" category, which also includes time and savings deposits maintained by domestic banks with other U.S. banks and depository institutions.

Balances With Federal Reserve Banks

Since enactment of the Federal Reserve Act of 1913, member banks have been required to maintain balances with their district Federal Reserve bank or branch equal to a specified percentage of their public deposits. This account, along with a bank's cash in vault, constitutes a bank's legal reserves. In addition to meeting reserve requirements, this account is used by banks to facilitate their financial transactions. For example, it is used as a channel for the payment of checks drawn on the bank and for the collection of incoming checks. This account is also used to effect payments to the U.S. Treasury and to other banks, or to collect from them. When banks borrow from the

Federal Reserve or other banks, this account is credited with the loan proceeds, and then debited at the time of repayment. At year-end 1982 all insured banks held 12.6 percent of their cash assets in the form of balances with the Federal Reserve banks (see Table 11.1).

Origin and Evolution

Wherever commercial banking has developed, the need for cash reserves has been demonstrated. At first the size of cash reserves held by commercial banks was merely a product of individual bank experience. The epidemics of bank failures in many nations proved, however, that banks were operating beyond the bounds of prudence. This fact led U.S. banking authorities to introduce prudent liquidity standards to ensure commercial bank ability to meet withdrawals of deposits in cash. Provisions for legally required reserves first appeared in the United States in 1863, with the passage of the National Bank Act. National banks located in central reserve cities were required to hold reserves equal to 25 percent of their deposits. Banks in reserve cities also had to keep reserves of 25 percent, but half could be in the form of deposits with national banks in central reserve cities. All other national banks, referred to as country banks, were required to keep reserves of 15 percent of their deposits, but 60 percent could be in the form of deposits with national banks in reserve and central reserve cities.

Because of the absence of a central bank in the United States, reserve regulations provided for a considerable degree of pyramiding—part of the reserves of country banks consisted of deposits with reserve city banks and part of these in turn were redeposited with central reserve city banks. The Federal Reserve Act of 1913 preserved the geographic classification of banks but modified reserve provisions, extending them to all member banks (national banks and state member banks), and required the maintenance of reserve balances with Federal Reserve banks. The Banking Act of 1935 authorized the Board of Governors to vary reserve requirements at its discretion over a substantial statutory range—an authority it has held ever since.

Although reserves were initally envisioned as a safeguard of bank liquidity, their original character has changed. Statutory regulations do not permit legal reserves to be depleted for any extended period of time. Indeed, the deviation allowed from legally required reserves is generally very little; excess or deficiency is limited to 2 percent of required reserves and can be carried forward up to the next statement period, but not beyond. Deficiencies in excess of this percentage are generally subject to a penalty equal to the discount rate plus two percentage points. Thus, required reserves can no longer be considered a significant source of liquidity, and hence a bulwark of protection. "Thus we find the paradox: in practice, a bank cannot depend on its legal cash-reserve requirement to meet deposit shrinkage; this must come mainly from other assets."[1]

In addition to possessing a low degree of liquidity, reserve requirements involve a loss of bank income. A bank's gross earnings, and in turn its net profits, are determined both by the amount of loanable and investable funds on hand and by the efficiency with which these funds are employed. Clearly, the required maintenance of legal reserves with regulatory authorities is a limiting factor on a bank's supply of loanable and investable funds, and hence on a bank's earnings prospects.

The function of legal reserves today is a very basic one. Their existence is justified not on the grounds of enforcing minimum liquidity standards of managerial prudence, but on providing a tool of monetary policy. Indeed, it is now generally recognized that reserve requirements serve primarily as a control device through which monetary authorities can influence the availability and cost of credit. By altering reserve requirements upward or downward monetary authorities can effectively decrease or increase the ability of commercial banks to lend and invest, and therefore affect the volume of bank deposits, the major part of the money supply. This manipulation of reserve requirements is, of course, dictated by the objectives of monetary policy.

Current Structure of Reserve Requirements

In 1972 the Federal Reserve System abandoned the traditional criterion of geographical location (reserve city, city, or country) in the determination of member bank reserves. Instead, it adopted a system of reserve requirements that, depending upon the type of deposit involved, provided for a multitiered structure of required reserves. For demand deposits reserve requirements were graduated according to deposit intervals and applied to those intervals of the deposits of each bank. For time deposits the reserve schedule was based on the maturity classification.

Enactment of the DIDMCA in 1980 brought important changes in reserve provisions. To increase Federal Reserve control over the monetary system, this act introduced uniform reserve requirements for all depository institutions (including commercial banks, mutual savings banks, savings and loan associations, and credit unions). Recognizing that all depository institutions offer at least one type of transaction deposit that is part of the money supply, it subjected these deposits to a uniform reserve requirement. Of all other deposits, only certain types of managed liabilities were subjected to reserve requirements. Under the terms of the DIDMCA, reserve requirements were imposed on three categories of deposits:

- Transaction accounts (demand deposits, NOW accounts, share draft accounts, ATS accounts, and any other account through which an automatic or telephone transfer of funds can be effected)
- Nonpersonal time deposits (time deposits of businesses and governments)
- Eurocurrency liabilities (deposit borrowings of U.S. banks from their offshore branches and foreign depository institutions).

Transaction accounts subject to reserve requirements are the total transaction accounts less cash items in process of collection and deposits due from banks. Cash items are excluded because they represent deposit liabilities, subject to reserve requirements, of other banks. Deposits due from banks are excluded because they are interbank deposits, which by definition are not part of the money supply. The derived net transaction accounts figure is subject to a two-tiered reserve requirement (see Table 11.2). At the present time the first $26.3 million is subject to a 3 percent requirement; amounts in excess of this figure, to a 12 percent requirement. Unlike the requirement for the

Table 11.2. Reserve Requirements of Depository Institutions (percent of deposits)

Type of Deposit and Deposit Interval	Depository Institution Requirements After Implementation of the Monetary Control Act	
	Percent	Statutory Range (percent)
Net transaction accounts		
$0-$26.3 million	3	3
Over $26.3 million	12	8-14
Nonpersonal time deposits by original maturity		
Less than 2.5 years	3	0-9
2.5 years or more	0	0-9
Eurocurrency liabilities		
All types	3	none

Source: *Federal Reserve Bulletin*, September 1983, p. A8.

first tier of accounts, which remains fixed, the act gave the Federal Reserve Board authority to alter the requirement on the remaining accounts within the range of 8-14 percent. The act also authorized the Federal Reserve Board to adjust the breakpoint figure annually, to reflect the growth in the transaction accounts held by all depository institutions. Thus, from the $25 million that was initially set by the act, the breakpoint has gradually been adjusted to the present $26.3 million level.

As implied by the current reserve requirement on transaction accounts, small deposit institutions are generally favored over large ones. The Garn-St. Germain Act of 1982 carried this further by providing that the first $2 million of reservable liabilities (transaction accounts, nonpersonal time deposits, and Eurocurrency liabilities) at all depository institutions would be subject to a zero percent reserve requirement. The Federal Reserve Board is authorized to adjust this amount annually. This provision completely exempted some 24,600 institutions, including approximately 18,400 with total deposits of less than $2 million. At the other extreme, institutions with net transaction accounts in excess of $26.3 million are subject to the highest reserve requirements. Clearly, the intent of the Federal Reserve Board is to control the larger institutions more effectively because of their growing role and importance in the financial system. These institutions, in addition to the private and public deposits they hold, are the depositories for many small and medium-size deposit-type financial intermediaries. Their failure would contribute to the collapse of these intermediaries and undermine the country's economic life.

The DIDMCA provided no reserve requirements for the time and savings deposits of individuals and households. However, it stipulated requirements for the time and savings deposits owned by a depositor that is "not natural person." Clearly subject to this requirement are large CDs, which represent the major type of nonpersonal time deposits. The reserve requirement against these deposits was set at 3 percent, applying initially only to maturities under four years. Here, too, the Federal Reserve Board was given the power to alter these requirements within the range of 0 to 9 percent, and to change them according to maturities.

On Eurocurrency liabilities the DIDMCA gave the Federal Reserve Board unlimited power, leaving the matter of reserve ratio or statutory range of permissible ratios to its discretion. The intent of this provision was to give the Board a free hand in preventing banks from relying on foreign deposit borrowing to fund domestic activities on a reserve-free basis. Required reserves against such borrowing were set at 3 percent.

To provide for an orderly transition and to facilitate the compliance of all depository institutions with its reserve provisions, the DIDMCA provided for phase-in periods. All existing nonmember banks and thrift institutions were given an eight-year phase-in period ending on September 3, 1987. In the course of this period, these institutions were permitted to maintain reserves with certain approved institutions (such as correspondent banks that are members of the Federal Reserve), provided the latter passed through the reserves to the Federal Reserve System. Existing member banks were given approximately a three-year phase-in period from the November 13, 1980, effective date, depending upon whether their new required reserves were greater or less than their old ones. All newly established depository institutions were given a two-year phase-in period from the date they opened for business.

The reserve requirements described in the preceding paragraphs do not exhaust the reserve provisions of the DIDMCA. This act also provided for supplemental reserves on transaction accounts of not more than 4 percent, if deemed essential by the Federal Reserve Board. However, unlike the basic reserves described above, supplemental reserves would earn interest at a rate to be determined by the average earnings on the Federal Reserve's portfolio. A final provision of the DIDMCA grants the Federal Reserve Board emergency powers in dealing with extraordinary circumstances, authorizing it to impose on depository institutions additional reserve requirements at any ratio on any liability. These reserves may be imposed for up to 180 days and require, because of their extraordinary nature, prior consultation with the appropriate Congressional committees.

Although the above reserve provisions apply to all banks and other deposit institutions, it is worth noting that state banks that are not members of the Federal Reserve System must also comply with the reserve requirements of their respective states. Although there is significant variation from one state to another, state reserve requirements are in many instances similar to those of the Federal Reserve. More important, state laws define required reserves much more broadly than does the Federal Reserve. For example, many states qualify as legal reserves—in addition to vault cash—correspondent bank balances, cash items in process of collection, and, in some cases, federal and state government securities.

Calculating Reserve Requirements

To facilitate compliance with reserve requirements, the Federal Reserve has developed standard operating procedures for banks to follow. Institutions with total deposits under $15 million (small depositories) file a report of their deposits once each quarter, in March, June, September, and December. The quarterly reporting period covers the seven-day period that begins on the third Tuesday of the given month and ends the following Monday. The average daily deposits of this one week (also referred to as the computation period) determine the daily average required reserves for each week of a full calendar quarter (maintenance period) beginning one month after the computation period. For example, a bank's average daily deposits the week of the third Tuesday to the following Monday in September will determine the required reserves for each week from the third Tuesday in October through the second reserve week in January. Similarly, a bank's average daily deposits during the third reserve-computation week in December will set the weekly required reserves for the quarter running from the third Tuesday of January through the second reserve week in April, and so on. The quarterly reporting system for small depository institutions was introduced by the Federal Reserve System in order to ease reporting requirements for these institutions.

For institutions with total deposits over $15 million, required reserves are to be satisfied on the basis of two different accounting systems: the contemporaneous reserve accounting system, which applies to transaction accounts, and the lagged accounting system, which applies to nontransaction accounts. Introduced on February 4, 1984, the contemporaneous reserve accounting system requires depository institutions to post reserves against their checking-account deposits on the basis of the current level of those deposits. A schematic presentation of this system is provided in Figure 11.1. The reserve computation period for all the reservable liabilities of a bank stretches over a two-week period beginning on a Tuesday and ending on a Monday. The maintenance period for transaction accounts is almost concurrent, beginning on a Thursday and ending two weeks later on a Wednesday, affording banks only a two-day lag to make final adjustments in their actual reserve position and meet reserve requirements on the settlement date. For nontransaction accounts the two-week maintenance period begins 17 days after the end of the computation period. As a result bankers have a 30-day lag from the end of the computation period to the settlement date to satisfy reserve requirements on nontransaction accounts. This lag gives ample time to adjust actual reserve balances. Moreover, since reserve requirements against nontransaction accounts are small, bankers have minimal problems in meeting required reserves against them. Most reserve management problems relate to transaction accounts.

Figure 11.1. Reserve Computation and Maintenance Cycle under the Contemporaneous Reserve Accounting System

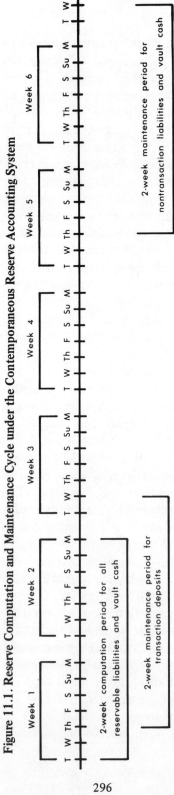

Source: Board of Governors of the Federal Reserve System.

Subjection of the transaction accounts of all depository institutions to the contemporaneous reserve accounting system is expected to enable the Federal Reserve to exercise more effective control over the supply of money. Prior to its introduction in early 1984, the Federal Reserve provided for lagged reserve accounting for all deposit accounts. Introduced in 1968, this system made no distinction between deposit types, and required reserves for all reservable liabilities —for any given week—were satisfied two weeks later. Over the years use of the lagged reserve accounting system drew considerable criticism from economists. The essence of their criticism was that by allowing banks a two-week lag to scramble for reserves on the settlement date, this system contributed to wide swings in the rates of growth of the money supply, thus undermining the effectiveness of monetary control. These critics contended that the Federal Reserve's inability to keep the money supply within bounds in the months following October 1979 was in part attributable to the interference of the lagged reserve accounting system.

Table 11.3 reproduces a member bank's weekly "Report of Transaction Accounts, Other Deposits, and Vault Cash" (form 2900), filed with the district Federal Reserve bank or branch that holds its reserve account. This report identifies the daily volume of deposits of the sample bank on a seven-day basis, from Tuesday through the following Monday. With the bank closed on Saturday and Sunday, deposit data for these two days are the same as those recorded the preceding business day—in this case, Friday. The same principle applies to holidays. Daily deposits and vault cash figures are aggregated in column 8 and averaged in column 9. This report and a similar one to be filed by the bank the following week, are combined to calculate required reserves. Whatever the amount of required reserves may be, it should be borne in mind that because of differing reserve accounting systems, the maintenance period for these reserves is different; for transaction accounts it is nearly contemporaneous, while for other reservable liabilities it is lagged. Thus, in any 14-day maintenance period banks' actual reserve balances must satisfy requirements for different deposit accounts. Regardless of what requirements are being met in a given maintenance period, the process of computing required reserves is always the same. The only differences are in the data inputs.

Table 11.4 identifies the steps involved in determining the sample bank's required reserves. The starting point is the member bank's average daily deposit balances during a given 14-day computational period. To simplify the process we may use the data of Table 11.3 (specifically of column 9) and assume that they reflect 14-day averages.

Table 11.3. Report of Transaction Accounts, Other Deposits, and Vault Cash (millions of dollars)

Report All Balances as of the Close of Business Each Day to the Nearest Thousand Dollars

Item	Column 1 Tuesday	Column 2 Wednesday	Column 3 Thursday	Column 4 Friday	Column 5 Saturday	Column 6 Sunday	Column 7 Monday	Column 8 Total	Column 9 Daily Average
A. TRANSACTION ACCOUNTS									
1. Demand deposits									
a. Due to banks	20,383	20,036	20,035	20,148	20,148	20,148	20,227	141,125	20,161
b. Due to other depository institutions	12,325	12,218	12,385	12,101	12,101	12,101	12,118	85,349	12,193
c. Of U.S. government	5,012	5,062	5,352	5,347	5,347	5,347	5,353	36,820	5,260
d. Other demand	106,622	106,005	105,291	105,654	105,654	105,654	107,498	742,378	106,054
2. ATS accounts	12,894	12,684	12,830	12,576	12,576	12,576	12,568	88,704	12,672
3. Telephone and preauthorized transfers	3,102	3,131	3,190	3,200	3,200	3,200	3,191	22,214	3,173
4. NOW accounts (including "Super NOWs"), share drafts	72,455	69,511	69,295	70,563	70,563	70,563	71,269	494,219	70,603
5. Total transaction accounts (must equal sum of items A.1 through A.4)	232,793	228,647	228,378	229,589	229,589	229,589	232,224	1,610,809	230,116
B. DEDUCTIONS FROM TRANSACTION ACCOUNTS									
1. Demand balances due from depository institutions in the United States	22,580	16,629	4,454	5,565	5,565	5,565	4,666	65,024	9,289
2. Cash items in process of collection	26,568	33,285	38,299	40,961	40,961	40,961	38,290	259,325	37,046

298

C. OTHER SAVINGS DEPOSITS, INCLUDING MMDAs

1. Money-market deposit accounts (MMDAs), personal	376,247	375,436	375,698	375,769	375,769	375,769	375,332	2,630,020	375,717
2. Money-market deposit accounts (MMDAs), nonpersonal	25,821	26,238	24,873	25,838	25,838	25,838	25,818	180,264	25,752
3. Other savings deposits personal	285,563	285,525	286,408	285,650	285,650	285,650	285,744	2,000,190	285,741
4. Other savings deposits, nonpersonal	14,172	14,276	14,136	14,111	14,111	14,111	14,080	98,997	14,142
5. Total other savings deposits, including MMDAs (must equal sum of items C.1 through C.4)	701,830	701,475	701,115	701,368	701,368	701,368	700,974	4,909,471	701,353

D. TIME DEPOSITS

1. Personal	2,130,885	2,127,303	2,138,075	2,169,168	2,169,168	2,169,168	2,137,217	15,040,984	2,148,712
2. Nonpersonal with an original maturity of less than 2.5 years	80,909	81,110	81,990	81,283	81,283	81,283	81,283	569,141	81,306
3. Nonpersonal with an original maturity of 2.5 years or more	4,180	4,180	4,198	4,198	4,198	4,198	4,198	29,350	4,193
4. Total time deposits (must equal sum of items D.1 through D.3)	2,215,974	2,212,593	2,224,263	2,254,649	2,254,649	2,254,649	2,222,698	15,639,475	2,234,211

E. VAULT CASH

	9,897	10,409	9,405	9,489	9,489	9,489	9,405	67,583	9,655

Source: Prepared by author.

Table 11.4. Calculation of Required Reserves

Item	14-Day Averages of Daily Data (thousands of dollars)	Required Reserves (percent)	Reserves (thousands of dollars)
Transaction accounts			
Total transaction accounts	$ 230,116		
Less deductions	46,335		
Net transaction accounts	183,781		
Initial amount subject to reserves	26,300	3	$ 789
Remaining amount subject to reserves	157,481	12	18,898
Total transaction reserves			$ 19,687
Savings and time deposits			
Nonpersonal savings			
Money-market deposit accounts	23,652[a]	3	710
Other savings	14,142	3	424
Nonpersonal time < 2.5 years	81,306	3	2,439
Other reservable obligations	0	3	—
Eurocurrency transactions	0	3	—
			$ 3,573
Total reservable deposits and obligations			23,260
Vault cash			9,655
Daily average balance to be maintained at the Federal Reserve bank (before carry-over)			13,605

[a]Adjusted to reflect the current $2.1 million in reservable liabilities subject to zero percent reserve requirements. These funds are to be deducted from money-market deposit accounts; if these are nonexistent or contain less than the allowable exemption, then the funds are to be deducted from net NOW accounts, net other transaction accounts, nonpersonal time deposits, or Eurocurrency liabilities, in that order.

Source: Prepared by author.

Transaction account balances would first be netted out by deducting demand balances due from depository institutions in the United States and cash items in the process of collection. The resulting net figure is then subjected to the statutory reserve requirements of Table 11.2. Accordingly, the first tier of net transaction accounts ($26.3 million) subject to reserves is multiplied by 3 percent and the excess by 12 percent. Similarly, the bank's nonpersonal time and savings deposits subject to reserves are multiplied by the corresponding reserve requirements stated in Table 11.2. The same process is followed for other reservable liabilities, if any. The final step involves the adding of the various amounts of reserves against the different accounts and subtracting vault cash to determine the average daily required reserves to be held at the Federal Reserve bank. In the example given in Table 11.4, the sample bank must maintain an average daily balances of $13.6 million for the reserve period under consideration.

Banks do not have to meet required reserves each day. A shortage early in the reserve maintenance period can be offset by a surplus later on, and vice versa. Despite the flexibility afforded by the use of averages and lagged accounting, bankers do not always succeed in meeting their reserve target. Recognizing this difficulty, the Federal Reserve has followed the policy of providing for a carry-over allowance, which permits banks to carry forward into the next reserve period a reserve deficiency or excess (limited to 2 percent of the average daily required reserves for the current maintenance period). In the example of Table 11.4, the maximum allowable carry-over of reserve deficiency or excess into the next reserve period would be $272,100. An excess or deficiency cannot be carried forward to additional periods following the period in which the excess of deficiency occurs. However, alternation of reserve excesses and deficiencies from one period to another is permitted, provided the amounts involved in the carry-forward process are within the allowable range. In other words, a deficiency in one period can be offset by an excess in the next period, and vice versa.

A bank with reserve deficiencies in two consecutive periods, or a reserve deficiency of more than 2 percent in any reserve period, is subject to a penalty. As indicated earlier in this section, the penalty rate on the deficiency is two percentage points over the going Federal Reserve bank discount rate. If the bank is consistently deficient, the Federal Reserve bank may enforce reserve requirements through moral suasion (by suspending membership privileges, or denying a bank holding company application, for example). Ultimately, the Board of Governors may revert to the courts and initiate cease-and-desist proceedings against the violators. To avoid the penalties and sanctions, banks try to manage their reserve positions in a manner consistent with prescribed reserve accounting procedures.

Cash in Vault

Banks hold relatively little cash in their vaults to meet their day-to-day operating requirements. Such cash usually represents only a small percentage of the bank's primary reserves and is held to meet daily requests for coins and paper money. As might be expected, vault cash requirements vary widely among banks, and at any particular bank they vary from season to season. Experience teaches each bank when the heavy drains come (that is, on an annual, monthly, or weekly basis) as well as the times when a heavy cash inflow may be expected.

Since banks are the public cash depots, management must look at it as a service function not only to keep on hand the cash that regular and exceptional circumstances will call for, but also to keep it in the denominations and form that are demanded. Most banks replenish their cash supplies from the nearest Federal Reserve bank or branch, though some still get direct shipments from their city correspondents. The amount of cash in vault, then, is frequently related to the distance between a bank and its cash source, distance being measured in terms of the length of time needed to acquire such cash.

During the early 1960s the reserve-requirements regulation changed to permit member banks to include vault cash in computing their required reserves. This seemed justified on two counts: currency, which is the main component of vault cash, is chiefly in the form of Federal Reserve notes, which basically are the same as reserves in the Federal Reserve banks; and banks located a considerable distance from the Federal Reserve banks must hold more vault cash than those closer to their source of new currency.

Although member banks can count vault cash in meeting reserve requirements, they frequently try to minimize these holdings. Not only is it a question of a nonearning asset; it is also a problem of surety (that is, the risk of armed robberies or defalcating tellers). The least-cash-possible principle has been gaining widespread acceptance among banks. Thus banks with excess vault cash resulting from favorable over-the-counter balances may use them to replenish their reserves with the Federal Reserve banks or with correspondent banks, to pay off their borrowings from the Federal Reserve bank, or to increase their earning assets. At year-end 1982 vault cash accounted for only 9.3 percent of the cash assets of all insured commercial banks.

MANAGING THE MONEY POSITION

Since cash assets produce no income, every effort is made by banks to manage them as effectively as possible. Effective cash management involves keeping the amount of funds held to meet legal and day-to-day operational requirements at a minimum. In many banks this task has been assigned to the money manager. In well-managed banks the money manager will carefully evaluate the cost-benefit relationship of the demand-deposit balances held with correspondent banks. He or she will strive to process and collect cash items as rapidly as possible, so that the bank can benefit from their early conversion from nonearning to earning assets. The money manager will take into account seasonal fluctuations and the bank's proximity to the Federal Reserve bank when determining the amount of vault cash holdings at any specific time. The most time-consuming task, however, is to make sure that the bank meets its legal reserve requirements within the time constraints discussed in the preceding section. Controlling the volume of bank balances at the Federal Reserve bank is a demanding task. The manager must see to it that during any maintenance period, reserve balances are, on average, at the target level, given the 2 percent carry-over provision—that is, neither too high (because excess reserves cause the bank to sacrifice earnings) nor too low (because a reserve deficiency would be subject to a penalty charge).

To attain this objective, the money manager must develop a reserve strategy. A basic component of this strategy is the bank's required reserves. Because of the contemporaneous reserve accounting system, the reserve computation period and the reserve maintenance period overlap by 12 days. As a result the money manager can establish only a tentative reserve target through the maintenance period until the exact reserve requirement is known at the end of the reserve computation. Once the reserve target is known, the next step is to meet it—that is, to ensure that the bank's reserve position matches the current period's requirement. The difficulty of this task stems from the effect that daily transactions may have upon reserve balances as the settlement date approaches. As stated earlier in this chapter, reserve balances at the Federal Reserve bank are affected daily by all the transactions through which payments flow into or out of the bank. Obviously, the larger the bank, the greater the number of transactions affecting its daily reserve position, and hence the more complicated the task of the money manager. Indeed, in many large money-center banks the size and frequency of transactions are such as to warrant continuous oversight of these banks' reserve positions. By contrast, smaller banks generally experience transactions of more limited size and frequency, which reduces the need for constant monitoring of reserve balances. Regardless of size, the need to meet reserve requirements within the maintenance period is similar for all banks.

Forecasting the Reserve Position

Because of the immediate and unpredictable effect of daily trans-actions upon reserve balances, many banks try to forecast their ex-pected positions on a day-by-day basis during the maintenance period. The large money-center banks incorporate reserve management into their overall asset planning process. As a result the reserve position of these banks is forecast by econometric models and is controlled with-in the framework of their other activities and plans. Other banks try to forecast their reserve positions through use of simpler statistical techniques. One such technique involves identifying the various trans-actions affecting reserve balances daily, measuring their effect on the bank's reserve position carried forward from the preceding day, and deriving the bank's new net reserve position for each day. Since the outcome of future events cannot be predicted with complete certainty, probabilities may be incorporated into these computations. In other words, probability coefficients may be attached to the range of likely reserve positions for each day. The ensuing computations would de-termine the mean reserve position and deviations (weighted for prob-ability) from that mean. On the basis of these data, the money man-ager will then plan the course of action to be followed in order to meet reserve requirements. Other banks, especially small ones, do not engage in any formal planning. The money manager has some idea of the seasonal and other influences on the bank's reserve position at particular times of the year.

However rigorous or lax the methodology used, the resulting fore-casts or anticipations should be based on all the transactions that in-fluence a bank's reserve position on a daily basis. These reflect all the different services offered by the banks and the scope of its operations. Some of the more important kinds of transactions deserve mention. The net clearing of checks is the principal factor influencing a bank's reserve position. Frequently this figure is forecast on the basis of known influences and recurring seasonal patterns. Loan contracts must be taken into consideration because they represent funds flow-ing out as loans and back in as scheduled payments. Maturity dates for securities and certificates of deposit are also noted.

Other transactions incorporated into these forecasts include the planned purchases and sales of securities, currency and coin orders, transfers of funds into or out of correspondent accounts, and Treasury calls on tax and loan accounts. The financial officers of important corporate customers may be contacted to provide information on their plans for large deposits or withdrawals. Some of these officers may be willing to cooperate with the bank and provide advance notice of their future transactions on a regular basis.

This and other information is collected by the money manager's office or—as it is generally referred to—the money desk, and is used to estimate the resulting change in reserve balances from one day to another and to determine the bank's net reserve position for each day of the maintenance period. In time the money desk will have the opportunity to cross-check each day's forecast against actual figures and to test the validity of the underlying assumptions. Differences between actual and expected amounts can be studied, and the insights gained will contribute to more realistic forecasts in the future.

Adjusting the Reserve Position

However closely monitored and well-managed the reserve position may be, problems are unavoidable. Unforeseen inflows or outflows can occur at any time during the maintenance period, and it is up to the money desk to decide what course of action is warranted and when to put it into effect. Clearly, developments early in the maintenance period offer more latitude for adjustment than last-minute ones. In the latter instance any adjustment may be very costly, since other banks are in the market at the same time, trying to balance their reserves before the close of the settlement date. A need for corrective action frequently surfaces on Fridays. Since most banks are closed during the weekend, the reserve balance that the bank achieves Friday afternoon will also be its balance for Saturday and Sunday. Thus, a large Fed Wire inflow late on a Friday afternoon, assuming a reasonably balanced reserve position, would result in sizable excess reserves. If Monday is a holiday, the bank would be locked into a surplus reserve position for three days. Unless the money manager anticipates offsetting transactions during the remaining working days of the maintenance period (such as Tuesday and Wednesday), the bank will forgo income unnecessarily. In such a case the money manager may adjust the bank's excess reserve position by placing these funds profitably—by selling federal funds, purchasing securities through repurchase agreements, or purchasing securities outright (such as Treasury bills).

The opposite situation will arise if a bank sustains an outflow of funds. For example, an unexpected outflow on the settlement date, assuming a reasonably balanced reserve position, would result in a reserve deficiency and a need for immediate corrective action. The money manager of the bank would have a choice of alternatives in the final hours of the reserve period. A decision will have to be made and transactions executed in short-term liabilities or in short-term assets. In other words, it is a matter of deciding between using liability-management or asset-management techniques in adjusting the bank's reserve position. In the former instance, funds may be raised quickly by purchase of federal funds, borrowing of Eurodollars, selling of securities under repurchase agreements, or borrowing from the Federal Reserve bank. Any of these techniques ensures the immediate availability of funds and makes possible the rapid adjustment of a bank's reserve position. Alternatively, the money manager may opt to sell short-term assets or use the proceeds of maturing short-term assets to adjust the reserve position.

Two of the considerations that weigh significantly in deciding which of the alternatives to use will be the duration for which the additional reserve funds are needed and the cost involved in choosing one alternative over another. It may, for example, be found more costly to sell securities than to borrow from another bank, particularly if the market price of securities has declined or if the additional funds to correct the bank's reserve position are needed only overnight. Again, it may be found more desirable to borrow funds than to call in outstanding loans. The methods more frequently used by money managers for short-run adjustments are the liability-management techniques mentioned above (other liability-management techniques are not customarily relied upon because they take more time to execute). But to effect long-run adjustments in the reserve position, money managers are more likely to liquidate short-term assets. In the final analysis the choice between using asset or liability liquidity in adjusting the bank's reserve position is entirely up to the individual bank. Not infrequently such choice reflects the overall reliance of bank policy upon either type of management: asset or liability.

NOTE

1. Roland I. Robinson, *The Management of Bank Funds*, 2nd ed. (New York: McGraw-Hill, 1962), p. 71.

SUGGESTED REFERENCES

Brick, John R. *Commercial Banking, Text and Readings*. Haslett, Mich. Systems Publications, 1983.

Cargill, Thomas F., and Gillian G. Garcia. *Financial Deregulation and Monetary Control*. Stanford, Calif.: Hoover Institution Press, 1982.

Gilbert, R. Alton. "Lagged Reserve Requirements: Implications for Monetary Control and Bank Reserve Management." *Review*, Federal Reserve Bank of St. Louis, May 1980, pp. 7-20.

Hempel, George H., Alan B. Coleman, and Donald G. Simonson. *Bank Management, Text and Cases*. New York: John Wiley and Sons, 1983.

Hoffman, Stuart G. "Reserves Management Strategy and the Carry-Forward Provision." *Monthly Review*, Federal Reserve Bank of Atlanta, August 1976, pp. 102-09.

Knight, Robert E. "Guidelines for Efficient Reserve Management." *Monthly Review*, Federal Reserve Bank of Kansas City, November 1977, pp. 11-23.

Laufenberg, D. E. "Contemporaneous versus Lagged Reserve Accounting." *Journal of Money, Credit and Banking*, May 1976, pp. 239-45.

Mason, John M. *Financial Management of Commercial Banks*. Boston: Warren, Gorham, Lamont, 1979.

McKinney, George W., Jr., and William J. Brown. *Management of Commercial Bank Funds*. Washington, D.C.: American Institute of Banking and American Bankers Association, 1974.

"Member Bank Reserve Requirements—Heritage from History." *Business Conditions*, Federal Reserve Bank of Chicago, June 1972, pp. 2-18.

The core function of commercial banks is the granting of credit. Although banks offer a wide spectrum of financial services, lending has traditionally been their main function. Banks profess experience, expertise, and flexibility in lending, which give them a clear competitive advantage over all other financial institutions. Bank credit has been responsible for the development and growth of many small and moderate-size businesses that otherwise would have withered and died. By providing credit, banks have contributed to the growth of their respective communities and the advance of local economic well-being.

Aside from its public service character, bank lending is a quite profitable activity. In fact, it is the most profitable activity of commercial banking, and hence the greatest contributor to bank profits. Income from loans and loan-related activities accounted at year-end 1982 for 78.5 percent of total operating income. The remaining 21.5 percent was contributed by the many other activities of commercial banks.

The loan function is important on other grounds. Lending is instrumental in creating and maintaining good deposit relationships, which are essential for the furthering of bank lending. The close and continuing contact established with the borrower is also instrumental in broadening the market for other bank services.

The above helps explain the prominent place of loans among bank assets and, more specifically, vis-à-vis investments, a bank's second major category of earning assets. There are distinctive differences between the acquisition of each of these assets. As noted earlier, investments constitute open-market purchases of securities, some of which serve as secondary reserves, while loans constitute direct customer demand for funds. Investments are evidences of interest-bearing debt offered for sale in the open market, and the acquiring bank does not anticipate establishing a continuous or permanent relationship with the issuing company. In other words, the acquisition of securities is generally conducted impersonally and is influenced by objective criteria, such as relative interest rate, quality of the issue (rating), maturity, and marketability. Banks purchase these securities either at the time they are issued or later on, by acquiring them from other investors in the open market. A loan, on the other hand, is arranged through direct, face-to-face negotiation between the borrower and the lending bank, and hence is personal. Bank lending is thus influenced significantly by subjective criteria, such as the borrower's character, the type and length of the borrower's relationship with the bank, and the new business potentially generated for the bank.*

These differences between loans and investments make apparent the need for well-formulated loan policies and practices. Sound lending policies and practices are reflected in the quality of the loan account and, hence, in bank solvency. Throughout most of the history of commercial banking, the quality of the loan portfolios has been closely linked with banks' solvency. This traditional link between the quality of loans and banks' solvency exists because banks' loan portfolios contain the bulk of their assets. This chapter will provide a historical overview of the evolution of loan portfolios and will describe the current nature and scope of commercial bank lending activity. The historical view is essential because it ties past experiences to the present and focuses upon the factors that have influenced and shaped loan portfolios then and now.

EVOLUTION OF THE LOAN PORTFOLIO: A HISTORICAL VIEW

Loan portfolios have existed since the early days of commercial banking, in response to theories of bank liquidity management. Four different theories of liquidity can be identified: the commercial-loan theory, the shiftability theory, the anticipated-income theory, and the liability-management theory. The first three relate to asset management, and the last focuses on the management of liabilities.

The Commercial-Loan Theory

The commercial-loan theory of credit—also referred to as the "real bills doctrine"[1]—dates back to the eighteenth century and is of English origin. Formulated by Adam Smith in *The Wealth of Nations*, it influenced commercial banking activity in the United States from

---

*The line of distinction between loans and investments is often only a fine one. Thus, we may find hybrid types that defy watertight classification in one category or the other. Examples of such hybrid types are the loans made by a group of banks (syndicated loans) to a single borrower and the private placement of corporate bonds with financial institutions.

colonial times through the 1930s. It exerted significant influence on the National Bank Act of 1863 and the Federal Reserve Act of 1913, the cornerstones of U.S. banking legislation.

According to this theory, the earning assets of commercial banks must be in the form of short-term, self-liquidating loans extended to businesses for the financing of their inventory needs. In other words, banks should be financing the processing of goods and their movement from the production to the consumption stages. These loans were viewed as self-liquidating because they generated the means for their repayment—that is, the goods acquired or produced on credit, when sold, provided the funds to repay the loan. By financing this type of loan, banks, it was held, would possess the most liquid earning assets, and therefore would be able to meet their demand-deposit liabilities when called upon to do so. Banking was thus related to the financing of commerce, which helps explain the original reference to the institutions extending this kind of loan as "commercial" banks.

The commercial-loan theory encompassed elements of bank management and monetary policy. According to this theory, if banks were to limit their lending to advances for short-term commercial purposes, the supply of money would have the desired elasticity. It was reasoned that if trade increased, this increase would give rise to a large volume of real bills (promissory notes). As these real bills are discounted at banks, demand deposits will increase, and so will the quantity of the circulating medium of exchange. Control over the quality of credit was therefore sufficient to ensure that the proper quantity of money would follow. The expansion of the circulating medium of exchange was expected to be in proportion to the growth in the volume of business activity. Similarly, if business is declining, fewer real bills will be created as older ones mature and are paid off, and consequently the total of discounted loans in bank portfolios will diminish—and with it the total of demand deposits. A contraction of the circulating medium of exchange was therefore expected to accompany a decline in business activity.

The quantity of money in circulation at any time was thus viewed as being in direct relationship to the state of business activity. By creating deposits against good self-liquidating commercial notes, banks were expected to provide a system that would be automatic, sound, and adjusted to the needs of trade. The role of commercial banks was therefore presumed to be passive—banks accompanied and facilitated changes in business but did nothing to induce them.

The commercial-loan theory has three basic weaknesses. First, it ignores other types of credit needs, such as loans to finance the acquisition of equipment and machinery, or the purchase of residential and nonresidential property and consumer goods. As a result other kinds of financial institutions—such as savings and loan associations, credit unions, and finance companies—were formed to serve these credit needs of individuals and businesses. Second, it rests on an overly cautious view regarding deposit withdrawals. It assumes that all demand depositors will withdraw their funds at the same time. Experience has shown that demand deposits possess a higher degree of stability than is assumed by the theory. Since withdrawals are to a large extent offset by simultaneous deposits, the bank need not confine itself to short-term placement of these funds. Third, in periods of recession or depression, loans may not be self-liquidating because many borrowers have difficulty in repaying them. But under normal circumstances, too, short-term loans may not be self-liquidating. For example, a firm's continued need for working capital or use of the loan proceeds to purchase long-term assets may force the bank to renew the loan. Thus, what was officially characterized as a short-term loan may effectively become long-term.

Despite the limitations of the commercial-loan theory, many bankers still favor short-term, self-liquidating loans over other types. Risk exposure is easier to evaluate and is generally more limited than with other loans. Also, even though banks have numerous options for meeting their liquidity needs, these loans continue to represent an important source of liquidity.

The Shiftability Theory

This theory holds that as long as a bank's assets are shiftable (readily marketable), its liquidity is adequately maintained. For example, if loans can be discounted to the Federal Reserve bank or if their collateral can be readily sold in the event of default, they are deemed to be sufficiently liquid. Similarly, securities, which can easily be converted to cash, possess a high degree of liquidity. In essence, the shiftability theory considers the marketability of an asset to be the main source of liquidity, and hence to be the qualifying attribute for its acquisition by a bank.

Originated by H. G. Moulton in 1918,[2] this theory became increasingly popular during the long bull market of the 1920s. Entry of the United States into World War I and the need to finance the war led to the issuance of large—by contemporary standards—amounts of government bonds (the Liberty Loan bonds and later the Victory Loan bonds) that raised public debt from $1 billion to $26 billion. To encourage banks to buy these bonds, the Federal Reserve System amended the Federal Reserve Act and allowed banks to offer these securities as collateral against their borrowings from Federal Reserve banks. Advances collateralized by government securities were thus placed on an equal footing with the discounting of real bills at the Federal Reserve banks. This development, along with the growth of a national market for government issues, made these securities an attractive asset for commercial banks. Convinced that government securities were more marketable than loans, and hence a superior source of liquidity, banks were drawn into the government securities market.

Although prior to World War I it was considered inappropriate to purchase or hold securities, some banks held such securities among their assets. This was generally true of national banks, which were required by law to maintain securities as collateral against their issues of bank notes. In all other instances, holdings of securities were in violation of the prevailing principles of banking theory, if not of practice.

The booming securities markets in the 1920s led banks to include corporate bonds and foreign bonds in their investment holdings and to engage in investment banking activities. Banks' investment excesses during this decade were criticized in the early 1930s and led to legislation that restrained much of their investment activities. The legislation of this era and, more important, the prevailing economic conditions led banks to expand their holdings of government securities to sizable proportions. Economic conditions were affected by two major events: the depression of the 1930s and World War II. In the 1930s the depression brought in most countries both a sharp decline in the private demand for loans and a substantial increase in government borrowing to finance budgetary deficits. Throughout World War II commercial banks bought substantial amounts of government securities, as a result of both a huge increase in government borrowing and a contraction in the demand for loans by private borrowers.

Commercial banks thus became important holders of government securities, which far outstripped the volume of bank loans. The paramount position of the Treasury among commercial bank borrowers is reflected in the relevant data of the era. In 1945 Federal Reserve member bank holdings of U.S. government securities reached an unprecedented height, accounting for 73 percent of the earning assets of all member banks. If all other securities held by these banks are taken into consideration, investments constituted 79 percent of their earning assets and loans but 21 percent. The change in the composition of commercial banks' earning-asset portfolios during this period and the general trend since the 1830s is shown in Figure 12.1. Drastic

Figure 12.1. Pattern of Loans and Investments in Total Earning Assets of Commercial Banks, 1834-1975 (percent)

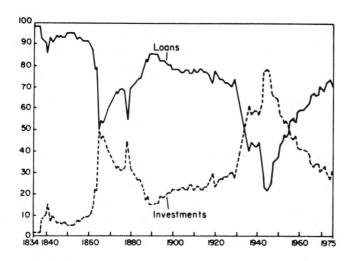

Note: Data are based upon all commercial banks except for the period 1865-95, when national bank statistics were used.

Sources: U.S. Department of the Treasury, *Annual Report of the Comptroller of the Currency*, 2 vols. (Washington, D.C.: U.S. Government Printing Office, 1897); U.S. Department of Commerce, Bureau of the Census, *Historical Statistics of the United States: Colonial Times to 1970*, 2 pts. (Washington, D.C.: U.S. Government Printing Office, 1975); Board of Governors of the Federal Reserve System, *All-Bank Statistics: United States, 1896-1955* (Washington, D.C.: Federal Reserve System, 1959); *Federal Reserve Bulletin*, various issues.

as it may have been, this shift in banks' earning-asset portfolios was but a deviation from a historic asset distribution pattern in commercial banking. Indeed, throughout banking history loans have exceeded investments, usually by a wide margin. This normal asset pattern also characterizes the post-World War II period.

The Anticipated-Income Theory

With the end of World War II, the composition of the earning assets of commercial banks began to change as resources shifted back from the government to the private sector. The spectacular rise in the loan demand of the immediate postwar years provided commercial banks with strong incentives to expand their loan portfolios, and hence to increase bank earnings. However, the almost exclusive reliance of Federal Reserve policy throughout this period on bank credit restraint to promote a sustainable rate of economic growth and to counter inflationary pressures led commercial banks to monetize part of their holdings of government securities in order to meet the postwar credit needs of the nation's expanding economy. Thus banks began to make loans that were of longer maturity, covered a much wider variety of borrowers, and extended to many more purposes than originally envisaged. More important, however, this move reflected the ongoing changes in banking attitudes. The sharp decline in the demand for loans in the 1930s had generated substantial pressures upon banks to seek and consider new outlets for their funds. These pressures, accentuated by the banks' dwindling proportion of savings flowing into nonbank financial institutions, forced important changes in bank attitudes toward extending maturities in their loan portfolios. Moreover, bank management had acquired more experience in meeting deposit withdrawals and had gained more confidence in its ability to design portfolios that were only partly composed of short-term or highly liquid assets. In other words, they had found that through prudent asset management, a mixture of very liquid and not-so-liquid assets could achieve the desired degree of overall liquidity.

Thus, the loan portfolios of commercial banks in the postwar years have included such items as intermediate- and long-term loans to consumers, homeowners, and business firms that would not qualify as liquid assets under the traditional theory of bank liquidity and would qualify only in part, if at all, under the shiftability theory. However, loans of this type do qualify under the "anticipated-income theory" of liquidity developed in 1949 by Herbert V. Prochnow.[3] This theory argues that a bank can maintain its liquidity if loan repayments are scheduled on the basis of the anticipated income of the borrower rather than the use made of the funds or the collateral offered. Thus, in making loans of the type cited above, this theory suggests that banks should rely on debtors' income and its coverage of debt-service requirements. This coverage is determined on the basis of inclusive cash-flow projections, which ordinarily provide a reliable indication of the quality of the loan being financed. Hence, the future cash flow of the borrower, rather than the nature of particular transactions being financed, assures the self-liquidating character of a loan because it will determine a borrower's overall ability to meet interest and principal payments as they fall due. If the debtors' anticipated income is estimated correctly, the bank will have a flow of funds that can be used to meet depositors' claims and/or other loan demands. During normal times bank lending of this type would function in about the same way as bank lending based on the commercial-loan theory of liquidity.

The Liability-Management Theory

Since the early 1960s the loan portfolios of commercial banks have been affected by the emergence of a new theory, which became known as the liability-management theory. As stated earlier, liability-management banking was originated by large New York City banks under strong pressures at the time: growing demand for loans as the economy experienced recovery from the 1960-61 recession, plus an inadequate growth of deposits at these banks. According to this new doctrine, it is no longer necessary for a bank to observe traditional liquidity standards if it can go into the market and bid for funds whenever it experiences a need for liquidity. In other words, a bank can meet its liquidity needs by creating additional liabilities. There are a number of possible sources on which the individual bank may draw to meet liquidity needs during the last phase of periods of cyclical expansion, such as issuing CDs, purchasing federal funds, borrowing at the Federal Reserve, issuing short-term notes, and borrowing from the Eurodollar market. The importance of these sources and the impact of Federal Reserve regulation upon their effectiveness have been discussed in chapters 6 and 7.

Liability management has been viewed as a major banking innovation and, as such, it has significantly influenced the outlook of bankers. It is a far cry from traditional banking and the need for short-term, self-liquidating commercial loans. Bank lending is symptomatic of new attitudes that are becoming increasingly general in the banking industry. There is no longer such a thing as a standard bank loan or borrower. Although some classes of borrowers and loan arrangements are more characteristic than others, bank lending has been evolving in response to new opportunities. For the most part opportunity has been the mother of innovation, to paraphrase an old saying. The fact that banks have been so alert to opportunities and so resourceful in exploiting them is a plus factor in any assessment of the U.S. financial system.

One of the relatively new areas of banking activity, and an adjunct to business lending, is lease financing. It began in the early 1960s and today involves a sizable number of banks. It is a unique means of financing the capital-goods needs of businesses without actually lending to them. Finance leasing of equipment ranges from office equipment to commercial aircraft and oceangoing tankers. The bank purchases the asset at the request of the lessee, who assumes virtually all responsibilities of ownership, including maintenance and payment of insurance and taxes. The profitability of leasing derives primarily from the bank's ability to depreciate the leased chattel for tax purposes.

LENDING ACTIVITY OF COMMERCIAL BANKS

Although loans can be classified in a variety of ways, the most meaningful presentation of statistics on the lending activity of commercial banks is by borrower or purpose for which funds are used. This criterion is commonly employed by regulatory authorities in identifying the scope and magnitude of the lending activity of commercial banks. Table 12.1 presents information regarding the loans of all insured commercial banks in 1982. At the close of 1982, loans outstanding totaled more than $1 trillion, compared with a mere $38 billion in 1947. The various types of loans and their relative importance are shown in Table 12.1 and reflect the current pattern of customer credit demands. The first three loan categories are the dominant ones, accounting for about 85 percent of the total. The various types of loans made by banks are discussed below.

Commercial and Industrial Loans

More than one-third of all loans granted in 1982, according to Table 12.1, were commercial and industrial loans. These loans are usually much more important, both relatively and absolutely, for large money-center banks than for middle-size and small banks. Part of the rise in large money-center bank lending came from foreign business borrowing. These loans involved the financing of plant expansion or working capital needs of businesses located in less-developed countries, where credit has generally been tighter and, hence, relatively expensive.

Some of the loans extended to businesses are secured and others are not. The businesses that can borrow on an unsecured basis usually have an adequate capital base, a record of meeting their financial obligations promptly, a good earnings performance, a potential for growth, and, above all, an efficient and effective management. These firms generally constitute the elite of their respective business communities and are a bank's most creditworthy customers. As a result these firms—customarily referred to as prime borrowers—are charged the lowest rate of interest, or prime rate, on short-term loans.

Loans to businesses take different forms, depending upon the needs being financed. Some of the more important financial arrange-

Table 12.1. Loans of All Insured Commercial Banks, December 31, 1982

Type of Loan	Amount (millions of dollars)	Percent of Total
Commercial and industrial loans	$ 382,481	37.0
Real estate loans, total	300,139	29.1
Construction and land development	52,439	
Secured by farmland	8,373	
Secured by 1- to 4-family residential properties	159,350	
Secured by multifamily (5 or more) residential properties	7,653	
Secured by nonfarm nonresidential properties	72,323	
Loans to Individuals, total	192,918	18.7
To purchase private passenger automobiles on installment basis	58,595	
Credit cards and related plans	36,793	
To purchase mobile homes (excluding travel trailers)	9,762	
All other installment loans for household, family, and other personal expenditures	48,048	
Single-payment loans for household, family, and other personal expenditures	39,721	
Loans to financial institutions	73,767	7.1
Loans to finance agricultural production and other loans to farmers	36,150	3.5
Loans for purchasing or carrying securities	13,719	1.3
All other loans	33,627	3.3
Total loans, gross	$1,032,802	100.0

Note: Details may not add to totals due to rounding.

Source: Federal Deposit Insurance Corporation, *Statistics on Banking*, (Washington, D.C.: FDIC, 1982), p. 41.

ments that banks have traditionally extended to businesses are discussed in the following paragraphs.

Open Line of Credit

Assume that a company that has been a regular customer of a bank determines from its cash-flow forecast a need for a certain amount of funds at the low point of the season. The company may request a seasonal loan in the form of a line of credit for a period usually not exceeding 90 days, supporting this request with current and forecast financial statements. If the request is approved by the bank, the company will have access to a credit facility that it can use as needed during the specified period. Open lines of credit are unsecured and are usually made available on a floating-rate basis; that is, the rate charged is tied to the bank's prime rate. In essence the open line of credit is an informal arrangement, oral or written, whereby a bank agrees to lend up to a stated maximum amount to a firm for a specified period of time. The bank is not legally bound to supply the funds. For example, the bank has the legal right to refuse the loan request in the event of an extreme shortage of loanable funds resulting from tight credit conditions. Although this arrangement is not a binding contract, banks tend to feel a moral obligation to honor requests made under open lines of credit.

Standby Commitment

This is a more formal and binding arrangement. Here the bank enters into a formal contract with the borrowing company and commits to extend to it the agreed-upon amount for the specified period of time. For this commitment the borrower pays a fee (commitment fee) that ranges between 0.25 and 0.75 percent (on an annualized basis) of either the unused portion of the commitment or the entire amount, regardless of usage. The agreement customarily contains provisions covering the amount of the facility, the time-availability of funds, the rate of interest charged (which is usually floating), and security.

Working-Capital Loans

Many businesses have credit needs that cover a period longer than a season. For example, a manufacturing concern with a long production cycle may need to borrow working capital to acquire raw materials and to finance the production process until the goods are sold. Such a company needs a working-capital loan to draw upon. Repayment of the loan will be made from the current sales of the firm and the conversion of accounts receivable to cash. Some banks require the borrowing company to stay out of debt to the bank for at least one or two months during the year. This "annual cleanup" provision is intended to ensure that the facility is not used as a means of permanent financing through continuous renewals. It also gives the bank the opportunity to reevaluate the borrower periodically and to decide whether to continue its financing.

Transaction Loans

A transaction loan is a short-term loan designed to finance a one-time transaction, such as the purchase of machinery. Transaction loans may also be obtained to take advantage of market opportunities. If the borrower is unable to repay the loan at maturity, the terms may be renegotiated.

Revolving Credit

This arrangement has some similarities to the standby commitment. Like standby credit, this is a formal, contractual agreement that obligates the bank to make funds available to the borrower on demand. The borrower pays a fee for this commitment ranging from 0.50 to 0.75 percent of either the unborrowed amount or the entire commitment. Unlike the standby credit, however, the revolving credit represents a specialized arrangement that provides for both the seasonal and the longer-term working-capital needs of businesses. Revolving credits usually run for three to five years and represent a form of intermediate credit. The following example identifies the sort of circumstances that give rise to a revolving-credit facility. Assume a firm is planning to expand its operations on a regional scale. Uncertain of the precise amount of funds needed or the timing of their disbursement, it may apply for a revolving credit. If the request is approved, funds will be taken down as needed and repaid at the borrower's option, with the bank committed to continue lending up to the maximum amount stated in the revolving-credit agreement until its expiration. The details covering the revolving credit are customarily spelled out in the agreement, which contains provisions on amount of credit, rate of interest charged, maturities of the notes, and security. Reflecting the particular needs of individual borrowers, revolving-credit agreements often include a provision that at their expiration, the entire amount borrowed will be incorporated into a term loan.

Term Loans

This is an intermediate type of credit. A term loan is usually defined as a loan to a business firm with an original maturity of more than one year. In the early and experimental period of term lending, maturities tended to be short—from one to five years. As banks became more confident of their ability to provide such credit safely, term loan maturities have extended up to ten years, and not infrequently they exceed this limit.

Most term loans are amortized regularly (monthly, quarterly, semiannually, or annually), according to an installment schedule. In some cases repayment provisions may call for a large portion of the loan (such as 15-20 percent of the principal) to be paid at the end in the form of a balloon payment. The purpose of such a provision is to permit the borrower an increased cash flow in the early years of the loan and thus afford greater financial flexibility. Occasionally repayment provisions may call for installments of irregular size and timing, based on the borrower's cash-flow projections. Term loans are thus easily adapted to financing the credit needs of a business whose ability to repay is related to its anticipated earning power.

Term loans have been sought by and made to businesses that are either too small to raise money in the capital market by the sale of bonds and stocks, or have access to such markets but find term borrowing more advantageous for a variety of reasons: loan maturity or repayment schedule is tailored to borrower's needs; there is greater flexibility in dealing with a single lender than with a large number of bondholders; capital market conditions may be unfavorable for the issuance of securities. Looked at from the side of the bank, term loans replace intermediate- and long-term corporate bonds, which a bank would otherwise be buying and carrying in its bond portfolio, and have the added advantage of protective provisions in the loan agreement that permit the bank to exercise more control over the debtor and its activities than would be true if it carried bonds. Term loans are usually made to businesses for the purpose of financing working-capital increases and the purchase or improvement of fixed assets (plant, equipment, and machinery). They represent one of the few means available for the financing of fixed capital by small and medium-size firms.

A special type of term loan is the bullet loan. This loan provides for regular interest payments throughout the life of the loan and a single principal (balloon) payment at maturity. In this respect it resembles a bond issue. Bullet loans mature between five and ten years, and are usually made on a floating-rate basis. These loans may be repaid, in whole or in part, prior to maturity without penalty.

Project Loans

These loans are among the most profitable loans made by banks. Project loans usually finance the construction of high-risk, high-cost projects that are beyond the financial capacity of a single creditor. Such multibillion-dollar projects include refineries, pipelines, and mining facilities. In some instances these projects are undertaken by private interests that contribute equity capital to create a new legal entity that will own and operate the facility. The sponsor-owners then approach various banks to secure a project loan, which usually accounts for 80-90 percent of the venture's capital. The lender assumes several significant risks in the financing of a project. These are highlighted below and reflect the experiences of both domestic and foreign banks in the financing of major international projects.

In the first place, the lender assumes a credit (default) risk, the risk that the borrower will fail to meet contractual obligations when due (make timely payments of interest and/or principal). In evaluating this risk a bank encounters a number of difficulties. The borrower has no financial history. Moreover, the project being financed is new, which means that the merit of the loan must be based solely on long-range forecasts. One such forecast is the project's cash flow, which will determine amortization of the loan. Since projects typically require a long time to complete, the project's cash flow during the construction period will be nil. As a result the bank should allow a grace period in loan amortization. What this means is that the bank should fund (accrue) interest payments throughout the construction phase. From the moment the project is completed and operations begin, any estimates of cash flows for debt service are based on subjective judgment, since the market prices for end products or services are difficult to forecast and the borrower has little, if any, control over them. Regardless of prices, however, if operations prove unprofitable, the bank will have a difficult time selling the physical facilities and avoiding any losses on the loan.

Completion delays are another risk lenders must face, since such long-term projects are frequently subject to delays and disruptions. This risk is higher in projects that are a part of an extended system. For example, if a project provides for the financing of a plant designed to supply chemicals, delays in the construction of the plant or in the transportation facilities may delay operation of the project over an extended period of time.

If the project is in a foreign country, the bank is also exposed to country risk during both the construction phase and the subsequent operation. This risk refers to the political, economic, social, and legal conditions in the country of the borrower that may adversely affect repayment of the loan. For example, the host government may nationalize the venture, or its operations may be disrupted by political tensions, civil unrest, violence, or rebellion. The profitability and eventual viability of the venture may also be affected by such economic measures as heavy taxation, increased royalties, and government red tape. Moreover, religious, tribal, linguistic, or other social differences may eventually lead to political and economic tension and undermine company operations. These and other forces (such as foreign-exchange controls and currency devaluation) may make it impossible for the company to meet its obligations on time. A bank's country risk exposure is moderated if the project is owned by the government or if the government is one of the project's sponsors.

There can also be an interest-rate risk if the project is financed at a fixed rate of interest. This risk can be shifted to the borrower by financing the project on a floating-rate basis. Thus, an increase in interest rates is passed on to the borrower. If the project's profit margins are significant, the added interest cost will be absorbed without difficulty. Otherwise, an undue burden is placed upon the project, undermining its financial viability.

These risks, though seemingly formidable, can be reduced in a number of ways. Banks can shift the risk to sponsors by requiring their guaranty of debt servicing. Guaranties by the parent companies are particularly common. Banks also limit their exposure by forming, or participating in, a syndicate that assumes the financing of the project. It is a common practice for banks to form a syndicate to participate in a large loan to a borrower, regardless of whether the borrower is a domestic or a foreign concern. As a result a bank's risk exposure is limited to the amount of the participation in the syndicated loan. In addition, banks try to reduce their exposure by diversifying their credits. In the case of foreign loans, they try to spread them over several countries rather than concentrate them in a single country.

Letters of Credit

Businesses that engage in international activities make frequent use of letter-of-credit financing. This financing may take the form of a commercial letter of credit or a standby letter of credit. The commercial letter of credit relies on a bank's substituting its own reputation for that of a buyer who is unknown to the seller. The seller then looks to the bank for payment, which is made either immediately or within a specified number of days after the date of the draft. The international effectiveness of this form of financing has encouraged its increasing use in domestic transactions.

The standby letter of credit is a bank's guarantee of payment to a third party should the client (in whose favor the letter is issued) fail to meet his financial obligations or perform according to a contract. The issuing bank is not ordinarily expected to make any payments; however, if it does, the borrower is obligated to repay the bank promptly. In domestic transactions standby letters of credit are used, as stated in Chapter 7, as backup for the issuance by companies of commercial paper and other obligations. Standby letters of credit also have application in international transactions. This type of credit has been used extensively by large banks to guarantee the performance of American companies under contract to foreign concerns. Standby letters are customarily requested by these concerns (such as foreign governments) as evidence of good faith in fulfilling the terms of the contract. These contracts may call for the construction of dams, military installations, or even villages. Although some transactions involve a higher degree of risk than others, letter-of-credit financing is popular with banks because of the income derived from fees.

Loan Participations

An outgrowth of correspondent banking has been the development of loan participations, which involve the purchase or sale of commercial loans to other banking institutions. Various reasons have given rise to the development of this practice. Certain banks, because of the strong loan demands in their communities, resort to selling some of the loans in their portfolios to other banks to replenish their liquidity. Another reason is the unavailability of local loan outlets, which induces banks to acquire loans originated by other banks. In addition, the credit needs of a business may exceed the legal lending limit of a bank (15 percent of the bank's capital for unsecured loans). Rather than turning down the loan request, with potentially adverse implications, the bank may sell the amount in excess of its credit limit (known as overline) to a correspondent bank. A final reason for loan participation is the need to control risk in the portfolio by spreading loans among different borrowers and over different geographic areas.

In recent years nonbank financial institutions have become increasingly involved in loan participations. Insurance companies and pension funds are significant buyers of loans originated and packaged by commercial banks. Since these institutions generally prefer longer-term credits than banks do, frequently they join a bank and fund a loan together. For example, in a 15-year loan to a business, it may be agreed that the principal payments made in the first seven years go to the bank and the payments made in the last eight years go to the insurance company. The interest rate charged may differ for each portion of the loan because of differences in the degree of risk assumed. For example, the rate of interest paid to the insurance company may be higher than the rate paid to the bank.

When considering a loan participation, a bank should always review all information available about the borrower, just as with any other loan request. Some participants have sustained losses because they failed to exercise their independent judgment, relying instead on the credit experience of the originating bank. Such was the case with many of the leading U.S. banks, which in the early 1980s bought $2 billion of energy-related loans originated by the Penn Square Bank. The drastic decline in gas and oil prices experienced during these years precipitated the failure of the bank and sizable losses in the portfolios of the participant banks.[4]

Consumer Loans

Consumer credit is defined by the Federal Reserve's Board of Governors as loans to individuals for household, family, and personal expenditures (except for real estate mortgage loans). Consumer credit is of two types, noninstallment and installment. Noninstallment is all consumer credit that is scheduled to be repaid in one lump sum. Service credit (such as doctors' bills), nonrevolving charge accounts granted by merchants, and all single-payment loans to individuals are examples of noninstallment credit. Banks generally dominate this type of credit, essentially because other consumer credit suppliers prefer to lend on an installment basis in order to obtain a rate of return high enough to cover the cost of their funds and operating expenses. Installment credit consists of all consumer credit that is scheduled to be repaid in two or more payments. Clearly, the convenience to the borrower of repaying a portion of the debt each month or payday, rather than at one time, has contributed to the phenomenal use of installment credit, which at year-end 1982 amounted to $345 billion (80 percent of the total consumer credit outstanding from all sources). Banks are the primary source of installment credit, surpassing retailers and all other financial institutions supplying such credit. At year-end 1982 banks' installment loans amounted to $152 billion, which represented 44 percent of the total installment credit outstanding. Some of the more important types of installment credit are described below.

Automobile Loans and Loans to Finance Other Consumer Goods

The dominant type of installment credit extended by banks is the auto loan, financing the purchase of a new or used automobile. Other consumer goods financed through installment loans include mobile homes, household appliances, boats, and furniture. Banks handle this type of financing in two ways: lending directly to the borrower or purchasing dealer installment contracts. The chief benefit of indirect lending is that it provides a means of acquiring a substantial volume of loans without incurring the costs in money and manpower of attracting and assessing each individual borrower. However, there are several drawbacks to this type of financing. Because the bank forgoes the opportunity to evaluate the individual customer, it must rely on the judgment and standards of the dealer who extends the credit. As a result there may be a greater possibility of failure, fraud, or forgery. Since the credit transaction is in effect secured, from the dealer's point of view, by the item purchased, the dealer may be less than meticulous in appraising a customer's creditworthiness, reasoning that if payments stop, the item can be repossessed. Similarly, the customer may not take seriously the obligation to meet the installment schedule, reasoning that the only risk is the repossession of the item purchased. Finally, the bank, by purchasing paper in volume, cannot build a customer relationship with the actual beneficiaries of the credit.

Revolving Credit

Another type of installment credit is the revolving credit, which includes credit cards and check credit plans. Banks began to issue credit cards in the early 1950s, following entry into this field by other major issuers, such as oil companies, department stores, and travel and entertainment firms. Although they were relative latecomers, banks played a decisive role in the success of credit cards in the United States and abroad.

Each cardholder has a prearranged line of credit with the bank issuing the credit card. When making a purchase with a credit card, the buyer signs a sales draft of a retail merchant, who presents the draft to the bank for full payment minus a service charge ranging up to 6 percent. The sales draft is then mailed to the credit card holder by the bank that issued the credit card. The cardholder has the option of paying the draft in full, typically within 25 days, or paying only a portion, with the remainder paid in installments. Banks' income from these operations consists of the service charges and the interest rate charges to consumers on the unpaid balance.

The increased popularity and use of credit cards has greatly diminished the other type of revolving credit, check credit plans. Check credit plans involve only two parties, the bank and the consumer. After appropriate screening, the bank provides a consumer a prearranged line of credit that is utilized when the individual writes checks above the limits of his account. These plans are customarily referred to as overdraft accounts. A similar type of plan involves the use of specially coded or denominated checks that are used to purchase goods and services. The bank sets up a special checking account to pay these checks and charges the individual interest on the unpaid balance.

Consumer Protection Laws

In recent years there has been a tremendous increase in legislation that provides protection for the consumer.* The first, passed by Con-

---

*Bank compliance with consumer legislation is customarily determined by bank examiners. In addition, consumer complaints against the practices of individual banks are brought to the attention of the appropriate supervisory agency *(Continued on page 326)*

gress in 1969, is known as the Consumer Credit Protection Act or, more commonly, the Truth in Lending Act, enforced under the Federal Reserve System's Regulation Z. One part of this act extends consumers the right to rescind, within three business days, any credit transaction in which their residence is used as collateral. This provision allows consumers time to think about the transaction and make up their minds. Another part of this act regulates the advertising of credit terms and provides for full disclosure of details to enable consumers to reach intelligent decisions. The most important section of this act, however, requires lenders to provide borrowers complete information concerning the cost of credit. Lenders are required to disclose to borrowers the annual percentage rate (APR) of the finance charge on a consumer loan. The finance charge includes all the various charges that are incidental to the extension of credit: interest, loan fee, finder's fee or similar charge, transaction or service charge, points, premium for credit life or other insurance, and investigation or credit report fee. The annual rate equivalent of the finance charge constitutes the loan's rate. The intent of this provision is to have the cost of credit presented to borrowers in a standardized way so that they can shop for the best credit terms.

Prior to this law, when buying a car or obtaining an installment loan, borrowers were frequently quoted "add-on" rates of interest. For example, on a $6,000 four-year loan the consumer knew that the rate applied on the loan was 8 percent and the finance charge $1,920 ($6,000 x .08 per year x 4 years). His monthly payments, according to the add-on method, came to $165 ($6,000 + $1,920 = $7,920 ÷ 48 months). Use of this method, however, results in a higher effective rate, since the borrower does not have full use of the amount borrowed for the whole time period. An approximate estimate of this rate can be obtained by means of a simple formula, known as the constant ratio:

$$R = \frac{2mA}{L(n+1)}$$

where R = approximate interest rate on installment loan

(Continued from page 325)
by the Consumer Banking Affairs Units, which were established by the Federal Reserve banks to function as complaint clearinghouses. Complaints against state member banks are investigated by the Federal Reserve banks, while complaints against insured nonmember banks and national banks are investigated by the FDIC and the Office of the Comptroller of the Currency, respectively.

m = number of payment periods per year
A = dollar amount of interest charged
L = amount of loan
n = total number of payments needed to discharge the debt.

The application of this formula to the example above is as follows:

$$R = \frac{2 \times 12 \times \$1,920}{\$6,000\ (48+1)} = 15.7 \text{ percent.}$$

If the loan is discounted and the interest is deducted in advance, the effective rate paid would be even higher (23 percent). This example helps explain why lenders are required to quote all installment loans on an APR basis. Detailed interest tables, based on an actuarial method of computation, enable loan officers to provide consumers with instant APR quotations.

Another protection accorded the consumer by the Truth in Lending Act is in the case of lost or stolen credit cards. The consumer is responsible only for the first $50 of charges made by unauthorized users before the loss is reported.

The Fair Credit Billing Act, implemented in October 1975, is an amendment to the Truth in Lending Act. Also enforced under Regulation Z, it requires merchants and banks to inform consumers of their rights and the procedural steps to follow in filing complaints about billing errors.

This act also protects consumers who purchase defective merchandise, so long as the transaction is over $50 and the customer lives in the same state or within 100 miles of the place where the transaction occurred. According to this act, the consumer may refuse to continue paying the seller, or any third party that purchased the debt contract, until the complaint is resolved.

The Fair Credit Reporting Act of 1971 deals with the protection of the consumer against obsolete or inaccurate information provided by consumer reporting agencies. These agencies are responsible for safeguarding the privacy of the consumer, and restrictions are placed upon the distribution of information. If a loan request is denied because of information contained in a credit report, a bank must disclose to the consumer the substance of the information and the name of the credit reporting agency.

The Equal Credit Opportunity Act was implemented in 1975 as a guarantee that credit is extended fairly and impartially. It prohibits discrimination against credit applicants because of race, color, religion, ethnic origin, sex, marital status, or receipt of income from public assistance programs. If credit is denied on these grounds, creditors are liable to the aggrieved individual for actual and punitive damages. The provisions of this act are implemented by the Federal Reserve System's Regulation B.

Real Estate Loans

As shown in Table 12.1, real estate loans accounted for 29.1 percent of total bank loans at year-end 1982. These mortgages represented the financing of ownership, construction, and remodeling of both housing and commercial and industrial facilities. Real estate loans are also made to farmers for the purchase of farmland. This type of real estate credit, however, is relatively insignificant. Banks have become important real estate lenders over the years. Their relative importance as a source of real estate credit can be sensed from the following data. At year-end 1982 total mortgage credit from all sources amounted to about $1.7 trillion, of which 62 percent was provided by financial institutions (including banks) and 38 percent by U.S. credit agencies and individuals. Banks ranked second in importance only to savings and loan associations and ahead of all other mortgage credit suppliers, accounting for 18 percent of the market.

Mortgage loans are a typical example of a long-term credit, the maturity varying between 10 and 30 years. Real estate loans also exemplify secured credits, since the owner has some equity in the property that is offered as collateral for the loan. Thus, even if the value of the property declines, the owner's equity provides a margin of safety against losses.

Residential Mortgages

Over half of banks' mortgage loans are for residential properties—that is, they are secured by one-to-four-family residential properties and multifamily properties. The former, single-family mortgages, are the principal type of residential mortgage held by commercial banks because of the high risk involved in the financing of multifamily mortgages (such as apartment buildings). Most of the residential mortgages in banks' loan portfolios are "conventional"—that is, they are not backed by a governmental agency. However, banks also hold a sizable number of residential mortgages that are insured by the Federal Housing Administration (FHA) or guaranteed by the Veterans Administration (VA). In case of default, the ownership of the property is shifted to the government agency and the bank is reimbursed for its losses. Yet most banks favor conventional loans over FHA and VA loans for a number of reasons. Since government-backed mortgages require minimal (FHA loans) or no (VA loans) down payment, the borrower tends to be more prone to nonpayment and default during difficult economic times. In addition, much less red tape is involved in extending, supervising, and foreclosing on conventional loans. There has also been an increase in the availability of private mortgage insurance modeled after that of FHA. The principal reason for the preference for conventional mortgages is that banks earn more money on these mortgages then they do on VAs and FHAs, whose rates are administered by the government and generally trail other market rates. However, one distinct advantage that government-backed mortgages have over conventional mortgages is that the secondary market for FHA-insured and VA-guaranteed mortgages is widespread among various types of financial institutions.

The Secondary Mortgage Market

The functioning of a secondary market for residential mortgages enhances the liquidity of the mortgage portfolios of banks and other real estate lenders. Three financial intermediaries form the basis of the secondary market: the Federal National Mortgage Association (FNMA or Fannie Mae), the Government National Mortgage Association (GNMA or Ginnie Mae), and the Federal Home Loan Mortgage Corporation (FHLMC or Freddie Mac).

Established in 1938, Fannie Mae was transformed into a private corporation in 1968. Functioning under the supervision of the Secretary of Housing and Urban Development (HUD), Fannie Mae holds auctions at regular intervals in which it buys (or commits to buy) government-backed and conventional home mortgages. Institutions short of loanable funds are thus in a position to continue their mortgage lending activities in periods of tight money. Fannie Mae sells these mortgages in regions where there are surplus funds and limited mortgage outlets. In essence, by alternately buying and selling mortgages, it improves the liquidity of the secondary mortgage market and contributes to its stability. Its activities are financed from commitment fees earned, mortgage repayments, and the sale of securities (such as debentures and short-term notes).

Ginnie Mae, created in 1968, is part of HUD. One of its activities includes the purchase of mortgages of low- and middle-income projects (tandem plan). Ginnie Mae buys these mortgages on the basis of a prior commitment to the originating institutions, and sells them to private investors, absorbing any loss in the differential between the purchase and sale prices. In this way it subsidizes and supports low-income housing. In 1970 Ginnie Mae initiated a "pass-through" program, which supports private organizations that pool government-backed home mortgages and issue securities against them. GNMA guarantees the payment of interest and principal on the securities of the pool. The private creators retain responsibility to collect all payments and pre-payments, which are "passed through" each month to the holders of the securities.

Freddie Mac was established in 1970, its capital subscribed by the 12 regional Federal Home Loan banks. It supports the mortgage market by purchasing residential mortgages that it pools, then selling shares or participation certificates (PCs) in the pool. PCs range from $100,000 to $5 million in value. In addition it sells guaranteed mortgage certificates (GMCs), which are also issued against mortgage pools and—like Ginnie Mae pass-through securities—appeal to bond investors. Freddie Mac funds its activities by selling debt securities in the open markets.

Interest Rates on Mortgages

Some states have enacted legislation imposing ceilings on interest rates for mortgages. When market rates for these mortgages rose above the ceiling rates, the supply of funds dissipated and new mortgages declined sharply. Because of this the DIDMCA of 1980 overruled state usury ceilings on mortgage loans, unless states reenact them within three years.

The removal of ceiling rates permits banks' mortgage loan rates to fluctuate in response to other capital-market rates. Considering the sharp increases in interest rates and the costs of housing experienced in recent years, many observers have expressed concern that young people can no longer afford to buy homes. However, the impact of these trends has been moderated by the proliferation of an ever increasing number of mortgage repayment plans, a smorgasbord of mortgage loan instruments from which the borrower can select according to his or her particular needs and expectations. These plans differ from the traditional fixed-rate mortgage, which is characterized by equal fixed monthly payments for the life of the loan.

One such mortgage instrument is the graduated-payment mortgage (GPM), which has a fixed interest rate and maturity and a specified schedule of monthly payments. These payments are purposely set at a low level in the initial years of the loan and increase gradually to cover the interest and fully amortize the loan. Thus, the GPM is particularly attractive to young, first-time homebuyers who cannot afford the initial payments of a traditional mortgage but whose income and debt-servicing capacity is expected to grow over time. A related plan is the flexible-payment mortgage, which in the early years of the mortgage (for instance, the first five years) provides for low monthly payments covering only the interest on the loan. Later payments increase to cover the remaining interest and retire the principal of the loan by its maturity. The deferred-interest mortgage is also associated with low initial mortgage payments because of a lower interest rate; in return the lender receives the deferred interest plus a fee upon sale of the house. This plan is attractive to families that expect to live in a house for a limited number of years (such as five years) and plan to repay the lender out of the appreciation realized at the time of the sale.

The balloon-payment mortgage is typically made for a period of three to five years without any commitment by the lender to renew it at maturity. Monthly payments are based on a regular amortization period (such as 25 to 30 years) and a fixed interest rate. When the loan matures, the entire balance must be paid in one lump sum, a balloon payment. Since the lender is under no obligation to refinance, the borrower must secure a new loan for all or a portion of the balloon payment. Recent experiences in California indicate that borrowers who failed to receive new financing were forced to sell their homes at a sacrifice.

The growing-equity mortgage (GEM) is a relatively new instrument that provides for increases in monthly payments at the rate of 4-7.5 percent a year. As a result the loan is fully amortized in a shorter period than otherwise (for instance, in less than 15 years). Because of the accelerated payback, most lenders are willing to give borrowers a break on the interest rate. The appeal of this plan to the borrower stems from the fixed interest rate; the nominal increases in payments, which are known with certainty; and the relatively smaller amount of total interest paid on the loan because of its shorter average life.

The shared-appreciation mortgage (SAM) is a fixed-rate loan, usually for a period of ten years. Mortgage lenders make these loans at rates below market levels in return for one-third of the gains realized upon the sale of the property. The reverse-annuity mortgage (RAM) is a fixed-rate plan that enables retired people to use the equity in their homes to supplement their retirement income. Under this plan the lender, instead of advancing the borrower a lump sum, pays a fixed annuity each month over the life of the loan (for instance, over ten years). The debt (cash advances and accumulating interest) is to be repaid out of the borrower's estate. One drawback of this plan is that if the property value declines in the meantime, the value of the collateral may be less than the amount of the loan. Also, problems arise if the borrower outlives the loan and the value of the house has not increased enough for a new reverse annuity to be issued.

The renegotiable-rate mortgage (RRM) or rollover mortgage (ROM) is written with a fixed rate for a fixed period. Its renewal is guaranteed every three to five years, with the interest rate determined each time according to market trends. One drawback to this type is the possibility of a sharp increase in monthly payments after a renewal.

The adjustable-rate mortgage (ARM) provides for upward or downward adjustment in the interest rate over the life of the contract, in response to variations in a specific reference rate or index. Among the most commonly used indexes are the market rates of interest on U.S. Treasury securities (such as Treasury bills and Treasury issues of one, three, and five years' maturity) and the national average mortgage contract rate, computed monthly by the Federal Home Loan Bank Board. Whatever the index may be, some lenders try to entice borrowers by setting the interest rate on ARMs, for an initial period, below the rate for conventional, fixed-rate mortgages. After the initial period rates are adjusted according to fluctuations in the key rate. Other lenders limit the amount by which the interest rate can increase at adjustment time, but generally there is no cap on how much the rate can rise over the life of the loan. As a result a sustained upward trend in interest rates means steadily escalating mortgage payments. Thus, a major disadvantage of the ARM is that monthly payments may rise appreciably and even go beyond the borrower's capacity to pay. To overcome this problem, homeowners have been allowed a number of options: pay off excess interest in a lump sum upon sale of the house; have the loan's maturity stretched beyond the original date; authorize adjustments in both the maturity of the loan and monthly payments. From the lender's point of view, the ARM offers returns that vary with the overall level of interest rates. More important, it permits lenders, especially thrifts, to match the variable-rate nature of some of their liabilities with a portfolio of correspondingly variable-rate loans. This contributes to rendering earnings from lending activities reasonably stable.

There is no certainty as to which of the alternative mortgage instruments, if any, will prevail, though lenders appear to favor the renegotiable-rate mortgage. The default record of alternative mortgage plans and the ongoing consolidation process in the financial sector will refine lender preferences among the various types of mortgages.

Regulations Protecting the Borrower

In addition to the credit laws discussed in the preceding section, consumers are protected by legislation specifically related to mortgage loans. These are summarized below.

The Real Estate Settlement and Procedures Act (RESPA) was enacted in 1974 and amended the following year. Administered by HUD, this law requires a lending institution, including a bank, to provide mortgage loan applicants with good-faith estimates of all the settlement costs that will be incurred in a given transaction. The lender retains the settlement statement along with a signed receipt from the borrower acknowledging disclosure of such information.

The Home Mortgage Disclosure Act (HMDA) was passed by Congress in 1975 to discourage redlining, the practice of refusing mortgage loans in blighted or declining neighborhoods. This law requires banks and other lending institutions to compile, and make public, information on the geographical locations of the properties on which they have made mortgage loans. The objective of this legislation was to provide depositors with information about the lending activities of banks and, through public pressure, to discourage redlining. This act has a major limitation. Although disclosure of information about the lending activity of an institution is important, it is nevertheless incomplete, since it is not accompanied by information about the demand for loans in the various geographic areas under consideration.

In 1977 Congress passed another important piece of legislation, the Community Reinvestment Act (CRA). This act requires federal regulatory agencies to determine whether banks and thrift institutions attend to the credit needs of the communities in which they are chartered. Thus, according to this legislation, banks are required to formulate explicit CRA statements outlining their willingness to meet their community's credit needs and the types of loans they will extend. These policy statements are periodically reviewed by bank examiners from the federal supervisory agencies (the Federal Reserve System, the FDIC, and the Office of the Comptroller of the Currency), to ensure that low- and moderate-income individuals are not being systematically discriminated against. In addition to the periodic reviews conducted by examiners, regulatory agencies determine institutional compliance with CRA provisions when a lender applies for a branch, office relocation, merger, or acquisition. This power of enforcement allows the CRA more far-reaching authority than that of the HMDA, and necessitates adherence on the part of bankers to the evaluation criteria set up by federal agencies.

Loans to Financial Institutions

At the end of 1982, this category of loans accounted, according to Table 12.1, for 7.1 percent of all bank loans. Recipients of these loans were such financial institutions as correspondent banks, foreign banks, investment banks, savings and loan associations, credit unions, and finance companies. Finance companies, though important consumer lenders, rely heavily for their funds upon commercial banks, which extend them loans under lines of credit. Since their credit needs are continuous, finance companies follow the practice of satisfying "clean-up" provisions by rotating their borrowing, paying off one bank's loans with loan proceeds from other banks.

Investment bankers also depend on bank credit to finance their security underwriting and placement activities. Loans of this type are generally made by the regional and money-center banks.

Loans to Farmers

For a great number of U.S. banks this type of loan constitutes a dominant loan portfolio category. Indeed, for many rural banks farm loans account for a sizable portion of total loans. Farmers generally borrow from banks to finance recurring seasonal expenses and intermediate-term investments. The former are such items as seeds, fertilizers, sprays, and feed for livestock. In the latter instance farm loans finance land improvements and the purchase of machinery and equipment, trucks and automobiles, and other consumer durable goods.

Despite the importance of farm loans for rural banks, for the banking industry as a whole, farm loans accounted for only 3.5 percent of the total loans outstanding at year-end 1982 (see Table 12.1). This means that commercial banks are not the primary source of funds for farm credit. Indeed, banks are exceeded in importance by lenders that specialize in farm credit and offer farmers loans at subsidized rates. These lenders are federal agencies—Federal Land Banks, Federal Intermediate Credit Banks, and Banks for Cooperatives—and make up the U.S. farm credit system.

Loans for Purchasing and Carrying Securities

Although this category of loans has experienced significant increases over the years, its relative importance in 1982 was the same as in 1978 (1.3 percent of total loans). This means that these loans grew during this period at the same pace as total loans. This category refers to credit extended to individuals for the purpose of purchasing corporate stock and other securities.

Because of the excessive speculation of the late 1920s and the stock market crash, the Securities Exchange Act of 1934, with amendments, authorized the Board of Governors of the Federal Reserve System to apply selective credit controls over this type of loan. As a result Regulation U has since been applied to loans made by lenders on all securities listed on national stock exchanges and selected over-the-counter securities. According to Regulation U, purchase of these securities on credit is subject to margin requirements. The term "margin" refers to the proportion of the total value of the securities that the buyer must deposit with the lender. In 1972 the margin requirement for stock was set at 65 percent; it was lowered to 50 percent in 1974, and maintained at this level until 1983. The Board of Governors of the Federal Reserve has the power to change minimum margin requirements within the range of 25 to 100 percent. The securities acquired on margin are pledged as collateral at the time the loan is made.

Another type of credit in this category is loans made to brokers and dealers for the purpose of financing customers' margin accounts and dealer security inventories, which must be carried in order to make a market in them.

All Other Loans

This last category of bank loans, accounting for 3.3 percent of total loans at year-end 1982, is made up of two groups: loans to foreign governments and official institutions, and loans not elsewhere classified. Loans to foreign governments have grown in recent years to become a major class of loans. Since the mid-1970s, following the dramatic rise in oil prices and the recession of 1974, an increasing number of foreign governments have entered the credit markets and borrowed from U.S. banks for a number of purposes. Some of the more important needs for which governments have borrowed money include acquiring foreign exchange to finance seasonal export/import variations and funding infrastructure projects, such as highway or railroad construction. Funds may also be borrowed to fund social welfare projects, such as the building of hospitals or schools or, on a short-term basis, to cover expected deficits in government operations. From a legal perspective American bankers distinguish four different levels of foreign government borrowers:

- Governments at the national (federal), provincial (state), and local levels
- Ministries of the national government and central banks
- Statutory authorities and agencies at all government levels
- Public-sector industries, development banks, and other banking institutions owned by the government.

This classification system permits a more realistic evaluation of the prospective borrower by readily identifying its importance in the government hierarchy, and by recognizing the supervisory authority responsible under law or policy in the event of nonpayment. These considerations play a decisive role in evaluating the quality of the loan, and dispel the notion that the government nature of the would-be borrower automatically assures repayment.[5]

The other component of this loan group is loans to official institutions. These include such international and regional organizations as the International Bank for Reconstruction and Development, the Inter-American Development Bank, and the Asian Development Bank.

The second group of loans included in the "all other" loans category is an assortment of credits not elsewhere classified, such as loans to nonprofit organizations: churches, hospitals, educational and charitable organizations, clubs, and similar associations. Also included are loans to individuals for investment purposes (excluding loans secured by real estate and those for the purchase of securities) and unplanned overdrafts on checking accounts. The last approach to extending credit was quite rare in the United States until the introduction of credit cards and check credit plans. By contrast, this form of financing has been very popular in Great Britain and other European countries, and often is the predominant form of lending. Both tradition and the absence of well-developed European capital markets have contributed to making these overdrafts "evergreen"; that is, they are not called in for payment and the bank charges interest on the negative balances in the borrower's account. In essence, then, overdrafts are functioning in these countries as a means of financing businesses' medium-term needs for capital.

NOTES

1. Lloyd W. Mints, *A History of Banking Theory* (Chicago: University of Chicago Press, 1945), p. 9; see also pp. 27-29.

2. On the "shiftability" theory of liquidity, see H. G. Moulton, "Commercial Banking and Capital Formation, III," *Journal of Political Economy* 26, no. 7 (July 1918): 723; Waldo F. Mitchell, *The Uses of Bank Funds* (Chicago: University of Chicago Press, 1925), pp. 15-17, 19ff; Rollin G. Thomas, *Modern Banking* (New York: Prentice-Hall, 1937), pp. 161-69.

3. Herbert V. Prochnow, *Term Loans and Theories of Bank Liquidity* (New York: Prentice-Hall, 1949).

4. Christian Hill and Richard B. Schmitt, "Energy-Loan Losses, Bigger Than Expected, Figure to Climb Higher," *Wall Street Journal*, November 14, 1983, pp. 1, 13.

5. Emmanuel N. Roussakis, ed., *International Banking: Principles and Practices* (New York: Praeger Publishers, 1983).

SUGGESTED REFERENCES

Brick, John R. *Commercial Banking, Texts and Reading*. Haslett, Mich.: Systems Publications, 1984.

Brockschmidt, Peggy. "The Secondary Market for Home Mortgages." *Monthly Review*, Federal Reserve Bank of Kansas City, September-October 1977, pp. 11-20.

"Complying with Consumer Credit Regulations: A Challenge." *Federal Reserve Bulletin*, September 1977, pp. 769-73.

"Coping with Consumer Credit Regulations." *Issues in Bank Regulation*, Winter 1978, pp. 3-5.

"Equal Credit Opportunity." *Federal Reserve Bulletin*, February 1977, pp. 101-07.

Guidelines for Upstream-Downstream Correspondent Bank Loan Participations. Philadelphia: Robert Morris Associates, 1975.

Hodgman, Donald R. *Commercial Bank Loan and Investment Policy*. Champaign: Bureau of Economic and Business Research, University of Illinois, 1963.

Jessup, Paul F. *Modern Bank Management*. St. Paul, Minn.: West Publishing Co., 1980.

"Loan Commitments at Selected Large Commercial Banks: New Statistical Series." *Federal Reserve Bulletin*, April 1975, pp. 226-29.

Merris, Randall C. "Loan Commitments and Facility Fees." *Economic Perspectives*, Federal Reserve Bank of Chicago, March/April 1978, pp. 14-21.

Peterson, Richard L. "Factors Affecting the Growth of Bank Credit Card and Check Credit." *Journal of Finance*, May 1977, pp. 553-64.

Sale, Alvin T. "Floating Rate Installment Loans: An Option for Increased Profitability." *Journal of Retail Banking*, September 1980, pp. 1-6.

Savage, Donald T. "CRA and Community Credit Needs." *Bankers Magazine*, January-February 1979, pp. 49-53.

Sivesind, Charles M. "Mortgage-Backed Securities: The Revolution in Real Estate Finance." *Quarterly Review*, Federal Reserve Bank of New York, Autumn 1979, pp. 1-10.

Small, Thomas A. "Letters of Credit for the Commercial Lender." *Journal of Commercial Bank Lending*, August 1980, pp. 5-13.

Wood, Oliver G., Jr. *Commercial Banking*. New York: D. Van Nostrand, 1978.

Woodworth, G. W. "Theories of Cyclical Liquidity Management of Commercial Banks." In Thomas G. Gies and Vincent P. Apilado, eds., *Banking Markets and Financial Institutions*, pp. 155-67. Homewood, Ill.: Richard D. Irwin, 1971.

Within the confines of law and regulation, the board of directors of each individual bank tries to create a framework for safe, sound, and profitable lending. As with all other aspects of banking activity, the board of directors ensures uniformity in lending practices through the formulation of a formal lending policy. This policy is in written form and is periodically reviewed, as warranted by changing economic conditions. Some of the key questions addressed by this policy are the size of the loan account, desirable maturities, types of loans, and the terms under which loans may be made. Once the loan policy has been formulated, the board must provide the administrative framework for its implementation. This chapter reviews the factors relevant to policy formulation, and describes the organizational structure and the procedures whereby loan policy is implemented.

SIZE OF THE LOAN ACCOUNT

Bankers continually face the question of how large the loan portfolio should be, a question that is especially significant because loans represent the bank's most lucrative activity. Banks may be tempted to increase the size of the loan portfolio in order to increase profitability, but the too liberal granting of loan requests can lead to losses through failure to collect. On the other hand, a conservative stance on the size of the portfolio may cause the bank to forgo earnings unnecessarily. There is no formulaic answer regarding the size of the portfolio; each bank must determine portfolio size for itself. The starting point is the accurate assessment of the credit needs of the community or market a bank serves or intends to serve. It has long been recognized that the basic responsibility of a bank lies in serving the credit needs of its community. There is no greater service that a bank can perform for a community than to provide the loans needed by creditworthy businesses and individuals.

In small communities this need for credit can be assessed by the actual demand for loans. In such communities bank officers and directors are usually in a position to have an intimate knowledge of most of the economic activity of the area and the developments that may be shaping up. In large communities such knowledge can be obtained through formal forecasting of expected credit needs. Loan officers of banks in such communities customarily provide this information after contacting their principal corporate clients and identifying their future credit needs. This information is then evaluated within the framework of the economic growth of the community. Large money-center banks frequently rely on national econometric models to identify the expected demand for and supply of funds in the private sector in the year ahead. Since it is the role of banks to bridge the gap between the supply of and demand for funds by extending loans, this information sets the parameters within which the bank can determine its own share of the market. In whatever type of community a bank may operate, its management must know the credit needs of its present and potential customers, both for the short and for the long run, as a basis not only for establishing loan policies but also for determining the bank's liquidity needs and investment policy.

When bank management has a fairly clear concept of what volume and character of loan demands the bank will be called upon to meet, it must appraise its own willingness and ability to meet those demands. In some communities local demand for loans is strong and practically insatiable, while in more developed and stable communities, bank management may have to seek out opportunities for sound loans. In either case the controlling principle should be the community's credit needs and the bank's capability to meet those needs.

Once liquidity provisions have been made (primary and secondary reserves) and there is adequate capital for absorbing loan losses, a bank should be in a position to make all the sound loans it can. In other words, given adequate liquidity and capital protection, a bank's ability to expand its loans is limited only by its resources. If a bank's resources are inadequate to meet the full volume of loan demands, management may proceed to fill them indirectly. Bank management may provide for the financing of specific loan demands by participating in or negotiating placement of the requested loans with correspondent banks or other financial institutions, itself retaining the servicing of such loans as a means of sustaining continuous relationships with its own customers. A bank's ability and willingness to accommodate local loan demands directly or indirectly is the most important factor in creating and maintaining depositor relationships. In addition, such ability and willingness to lend contribute to the economic well-being of the community and thereby broaden the market for bank services, so that the bank shares in the prosperity it has helped to bring about.

Over the years management has developed certain criteria that assess the overall loan commitments of a bank in terms of its capacity to lend. These criteria are various key balance-sheet relationships expressed in the form of ratios. Foremost among these are the loans-to-deposits ratio and the loans-to-capital ratio. As implied, these ratios aim to show the relationship of a bank's loans to its deposits and to its capital accounts. Of these two ratios the more widely used is loans-to-deposits. Because it is readily computed and compared, this ratio is in general use as a yardstick for asset management. Specifically, it is used to demonstrate the extent to which available resources have already been used in accommodating the credit needs of customers. The presumption is that the higher the ratio of loans to deposits, the less able a bank will be to make additional loans.*

Commercial bank managements have come, at various times, to accept a certain ratio of loans to deposits as being an acceptable determinant for the size of the loan portfolio desired. As might be expected, this ratio experienced considerable variation over the years, reflecting the prevailing economic conditions and, more specifically, the credit demand of these years. Since 1914, for example, the average loans-to-deposits ratios for all commercial banks in the United States has varied from a high of 80 percent loans in 1920 to a low of 17 percent in 1944.

The loans-to-capital ratio measures the extent to which a bank's loan losses may be safely absorbed by its capital account without jeopardizing the bank's continuing viability. Here, too, management has come to accept a maximum desirable ratio of loans to capital; the loans of a bank should not be more than seven times the capital funds of that bank.

These ratios have become critical guides for commercial bank managements. Not infrequently a bank's management may feel uncomfortable when its ratios get too far out of line with those of other banks regarded as comparable in size and character. Apart from the questions that may be raised by the top management's conflicting assessments of the uncertain future, there are likely to be pressures generated by the inquiries of large corporate depositors and other

---

*This ratio is frequently used by management as a liquidity indicator because, by showing the relationship of a bank's loans to its deposits, it also reveals the amount of funds still readily available for liquidity purposes.

individuals whose good opinion is important to the welfare of the individual bank. Bankers do not permit the judgment of such influential outsiders to substitute for their own, but they are forced to concede it some weight or risk adverse action, such as transfer of important deposit accounts to competitors. The attitude has thus developed that whenever these ratios approach what is considered the maximum acceptable ratio for all banks or for banks of a certain size and character, management should try to become more cautious and selective in its lending policies.

However important the ratios concerning limits to overall lending capacity may be, they must not be taken to imply that they are in any sense magic numbers. True, some element of tradition clings to particular values for these ratios; such tradition, however, must be flexibly interpreted in the light of the current situation. These ratios become especially meaningful if interpreted in the light of such relevant magnitudes as the composition of the loan portfolio (by maturities and by major loan types), the size and composition of the bond portfolio, business expectations, management philosophy, and respectability in comparison with all commercial banks or with other banks of the same size and character.

LOAN MATURITIES

Because loan maturities have implications for both bank liquidity and risk exposure, it is important that the board of directors formulate a clear policy defining an acceptable distribution of maturities in the loan portfolio. In terms of maturity, a bank's loan portfolio may be classified into short-term, intermediate-term, and long-term loans. Short-term loans are usually defined as those with a maturity of one year or less, intermediate-term loans are from one to eight (or occasionally ten) years, and long-term loans are in excess of ten years.

Short-term loans are of two types: demand and time. Demand loans are those that the borrower may repay, or the lender may demand payment of, at any time. The most common example of demand credit is loans to brokers and dealers for financing their inventories of securities and their customers' margin accounts. Because the bank can call the loan at any time, on one day's notice, these loans are also known as call loans. Rate quotations on these loans are customarily made by large money-center banks.

Time loans are extended for a definite period, up to one year. The traditional type of such credit, as we saw in Chapter 12, has been self-liquidating loans to businesses. In its pure form this loan is customarily employed to finance the seasonal inventory needs of businesses and is repaid from the sale of the inventory and the conversion of accounts receivable into cash.

Intermediate-term loans, by definition, are those whose maturities fall between the short-term and long-term categories. One example of intermediate credit is consumer loans, which are usually made for a period of two to three years. Term loans to businesses are another example of intermediate credit. (Both types of loans were discussed in Chapter 12.)

Loans with a maturity of ten years or more when contracted are characterized as long-term. The most common type of long-term loan is the real estate loan. Originally, lending on the security of real estate was considered unduly illiquid, and hence inappropriate for commercial banks, whose liabilities were so largely payable on demand. Indeed, before the Great Depression mortgage loans were made with lump-sum maturities. These loans were seldom paid at the initial maturity and were renewed frequently. The monthly amortization feature came with the establishment of the Federal Housing Administration (FHA) in 1934 and with the initiation by this agency of a mortgage insurance program. The improved liquidity of mortgages that resulted from the monthly payments, along with the backing of real estate loans by federal agencies (FHA and VA) and the creation of a secondary market, contributed to making real estate loans more popular. In the years immediately after World War II, banks entered this market, and they have since become important real estate lenders. Real estate loans are a basic outlet for the time deposit funds of commercial banks.

Loan maturity distribution in the portfolio reflects a bank's maturity policy. Such a policy must be flexible, permitting adjustments in the portfolio that reflect changing economic conditions. Blind adherence to a given maturity structure does not benefit the bank, its depositors, or its stockholders. The cyclical nature of the economy and its impact upon the monetary system require the change or shift of emphasis in maturity policy, in order to give recognition to changes in the strength of loan demand. During periods of slackened loan demand, which normally coincide with business recession and monetary ease, banks should engage primarily in short-maturity loans. Conversely, during periods of peak loan demand, which normally coincide with high business activity and monetary restraint, banks should emphasize term lending. This shift in loan maturity policy to reflect changes in the market conditions and the demand for loans enables a bank to substantially improve its long-range rate of income. By refusing to make loans other than those of short term in periods when loan demand and (consequently) interest rates are low, banks are in a position to make rather large term loans at the height of loan demand and command unquestionably higher rates of interest. By following this pattern of loan maturity policy, banks provide themselves with portfolios that stretch over succeeding periods of lesser loan demand and income.

In practice, however, banks have often deviated from this pattern. In other words, during periods of slackened business activity and loan demand, they have been willing to extend term loans, while in periods of high business activity and loan demand they have tended to reduce term loans and to engage primarily in short-term lending. Clearly, this pattern of maturity policy is not as profitable over the long run. Its use, however, is understandable, because short-term lending presumably adds to a bank's flexibility and ability to accommodate a larger number of customers, and permits adherence to custom and tradition.

TYPES OF LOANS

The types and proportions of loans carried in the portfolio vary greatly from bank to bank. This variation generally reflects factors both external and internal to a bank. These factors include the economic character of the area in which the bank is located, the kind and stability of deposits held, the background and evolution of a particular bank, and the preferences of management within the framework of current opportunities and pressures.

Economic Character of the Community

The economic character of the area in which a bank is located largely determines the fields of lending in which it will specialize. In a unit banking system, the bank is more closely tied to a single community than is the case in a branch banking system. Thus, banks located in areas where the economy is predominantly agricultural inevitably find themselves engaged primarily in agricultural and real estate loans. In consequence banks in these areas have far greater proportions of these types of loans in their portfolios than do banks located in large urban centers. The latter banks build loan portfolios predominantly with commercial and industrial loans, consumer loans, and mortgage loans. And if one of these centers functions as the national money market, then its larger banks can reasonably be considered as money-market banks—a fact that would account both for the great proportion of loans for the purchasing of securities found in their loan portfolios and for the importance of correspondent bank accounts among their deposit balances.

Under the branch banking system, banking is generally conducted by a few large metropolitan banks with branches statewide. This characteristic of branch banking contributes to a highly diversified commercial bank loan portfolio with risks spread over different companies, industries, occupations, individuals, and geographical areas. At the same time, however, branch banking renders loan portfolios impersonal—that is, less representative of the specific needs of local communities and groups of individuals. In any case, whether the area served by a bank is local, regional, or statewide is a matter of legal prescription.

Banks whose communities include blighted or declining neighborhoods are torn between the desire to meet the credit needs of their communities and the need to make prudent loans. Increasingly in recent years bank boards have become sensitive to charges of redlining, the practice of using geographic location as a criterion to reject loan requests. As was discussed in Chapter 12, legislation has been enacted to discourage discriminatory loan policies. Bank boards must formulate policy that defines the bank's role in meeting the community's credit needs.

Stability of Deposits

The types of loans in a bank's portfolio reflect, in part, the composition of maturities and the stability of bank deposits and other liabilities. A general practice that banks have sought to follow over the years in the employment of their funds is to match the maturity of their liabilities with assets of corresponding maturity. This principle underlies the commercial-loan theory of lending, which, as we saw in Chapter 12, argues in favor of short-term, self-liquidating loans in recognition of the demand-deposit character of bank liabilities. Since the end of World War II, the gradual increase in banks' time and savings deposits and their importance, relative to total deposits, have led banks to increase their intermediate-term and long-term lending. Business term loans and many consumer loans constitute examples of the former, while mortgage loans exemplify the latter. These loans are generally financed out of the more stable savings deposits, while the more volatile demand deposits are used to finance short-term loans to businesses. Clearly a fluctuating deposit base, which is typical of banks in rural areas or single-industry communities, is less susceptible to longer-term financing.

Background and Evolution of Bank

Given the economic characteristics of its market and the stability of its deposits, a particular bank's opportunities to make loans also depend on the established patterns of business contacts and loan practice that its management has developed over the years. These patterns—which may have been the result of special talents or tastes of the bank's leading loan or executive officers, or of incidentally useful connections or conditions—also tend to develop institutional roots in highly trained and specialized lending officers, special reputations, and the like, which bestow upon the individual bank a particular character that is shown in the type of business it does and is expressed in the composition of its loan portfolio.

This helps to explain how some banks have become known as, for example, shipping, textile, electronics, or oil banks. Specialization of this type can be profitable, particularly where a degree of expert knowledge not common in the banking industry prevents other banks from competing effectively. It does, however, open the bank to a potential peril. Clearly, substantial loan concentration in the portfolios of such banks would be unavoidable. Such concentration, however, can be partly offset by seeking credit outlets in contrasting industries or in industries not subject to the same cyclical influences. This move, coupled with a good income investment policy, geographically and/or industrially diversified, can hold the risks of loan concentration within tolerable margins.

Management Preferences

The foregoing influences set the framework of possibilities within which bank management makes policy decisions pertaining to the composition of the loan portfolio. Not only is there ample choice within this framework, but the framework itself is not unalterable and may be changed gradually and within limits by the additions to established patterns fostered by current policy. The preferences of management with respect to loan portfolio composition, as these are affected by such considerations as yield, risk of loss, and liquidity (average rate of loan payoff), have a strong affect upon the actual composition at any time. This is especially true during a period of monetary restraint. During such a period the general demand for credit is so strong that banks are confronted with more loan requests in practically every category than they can possibly accommodate. Then, more than in any other phase of the business cycle, management exerts a decisive influence upon the types and volume of loans to be made.

Management's preferences for proper balance in the portfolio among the various loan types are expressed in the form of limits upon various loan categories. These limits are not firmly fixed for all time, but are flexibly adjusted or altogether eliminated in line with changing conditions. Limits on specific categories take the form of absolute magnitudes or of percentage relationships that broaden loan categories, or of relationships to time (including savings) deposits or to capital accounts. These limits become especially important when the initial phases of a restrictive credit policy set in, for it is during this time that management adopts a more cautious and selective approach in the extension of loan funds. The implementation of such an approach affects all loan categories and all borrowers. However, there are significant differences in the degree of this effect and in the manner of its transmission for major loan categories and for the individual borrower.

The categories that are the first to feel the impact of credit restraint vary, depending on the character of the loan market in which the bank finds itself. A restrictive lending policy affects primarily the bank's major lending categories (those that constitute the overwhelming bulk of the loan portfolio). Regulation of such categories is both an effective and a necessary instrument of general loan policy.

The loan categories that usually feel the impact of credit restraint most are real estate loans, consumer loans, and loans to brokers and dealers. By contrast, commercial and industrial loans, unless they constitute the overwhelming bulk of the loan portfolio, tend to feel the effects of a restrictive policy less. This must not be taken to imply that commercial and industrial loan applicants will not be required to meet the higher standards that are progressively imposed as credit tightens, or that they will receive priority over others seeking loans. The great diversity among borrowers within loan categories does not permit such a generalization to hold. But it does imply that commercial and industrial borrowers who can meet the higher standards will be the last to be turned down as a bank's lending limit is approached. There are a number of reasons for this privileged position of commercial and industrial borrowers. The cost of administering large business loans is generally low. There are certain economies of scale achieved in making a $1 million loan rather than 50 small mortgage loans or even a larger number of consumer loans. Another reason for their preference over other types of loans is that they are considered essential in maintaining the bank's lending base in the form of commercial deposits. It is basically the deposit balances (compensating balances) provided by the borrowers that place commercial and industrial loans first in management preference vis-à-vis the loans in the other categories during a period of credit stringency.

TERMS OF LENDING

Although there is significant variation in the terms of provisions of loan contracts, some generalizations may be made regarding this domain of lending policy. Some of the more important loan terms covered by bank policy, as determined by the board, include the rate of interest, compensating balances, provisions to protect against defaults, and repayment schedule.

Rate of Interest

The rates of interest that banks charge on loans at any given time generally reflect the state of the economy—that is, of monetary and fiscal policies and the demand for credit. These forces provide the background against which individual banks define their interest rate policy. This policy does not identify the specific rates that should be charged on the various kinds of loans made by a bank; instead, it provides guidelines to be taken into account by loan officers in the pricing of loans. The objective is, clearly, to treat the borrower fairly and earn for the bank a reasonable rate of return. If the rate quoted is too low, the bank will be forgoing income unnecessarily, while if it is too high, it may drive its customers to borrow elsewhere. Any consideration of the factors that enter into loan pricing must start with a discussion of the prime rate, which forms the basis on which other lending rates are formulated.

Role of the Prime Rate

The prime rate is the interest rate that banks charge their largest and most creditworthy customers. Large, preferred corporate clients have traditionally been granted short-term loans at the prime rate. It is considered an administered rate because it is adjusted by banks according to prevailing money-market conditions. This rate was first introduced in 1933 and represented the efforts of certain large banks to prevent the emergence of a price war among themselves in meeting the slack demand for bank loans that characterized the 1930s. Equally concerned about the adverse effects of a price war, the U.S. Congress allowed large banks to post a 1.5 percent prime rate as a minimum acceptable return on loans to creditworthy customers. Thus, the concept of a bank-imposed "floor" loan rate became an important feature of U.S. commercial banking, with rate changes initiated at various intervals by the leading banks. Once a change was announced, other major banks, and then smaller banks, followed suit. The rationale for this reaction was that if a large money-market leader deemed this change appropriate, it must be both needed and warranted by market conditions. Changes in the prime rate were given significant coverage in the financial press and the financial community, for they signaled changes in short-term bank lending rates in general and a possible movement in longer-term lending rates.

From the late 1960s on, two developments reduced the significance of the prime rate. First, the increased reliance of banks on money-market funds to finance their loan demands caused greater volatility in the cost of funds and resulted in greater and more frequent changes in the prime rate. This development, along with an apparent desire for publicity, led an increasing number of banks to join in the act of announcing prime rate changes. The resulting diversity reduced market sensitivity to rate changes and mitigated the importance of prime rate changes by the larger and more influential money-center banks.

Second, beginning in 1977 and continuing through the early 1980s—a period of record high prime rates (in mid-December 1980 the prime rate reached an unheard-of 21.5 percent)—there were widespread reports of loans to preferred customers at rates below prime. Recipients of these loans were generally large corporations with impressive credentials and access to alternative sources of funds, including the open market (such as borrowing through issuance of commercial paper). The practice of lending below prime quickly spread throughout the country, and in the early 1980s many medium-size and small banks regularly offered their corporate customers discounts from the announced prime rates. As a result the following trend developed: high-quality borrowers obtained loans at a discount from the prime rate while medium-quality borrowers received loans at prime. This practice was an important deviation from the traditional definition of the prime rate, and soon gave rise to a rush of lawsuits and Congressional criticism. The rising controversy led banks to adopt one of two strategies: delete the term "prime rate" from their loan documents and operational language, and replace it with the term "base rate," or keep the term but change its formal connotation as the "lowest" or "best" lending rate. Citibank and the First National Bank of Chicago are in the first group; Morgan Guaranty, Bank of America, and Chase Manhattan, in the latter.

Introduction of Floating Rates

Traditionally loans to businesses were made at fixed rates—that is, the rate charged did not change over the life of the loan. However, the higher cost of funds experienced in the late 1960s and its effects on profitability were instrumental in bringing about a change in banks' pricing strategies. To keep a profitable spread between their revenues and their cost of funds, in the late 1960s banks began to shift gradually to floating prime rates. The floating prime rate is linked to an open-market rate, such as that on commercial paper or Treasury bills. Often the secondary market rate on negotiable CDs is used to link the prime closely to the bank's cost of funds. Whatever the formula used, fluctuations in money-market rates cause adjustments in bank prime rates that, in turn, affect the amount of interest payments made by borrowers. For example, in a line of credit extended to a low-quality borrower at a rate of 2 percent above prime, interest rate charges will automatically change as the prime rate changes. Thus, if in response to fluctuations in money-market rates the prime rate rises from 9 to 10 percent, the loan's rate will increase from 11 to 12 percent; if the prime rate falls to 8.5 percent, the borrower will be charged an interest rate of 10.5 percent.

The floating-rate concept of loan pricing acquired new impetus in the early 1980s. With profits undermined by competition and a recessionary economy, banks began to make floating-rate consumer loans. By mid-1983 banks in at least a half dozen states were making variable-rate consumer loans. The floating rate on these loans made them a perfect match for banks' floating-rate money-market deposit accounts. Borrower acceptance of floating-rate consumer loans is expected to be better than that of variable-rate mortgages. With the maturity of consumer loans much shorter (usually up to four or five years), borrower exposure to rate fluctuations is more limited. To enhance the acceptability of these loans, banks were advertising auto loans at rates that were generally below the corresponding fixed-rate loans. In July 1983, for example, the Bank of America was marketing floating-rate auto loans priced at 12 percent, 2.5 percentage points less than its fixed-rate auto loans. Rates are adjusted quarterly, in line with the yield of three-month Treasury bills.

Variable-rate lending is also making headway in the area of mortgage financing. Indeed, as seen in Chapter 12, adjustable rates are becoming a common feature of mortgage instruments. Since the mid-1970s,when they made their first appearance in California,variable-rate mortgages have gained increasing acceptance among lenders because they offer returns that are competitive with going market rates. In addition, they provide greater flexibility in adjusting these long-term assets to the changing cost of funds.

With the advent of the floating-rate loan, the profitability of loan portfolios has been enhanced. In addition, the flexibility of the floating-rate loan gives bankers an important tool for coping with the increasingly competitive environment in which they must operate.

Loan Pricing

Clearly, if a loan is to be profitable, it must earn a rate of interest higher than the cost of the funds to the bank. How much higher is a function of a number of factors. Interest rates reflect the amount of risk involved. Small businesses have a higher rate of failure than large businesses and usually are charged more. The maturity of the loan is also considered, since the longer the loan period, the greater the uncertainty that repayment will be made in full. All of the costs involved in originating and servicing the loan—the costs of checking the borrower's credit history, of appraising collateral, and other administrative costs—must be covered by the interest charged. Installment loans have relatively high rates of interest because of the bookkeeping involved in recording the payments and the time required to make this type of loan. Moreover, small loans usually carry high interest rates because they have high administrative costs per dollar lent. In order to entice borrowers, the bank must offer loans at rates that are competitive with the costs of alternative sources of funds available to the borrower (such as other domestic or foreign banks or the money and capital markets). The bank must also weigh the opportunity cost of the loan by comparing it against other possible uses for the same funds. Finally, the applicant's relationship with the bank must be considered. Evaluating a business loan application goes beyond estimating the profitability of the individual loan. It also entails assessing the overall profitability of the applicant's relationship with the bank. The loan is but one element in that relationship, which may include maintaining deposits and using other bank services. The essence of a banking relationship, after all, is that business customers expect banks to meet their credit needs and banks expect loan customers to use the bank's other services.

Ignoring the benefits derived from the long-standing relationship with the corporate customer means risking loss of the customer's other business, then and in the future. Further, that customer may be responsible for attracting other customers to the bank, thus contributing to an expansion of the bank's business. For these reasons banks try to accommodate their steady customers' credit needs whenever possible.

A widely used approach to assessing the overall profitability of a corporate customer to a bank is called customer profitability analysis (CPA). This analysis is similar in principle to the standard account analysis (SAA), which determines the revenue generated by an account, the expenses of servicing it, and the resulting net profit or loss. The SAA is used primarily to determine appropriate compensating balance requirements for nonborrowing customers who use the bank's other services (such as wire transfers and lock box services) for which it charges fees. The CPA goes further, considering in addition such services as loans, investment counseling, and data processing in order to gauge a customer's overall profitability.

When the business loan applicant is a new customer, the bank has less information on which to base its profitability assessment, but the same issues apply: the bank forecasts the future profitability of the customer as a whole in deciding whether to grant the loan. Occasionally loan officers may extend loans to young and struggling businesses that other banks consider marginal credits. These loans constitute promotional lending. Several large U.S. companies owe their development and growth to aggressive and imaginative loan officers who recognized their potential and took greater-than-average risk to assist them in their modest beginnings. These companies never ceased to patronize the bank that extended them their first loan.

Compensating Balances

A customary feature of a short-term unsecured business loan is the compensating balance requirement, which obligates the borrower to maintain demand or time deposits with the lending bank as part of the loan agreement. Alternatively, this requirement may be applied against the credit facility; that is, borrower balances are expected not to drop below an agreed-upon percentage of the loan amount. The way this requirement is applied varies. In some banks it is applied rigidly: borrowers' balances are expected to be maintained at the minimum or not to fall below it throughout their indebtedness to the bank. Frequently, however, borrowers are given more latitude—the deposit balance must equal the specified minimum on the average or over the course of the year. Clearly, the former rule is much more burdensome to the borrower. Average balance requirements vary among banks and are influenced by prevailing money-market conditions. Generally, however, they run from 10 to 20 percent, with 15 percent being most common.

The requirement of maintaining compensating balances has an important effect on the cost of the loan. If the requirement is 20 percent and the borrower needs $80,000, the loan raised must amount to $100,000. Assuming that the interest rate charged is 15 percent, the effective cost of the portion of the loan usable by the borrower is 18.75 percent ($15,000 ÷ $80,000). The underlying assumption is, of course, that the borrower will use the entire amount of the loan. Since businesses frequently maintain some funds in their loan accounts, however, there is redundant borrowing (the difference between the level of these funds and the compensating balance amount).

Banks place more emphasis on compensating balances as qualification for loan accommodation in a period of credit stringency. During such times a borrower's legitimate claim on a bank for a loan is expected to be a multiple of his or her average balance, a figure that is gradually reduced (thus increasing the compensating-balance requirement) as the bank's credit-granting capacity approaches its maximum. Although the compensating balance increases the effective rate of interest on a loan, this does not constitute the full explanation for management's concern. The deeper significance of the compensating balance lies in the relationship of a bank's lending capacity to its deposit base. In order for a bank to be able to lend, it must have deposit funds, and borrowers must be disciplined to contribute to giving the bank lending power. Finally, the compensating balance constitutes a protective device for the bank in dealing with borrowers whose credit is not above reproach. Thus, if a borrower's default appears imminent, the bank can apply the balance on deposit against the loan, thereby offsetting a portion of it. This legal practice (right of offset) enables a bank to obtain a slightly better settlement than would otherwise be possible; that is, it enables the bank to become a general creditor for the remainder of the loan rather than being a general creditor of the bankrupt customer.

The popularity of compensating balances has been affected adversely in recent years by banks' growing reliance on profitability analysis. Cost-benefit analysis of corporate accounts focused on two inefficiencies of compensating balances as a pricing mechanism: the need to maintain legal reserves against these balances and to pay FDIC assessments. As a result a number of large banks have replaced compensating balances with fees or higher loan rates. This move is a departure from the traditional belief that lending is primarily a tool for developing a bank's current and potential deposit base.

Protection Against Default

In extending a loan a bank is always concerned with its ultimate collectability. If the borrower's current financial condition and past record of repayment are good, and loan collectability is expected from the liquidation of the transaction being financed or from anticipated profits, the bank will make the loan on an unsecured basis. Contrary to what is generally believed, large loans to businesses are frequently made on an unsecured basis. Moreover, consumer loans may be made on an unsecured basis because of borrower integrity, income, and past record of repayment. However, in a great many cases concern over the applicant's weak credit history may lead the bank to ask the borrower to pledge a specific asset or offer some other form of protection. Also, loans to rapidly expanding enterprises or to small or new businesses present a greater amount of risk and, therefore, necessitate bank protection. Long-term loans, because of the degree of uncertainty and potential risk involved, may require an extensive loan agreement to protect the lender.

There are various forms of protection available to a bank. The most common type is the direct pledge of assets. Lending against collateral is customarily referred to as asset-based financing. Various types of assets may be pledged as collateral, including real estate, equipment, corporate stocks and bonds, and accounts receivable. Since the purpose is to lessen the possibility of a loss if the loan is not repaid, banks have adopted certain criteria that determine the suitability of the collateral. First, the asset must be marketable—that is, it should be readily convertible into cash. A second desirable feature is that the asset has a relatively stable market value, so that the lender can ascertain in advance the approximate amount that can be realized should foreclosure become necessary. Further, the asset should not be perishable or subject to obsolescence due to changes in style or technology. Also, it is desirable that the asset entails a minimum of administrative expenses in maintaining control of it. Finally, the bank should obtain a first claim on the asset and its value should be greater than the face value of the loan it secures. The purpose of this safety margin is to protect the bank if it is forced to liquidate the asset because of borrower default. If the value of the collateral is not sufficient to cover the loan, the bank will have to obtain—in the event of a liquidation—a deficiency judgment and become a general creditor for the difference.

Frequently a loan applicant may substitute the guarantee of payment by another party for collateral. For example, when the loan request comes from the subsidiary (such as the production or marketing unit) of a corporation, the latter may offer its guarantee in support of the loan. Parent support is ordinarily justified on the ground that the operations of the subsidiary are financially an integral part of the parent's. Assuming the explicit guarantee of the parent, the bank's risk is no different from that assumed in a direct loan to the parent itself.

Guarantees are also sought and received by lenders in support of loans to veterans and small businesses. In the former instance, as stated in Chapter 12, the Veterans Administration guarantees all real estate loans to former servicemen. Small businesses may obtain loans with the guarantee of the Small Business Administration (SBA). One of the conditions for such a guarantee is inability of the borrower to obtain funds from commercial banks on a reasonable basis. Rural businesses and farmers also may obtain loans from banks with the guaranty of another governmental agency, the Farmers Home Administration.

In addition to collateral and guarantees, there are other forms of protection. One is the incorporation of covenants into the loan agreement, especially common in term loans to businesses. These covenants are of three types: affirmative, negative, and restrictive. An affirmative covenant, for example, requires the borrower to submit audited financial statements at the end of each year and unaudited statements at more frequent intervals. Other affirmative covenants may require the borrower to maintain minimum balance-sheet ratios; to hire an officer (such as a vice-president for finance) to ensure efficient financial management; and to carry "key-man" insurance on senior management personnel who cannot be easily replaced. Negative covenants restrain the borrower from certain actions, such as pledging assets while the loan is outstanding, entering into a merger with another concern, or offering a guarantee on loans to third parties. Restrictive covenants limit the latitute of management action, such as restricting dividend payments and potential borrowing, and setting ceilings on salaries, bonuses, and advances to officers and employees.

Still another form of protection normally required in loans to proprietorships and partnerships is obtaining the endorsement of principals and their spouses, thus rendering them responsible for the debt of the firm. In the cases of small or closely held corporations whose owners have also extended loans to the business, banks customarily request subordination of this debt to the bank's loan. The amount owed to principals thus serves essentially as additional capital protecting the bank's claim in the event of liquidation.

A final form of protection for the bank consists of the default provisions customarily included in loan contracts. Failure to comply with contractual obligations (such as to pay principal and interest when due or to observe the provisions of the loan agreement) makes the loan immediately due and payable. Term loan agreements customarily include a clause, known as an acceleration clause, that provides for the immediate repayment of the loan if certain provisions are violated.

Loan Repayment

The timing of loan repayment is a basic feature of a bank's lending policy. Loan repayment is generally agreed upon prior to the extension of the loan and should represent a realistic evaluation of the customer's ability to repay. The objective is to secure repayment through liquidation of the transaction being financed or the scheduled flow of earnings, rather than through forced foreclosure and subsequent sale of the pledged collateral.

When a bank is forced to sell collateral at a price below the market level, both the borrower and the community as a whole suffer. This effect is especially acute when the economy is already sluggish. The collapse of the real estate market in the 1930s in generally blamed on just such a trend. Mortgage loans extended in the 1920s were based on collateral values rather than on a realistic appraisal of the customer's ability to repay. As a result defaults occurred in the 1930s, forcing foreclosures in large enough numbers to depress the real estate market as a whole.

Repayment terms exhibit significant variation, depending on the type of transaction being financed. Loan repayments may range from a few weeks to 25 or 30 years, as is the case of mortgage loans. The terms may require a lump-sum repayment or repayment according to an installment schedule. Lump-sum loans, usually called straight loans, require complete repayment of principal on an agreed-upon date, with interest being paid at maturity or at various intervals during the life of the loan. More common, however, are installment loans, which require incremental repayment at fixed intervals: monthly, quarterly, semiannually, or annually. This type of loan is less formidable for an individual to manage and even aids in the budgeting of income.

Although installment terms are seen most often in consumer and real estate loans, businesses also avail themselves of this type of arrangement. At times banks will offer different terms of installment repayment, such as a larger, balloon payment at the end. This often necessitates the arranging of a new loan to cover repayment of part of the balloon payment. A balloon payment is normally set up to allow the borrower more flexibility at first, trusting that he or she will be able to pay off the full loan when it reaches maturity.

Another form of installment loan calls for payments at irregular intervals or in varying amounts. Agricultural loans are frequently of this type. Because of its dependence on weather, size of crops, and control of insect infestations, agriculture does not lend itself to a regular method of loan payment. Regular and equal payments similar to those in consumer credit are found only in loans financing dairy and poultry activity.

Borrowers often opt to repay their loans before they come due. Banks are usually in favor of such actions because they indicate the borrower is financially stronger. However, banks do not favor repayments made from funds borrowed elsewhere at lower interest rates. In such a case they may impose a stiff penalty for prepayment. This is especially true for term loans to businesses.

ADMINISTRATION OF THE LOAN POLICY

The administrative framework for carrying out the lending function is an integral part of loan policy. In other words, loan policymaking extends to the establishment of an effective lending organization and the adoption of the necessary procedures for the proper execution of the lending function. Specifically, the directors must determine the organizational structure of the lending function, set procedures for the review of loan applications, and identify the steps to be taken when the borrower fails to meet contractual responsibilities.

Organizing the Lending Function

The lending organization varies considerably from one bank to another, reflecting, among other things, differences in the sizes of the banks, the types of loans made, the quality of management, and the attitude of the boards of directors toward the delegation of authority. Generally speaking, the legal responsibility for bank lending rests with the entire board of directors. It is customary, however, to assign responsibility for supervising the lending function to a senior management member or to a loan committee that will ensure that loans are made in accordance with the law and the bank's own policies. In small unit banks, for example, this responsibility is assigned to the chief executive officer. Thus, the president of such a bank is at the same time the principal lending officer, and therefore handles all types of loan requests, whether for consumer, business, or real estate purposes. Other officers may be charged with performing limited lending functions along with their other activities. Under no circumstances, however, should the outside directors be actively involved in the granting of loans. Such involvement is a poor loan policy, not only because of their lack of technical or specialized knowledge but also because of their community affiliations with political, social, and business interests.

In large unit banks there is usually more delegation of authority and lending specialization. In such banks it is customary for the board of directors to assign to a loan committee the responsibility for supervising the lending function. This committee may be composed of a specific number of directors (directors' loan committee) or of loan officers (officers' loan committee). The latter holds especially true for larger banks, which, in response to specialized loan demand, usually have the lending function carried out by such specialized departments as consumer, real estate, agricultural, and business or commercial. In such cases the officers' loan committee may be composed of officers of the same loan department (intradepartmental committee). With an organization of that kind, very few, if any, loan requests would be referred to the board of directors for action.

The delegation of lending authority by the board of directors extends beyond the establishment of a loan committee. The board, at the recommendation of management, also assigns maximum dollar lending limits, for both secured and unsecured loans, that authorize loan officers to decide independently of the committee on requests within their assigned limits. These limits are subject to periodic review by the board and generally vary according to the size of the bank and the experience of the loan officer. A generally accepted approach is to assign lending limits by title. For example, the assigned limits may be scaled as follows: commercial loan officer, $50,000; assistant vice-president, $100,000; vice-president, $500,000; senior vice-president, $1,000,000. To expedite the loan decision process, some banks allow banking officers to combine their lending limits. Thus, two bank officers with loan limits of $100,000 each might jointly approve a $200,000 loan request. Combinations of lending limits are especially useful in situations requiring fast responses.

Just as with unit banks, the lending organization of branch banks exhibits important variation. It is not uncommon, however, for branch officers and managers to have a limited loan authority. In such instances loan requests above these limits must be referred to the head office for consideration by the branch's regional supervisor. If the specific request is higher than the supervisor's limit, it is referred to the bank's loan committee. Clearly, a high degree of centralization in lending authority is undesirable because of its detrimental effects. Such centralization results in significant delays; drastically reduces the element of personal contact, which is so important in credit evaluation; and gives rise to poor customer relations.

Assessing Loan Requests

In deciding upon loan requests, lending officers must have all relevant information about the applicant. While in small banks the loan officer must evaluate the creditworthiness and debt-repayment capacity of the loan applicant, in larger banks this task of credit analysis is performed by the credit department. The functions of the credit department are basically the same in all banks: it assembles, records, and analyzes credit information, with the objective of ascertaining the degree of risk associated with each loan request and determining the amount of credit the bank can prudently extend in each case. In some banks the credit department may make recommendations on a credit request; in others it may not. In any case the final decision is left to the lending officer and/or the loan committee.

Scope of Credit Analysis

In analyzing a loan request, the loan officer or credit analyst (depending upon who performs the credit analysis) will analyze a variety of factors, commonly referred to as the five C's of credit: character, capacity, capital, collateral, and conditions.

Character implies not just a willingness to pay off debts but also a strong desire to settle contractual obligations in accordance with the terms of the contract. When the borrower is an individual, character is largely a function of moral qualities, personal habits, style of living, business and personal associates, and general standing in the business and social communities. When the borrower is a company, character is a function of management integrity and reputation and standing in the business and financial communities. In the final analysis the reputation, integrity, and standing of a company's management are primarily a reflection of the character of the individuals responsible for the formulation and execution of company policies. Whether the borrower is an individual or a business, the previous record of meeting financial obligations plays a major role in evaluating character.

Capacity has both legal and economic connotations. From a legal perspective lenders are interested in knowing whether the party requesting the loan can legally obligate itself to borrow. In lending to a partnership, the loan officer should ascertain that the signing partner has legal authority (such as a power of attorney from the other partners) to obligate the partnership. Similarly, in lending to a corporation it is advisable to examine the corporate charter and bylaws to determine who has the authority to borrow for the corporation. In the absence of any explicit statement, a bank may accept a corporate resolution, signed by the board of directors, that identifies the person who has authority to negotiate for the company and sign the loan contract.

From an economic perspective capacity implies the ability to meet loan payments as they come due. The analytical measure utilized to determine a borrower's debt repayment capacity is cash flow, defined as net income plus depreciation and other noncash charges, minus other noncash income. The essence of cash-flow lending is that it enables a bank to analyze a company's financial projections and, if they are acceptable, develop a repayment schedule that reflects its ability to generate cash. An outgrowth of the anticipated-income theory, cash-flow lending has been extensively relied upon in the evaluation of loan requests. If the borrower is an individual, ability to generate income depends in part on business experience, education, good judgment, ambition, maturity or age, and shrewdness. For a corporation its power to generate income depends upon the quality of goods and services sold, cost and availability of raw materials and labor, competition, profit-sensitivity to cycles, effectiveness of advertising, and company location. In recent years, however, it has been increasingly recognized by banks that the single most important income-generating factor for a company is the quality of its management. Studies have concluded that inexperience, incompetence, neglect, and fraud are among the chief causes of business failures. Thus management should be able to adapt to changing conditions, replace inefficient practices with more efficient ones, take advantage of opportunities as they arise, and ensure that the company products have price and/or quality appeal.

A company with a sizable capital base is a more acceptable credit risk than one that is highly leveraged. The utilization of capital to purchase quality assets is an important factor in determining the financial strength of the company. A borrower's ability to obtain credit would thus be greatly affected by the amount and quality of the assets owned. For example, a manufacturer that owns modern machinery and equipment will be more certain of obtaining credit than will its counterpart with obsolete machinery and worn-out equipment. Similarly, a retailer with attractive premises and adequate stock will be favored over a counterpart with run-down premises and inadequate stock.

A bank may request a would-be borrower to provide collateral for the loan. In some cases collateral is pledged because the loan is longer-term, which increases the risk factor for the bank; in other cases security is requested in order to increase the borrower's sense of responsibility. In most cases assets are pledged because they improve a lender's claim against a borrower. Broadly speaking, the proper function of collateral is to minimize the risk of loss to a bank if, for unforeseen reasons, the borrower's income or profits fail to materialize sufficiently for repayment of the loan. In other words, the purpose of the collateral is to provide a bank with a second way out of a loan, and not to be the primary source of repayment. This view is exemplified by the axiom that collateral does not make a bad loan good but makes a good loan better.

A final factor to be considered by the loan officer in deciding on a loan request is conditions—the economic environment within which the borrower operates. To properly evaluate this factor, the loan officer must become familiar with the characteristics of the industry with which the firm is associated. This aspect of credit analysis has become increasingly difficult in recent years as more companies have grown into multiproduct and multinational concerns.

The kind of information for which the loan officer should look includes effect of economic conditions upon the industry (cycle sensitivity), the industry's output relative to gross national product, market structure, applicant's position in the industry, impact of technology (and technological changes) on the demand for the industry's product or its capital requirements, distribution methods, trends in industry profits, and the extent to which the industry is regulated by the government. Answers to these and related questions will enable the loan officer to obtain a comprehensive understanding of the dynamics of the industry, a basic input for a more pragmatic appraisal of the relative strengths and weaknesses of the firm.

Sources of Credit Information

Any evaluation of the applicant's creditworthiness has to rely on information. The bank certainly needs to accumulate information that will be used to evaluate the borrower's character, capacity, capital, collateral, and industry characteristics. Collecting information is the function of credit investigation, the scope of which varies from case to case, depending upon such considerations as type of loan, size, maturity, and collateral offered. Although a bank may draw upon several sources of credit information, some of the more important ones include an interview with the party requesting the loan, the bank's credit files, external sources, an in-person visit to the applicant's premises, and the applicant's financial statements.

It is customary for a loan officer to interview a would-be borrower for the purpose of developing credit information. During the interview the loan officer has the opportunity to inquire—or obtain additional information—about the history of the company, experience and background of the principal officers, the nature of the business, profitability of operations, extent of competition in the marketplace, and availability of resources for the smooth functioning of the business. Other information that the loan officer can obtain during the interview pertains to the purpose for which the proceeds of the loan are to be used. Knowledge of the purpose of the loan is important not only because of risk considerations but also because it enables the loan officer to relate repayment to the nature of the transaction being considered for financing. For example, project loans (for instance, to finance the development of raw materials, oil, mineral and other resources) call for repayment provisions tailored to the cash flow of the project being financed. The interview, moreover, provides the loan officer with an initial impression of the sincerity, integrity, and capability of the party requesting the loan. Finally, the interview is an appropriate time for asking the loan applicant to submit financial statements and any other additional information, and to arrange for a visit to the company.

A bank's credit files can be an important source of information for a loan officer. Banks establish for each borrower a file containing detailed information on the credit relationship with that client. By studying a prospective borrower's file the loan officer can see how well the customer complied with the terms and conditions of previous loans and can assess the bank's overall credit experience. The information contained in these files, though confidential, is customarily shared with other banks when they consider extending credit to the same client. Even if the borrower approaches the bank for the first time, a credit file may exist if the borrower is a sizable concern in the area in which the bank is located (a "prospect file").

Apart from the loan interview and the bank's own records, a loan officer may also make use of external sources of credit information. One such source is other banks; although banks compete vigorously among themselves, they share credit information when approached by the same customer. Another source of credit information is credit-reporting agencies. Payment and employment information on individuals is customarily supplied by credit bureaus that may be local, regional, or national. For businesses there are various credit-reporting agencies. One of the best-known is Dun and Bradstreet. This agency collects information on businesses in the United States and abroad, and publishes it on a firm-by-firm basis. Dun and Bradstreet also issues written credit reports that provide more detailed information on individual firms. These reports contain a brief history of the company, its principal officers, the nature of the business, ownership, operating data, and other financial information. Other external sources of credit information are the suppliers and customers of the prospective borrower; public records (where reference is made, for example, to pending lawsuits, bankruptcy proceedings, and transfers of propery); trade journals, which report developments and trends in the particular industries in which bank customers are engaged; public accounting firms; commercial publications (such as Moody's and Standard and Poor's); and newspapers, magazines, circulars, bulletins, and directories.

The financial status of a loan applicant and the quality of its management can often be determined by the loan officer through a visit to the applicant's business. Such a visit will give the loan officer firsthand information on the condition and efficiency of its physical facilities; the extent of management sophistication in terms of nature and method of operation, and financial planning; and employee attitude toward management policies.

One of the most important sources of credit information is the applicant's financial statements. Because financial statements identify the expected ability of a would-be borrower to repay indebtedness, their submission is generally required. A firm usually must submit audited condition and income statements, covering the last three to five years, so that the loan officer can obtain a feeling of company direction. The loan officer will need to inquire about each important account and determine whether the figure cited represents a fair and accurate statement of the value involved. Clearly, such evaluation may result in the trimming or adjustment of items from what was originally reported by the applicant.

This approach provides a pragmatic picture of the prospective borrower's financial position. A generally accepted practice is to record the applicant's financial information on standardized forms known as spread sheets. These permit consistency in the presentation and organization of financial data, and facilitate comparisons of several annual financial statements. If, in the bank's judgment, the applicant has misclassified any items—if, for instance, an item is classified as a current liability but actually belongs in the long-term category—the bank will reclassify them accordingly. A sample of spread sheets for balance sheet and income statement data is provided in Figures 13.1 and 13.2. Analysis of financial information is effected through certain widely used techniques, which are presented in the appendix to this chapter.

The credit information and analysis of the pertinent data, whether of businesses or consumers, constitute a bank's written record of its investigations. Because of the present and potential importance of such information for the bank itself and for other banks, an effort is made to preserve it in an orderly fashion—in an individual folder or file readily available for the use of the loan officer, loan committee, and even the board of directors. The credit department must keep these files up to date as new information comes to its attention. By

Figure 13.1. Sample Spread Sheet Form: Balance Sheet Analysis

| Name | CPA | | | | | | |

AMOUNTS IN $ M / $ MM	F I	DATE TYPE						
FINANCIAL SUMMARY								
Current Assets								
Current Liabilities								
Working Capital								
Long Term Debt								
Tangible Net Worth								
Net Sales								
Net Income (Before Extra. Items)								
BALANCE SHEET								
1. Cash								
2.								
3. Allowance for Bad Debts								
4. Net Receivables								
5. Inventory								
6.								
7. (ASSETS) Total Current Assets								
8. Net Fixed Assets								
9. Inv. & Adv. - Subs. & Affil.								
10. Prepaid Expenses								
11.								
12. Intangibles								
13.								
14.								
15. Total								
16. Notes Payable — Banks								
17.								
18.								
19. Current Maturities								
20. Accounts Payable								
21. (LIABILITIES) Accruals								
22. Income Taxes								
23.								
24. Total Current Liabilities								
25. L/T Senior Debt								
26.								
27. Deferred Taxes								
28.								
29. Total Liabilities								
30. Preferred Stock								
31. (NET WORTH) Common Stock								
32. Paid in Capital								
33. Retained Earnings								
34.								
35. Net Worth								
36. Total								
37. Lease Commitments								
38. Contingent Liabilities								
39. (INV.) Finished Goods								
40. Work in Progress								
41. Raw Materials								
42. (FIXED ASSETS) Land & Buildings								
43. Machinery, Equip.								
44. Gross Fixed Assets								
45. Accumulated Depreciation								
46. Old Retained Earnings								
47. Net Income								
48. Dividends								
49. Other								
50. New Retained Earnings								

Source: Provided by a bank.

providing a factual picture of the creditworthiness of the borrower, credit files are at the heart of the lending function and are essential prerequisites for the effective operation of a commercial bank.

As stated earlier, credit analysis does not involve decision making; at best it is a recommendation to loan officers and/or the loan com-

Figure 13.2. Sample Spread Sheet Form: Income Statement Analysis

	DATE PERIOD											
	INCOME STATEMENT											
51.	Net Sales/Revenue											
52.	Cost of Goods Sold											
53.	Gross Profit											
54.	Selling Gen. & Adm. Expenses											
55.	Depreciation											
56.												
57.	Operating Profit											
58.	Other Non Cash Charges											
59.	Other Income											
60.	Other Expenses											
61.	Interest Expense											
62.												
63.	Profit Before Taxes											
64.	Income Taxes											
65.	Net Income (Before Extra. Items)											
66.	Extraordinary Income (Charges)											
67.	Net Income (Loss)											
	ANALYTICAL & COMPARATIVE RATIOS											
68.	Net Sales Growth Rate %											
69.	Gross Profit Margin %											
70.	Net Income/Net Sales %											
71.	Net Income/Tang. N. W. %											
72.	Net Sales/Net Fixed Assets											
73.	Current Ratio											
74.	Quick Ratio											
75.	Days Receivable											
76.	Days Inventory											
77.	Total Liability/Tang. N. W.											
78.	Total Sen. Debt/Tang. N.W. & Sub. Debt											
79.	L. T. Debt/Tang. N. W.											
80.												
	SOURCES AND USES OF FUNDS											
81.	Net Profit After Taxes											
82.	Non-Cash Charges											
83.	Extraordinary Income (Charges)											
84.	Deferred Taxes											
85.	New Long Term Debt											
86.	Sale of Fixed Assets											
87.	Short Term Notes											
88.	Accounts Payable											
89.	Accruals											
90.	Other Current Liabilities											
91.	Other Liabilities											
92.	Minority Interest											
93.	New Capital											
94.	Total											
95.	Cash Dividend											
96.	Capital Expenditures											
97.	Long Term Debt Repayment											
98.	Cash											
99.	Accounts Receivable											
100.	Inventory											
101.	Other Current Assets											
102.	Investments											
103.	Other Assets											
104.	Intangibles											
105.	Total											
106.	Net Change In Working Capital											

Spread By:

Source: Provided by a bank

mittee, which will review the credit information and decide on the action to be taken. As is implied, in arriving at such decisions, loan officers are always expected to consider what is good for the bank. After all, the purpose of the lending policy is not to serve as an end within itself but to promote the objectives of the lending function.

Loan Monitoring

A necessary part of the loan officer's responsibility is to keep abreast of the loans outstanding. That is, once a loan has been made, the loan officer is usually responsible for supervising it. Loan supervision implies keeping in close contact with the borrower and monitoring his financial activities. This may include plant visits, securing the borrower's periodic financial statements, and reviewing requests for renewal or additional funds. And in the event of difficulty with the loan, the loan officer will exert every effort to collect the amount outstanding.

An essential corollary of active and aggressive lending is an effective collection system. Successful bank lending implies making good loans and keeping them current through a vigorous collection policy. Such a policy allows the bank to keep loan losses within tolerable limits.

The first explicit sign that a bank receives of a loan in distress is usually an indication from the borrower of inability to comply with the original repayment terms. Not infrequently a bank may see this difficulty approaching through its process of loan supervision. Whatever the case, with the first indication of customer delinquency, a bank should take appropriate measures. These measures may range from the revision of a borrower's payment schedule to meet new circumstances, to the implementation of strong-arm tactics. Prompt action may sometimes make the difference between the success and the failure of an active lending policy.

When delinquencies arise, they should be brought promptly to the attention of the loan committee or the board of directors. Detailed reporting is especially warranted when delinquent loans are large (as in the case in many commercial loans), with such reporting containing information on the cause of the delinquency and the subsequent measures instituted by the loan officer. On the other hand, small loans (consumer loans) may be referred to in the delinquency reports in a more generalized manner—in terms of aggregate amounts per type or class of loan.

Comparative data on delinquency rates, especially for consumer loans, are made available regularly through the publications of local credit bureaus, state bankers' associations, and the American Bankers Association. The direct comparison of these data with individual bank figures should provide a reasonable index of the soundness of a bank's lending and collection policies.

While the overall lending practices of banks are considered satisfactory, frequent criticism has been voiced about the loan administration of some banks. Such criticism has focused upon bank emphasis on collateral instead of on borrowers' ability to repay out of earnings (capacity); the failure to use information available; the use of inefficient, lenient, and tardy collection procedures; the tendency to equate loan size with borrowers' integrity and overall creditworthiness; the extension of too many loans on the basis of character references and outdated information; the giving of extensions and permitting of pyramiding of loans by marginal loan customers; and the extension of loans that do not contain adquate legal provisions to protect the bank in case of collection difficulties.

APPENDIX: TECHNIQUES OF ANALYSIS

Although inquiring about the nature and determining the true worth of accounts in financial statements are essential to intelligent analysis of the prospective borrower's business, item-by-item evaluation does not identify any key relationships between accounts or groups of accounts, nor does it make possible any judgment on the stability of the company's operations or the efficiency with which it is being managed. To address these and related questions, the loan officer must turn to such tools of financial analysis as cash flow, ratios, sources and uses of funds, and common-size analysis. Use of these tools helps the officer recognize exceptional situations quickly and distinctly, and encourages him or her to seek additional information, or clarification, from the would-be borrower. No single tool is complete; rather, each tool gives a different perspective on the prospective borrower's financial condition. Therefore, each of these tools should not be viewed as an end in itself, but as a means to reaching a reasoned decision. A brief description of some of the basic techniques used in the analysis of financial statements is provided below.

Common-Size Analysis

One of the simpler methods that the loan officer may use in analyzing financial statements is the common-size analysis, which expresses all related items as a percentage of a basic magnitude. For the purpose of this analysis, the basic magnitude is given the rating of 100 percent. Thus, all items in the income statement are expressed as a percentage of net sales, and all balance sheet items are expressed as a percentage of total assets or liabilities and equity. Once this is done and is extended to the financial statements of preceding years, the loan officer will be able to compare the relative importance of similar figures for previous periods and to identify any situations that appear to be out of line.

Trend Percentage Method

A related technique is the trend percentage method of comparison. This approach calls for establishing as base year the earliest year for which financial statements are submitted by the would-be borrower, and giving each item appearing in that statement a rating of 100 percent. If the corresponding accounts in subsequent years' statements are related to the base year, the lending officer will be able to detect the extent of the increase in each statement account, or group of accounts, over the base year and the revealed trend over the period under consideration. In some accounts the trend may be upward; in others, downward; in still others no definite trend may be evidenced. In addition to the direction of the trend, the loan officer will be able to compare the trends of individual accounts, or groups of accounts, over the period under consideration.

Sources-and-Uses Statement

Another useful method in investigating financial statements is the sources-and-uses-of-funds statement. Preparation of a sources-and-uses-of-funds statement is based on the computation of the net changes in the asset, liability, and net worth accounts from one balance sheet date to another. The net change in each individual balance sheet item is listed under separate "source" and "use" columns, depending upon what such a change represents. Changes that reflect increases in assets and decreases in liabilities and in net worth are recorded under the "uses of funds" column; decreases in assets and increases in liabilities and in net worth, under the "sources of funds" column. The purpose of this method is to readily identify the sources tapped by the would-be borrower to meet the need for funds during the period under consideration.

Cash Budgets

Cash flow is still another technique of value to the loan officer in the credit analysis function. Since borrowers are expected to pay off loans out of income rather than out of the sale of assets or through refinancing from another lender, the loan officer must look to their future income for debt retirement. Cash flows are thus prepared, for the most part, from information contained in projected income statements and balance sheets. Hence the importance of always checking the reasonableness of the borrower's projected data against the economic and industry forecasts for the period that the loan will be outstanding. Since the accuracy of a cash flow depends heavily on the assumptions underlying pro forma financial statements, the loan officer

Table 13.1. Cash Flow Analyses (millions of dollars)

	Company's Estimate of Most Likely Cash Flow					Bank's Estimate of Most Likely Cash Flow				
	1984	1985	1986	1987	1988	1984	1985	1986	1987	1988
Net income	-1	22	37	48	69	-5	-1	6	18	26
+ depreciation	51	56	60	63	57	48	51	52	55	58
Operating cash flow	50	78	97	111	126	43	50	58	73	84
+ other sources	11	8	12	13	1	11	8	11	10	1
Total operating cash flow	61	86	109	124	127	54	58	69	83	85
Change in net working investment	-69	48	-1	3	5	24	-6	-17	8	12
Capital expenditures	56	34	36	34	52	56	34	36	34	52
Other uses	7	6	0	1	11	1	12	0	0	1
Total uses	-6	88	35	38	68	81	40	19	42	65
Excess/(deficit)	67	-2	74	86	59	(27)	18	50	41	20
Change in short-term debt[a]	-29	-8	-7	5	-7	-29	-8	-7	5	-7
Available to service long-term (LT) debt	38	(10)	67	91	52	(56)	10	43	46	13
LT debt repayments	84	64	73	130	71	85	65	73	130	71
Excess/(deficit)	(46)	(74)	(6)	(39)	(19)	(141)	(55)	(30)	(84)	(58)

[a] Reduction in short-term borrowing as anticipated by loan applicant.
Source: Provided by a large New York bank.

may wish to develop cash flows under best, worst, and most likely assumptions when deciding the borrower's ability to service the debt.

Cash flows are normally requested from would-be borrowers for each year that the loan will be outstanding. These cash flows, in addition to predicting loan repayment, provide important insights into management competency. In other words, a company's sources of cash and its cash needs, and the relative amounts involved, project a clearer picture of the degree of efficiency with which the company is being managed. If, for example, the company's net cash generation is poor because of a rapid growth pattern, this raises questions about the soundness of credit practices, requirements for additional working capital, inventory policies, and payables policies.

An example of a cash flow analysis for a business firm is presented in Table 13.1. This table cites two cash flow versions: one submitted by the credit applicant and the other developed by the bank's credit analyst. The format is made up of the following components: total cash generated from operations, which includes net income plus depreciation and other sources of cash (such as decrease in noncurrent assets or increase in senior liabilities); total uses of cash, which includes capital and other expenditures as well as changes in net working investment (as determined by separate analysis of current accounts); changes in short-term debt, which may—or may not—constitute an additional source of cash, depending upon the direction of the change; servicing of already contracted long-term debt; and the resulting excess or deficit, which identifies the prospective borrower's ability to service the loan requested.

Ratio Analysis

A final technique in financial statement analysis is ratios. The objective of ratios is to highlight the internal relationship between figures reported in financial statements. If discriminately calculated and wisely interpreted, ratios can be of considerable assistance in the analysis of these statements. In other words, ratio calculations are helpful when the figures selected are reliable and come from accounts that bear a fundamental and important relevance to one another. Thus, though a large number of ratios can be computed, only a few are considered basic in analysis work. Table 13.2 lists the commonly used financial ratios, grouping them according to type.

Ratios are meaningless if analyzed in isolation. To provide insights regarding a company's performance, they must be compared against certain standards. Ratios lend themselves to two kinds of comparative analysis: time series and cross-sectional. The former provides

Figure 13.3. Industry Statistics for Retailers: Groceries and Meats (SIC #5411)

	Current Data					Comparative Historical Data				
	226(6/30&-9/30/81)		261(10/1/81-3/31/82)			6/30/77-3/31/78	6/30/78-3/31/79	6/30/79-3/31/80	6/30/80-3/31/81	6/30/81-3/31/82
ASSET SIZE	0.1MM	1-10MM	10-50MM	50-100MM	ALL	ALL	ALL	ALL	ALL	ALL
NUMBER OF STATEMENTS	245	162	60	20	487	351	358	409	453	487
ASSETS	%	%	%	%	%	%	%	%	%	%
Cash & Equivalents	9.6	10.4	9.5	7.7	9.8	10.9	11.2	11.1	9.3	9.8
Accts & Notes Rec. - Trade(net)	5.1	4.3	4.3	3.5	4.7	5.4	5.2	5.5	6.0	4.7
Inventory	35.0	31.6	28.7	32.1	33.0	34.1	34.1	33.5	33.5	33.0
All Other Current	1.7	2.2	3.1	2.0	2.0	1.9	1.4	2.2	1.7	2.0
Total Current	51.4	48.5	45.5	45.3	49.4	52.3	51.8	52.4	50.4	49.4
Fixed Assets (net)	38.6	39.3	45.3	43.4	39.9	36.8	36.3	37.1	38.1	39.9
Intangibles (net)	1.8	.9	.9	1.5	1.4	1.0	1.0	1.0	1.1	1.4
All Other Non-Current	8.2	11.3	8.2	9.8	9.3	10.0	10.2	9.6	10.3	9.3
Total	100.0	100.0	100.0	100.0	100.0	100.0	100.0	100.0	100.0	100.0
LIABILITIES										
Notes Payable-Short Term	5.2	2.9	1.6	1.6	3.8	4.7	5.2	5.2	4.9	3.8
Cur Mat-L/T/D	5.3	3.9	4.0	2.3	4.6	4.2	4.0	4.6	4.6	4.6
Accts & Notes Payable - Trade	18.0	23.4	25.7	23.3	21.0	20.8	21.3	20.5	21.6	21.0
Accrued Expenses	5.8	7.2	6.1	6.6	6.3	6.0	5.8	5.9	5.4	6.3
All Other Current	5.1	3.1	1.9	2.7	3.9	3.9	4.1	4.0	3.4	3.9
Total Current	39.3	40.6	39.3	36.6	39.7	39.5	40.4	40.2	39.9	39.7
Long Term Debt	25.1	22.0	18.5	24.6	23.2	21.9	21.9	23.2	24.2	23.2
All Other Non-Current	1.3	2.0	2.0	3.4	2.2	2.0	1.8	2.2	2.3	2.0
Net Worth	34.3	35.4	37.3	35.5	35.1	36.7	35.8	34.5	33.6	35.1
Total Liabilites & Net Worth	100.0	100.0	100.0	100.0	100.0	100.0	100.0	100.0	100.0	100.0
INCOME DATA										
Net Sales	100.0	100.0	100.0	100.0	100.0	100.0	100.0	100.0	100.0	100.0
Cost Of Sales	77.2	78.3	79.8	77.4	77.9	78.9	77.9	77.2	78.5	77.9
Gross Profit	22.8	21.7	20.2	22.6	22.1	21.1	22.1	22.8	21.5	22.1
Operating Expenses	20.5	20.3	18.0	20.3	20.1	19.2	20.0	20.2	19.7	20.1
Operating Profit	2.3	1.4	2.2	2.3	2.0	2.0	2.0	2.6	1.8	2.0
All Other Expenses (net)	.5	-.1	.6	.6	.3	.1	.1	.4	.3	.3
Profit Before Taxes	1.9	1.5	1.6	1.8	1.7	1.9	1.9	2.2	1.5	1.7
RATIOS										
Current	2.1 / 1.4 / 1.0	1.7 / 1.2 / .9	1.5 / 1.1 / .9	1.4 / 1.3 / 1.1	1.8 / 1.3 / 1.0	1.8 / 1.3 / 1.0	1.8 / 1.3 / 1.0	1.8 / 1.3 / 1.0	1.7 / 1.3 / .9	1.8 / 1.3 / 1.0
Quick	.6 / .3 / .1 (239)	.7 / .3 / .1 (160)	.5 / .3 / .2	.5 / .3 / .2 (479)	.6 / .3 / .2	.6 / .4 / .2 (347)	.6 / .4 / .2 (354)	.7 / .4 / .2 (405)	.7 / .3 / .2 (449)	.6 / .3 / .2 (479)
Sales/Receivables	0 999.8 / 1 390.0 / 3 139.0	0 999.8 / 1 331.5 / 2 151.0	1 376.7 / 2 214.8 / 3 123.2	1 271.1 / 2 186.5 / 3 113.7	0 999.8 / 1 327.5 / 3 133.7	0 963.0 / 1 319.7 / 3 113.0	0 999.8 / 1 325.1 / 3 120.7	0 999.8 / 1 315.7 / 3 121.7	0 999.8 / 1 261.6 / 4 932.	0 999.8 / 1 327.5 / 3 133.7

The table below is a comparative financial-ratio table (Robert Morris Associates format). Each data cell lists three stacked values (upper quartile / median / lower quartile); counts of statements are shown in parentheses.

Left section

Cost of Sales/Inventory	20.2 / 15.3 / 10.8	23.9 / 17.3 / 11.1	25.9 / 18.5 / 12.1	23 / 30 / 36	17 / 23 / 33
Sales/Working Capital	22.7 / 43.9 / -538.4	29.7 / 90.5 / -155.5	36.7 / 118.9 / 240.6	31.4 / 56.4 / 193.0	27.0 / 63.9 / 353.9
EBIT/Interest	(216) 6.5 / 3.2 / 1.4	(135) 6.8 / 2.8 / 1.5	(48) 7.8 / 3.8 / 1.0	(17) 5.3 / 4.3 / 2.3	(452) 6.7 / 3.1 / 1.5
Cash Flow/Cur. Mat L/T/D	(94) 4.5 / 2.3 / 1.3	(104) 5.3 / 2.6 / 1.1	(47) 9.5 / 3.0 / 1.4	(17) 8.1 / 5.5 / 3.2	(262) 5.5 / 2.7 / 1.4
Fixed/Worth	.6 / 1.1 / 3.0	.6 / 1.3 / 2.1	.9 / 1.4 / 2.1	1.0 / 1.4 / 1.7	.6 / 1.3 / 2.2
Debt/Worth	1.0 / 1.9 / 5.3	1.1 / 2.2 / 4.2	1.1 / 1.8 / 3.5	1.4 / 2.0 / 2.7	1.1 / 2.0 / 4.4
% Profit Before Taxes/Tangible Net Worth	(214) 48.5 / 25.2 / 12.0	(158) 35.0 / 20.8 / 9.0	33.6 / 20.7 / 4.8	29.6 / 24.1 / 12.4	39.7 / 23.4 / 10.6
% Profit Before Taxes/Total Assets	16.3 / 9.1 / 3.1	12.3 / 6.4 / 2.7	14.8 / 7.1 / 1.3	10.3 / 7.4 / 4.6	14.0 / 7.6 / 2.9
Sales/Net Fixed Assets	35.2 / 18.7 / 9.1	30.4 / 16.6 / 10.2	19.6 / 13.4 / 9.2	16.6 / 11.6 / 8.3	30.6 / 16.6 / 9.3
Sales/Total Assets	8.8 / 6.0 / 4.2	8.9 / 6.2 / 4.5	7.0 / 6.0 / 4.9	6.0 / 5.2 / 4.0	8.5 / 6.0 / 4.4
% Depr., Dep. Amort./Sales	(226) .6 / .9 / 1.4	(152) .6 / .8 / 1.2	(55) .7 / 1.1 / 1.3	(19) .8 / 1.1 / 1.4	(452) .6 / .9 / 1.3
% Lease & Rental Exp/Sales	(159) .6 / 1.2 / 2.0	(104) .7 / 1.1 / 1.6	(36) .4 / .9 / 1.1	(11) .1 / .5 / .9	(310) .6 / 1.1 / 1.6
% Officers' Comp/Sales	(126) 1.0 / 1.6 / 3.3	(63) .5 / .9 / 1.5			(200) .7 / 1.2 / 2.6
Net Sales ($)	701954M	3863019M	8212120M	6997804M	19774987M
Total Assets ($)	104275M	600747M	1375743M	1402253M	3483018M

Right section

Cost of Sales/Inventory	16 / 23 / 34	17 / 23 / 35	16 / 23 / 37	16 / 23 / 33	17 / 23 / 33
Sales/Working Capital	24.0 / 56.5 / -724.0	26.1 / 57.1 / -502.2	24.3 / 59.3 / -999.8	25.1 / 69.3 / -262.5	27.0 / 63.9 / -353.9
EBIT/Interest	(276) 11.0 / 5.2 / 2.0	(306) 9.9 / 4.5 / 2.0	(351) 8.2 / 4.0 / 2.0	(386) 5.8 / 2.9 / 1.5	(416) 6.7 / 3.1 / 1.5
Cash Flow/Cur. Mat L/T/D	(187) 5.6 / 2.5 / 1.1	(183) 5.2 / 2.5 / 1.2	(212) 6.9 / 2.9 / 1.6	(251) 6.1 / 2.6 / 1.2	(262) 5.5 / 2.7 / 1.4
Fixed/Worth	.6 / 1.0 / 2.0	.6 / 1.0 / 2.0	.6 / 1.0 / 2.1	.6 / 1.2 / 2.5	.6 / 1.3 / 2.2
Debt/Worth	.9 / 1.7 / 4.3	1.0 / 1.9 / 3.9	1.1 / 2.0 / 4.1	1.1 / 2.1 / 4.7	1.1 / 2.0 / 4.4
% Profit Before Taxes/Tangible Net Worth	(325) 45.4 / 25.7 / 12.5	(338) 43.3 / 25.6 / 12.8	(384) 48.1 / 29.2 / 15.7	(418) 38.5 / 22.7 / 9.1	(452) 39.7 / 23.4 / 10.6
% Profit Before Taxes/Total Assets	17.6 / 9.4 / 3.2	15.6 / 8.9 / 3.1	15.4 / 10.0 / 4.2	13.8 / 7.3 / 2.1	14.0 / 7.6 / 2.9
Sales/Net Fixed Assets	33.5 / 19.4 / 11.0	32.4 / 19.6 / 10.7	31.6 / 18.0 / 9.8	32.4 / 17.3 / 9.3	30.6 / 16.6 / 9.3
Sales/Total Assets	8.5 / 6.1 / 4.3	8.5 / 6.2 / 4.4	8.3 / 5.9 / 4.3	8.5 / 5.9 / 4.3	8.5 / 6.0 / 4.4
% Depr., Dep. Amort./Sales	(334) .6 / .8 / 1.2	(340) .8 / .8 / 1.2	(387) .8 / .8 / 1.3	(431) .9 / .9 / 1.3	(452) .6 / .9 / 1.3
% Lease & Rental Exp/Sales	(243) .8 / 1.2 / 1.8	(248) .7 / 1.2 / 2.0	(281) .7 / 1.1 / 1.6	(298) .7 / 1.1 / 1.6	(310) .6 / 1.1 / 1.6
% Officers' Comp/Sales	(146) .7 / 1.2 / 2.7	(150) .9 / 1.6 / 2.6	(166) .9 / 1.9 / 3.1	(178) .8 / 1.3 / 2.6	(200) .7 / 1.2 / 2.6
Net Sales ($)	10875054M	9990768M	11547799M	1948023M	19774987M
Total Assets ($)	1814079M	1571063M	1975848M	3477755M	3483018M

Note: M = thousand dollars; MM = million dollars.

Source: Robert Morris Associates, Annual Statement Studies (Philadelphia: Robert Morris Associates, 1982), p. 264. Reprinted by permission of Robert Morris Associates.

Table 13.2. Summary of Financial Ratios

Type and Name of Ratio	*Formula for Calculation*
Liquidity	
Current	Current assets
	Current liabilities
Quick, or acid, test	Current assets, inventory
	Current liabilities
Leverage	
Debt to total assets	Total debt
	Total assets
Debt to equity	Total debt
	Common equity
Interest coverage	Earnings before interest & taxes
	Interest charges
Fixed charge coverage	Earnings before fixed charges & taxes
	Fixed charges
Activity	
Inventory turnover	Cost of goods sold
	Average inventory
Average collection period (days)	Accounts receivable
	Annual credit sales/360
Fixed assets turnover	Sales
	Fixed assets
Total assets turnover	Sales
	Total assets
Profitability	
Net profit margin	Net profit
	Sales
Return on assets	Net profit
	Total assets
Return on equity	Net profit
	Common equity

Source: Prepared by author.

for interyear comparisons of borrower performance to determine the general direction in which the company's financial condition is moving; the latter, for comparisons with other firms in the same industry over a common period of time.

There are several sources of comparative financial ratios both for time series and cross-sectional analysis. Probably the source of industry average ratios most widely known and used by bankers is the *Annual Statement Studies* published by Robert Morris Associates (RMA). This publication provides financial data on more than 300 lines of business activity based on the financial statements of a sample of over 60,000 different firms. The data, which consist of 16 ratios and a common-size balance sheet and income statement, are presented on an industry-by-industry basis, with each industry subdivided into size categories. A standard page from the *Annual Statement Studies* is reproduced in Figure 13.3.* Another source of ratios is Dunn and Bradstreet's *Key Business Ratios in 125 Lines*. This publication provides 14 ratios, with the interquartile ranges, for 125 lines of business activity. The *Almanac of Business and Industrial Financial Ratios*, published annually by Prentice-Hall, is still another source. Ratios cover 170 lines of business activity and are based on samples of corporate tax filings with the Internal Revenue Service. Although quite accurate, these data have a drawback—they are available with a lag of two to three years.

LOOKING BEYOND ANALYTICAL TOOLS

Although analytical tools are important in evaluating the financial condition of a would-be borrower, it is necessary to supplement them with specific pertinent facts and direct contact with the borrower. After all, credit analysis is not cut-and-dried. It is as unique as each individual borrower. If a borrower's character is poor, the probability of respect for the terms of a loan agreement is low. Arriving at a reasoned decision thus requires use of analytical tools combined with intuitive judgment.

SUGGESTED REFERENCES

Conlin, Graham P. *Commercial Loan Review Procedures*. Philadelphia: Robert Morris Associates, 1978.

Crosse, Howard D., and George H. Hempel. *Management Policies for Commercial Banks*. 3rd ed. Englewood Cliffs, N.J.: Prentice-Hall, 1980.

Davis, Richard G., and Jack M. Guttentag. "Are Compensating Balance Requirements Irrational?" *Journal of Finance*, March 1962, pp. 121-26.

Gill, Edward K. *Commercial Lending Basics*. Reston, Va.: Reston Publishing Co., 1983.

---

*RMA cautions that the *Studies* be regarded only as a general guideline and not as an absolute industry norm. This is due to limited samples within categories, the categorization of companies by their primary Standard Industrial Classification (SIC) number only, and different methods of operations by companies within the same industry. For these reasons RMA recommends that the figures be used only as general guidelines in addition to other methods of financial analysis.

Hodgman, Donald R. *Commercial Bank Loan and Investment Policy*. Champaign: Bureau of Economic and Business Research, University of Illinois, 1963.

Kreps, Clifton H., Jr., and Edward F. Gee, eds. *Analyzing Financial Statements*. 4th ed. Washington, D.C.: American Institute of Banking/American Bankers Association, 1970.

Merris, Randall C. "Business Loans at Large Commercial Banks: Policies and Practices." *Economic Perspectives*, Federal Reserve Bank of Chicago, November/December 1979, pp. 15-23.

Morsman, Edgar M., Jr., *Effective Loan Management*. Philadelphia: Robert Morris Associates, 1982.

Nadler, Paul S. "Compensating Balances and the Prime at Twilight." *Harvard Business Review*, January/February 1972, pp. 112-20.

Park, Y. S. "Devaluation of the U.S. Prime Rate." *The Banker*, May 1982, pp. 45, 47, 49, 51-52.

Sihler, William W., ed. *Classics in Commercial Bank Lending*. Philadelphia: Robert Morris Associates, 1981.

Sinkey, Joseph F., Jr. *Commercial Bank Financial Management*. New York: Macmillan, 1983.

Stock, Keith L. "Asset-Based Financing: Borrower and Lender Perspectives." *Journal of Commercial Bank Lending*, December 1980, pp. 31-46.

From a functional point of view, the investment account may be said to straddle the lending operations of commercial banks. On the one side it provides the necessary degree of bank liquidity in the form of short-maturity, money-market instruments (secondary reserves). On the other side it employs whatever funds cannot be loaned to provide income for the bank in the form of long-maturity, capital-market instruments (bond portfolio). Liquidity, in the first instance, and income, in the latter, thus constitute the determining factors in the acquisition and holding of securities. This dual role of the investment account is not, however, identifiable in a bank's balance sheet, where reference to investment holdings is made only according to issuer. Since statistics also do not distinguish between secondary reserves and the bond account, discussion of banks' investments is kept at the general, or aggregate, level. This chapter thus identifies the different types of securities that banks may purchase and describes the regulations that govern such purchases. The last part of this chapter deals with the underwriting function and related investment activities of commercial banks.

ELIGIBLE INVESTMENT SECURITIES

Securities eligible for purchase by commercial banks may be classified according to obligor into the following categories: U.S. Treasury securities, agency obligations, state and local government issues, corporate debt, and other securities. These are discussed below.

U.S. Treasury Securities

Types

When its revenues from taxation are not large enough to cover its expenses, the federal government must make up the difference. On various occasions the Treasury Department, as fiscal agent of the government, has sold securities as a means of borrowing. As shown in Table 14.1, at year-end 1982 the total gross public debt of the U.S.

Table 14.1. Total Gross Public Debt of U.S. Treasury, 1982 (billions of dollars)

Item		*Amount Outstanding*
Total gross public debt		$1,197.1
By holder		
Held by U.S. government agencies & trust funds		209.4
Held by Federal Reserve banks		139.3
Held by private investors		848.4
Commercial banks	$ 131.4	
Insurance companies	38.7	
State and local governments	113.4	
Foreign and international	149.4	
All other	415.5	
By type[a]		
Marketable		881.5
Bills	311.8	
Notes	465.0	
Bonds	104.6	
Nonmarketable		314.0
Savings bonds and notes	68.0	
Foreign issues	14.7	
Held by U.S. government agencies and trust funds	205.4	
Other	25.9	

[a]Excludes $1.6 billion of noninterest-bearing debt.
Note: Details may not add to totals due to rounding.
Source: *Federal Reserve Bulletin*, September 1983, p. A33.

Treasury was about $1.2 trillion. If allowance is made for the portion of the debt held by accounts of the federal government itself, the net indebtedness of the U.S. Treasury was actually much less. Not all of the U.S. Treasury debt was "in the market." There are three major forms of nonmarketable debt: U.S. savings bonds sold to households, special dollar-denominated and foreign-currency-denominated Treasury issues held essentially by foreign central banks, and issues held by U.S. government agencies and trust funds. Thus, the marketable portion of the U.S. Treasury debt amounted at year-end 1982 to $881.5 billion, 73.6 percent of total debt.

As indicated in Table 14.1, there are three types of marketable Treasury debt: bills, notes, and bonds. At year-end 1982 Treasury bills amounted to $311.8 billion, 35.4 percent of the total marketable debt. Treasury bills (T-bills) are short-term obligations with original maturities of three, six, nine, or twelve months. Each issue is advertised and sold on an auction basis through the Federal Reserve banks and their branches, which perform the role of agents for the Treasury. Unlike the nine- and twelve-month bills, which are auctioned once a month, the three- and six-month issues are auctioned every Monday at 1:30 P.M. New York time, with payment made on the following Thursday. Interested investors, primarily financial institutions, submit their bids for particular quantities of specific denominations. The Treasury awards bids in full, starting with the highest price and going down to the one that exhausts the amount available of that issue, which is the total to be issued less the amount for which noncompetitive tenders have been received. Noncompetitive tenders (normally less than $500,000 each) from small investors are accepted in full, with such investors paying the average of the accepted competitive bids in the weekly or monthly bill auction.

The automation of the government securities market has resulted in the marketing of T-bills on a computerized book-entry basis. T-bills are customarily quoted on the basis of 100, even though the par, or face, value of each bill is $1,000. They are sold in denominations of $10,000 to $1,000,000, and are issued on a discount basis. In other words, the rate of return to an investor is determined by the difference between the par value of the bills and the price paid for them. For example, if an investor pays the Treasury $9,500 for a $10,000 T-bill maturing a year later, he or she will earn $500 (5.3 percent) on the investment if it is held to maturity.* Since there is an active secondary market in bills, the investor may sell them at any time before their maturity, receiving the current market price of the bills (which will be less than the par value).

---

*For T-bills of less than a year's maturity, the discount rate (D_r) may be determined on the basis of the bank discount method, which uses a 360-day year for simplicity. This formula is

$$D_r = \frac{\text{par value - purchase price}}{\text{par value}} \times \frac{360 \text{ days}}{\text{no. days to maturity}}.$$

The yield to maturity for this instrument is always higher because of consideration of the amount invested rather than the principal, and of a 365-day year rather than the 360 used in the above computation. Thus,

$$Y = \frac{\text{par value - purchase price}}{\text{purchase price}} \times \frac{365 \text{ days}}{\text{days to maturity}}.$$

Thus the discount rate on a three-month, $10,000 T-bill that costs $9,800 is

$$\frac{\$10,000 - \$9,800}{\$10,000} \times \frac{360}{90} = 8 \text{ percent.}$$

The yield to maturity of this bill is 8.277 percent.

A bill issued by the Treasury when it has special cash needs is the tax anticipation bill (TAB). The TABs are issued with six- or nine-month maturities and aim to attract the funds set aside by corporations to pay their federal taxes. They are set up to mature one week after the quarterly date when corporate taxes come due. Although they may be turned in for cash at maturity, corporations can redeem them at the Treasury for par one week earlier, in payment of their taxes.

The principal utility of Treasury bills for banks and other investors is liquidity. T-bills are liquid not only because their maturity is near but also because the secondary market in these obligations is very large. In fact it is so large that a $100 or $200 million sale of T-bills can be made almost casually, with minimal, if any, pressure exerted in the market. T-bills have thus evolved into the most popular money-market instrument. Commercial banks are large investors in T-bills, which they hold as part of their seasonal secondary reserve requirements.

As seen in Table 14.1, the largest concentration of marketable Treasury debt at the close of 1982 was in Treasury notes (52.8 percent of marketable debt). Treasury notes range in original maturity from one to ten years. With the passage of time, of course, the maturities of outstanding notes fall to five years or less, which renders them ideal for banks' cyclical secondary reserve needs. These notes bear a fixed rate of interest that is paid semiannually and is slightly above that on T-bills. They are also quite marketable and may be purchased in denominations ranging from $1,000 to $1,000,000. Treasury notes are available in either a registered or a book-entry form.

Treasury bonds, the government's typical instrument for long-term debt, have a maturity at issue of more than ten years. They are also very marketable and are issued in denominations of $1,000 to $1,000,000. Bonds, like notes, are available in registered or book-entry form and pay a fixed rate of interest semiannually. At year-end 1982 the value of bonds outstanding was $104.6 billion, 11.9 percent of the Treasury's marketable debt. The limited importance of bonds vis-à-vis the other forms of marketable debt outstanding is partially explained by interest costs. Short- and intermediate-term financing is customarily associated with lower rates of interest than is long-term debt, thus contributing to a reduction in the Treasury's interest expense. Most important, however, the maturity structure of the federal debt has been affected by legislative constraint on the interest rates that the Treasury can pay on long-term debt. Since the late 1910s Congress has restricted the interest rates that may be offered on

Treasury bonds* while leaving unregulated the rate that may be paid on short- or intermediate-term securities. Thus, during periods of high interest rates the Treasury, in view of its inability to compete effectively for funds in capital markets, relies extensively on short- and intermediate-term issues.

Investment Characteristics

Several features make Treasury obligations attractive to commercial banks. Government securities are unique in that they offer investors safety of principal and interest. The constitutional right of the federal government to tax and to print money assures its current and future capacity to service its debt. Because these debt instruments are so safe, their yields are generally lower than those obtained from corporate issues. An additional corollary of safety is that bank holdings of Treasury securities require less supervision, and hence administrative costs in managing them are relatively low. Another attribute of these securities is their availability in almost any desired maturity consonant with bank investment policies. In addition, they enjoy a high degree of marketability. The secondary market in which Treasury securities are traded is a very large one with great absorptive capacity. The market is dominated by a relatively small number of dealers, some of which are money-market banks, who stand ready to trade in Treasury issues. The average trading volume in Treasury securities in mid-August 1983 approached $48 billion a day, with T-bills accounting for more than half of such trading (see Table 14.2).

These qualities have expanded banks' use of government securities beyond the traditional domains of liquidity and income. One alternative use of U.S. Treasury obligations is as collateral for advances obtained from Federal Reserve banks. Another is their use in repurchase agreements. Still another is their use in meeting the pledging requirement on public deposits. More specifically, commercial banks

---

*The statutory interest-rate restriction on Treasury bonds originated with the Liberty Bond acts of 1917 and 1918, which introduced a ceiling interest rate of 4.25 percent. This ceiling did not cause any controversy for several decades because government bond yields in the secondary market rarely rose above it. In 1965, however, bond yields began to exceed the ceiling, placing the Treasury at a competitive disadvantage vis-à-vis other borrowers in the capital markets. Recognizing this problem, the U.S. Congress provided for the exemption of certain long-term debt issues of the U.S. Treasury from interest-rate ceilings, and also for the extension of the maturities of Treasury notes to ten years (instead of the earlier five years) to enable the Treasury to tap funds at competitive rates.

Table 14.2. U.S. Government Securities Dealers' Transactions for the Week Ending Wednesday, August 17, 1983 (average of daily trading)

Item	Volume of Transactions (billions of dollars)	Percent of Total
By maturity		
Bills	$25.1	52.2
Other within 1 year	.7	1.5
1-5 years	10.1	21.0
5-10 years	5.5	11.4
Over 10 years	6.8	14.1
Total	$48.1	100.0

Note: Details may not add to totals due to rounding.
Source: *Federal Reserve Bulletin*, September 1983, p. A34.

that accept federal government deposits are required to secure such deposits by pledging U.S. government securities against them. These securities, whether from the bank's liquidity account or the bond portfolio, are typically pledged with the bank's trust department to ensure the safety of these deposits in the event of insolvency. Their replacement by other types of securities is possible, although the Secretary of the Treasury reserves the right to require amounts in excess of 100 percent of the value of the deposit if the collateral is deemed to be of great potential risk.

This pledging requirement extends to state and local government deposits, with U.S. government securities, and sometimes the securities of state and local governments, usually pledged to ensure the safety of these deposits. Although this requirement is important, the extent to which it is enforced by local governments is more a matter of local custom than of careful consideration of the potential hazards involved.

All business decisions normally are accompanied by constraints on the range over which action can be taken. The alternative uses of Treasury securities described above constitute one such dimension of decision making for a bank. Money-market instruments, and more generally investment securities used in any of the above capacities, cannot be readily sold. Thus, to the extent that these securities are held for liquidity purposes, their efficiency as media of liquidity is thereby lessened.

Bank Holdings

As shown in Table 14.1, at the end of 1982 commercial bank holdings of Treasury securities amounted to $131.4 billion, which represented 11 percent of the total federal debt outstanding. The many qualities that these obligations possess made them the most important feature of bank investment portfolios for the three and a half decades ending in the late 1960s. The preponderance of U.S. Treasury obligations in bank portfolios, as shown in Figure 14.1, started in the early 1930s. With the loan demand generally low and the pressure on commercial banks to augment income rising significantly, banks became active buyers of investment securities. The sizable losses they had sustained, however, during 1929-31 had led to a shift in emphasis among alternative investment instruments and a more conservative approach to investment portfolios. This shift in emphasis favored the securities of the federal as well as of the state and local governments, though more markedly so those of the federal. The increase in the federal debt, which resulted from the Treasury's deficit financing (designed, in part, to stimulate the economy), gave commercial banks and other investors the opportunity to build up their portfolios of government obligations. Thus, from 1932 to 1935 bank holdings of government obligations doubled, and by 1934 the investment portfolio of com-

Figure 14.1. Investment Holdings of Commercial Banks, by Type of Security: 1914-74 (billions of dollars)

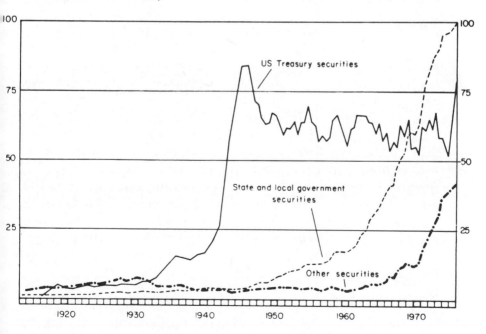

Source: Board of Governors of the Federal Reserve System, *Historical Chart Book* (Washington, D.C.: Federal Reserve System, 1974), p. 15.

mercial banks exceeded loans—a relationship that lasted until the latter part of 1955.

The war years accentuated the trend established during the prewar decade, with bank holdings of U.S. government securities reaching unprecedented heights. From 1941 to 1945 bank holdings of such securities increased from $22 billion to nearly $91 billion. This expansion was made possible on the supply side by the huge deficits of the federal government, and on the demand side by the use of the large amount of excess reserves accumulated by the banks during the 1930s and the additional reserves created by the Federal Reserve banks in support of the Treasury's requirements. In postwar years commercial banks have greatly reduced their holdings of Treasury obligations, prompted by the extraordinary postwar demand for loans. This reduction, however, was also occasioned by their desire to invest more substantially in the securities of state and local governments and profit from the tax-exemption feature of these issues. In the 1970s bank holdings of tax-free state and local government issues grew very rapidly— so much so that they became of primary importance in the portfolios of commercial banks. Thus, by March 31, 1976, state and local government obligations in commercial bank portfolios amounted to $100 billion, as against $85.4 billion in U.S. Treasury obligations and $38.4 billion in "other securities."

Agency Obligations

Another popular type of security traded in financial markets is the debt of government agencies. Established to support the financial needs of disadvantaged sectors of economic activity, government agencies issue their own debt securities and compete effectively for funds in financial markets. The activities of these agencies have expanded significantly over the years, as evidenced by the size of the agency debt outstanding. From a modest existence in the early 1950s, the market for agency debt has grown to a major component of the U.S. financial system, with $235 billion of securities outstanding on June 30, 1983. This debt encompasses the entire spectrum of maturities, ranging from short- to long-term. Like most Treasury issues many agency obligations enjoy an active secondary market, and price quotations are made available for many of these to banks on a daily basis by the financial press.

Types

Federal agencies issuing debt include the Export-Import Bank, the Federal Housing Administration, the Postal Service, and the Tennessee

Valley Authority. The securities of these agencies accounted for 14 percent of the total agency debt outstanding in mid-1983. Indications are that the debt of these agencies will gradually be reduced because of the activities of the Federal Financing Bank (FFB). Established in 1974 and operating under the Treasury Department, the FFB finances the activities of federal agencies by borrowing funds from the Treasury. If current trends continue, FFB securities issued to the Treasury will eventually replace all federal agency debt outstanding. What this means is that in time, government-sponsored agencies, which cannot borrow through FFB, will be virtually the only agencies tapping the markets for funds.

Government-sponsored agencies are in essence corporations sponsored, but not owned, by the U.S. government. These agencies account for the bulk of the agency debt outstanding (86 percent in mid-1983). These agencies are active in two markets, the residential mortgage market and the market for farm credit. The agencies included in this group are Fannie Mae and Freddie Mac, which provide a secondary market for mortgages; the Federal Home Loan Bank System, in essence the equivalent of the Federal Reserve System for savings and loan associations and other types of mortgage lenders; the Student Loan Marketing Association (SLMA or Sallie Mae), which supports the student loan program by purchasing insured student loans from, and making advances to, eligible lenders; and the Farm Credit Banks (Federal Land Banks, Federal Intermediate Credit Banks, and Banks for Cooperatives), which provide farm business services and make loans to farmers and cooperatives. Several of these agencies were formerly part of the federal government structure. However, to spare them the political and economic constraints of the federal budget and to allow them to achieve their full potential, the government converted these agencies to private ownership.

Investment Characteristics and Bank Holdings

Since agency securities do not constitute the direct obligations of the federal government, they tend to offer somewhat higher yields than those available on U.S. Treasury securities. Nevertheless, agency debt is extremely safe and is regarded by the investment community as having credit quality similar to that of U.S. Treasury issues. For it is the general belief that the federal government would not allow the default of any of these obligations. Agency issues have thus been treated as noncredit-risk assets and are usually reported in bank statements separately from other risk assets. Agency securities can be pledged as collateral by commercial banks for securing public deposits. At year-end

1982 all insured commercial banks held $76.4 billion of agency securities, which accounted for 21.3 percent of their total investment holdings.

State and Local Government Issues

Population pressures (increases in, and movements of, population) and the soaring costs of providing services have driven an increasing number of state and local governments to financial markets in order to finance their capital projects and budgetary deficits. These bodies include not only state, county, and municipal governments but also school districts and special districts, such as water or transportation authorities. The securities issued by these entities have come to be known as municipal bonds or "munis." The financing requirements of these various state and local governmental units have risen so rapidly in recent decades that between 1950 and 1980 state and local debts expanded from $24.1 billion to over $300 billion.

The major distinguishing feature of these securities compared with all other securities in the financial markets is that the interest paid to investors is exempt from federal income taxes, hence the reference to these securities as tax-exempts. Most states exempt their own securities from state income taxes as well. Exemption of the interest income of these securities from federal taxation dates from the late nineteenth century, when Congress passed a law to this effect. The implication of the federal income-tax exemption of these securities is that state and local governments can raise funds at lower interest costs than the federal government, since investors gain from the lack of taxation. These securities are thus appealing to investors who are subject to a high marginal tax bracket (such as commercial banks, casualty insurance companies, and wealthy individuals). By contrast, these securities do not appeal to such investors as pension funds, thrift institutions, and life insurance companies, which are subject to either relatively low or zero marginal tax rates.

Types

State and local government debt is both short- and long-term. Short-term borrowing by state and local government units is basically of three types: tax anticipation notes (TAN), which are used to bridge the gap between actual expenditures and anticipated tax receipts; public housing authority notes (HAN), which provide local housing agencies with working capital for public housing projects until permanent financing is secured through long-term bonds; and bond anticipation notes (BAN), which are used as temporary sources of financing particularly if credit markets are tight or interest rates are expected to fall.

These notes are generally backed by the "full faith and credit" of the issuing government unit. Housing authority notes are, in addition, guaranteed by the full faith and credit of the federal government, according to the Housing Act of 1949. These issues are thus especially attractive to investors because they are both tax-exempt and guaranteed by the federal government—that is, virtually free of credit risk.

The bulk of state and local government financing is on a long-term basis. There are two major types of municipal bonds, general obligation bonds and revenue bonds. General obligation bonds are the most common type of state and local government debt. From the investor's point of view, general obligations are generally safer than revenue bonds because they are backed by the full faith and credit of the issuing government; that is, the full taxing power of the issuer is pledged to assure payments of interest and principal when due. Despite this safeguard, the tangled financial problems of many large cities in the 1970s caused investors to reassess the credit standing of general obligations. The financial crisis of New York City in the mid-1970s and the prospect of default led the federal government to step in and guarantee loans made to the city. Investor concern about the credit standing of municipal obligations reached a climax in December 1978, when the city of Cleveland defaulted on its debt.

In addition to the financial crises of the large older cities, the "taxpayer revolt" of the late 1970s increased investor sensitivity to the creditworthiness of borrowing governments. This revolt started in California in the summer of 1978 with the passage of Proposition 13, which introduced limitations on real property tax rates. The effect of this law was to limit the taxing authority of the state, and hence its ability to finance new bond issues through tax increases. The success of the taxpayer revolt in California resulted in the creation of taxpayer lobbies in other states, and the passage of similar legislation. For many states this issue is a continuing problem hanging over the market for general obligation bonds.

Revenue bonds, the other major group of state and local obligations, lack any government backing and are payable only from the revenues generated by the project being financed through their issue. For example, dormitories and universities are frequently financed with revenue bonds, and student fees are used to pay them off. Also, roads and bridges may be financed with revenue bonds, to be repaid with tolls. The risk assumed by investors is that the revenues generated may not be sufficient for the payment of interest and principal, in which case the bonds will go into default. Since investors cannot foreclose on a university or a bridge, their only course of action is to wait and hope for a possible resumption of payments in the future.

In recent years various new types of revenue bonds have appeared in financial markets. One type is industrial development bonds, which finance the purchase of land and the construction of plants to attract new industry to an area. The new businesses lease the plant, and the rental payments are used to service the bonds. The benefits to the area are twofold: an increase in the number of local jobs and an increase in local tax revenues. Another type is hospital revenue bonds, issued to finance the building of hospitals. Once completed, these hospitals are leased to private or public agencies, with the lease income used to amortize the debt. Still another type is mortgage revenue bonds, whose proceeds are loaned to low- and moderate-income families for the purpose of buying a home. The home buyers' monthly mortgage payments go to service these bonds. A similar type is life-care bonds—or retirement community bonds—which finance housing for the elderly, with lease income going to servicing the bonds. Last, public housing bonds are issued to finance the construction of public housing projects, with rental revenues servicing these bonds. If revenues are inadequate to meet principal and interest payments, the Public Housing Administration makes up the difference through payments to the local authority that issued the bonds. Like HANs, these issues are tax-exempt and guaranteed by the federal government.

Investment Characteristics and Bank Holdings

With banks subject to high marginal tax rates, the tax-exemption feature of state and local government debt has a powerful appeal. So much so that the amount and relative importance of municipal securities in banks' investment portfolios have expanded dramatically over the years (see Figure 14.1). At the close of 1982, all insured commercial banks held $154.8 billion of state and local government securities, which represented 43.2 percent of their total security holdings, placing state and local issues at the top of banks' security holdings. These securities also qualify as collateral for securing fiduciary, trust, and public funds.

Unlike U.S. Treasury debt and agency obligations, state and local government issues exhibit a significant variation in quality; some issues are free of credit risk (such as those guaranteed by the federal government), while others contain different degrees of risk. In the case of general obligations, the degree of risk involved is determined by the ability and willingness of the issuing government to service its debt. The ability and willingness are, in turn, a function of such factors as the economic base of the community, the stability of employment, per capita income, and the current as well as future pattern of revenues available to service the debt. For revenue bonds risk exposure is a function of the profitability of the project being financed and debt service requirements.

The prime-credit issues of large, well-known state and local government units enjoy a national market. The great majority of tax-exempts, however, trade only on a regional or a local basis. Trading in these issues is rather inactive, and price quotations for most of them are not available on a regular basis. The thinness of the market for local issues has contributed to spreads (between the bid and asked prices) usually of 1.5 points, which in periods of tight money conditions may rise to 3 or more points. The dealers who are making a market in various state and local government issues and the inventories they carry are advertised in a daily publication, *Blue List*.

State and local government debt is issued in various maturities. Most issues, especially general obligations, have serial maturities. That is, a single bond issue is split into several different maturities. Coupon rates are lower on the shorter-term securities and gradually increase as maturities lengthen. Serial bonds thus offer banks and other investors a wide choice of maturities and yields. This approach contrasts with the practices of most corporate borrowers and the federal government of having all securities in the same issue come due on the same date (term bonds). The multiple-maturity approach is in essence a vehicle ensuring the gradual amortization of state and local debt.

Corporate Debt

Corporate debt is both short- and long-term. The former consists of commercial paper; the latter, of bonds, notes, and debentures. As we have seen in Chapter 7, commercial paper is the unsecured promissory notes of large, well-known financial and nonfinancial businesses with impeccable credit ratings. Issued on a discount basis, commercial paper matures anywhere from a few days to a maximum of 270 days. It is sold either directly to investors or through commercial paper dealers.

Bonds, notes, and debentures are the most common forms of long-term financing by corporations. Although this terminology is often used interchangeably, bonds are long term (usually), secured promises to pay, bought and sold on the open market; notes are similar to bonds except for shorter maturities; and debentures are unsecured long-term promises to pay. Prior to the early 1930s, corporate debt was of principal importance in the investment portfolios of commercial banks. Its primacy over all other security holdings stemmed from the limited availability of federal and municipal issues and management emphasis upon income. At the end of 1930, corporate issues amounted to $7.4 billion and accounted for over 50 percent of banks' investment holdings. By 1982 these issues amounted to a little over $5 billion and represented only about 1.4 percent of the investments of all insured commercial banks.

The reduced attractiveness of corporate issues for commercial banks is essentially attributed to several considerations. First, corporate issues entail a higher credit risk than is true of state and local government debt. Indeed, corporations can go into bankruptcy and disappear; however, examples of state and local governments disappearing are much less frequent. Second, with banks operating under higher tax rates, the after-tax yield of corporate issues is ordinarily lower than that of municipals of the same quality. Third, banks prefer to deal personally with their corporate customers and grant them loans tailored to their needs rather than finance them indirectly through the highly impersonal bond market. Last, the secondary market for corporate issues is rather limited compared with that for municipal bonds. Trading volume is low even for issues of some of the largest corporations with strong credit standing and reputation. Insurance companies and pension funds are the major institutional investors in this market.

Some of the larger U.S. banks include among their security holdings a less-known type of corporate debt, equipment trust certificates. These certificates are issued to finance the purchase of industrial equipment or rolling stock (such as locomotives, railroad cars, airplanes, and trucks), with such equipment pledged as collateral. The title to the assets acquired is normally held by a trustee—such as a bank's trust department—that leases the equipment to the company issuing the certificates. As the equipment is used and cash flow is generated, lease payments are made by the company to the trustee, which passes them on to the certificate holders. In time the certificates are retired and ownership of the assets is transferred to the borrowing company by the trustee. Although the collateral is generally of excellent quality and can be readily moved, the market for some of these assets may at times be quite soft, contributing to sizable investor losses in the event of borrower default on the certificates. Such, because of the world recession, was the state of the market for used planes in the early 1980s, when Braniff Airlines and Freddie Laker's Skytrain went bankrupt. As a result many secured creditors—including banks—were unable to collect in full. In the case of Braniff, company reorganization may lessen such losses.

Other Securities

This category is of marginal importance and includes the obligations of international organizations and foreign governments as well as corporate stock.

Issues of International Organizations and Foreign Governments

The growing financing needs of the world economy have led many international financial organizations to rely increasingly on international capital markets for funds. Through international bond issues these organizations are able to raise sizable amounts of funds to fulfill their objectives. Foremost among these organizations is the International Bank for Reconstruction and Development (IBRD or World Bank), which, established in 1945 under the Bretton Woods Agreement Act, makes loans to member countries in order to assist in the development of their resources. The World Bank is the primary institution of the World Bank Group, which includes two other institutions—both of which are financially assisted by, and are affiliated with, the bank—the International Finance Corporation, formed in 1956, and the International Development Association, set up in 1960. A sizable portion of the bonds issued by the World Bank is dollar-denominated. These bonds are backed in full by the commitment of the U.S. government because they represent the portion of subscribed capital for which the United States is subject to call. For practical purposes, therefore, these bonds belong in the federal debt category. Their yields are slightly above those of direct government obligations of the same maturity.

Other international financial organizations whose bonds are eligible investments for commercial banks are the Inter-American Development Bank, established in 1959, and the Asian Development Bank, formed in 1966. These institutions duplicate the functions of the World Bank Group in a particular region of the world and fund their activities through international bond issues. These bonds are backed in full by the callable capital, and hence the commitment, of the member countries of these organizations. Thus the bonds of the Inter-American Development Bank and the Asian Development Bank are considered of high quality, being rated Aaa by Moody's Investors Service.

Foreign governments and their political subdivisions have in many instances tapped U.S. financial markets through issuance of dollar-denominated bonds, frequently referred to as "Yankee bonds." Although U.S. investors sustained significant losses in the past with such issues, the record has improved greatly since World War II. Under current laws all foreign issuers—like domestic private borrowers—must comply with the registration requirements of the Securities and Exchange Commission (SEC) prior to the public offering of their bonds. Although domestic investors cannot take any legal action in the event of borrower default on these bonds, foreign public debtors usually make adjustment offers to U.S. creditors (for instance, exchange of an old issue for a new one with longer maturity or one paying lower interest). Most of the foreign public issues currently in the market are of high quality. For example, the bond issues of the governments of Australia, Canada, Norway, France, and Sweden are rated AAA by Moody's. The issues of the European Economic Community and the European Investment Bank have a similar rating.

Corporate Stock

As indicated in the opening paragraph of this section, included in this "other securities" category are eligible corporate stocks. The general rule is that a national bank, or a state bank member of the Federal Reserve System, may not purchase or acquire corporate stock except as permitted by law in special cases. Some of the special situations that account for stock ownership by commercial banks are the following:

- Member banks are required to purchase stock in their district Federal Reserve bank upon their admission to Federal Reserve membership. The amount of such purchase must equal 3 percent of a bank's capital stock and surplus. Additional stock must be acquired (or canceled) when a bank increases (or reduces) its capital and surplus. The stock is not transferable, and if a bank liquidates, such stock is canceled.
- A bank may own stock in an amount equal to its capital in a corporation organized to own the building in which the bank is located. The risk assumed by the bank is limited to the amount of its investment.
- A bank may own stock up to 15 percent of its capital and surplus in a safe deposit company that it has organized to engage in this type of activity. As in the preceding case, the parent bank is liable only for the amount of its investment.
- With the approval of the Board of Governors, a bank may invest no more than 10 percent of its capital and surplus in a corporation formed to engage in foreign activity.
- A bank may purchase unlimited amounts of stock in government-sponsored agencies (such as Fannie Mae and Sallie Mae), as well as

in corporations authorized under Title IX of the Housing and Urban Development Act of 1968.

•A bank may hold corporate stocks if such stocks served as collateral on defaulted loans. However, these stocks are to be disposed of as soon as can reasonably be done without undue loss. A reasonable holding period for these stocks is generally viewed as up to five years.

National banks may invest in equities indirectly through the purchase of convertible bonds or bonds with warrants attached. The cost of these securities, however, must be written down by the amount of the conversion feature or the value of the warrants, to reflect the true value of these securities as debt instruments. Banks are generally reluctant to buy these bonds to avoid significant charge-offs, especially when they are overpriced.

REGULATIONS INFLUENCING SECURITY SELECTIONS

Banks' investment activities are subject to a host of regulatory controls for the same reason that all other aspects of commercial banking are: safety of deposit funds. The main objective of investment regulations is to minimize bank losses resulting from the default risk inherent in certain securities. As part of his regulatory powers, the Comptroller of the Currency has issued investment regulations that apply to national banks and all state banks that are members of the Federal Reserve System. Some of these regulations were reviewed in the preceding section in connection with corporate stock, which banks are allowed to acquire only exceptionally. A more important part, however, deals with debt instruments, which constitute the core of banks' investment portfolios.

The regulations promulgated by the Comptroller of the Currency require all national and state member banks to diversify their security holdings among various issuers, and for this purpose they identify three classes of marketable instruments eligible for bank investment. Type I securities are essentially risk-free, and a bank "may deal in, underwrite, purchase and sell for its own account without limitation." This category includes U.S. Treasury obligations, debt issues of federal agencies, and general obligation bonds of any state or political subdivision within the state. In light of recent municipal defaults, such as Cleveland's, some Type I securities pose a limited risk. Therefore, even with Type I securities the Comptroller's caveat that the banks must exercise "prudent judgment" applies.

Riskier than Type I bonds, Type II securities include those issued by international organizations, such as the Asian Development Bank, the World Bank, and the Inter-American Development Bank, as well as certain bonds issued by local governments. The latter include state obligations for public housing projects and university buildings and dormitories. Regulations permit a bank to "deal in, underwrite, purchase and sell for its own account" Type II securities, subject to a 10 percent capital and surplus limitation.

The riskiest class of securities that banks may purchase is Type III securities, which includes all other obligations. Unlike Type I or II securities, banks may "neither deal in nor underwrite" Type III securities. A bank's portfolio may not contain Type III securities in excess of 10 percent of its capital and surplus accounts. The category includes state and local revenue bonds, corporate debt instruments, and foreign corporate or government bonds. Banks are expected to exercise a considerable amount of judgment with Type III securities because they are exposed to greater risk. In particular, a bank should consider the issuer's historical operating record and/or reliable estimates concerning the likely success of new projects. The bank must maintain a complete file on these and all other securities not backed by the U.S. government. This file allows the investment officer and the bank examiners to determine that a security is investment-grade.

OTHER INVESTMENT ACTIVITIES

In addition to holding securities in their portfolios, large banks also can deal in and underwrite securities, within certain prescribed limitations. Banks may not deal in and underwrite municipal revenue bonds or corporate bonds and stocks. They may, however, arrange for the private placement of these issues. The securities in which banks may deal and that they may underwrite must be kept separate from the investment account and are identified as trading account securities.

Dealing in Securities

The investment department of a bank may function as a dealer by standing ready to buy or sell a security at an established bid or asked quotation. The difference between the two prices is known as the spread. The spread realized by a dealer bank in specific transactions varies over time in response to fluctuations in the market prices of the securities owned. A dealer always maintains an inventory of securities because he or she rarely sells as much as is bought. In some instances the dealer may have a negative inventory, having sold (short) more than is owned, in which case additional securities will have to be purchased. In any case, the individual spreads and the frequency of transactions are determinants of the revenues dealer banks realize from this kind of activity.

Larger banks generally act as dealers. National and state member banks can deal only in Type I and Type II securities (U.S. Treasury and agency debt, general obligation municipal securities, and certain revenue bonds). As banks commit a certain amount of capital in support of dealer activities, these funds are customarily kept as a separate profit unit within the investment department. Banks dealing in securities advertise this function as an additional service to their customers as well as to smaller banks.

As a result of initiatives by the Federal Reserve System and the U.S. Treasury, the markets for federal government securities and agency debt have been automated since the 1970s. Moreover, indications are that the automation of the municipal securities market will be completed by 1985. Automation enables the ownership and transfer of securities in a computerized book-entry, instead of a physical, form. This automated program offers many advantages to both the Treasury and investors. It cuts the printing costs of the Treasury and eliminates the problem of counterfeiting. At the same time it protects the investors from loss and theft of the certificates and reduces handling and storage costs. The first efforts to introduce this program date from the late 1960s, when member banks asked their Federal Reserve banks to hold their U.S. Treasury securities in book-entry, rather than physical, form. This has led to the current system of transactions being effected by means of wire messages among all participating parties, eliminating the need for physical delivery of securities.

Underwriting Activities

As indicated earlier in this chapter, commercial banks have limited underwriting privileges. The term "underwriting" refers to the process of selling newly issued securities. The underwriter customarily agrees to buy from the issuing concern (such as a government entity) its entire new issue of securities for a specified amount of money, with the intention to resell such issue publicly for profit. Failure to sell the securities or adverse price fluctuations at the time of the public offering impose significant losses on the underwriter, who must still pay the issuer the agreed-upon sum of money.

Just prior to 1930, banks and their investment affiliates were responsible for the retailing of over half of all new debt issues coming into the market. The dominance of the security business by commercial banks seemed almost certain until interrupted by the Great Depression. Failure of a large bank in 1931, triggered by the failure of its investment affiliate, aroused Congressional concern over the tie between commercial banking and investment banking. As a result, the Banking Act of 1933 gave commercial banks one year to divest themselves of their investment affiliates and introduced important limitations on banks' underwriting functions. Thus, banks are permitted today to underwrite only Type I and Type II securities. Increasingly in recent years, however, there has been much controversy about whether to extend banks' underwriting activities. Banks have been lobbying against those who argue that extending their underwriting activities will lead to conflicts of interest between commercial and investment banking as well as the concentration of underwriting in the hands of a few large banks.

Commercial banks are actively involved in the underwriting of U.S. Treasury obligations through their participation in the auctions of Treasury bills, notes, and bonds. Banks are especially active in the underwriting of municipal bonds (general obligation and certain revenue bonds). Bidding for municipal securities is usually competitive as a safeguard against connivance. The announcement of a new municipal issue by the issuing unit of government is made through a published solicitation of bids. If the issue is small, large commercial banks in the area may bid individually to buy the issue. Large issues, however, require the formation of an underwriting syndicate. A syndicate is a temporary association of a group of banks and other underwriters who join together to spread the risk of underwriting and assist in the marketing of a specific issue. A large commercial bank in the area may lead or manage the syndicate formed to bid on the given issue. Prior to submitting any bids the syndicate members agree in advance on their responsibilities and liabilities in the event that the bid is successful.

Bidding for municipal issues involves a significant degree of risk for the underwriting banks. This is generally attributed to the erratic investment pattern of commercial banks, which play a dominant role in the market for tax-exempt securities. In periods of rising loan demand and expanding earnings, bank purchases of tax-exempts are generally limited. In fact, during the credit crunches of 1966, 1969, and 1973, the loan demand was so high that banks funded loans by selling off municipals. By contrast, during 1967, 1970, and 1976, when the demand for loans was low, banks became large investors in tax-exempts. This erratic participation of commercial banks in the municipal market has contributed to its increased volatility, which in many instances has forced state and local governments to postpone their market offerings until more opportune times. As a result the late 1970s experienced a gradual shift in the marketing of new municipal bonds from competitive bidding to negotiated sales. This shift, however, gave rise to growing concern over the higher interest cost and the added burden to the taxpayer associated with the negotiated sales approach.

In the past only regional banks or money-market banks participated in underwriting securities. Now, however, underwriting functions are being assumed by medium-size banks as well. Like dealer activities, the underwriting function is handled by a separate unit within the bank's investment department.

Private Placements

Although the Glass-Steagall Act prohibits the underwriting of corporate bonds and stocks by banks, it cannot prevent a bank's assisting a borrower in obtaining funds from other financial institutions, such as insurance companies or pension funds. Indeed, on several occasions since the mid-1970s, large money-center banks have accommodated businesses by arranging the private placement of their debt securities with nonbank financial intermediaries. The placement fees charged were, for obvious reasons, lower than the fees usually charged by investment bankers. For the borrowing concern the private placement is associated with lower costs, since it eliminates the underwriting fees and entails fewer legal restrictions than a public offering.

Another service provided by a bank involves aiding corporate clients in finding and negotiating merger opportunities.

SUGGESTED REFERENCES

Christy, George A., and John C. Clendenin. *Introduction to Investments*. 8th ed. New York: McGraw-Hill, 1982.

Darst, David M. *The Complete Bond Book*. New York: McGraw-Hill, 1975.

First Boston Corporation. *Handbook of Securities of the United States Government and Federal Agencies*. New York: First Boston Corp., biennial.

Groves, Harold M., and R. Bish. *Financing Government*. 7th ed. New York: Holt, Rinehart and Winston, 1973.

Hayes, Douglas A. "Bank Portfolio Management: Revolution in Portfolio Policies." *Bankers Magazine*, September-October 1980, pp. 21-24.

Hoffland, David L. "New York and the Municipal Bond Market." *Financial Analyst Journal*, March-April 1977, pp. 36-39.

Mayo, Herbert B. *Investments, an Introduction*. Chicago: Dryden Press, 1984.

Mote, Larry R. "Banks and the Securities Market: The Controversy." *Economic Perspectives*, Federal Reserve Bank of Chicago, March-April 1979, pp. 14-20.

Preston, Lewis T. "The Glass-Steagall Act: Barrier to Competition." *Morgan Guaranty Survey*, April 1979, pp. 6-11.

Ratti, Ronald. "Pledging Requirements and Bank Asset Portfolios." *Economic Review*, Federal Reserve Bank of Kansas City, September-October 1979, pp. 13-23.

Reilly, Frank K. *Investment Analysis and Portfolio Management*. Hinsdale, Ill: Dryden Press, 1979.

Robinson, Roland I., and Dwayne Wrightsman. *Financial Markets: The Accumulation and Allocation of Wealth*. 2nd ed. New York: McGraw-Hill, 1980.

12 *U.S. Code* 24, para. 7.

The regulatory provisions discussed in Chapter 14 constitute the framework within which a bank's board of directors formulates investment policy. Whether in detail or in general terms, this policy is put into writing to ensure consistency by all those involved in its implementation. To guard against the inflexibility of the investment function over a period of time, it is imperative that investment policy be periodically reviewed in the light of changing economic conditions.

Formulating a bank's investment policy generally implies the setting up of standards and the establishment of procedures for the management of a bank's investment account. Developing an investment policy offers a bank's board of directors a wider framework than for loans. Unlike the loan portfolio, the distributional character of which reflects local conditions and therefore can be controlled only within limits, a bank's investment account can be planned in advance and consequently can be tailored to bank wishes. Investment policy, therefore, has a unique element: it can be designed around the types of investment instruments that are available in the open market.

The basic considerations that underlie the liquidity aspect of a bank's investment account have already been considered in discussing a bank's secondary reserves (see Chapter 8). A notable part of investment activity, however, is still to be discussed, and this pertains to the other aspect of a bank's investment account, the residual employment of bank funds—the bond portfolio. A bank's bond portfolio may be defined as those securities not held as secondary reserves. This chapter identifies the objectives of the bond portfolio, outlines the basic criteria established by the board for the selection of securities, and describes alternative investment strategies in the management of the bond portfolio. The last part of this chapter reviews the organization of the investment function.

OBJECTIVES OF THE BOND PORTFOLIO

The objectives of the bond portfolio, as defined by the board, are basic to the determination of a bank's investment activity. They are generally the same for all banks: to provide supplementary liquidity and to generate supplementary income.

Supplementary Liquidity

Although banks try to forecast their liquidity needs over the next year and to maintain adequate secondary reserves, there is always the possibility of some unaccounted-for developments that may cause important deviations between the actual and the forecast deposit and loan demands. In addition, the bank must always be prepared for contingencies. For example, a natural disaster might cause a rapid decline of deposits and a delay in repayment of loans. A bank that experiences such unexpected demands on its liquidity positions may be forced to sell securities from its bond portfolios in order to increase the amount of funds raised from borrowing and selling of secondary reserves.

Supplementary Income

Except for tight money periods, when loan demand exceeds available resources, banks usually have residual funds that can be profitably invested in securities. These investments can be the determining factor in assessing a bank's profitability.

A bank's investments, as we saw in Chapter 14, are generally restricted by law to debt instruments. The income generated by these instruments is in the form of interest and capital gains (or losses). The interest income consists of explicit cash flows received periodically from the issuer over the lifetime of the bond. The size of these flows is determined by the bond's coupon rate, which is established at the time of its issue. A $1,000 bond bearing a 6 percent coupon rate would pay the investor $60 per annum until its maturity, regardless of the state of the economy. That is, regardless of whether the market rates of interest go up or down in the future because of changes in economic conditions, the bond will continue to generate $60 per year until its maturity. Capital gains (or losses) are realized if the bond is sold prior to its maturity and at the time of its sale the going market rates are lower (higher) than the bond's coupon rate.

Both interest income and capital gains (or losses) determine the yield a bank earns from a bond. There are two measures of a bond yield, the current yield and the yield to maturity. The current yield is derived by dividing the annual interest income of a bond by its market price. In other words, a bond with three years left to maturity, paying $60 per year, and bought for $948.62 offers a current yield of 6.3 percent. The current yield formula is $Y_c = R/P$, where Y_c stands for the current yield, R for the annual interest income from the bond, and P for its current market price. Current yield quotations for listed bonds are customarily provided by financial newspapers and are helpful for investors who finance their purchases through borrowed funds and wish to determine whether their borrowing cost is being covered.

Otherwise, the importance of this measure is limited because it assures that payments will continue forever. Moreover, it ignores that at maturity the investor will receive the face value of the bond, which is different from the market value. For these reasons the yield-to-maturity concept is considered a more meaningful and useful measure of a bond's rate of return. The equation for the yield to maturity is the one that was used in Chapter 9 to determine the effect of interest-rate changes on the value of a bond:

$$P = \frac{R_1}{(1+r)} + \frac{R_2}{(1+r)^2} + \frac{R_3}{(1+r)^3} + \cdots + \frac{R_n}{(1+r)^n} + \frac{M}{(1+r)^n}.$$

Here R_1 through R_n represents the annual income from the bond until it matures; P, its current market price; and r, the yield to maturity—that is, the rate of discount that makes the present value of the expected future stream of revenue equal to the cost of the asset. We can illustrate the application of this formula by making reference to the data of the example cited above. The equation would be

$$\$947.62 = \frac{\$60}{(1+r)} + \frac{\$60}{(1+r)^2} + \frac{\$60}{(1+r)^3} + \frac{\$1,000}{(1+r)^3}.$$

Solving for r, we find that the rate that makes the total present value of future income equal the cost of the asset is 8 percent.

An approximate yield-to-maturity estimate can be derived by means of a simple arithmetical computation. The formula that may be used in this respect is

$$\text{Yield to maturity} = \frac{\text{annual dollar coupon interest} \begin{array}{c} + \text{ annual accumulation} \\ \text{or} \\ - \text{ annual amortization} \end{array}}{\dfrac{\text{current market price} + \text{par value}}{2}}.$$

Using the information of the example illustrated above, we can calculate the approximate yield to maturity. The example mentioned a three-year bond, bearing a 6 percent rate of interest, acquired at the price of $948.62. Since this bond will be redeemed at maturity for $1,000, the investor will receive an appreciation of $51.38, which corresponds to an annual gain of

$$\frac{(\$1,000 - \$948.62)}{3} = \frac{\$51.38}{3} = \$17.127 \text{ per year.}$$

To determine the yield, we also need to ascertain average investment, which can be established by averaging the cost of the bond ($948.62) and the par value at maturity ($1,000). Using this information in the above formula, we have

$$\text{yield to maturity} = \frac{\$60 \quad + \$17.127}{\dfrac{\$948.62 + \$1,000}{2}} = \frac{\$\,77.127}{\$974.31} = 7.916 \text{ percent.}$$

If the bond was bought at a premium, the above calculation would differ in that we would need to amortize the premium on an annual basis, and hence charge it off to annual interest income.

Once the yield of a security has been determined, a bank's decision to acquire it will be based upon the spread, or difference, between that yield and the bank's cost-of-funds rate. As was indicated in Chapter 5, if an investment promises a rate of return exceeding the bank's cost of funds, its acquisition will make a positive contribution to profits and will enhance the wealth of stockholders. By contrast, investments that are expected to produce a return equal to, or less than, the bank's cost of funds will not be undertaken. Thus, among alternative investment opportunities a bank will undertake only those offering the highest spread possible for the same degree of risk.

CRITERIA IN THE SELECTION OF SECURITIES

The degree of detail by which the board of directors sets bond portfolio policy varies from bank to bank, and indicates the margin of latitude for maneuvering in the application of such policy. However detailed such policy may be, the basic issues covered include the quality of the securities to be bought, marketability guidelines, extent of diversification desired, tax considerations, and maximum maturities. Each of these is discussed below.

Quality

Although the bond portfolio is an important source of income, aggressive pursuit of income could undermine the bank's continued existence. To ensure the safe employment of funds in banks' bond portfolios, regulatory authorities have introduced certain qualitative standards for banks to follow in security purchases. In regulations promulgated by the Office of the Comptroller of the Currency and extended to state banks that are members of the Federal Reserve

System, ratings are presumptive evidence of investment quality and are considered a fair yardstick of quality differences among securities. In the Investment Securities Regulation, first issued in 1936, the Comptroller of the Currency, in defining the investment securities eligible for purchase by Federal Reserve member banks, describes them, from the standpoint of quality, as not "predominantly speculative in nature." Banks are thus implicitly referred to the published opinions of rating agencies to identify the rating classification assigned to a specific security. Considered eligible for a bank's portfolio are the general obligations that are readily marketable and are rated within the top four classes by leading agencies in their investment-rating manuals.

Two highly respected agencies that rate debt issues are Standard and Poor and Moody's Investors Service. They do not rate all the issues, but only those that are subject to default risk (municipalities and corporates) and enjoy a relatively broad market. Table 15.1 shows the rating system of each agency. Both systems attribute high ratings to securities of high quality (low risk) and lower ratings to issues of poorer quality (high risk).

A national bank or a state bank member of the Federal Reserve System can hold securities down through Moody's Baa or Standard

Table 15.1. Bond Ratings

Standard & Poor's		*Moody's*	
AAA	Highest grade	Aaa	Best quality
AA	High grade	Aa	High quality
A	Upper medium grade	A	Higher medium grade
BBB	Medium grade	Baa	Lower medium grade
BB	Lower medium grade	Ba	Possess speculative elements
B	Speculative	B	Generally lack characteristics of a desirable investment
CCC } CC }	Outright speculation	Caa Ca	Poor; may be in default Speculative to a high degree; often in default
C	Income bonds		
DDD } DD } D }	In default; rating indicates relative salvage value	C	Lowest grade

Note: Plus (+) and minus (−) are used to show relative strength within a rating category.

Sources: *Moody's Bond Record*, April 1978; *Standard and Poor's Bond Guide*, May 1978.

and Poor's BBB. If a bank holds a bond with a lower rating, examiners will advise the bank to sell it. The FDIC and state banking authorities maintain similar quality standards for banks under their jurisdiction.

Often banks may consider buying securities that are not rated (such as securities of small face value or of small localities)—for example, the nonrated obligations of a local governmental unit that holds deposits with the bank. Unrated securities are eligible for purchase by member banks, even though they enjoy limited marketability. The responsibility for proving the quality of these securities, however, rests with the bank's top management. Whether the securities are rated or unrated, the Comptroller of the Currency requires that every "bank maintain in its files credit information adequate to demonstrate that it has exercised prudence" in making its investment determination.

Although banks emphasize high-quality securities in their bond portfolios, some credit risk is unavoidable with state and local debt as well as corporate issues. Moreover, all intermediate- and long-term obligations entail significant interest-rate risk. Hence the question of what amount of risk is appropriate for the bond portfolio. A bank's main source of income, as well as of risk exposure, is its loan account. Since the funds employed in the bond account are residual, it follows that, as far as risk taking is concerned, the bond portfolio should be approached from the standpoint of a residual income producer. In other words, commercial banks should take bond portfolio risks that complement the risks taken in their loan portfolios. Thus, high-risk exposure in the loan portfolio would justify a high-quality and lower-income bond portfolio, and vice versa, depending upon the growth or stability of the local economy. Risk taking in the bond portfolio must therefore be kept within certain limits. The framework for risk taking is, to a great extent, determined by the amount of capital available for application against the portfolio. Acceptance of risks beyond the ability to absorb them (in the form of capital adequacy) should be avoided, as being outside the framework of a realistic and productive investment policy.

Marketability

Regulatory agencies view marketability as a criterion for quality. The reasoning is that if an obligation possesses quality, investors will be eager to purchase it, and vice versa. This approach raises the question of defining marketability. Although there are differing degrees of marketability, in general a marketable instrument is one that is actively traded and hence can be readily converted into cash through the securities market mechanism. A more refined approach would be to consider the differences between the bid and asked quotations for a security. Financial experts suggest that a margin of one point or more between such quotations is an indication of limited marketability.

Banks have every reason to emphasize marketability or shiftability in their portfolios. With deposits providing the overwhelming portion of loanable and investable funds, marketability ensures promptness in the disposition of the securities held and availability of supplemental liquidity in periods of severe financial strain. For banks that pursue an aggressive investment policy (that is, one geared to the cyclical nature of the economy), marketability considerations are of major importance. Such banks must be able to adjust, through sale, most of their portfolio when they desire to do so. In these instances marketability can be ensured by holding nationally known issues that are capable of attracting buyers under any market conditions.

Although marketability must be maintained throughout the investment portfolio, there will be instances in which management may be forced to deviate from this principle. This occurs when the community or municipality served resorts to a local issue to take care of its needs. In such a case banks, for reasons outside investment portfolio operations, may have to acquire the local issues, in whole or in part. It is generally the rule rather than the exception that such local credits are of limited marketability. By form, of course, these credits constitute investment of funds; in essence, however, they have all the characteristics of a local loan. It is only realistic, therefore, that such local credits be viewed as additions to the loan portfolio, in the form of term loans, rather than to the investment portfolio. For obvious reasons such credits should not be part of the fundamental considerations influencing bond portfolio management.

Of the various securities available in the market, obligations of the U.S. government enjoy the highest marketability. Their riskless character and the highly organized market available enable the holder to convert them into cash with minimal loss. These attributes have rendered U.S. government securities the most common and convenient type of security desired. Also of significant marketability are the obligations of U.S. government agencies and government-sponsored corporations that are traded in the same markets as the direct obligations of the federal government. Of the municipal and corporate securities, only those of the larger and more creditworthy issuers enjoy a national market.

Diversification

Closely related to quality considerations in the management of the bond account is the principle of diversification. Diversification is one of the fundamental and most significant rules of investment policy, whether it pertains to banks or to any other institutional and individual investors. A generally accepted method of reducing risk in the investment account to manageable proportions, it may be defined as a process of spreading risk, prompted by the need to minimize the effect of poor judgment and the impact of economic conditions on the investment portfolio. Diversification is effected through the purchasing or holding of investment issues consistent with the regulatory provisions discussed in Chapter 14. The holding of an assortment of securities in the portfolio, rather than a limited number of issues bunched at one time or in one place, tends to reduce losses by averaging them out over the long run.

Proper diversification can be ensured by providing in the investment policy of a bank that certain percentages of the investment portfolio be invested in particular types of securities or by establishing a ceiling on the funds that may be placed in specific types of securities. Clearly, the types of securities specified reflect the kind of diversification desired. Diversification may take various forms, such as by industry, geographical area, or type of security. Of these, two forms stand out in banking practice: diversification by industry and by geographical area, with the latter constituting the principal form of risk spreading in the portfolio.

Diversification by industry has significance only with respect to holdings of corporate securities. When corporate debt was the dominant investment in the portfolios of commercial banks, securities were classified into industrials, railroads, public utilities, and miscellaneous. Each of these groupings was further divided into subgroupings. Thus, industrial securities were subclassified, for example, into securities of heavy or capital goods industries and of consumer goods industries. Railroad obligations, once the aristocrats among bonds and a one-time bank favorite,* used to be distinguished, depending upon the principal type of service rendered, into such classes as passenger and agricultural lines. Public-utility holdings, too, were further classified into such categories as gas, light, and telephone. The degree of detail in the classification of corporate securities depended to a large extent upon the size of such holdings and the feasibility of such classification.

Diversification of corporate obligations by industry does not, of course, exclude the possibility of a geographic distribution of these securities within each of the groupings and/or subgroupings referred

---

*In the late 1890s and the early years of the twentieth century, railroad bonds were almost the only ones listed on the New York Stock Exchange.

to above. In such a case, risk spreading in corporates is by industry and geographic area. Because of the minor amounts of corporate securities in the investment portfolios of commercial banks, diversification in corporates is of limited significance. By contrast, the leading application of the principle of diversification is in state and local government securities, with risk spreading done on a geographic basis. Indeed, with municipal obligations constituting the largest holdings of investment securities in commercial bank portfolios, diversification becomes of special importance. As stated earlier, municipal securities represent debt of the various states and their political subdivisions. This debt has grown considerably over the postwar years, reflecting the increasing use of debt financing by state and local governments. Because of the large number of issuers and issues, there is a wide variation in the types of securities available. This variation is, of course, to be expected, since each issuer has a different economic base not only vis-à-vis other issuing governments, state or local, but also over time. Some states or localities are agriculturally oriented, some industrially, some commercially, while others are fairly diversified. In some the pace of economic change is slow; in others, faster. Some issuing governments are heavily indebted, others are less so. Differing portions of this debt are in the form of revenue obligations, supported by the earnings of some business venture, and in the form of general obligations, with the full taxing power of the issuing body pledged to assure repayment.

Clearly, of paramount importance in the geographic diversification of risk is the location of the issuing governmental body or obligor. In building up its portfolio of state and local government securities, a bank should seek to purchase—over and beyond such local issues as are required for reasons of good customer and community relations—securities that are dependent upon areas of the country beyond the local community. In doing so, a bank minimizes exposure of its bond account to the economic conditions of the local economy, and hence to the effects of area blight. Investing, therefore, in the municipal issues of other areas provides adequate hedging against local risk and safeguards the shiftability of the bond account. Inclusion of nonlocal, general-market, tax-exempt municipals in the bond account is advocated in view of the fact that a bank's loan account is itself, and by necessity, made up of local credits. Indeed, with the loan portfolio consisting basically of local credits, a large position in local municipals in the bond portfolio would only accentuate the concentration in assets subject to adverse developments in the local economy. Local concentration in lending, and hence in the loan account, is not only inevitable but normal and to be anticipated. Indeed, it is difficult for all but the very largest banks—under a unit banking system—to make loans throughout the country and therefore to effect real diversification in their loan portfolios. Management may not be able to diversify the bank's loan account as much as it would like to, but the bond account offers an opportunity for diversification. The investment portfolio offers management the opportunity to hedge against local risks by qualifying for it securities that have a different geographic, and hence economic, base. In planning investment operations, therefore, management may offset concentration in the loan account by following a policy of not duplicating it. In other words, the bond account must be viewed as complementary to a bank's loan account. This type of relationship constitutes an important test of diversification.

The bond account, therefore, offers management the only opportunity to achieve the diversification of a bank's earning assets. Hedging against local risks has long been regarded a sound banking practice. A word of caution must be added here, however, if management is to reap the full benefits of diversification. Diversifying against local risks in the portfolio means that a bank should avoid purchasing local or nearby open-market securities in favor of securities from issuers located in other areas. By doing so, however, management forgoes investing in quality securities with which it may be thoroughly familiar from its lending activities, and must rely instead upon outside investment advice and other data for its knowledge of specific credits issued by remote localities. This drawback makes it imperative for management to restrict its nonlocal investments to securities of unquestioned credit standing. Such a step should suffice to protect the portfolio against any fast-deteriorating situation and meet a prudent standard for geographic diversification.

Too much diversification is as undesirable as too little or none. Diversification must not be taken to imply the purchase of small amounts of securities from every eligible issue that comes along to round out the portfolio. Such interpretation would tend to render the portfolio position too difficult to manage, give rise to higher bookkeeping expenses, and reduce the marketability of individual holdings, since these would consist of small or odd lots. Too much diversification, therefore, can become cumbersome and is apt to reduce the effectiveness of the portfolio.

Tax Considerations

Tax considerations play an important role in the formulation of a bank's bond portfolio policy. Federal income tax laws affect the profitability of the bond portfolio and its contribution to the bank's net income in two ways. First, interest income from municipal securities is not subject to federal income taxes. Second, capital gains and losses from the sale of securities—defined as ordinary income that is customary to banking—are, with certain limitations, included in, or deducted from, the bank's ordinary income.

Importance of Tax-Exempts

Banks are subject to the standard corporation income tax rates. As of January 1, 1983, the tax structure was considerably simplified and included only five tax brackets.

Corporate Income ($)	Tax Rate (%)
0-25,000	15
25,000-50,000	18
50,000-75,000	30
75,000-100,000	40
over 100,000	46

Under this schedule the maximum rate applies to virtually all banks of any significant size. Thus, for a bank in the 46 percent marginal tax bracket, an 8 percent coupon rate of an Aaa-rated municipal bond is equivalent to a before-tax rate of 14.8 percent.* By contrast, for a bank in the lowest marginal tax bracket (15 percent), this same bond offers a before-tax equivalent rate of 9.4 percent. Thus, large banks subject to the highest marginal tax rates benefit most from investing in municipals, while small banks sacrifice gross revenues unnecessarily because alternative, taxable, instruments offer higher yields. It should be evident, then, that for banks in high marginal tax brackets, tax considerations may outweigh all others in the selection of securities, while for banks in low tax brackets, tax considerations may be insignificant in the determination of their bond portfolio policy.

The yields on tax-exempt bonds have varied over time. Figure 15.1 shows the average yields of high-quality municipal securities (Aaa), and their relationship to other bond yields, since the mid-1920s.

---

*The tax equivalent rate is calculated from the following formula:

$$\text{tax equivalent interest rate} = \frac{\text{coupon rate}}{(1 - \text{marginal tax rate})}.$$

Thus, $\dfrac{.08}{(1-.46)} = .148$ (14.8 percent).

Figure 15.1. Bond Yields, 1926-83 (percent)

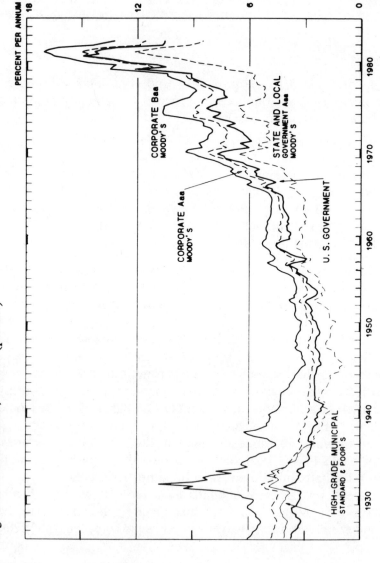

Source: Board of Governors of the Federal Reserve System, *Historical Chart Book* (Washington, D.C.: Federal Reserve System, 1983), p. 97.

During the 1970s and early 1980s there was a considerable fluctuation in the yield of tax-exempts, consistent with the general trends of the market. For example, in 1970 the yield to maturity for these securities was a little over 6 percent, and rose to an unprecedented 12 percent in 1982. This was comparable with a yield of 22.2 percent for a bank or a business concern in the 46 percent income tax bracket. There was a comparable fluctuation in the yields of other instruments during the same period, with corporate Baa-rated bonds rising to 17 percent in 1982.

The fluctuations of this period, as was generally true for preceding decades, reflected prevailing conditions in financial markets. The tight monetary policy of the late 1970s produced high rates of interest, which led to increases in the yields of outstanding securities. By contrast, the monetary ease of 1971-72 and 1975-76 caused low rates of interest and corresponding decreases in yields. In addition to the prevailing economic climate, the yield trends of this period reflected demand and supply forces in specific markets. For example, during the boom conditions of 1980, increases in the yields of municipals were accentuated by an oversupply of tax-exempts. When many state and local governments simultaneously seek funds through the issuance of bonds, the large volume of municipals being sold drives up the yield of these instruments.

In addition to showing the fluctuations in yields, Figure 15.1 shows the yield relationship between instruments of different risk. For example, Baa-rated corporate bonds yield more than Aaa corporates, which in turn yield more than risk-free U.S. government securities. The lowest yield in the market has been that of municipal bonds, because of their interest exemption.

Tax Treatment of Capital Gains and Losses

Federal income tax laws affect the profitability of a bank's investment portfolio through their treatment of capital gains and losses. Since passage of the Tax Reform Act of 1969, all gains and losses are included in, or deducted from, ordinary income. Both short- and long-term gains from the sale of securities must be treated as ordinary income for tax purposes. By the same token, short- and long-term capital losses can be used as offsets to taxable, ordinary income.

If the availability of current taxable income against which to offset net losses is rather limited, the bank can still benefit through the carry-back and carry-forward features of the tax law. Section 582 of the Internal Revenue Code indicates that, unlike other corporations, banks enjoy the privilege of carrying losses back against the income they realized in the ten preceding taxable years. This entitles the bank to receive a cash refund of taxes paid in the past ten years, beginning with the earliest year in the period. If the prior years' taxable income is less than the current loss, the unused portion of the loss can be carried forward for five years. By applying this provision, the bank will be able to reduce its exposure and pay lower taxes on its potential income than it would otherwise pay.

Maturity

An important supplement to quality and diversification considerations in the selection of securities is the factor of maturity. In the employment of funds in the bond portfolio, the policymakers are faced with the problem of determining the maximum maturity of the securities to be acquired. To maximize income, bank managers need to invest in long-term securities with high yields. However, if these securities are held to maturity, the bank will be exposed to a considerable amount of risk. The longer the maturities of the securities acquired, the greater the bank's exposure to credit and interest-rate risks.

With an investment involving credit risk (such as municipal and corporate issues), the likelihood of quality deterioration over time is greater than the chance of improvement. No such bond is good enough to buy and then forget. There is always the possibility that the credit standing of the obligor may change, with consequent implications for the credit quality of the outstanding debt. If the issuer is a state or local government unit, various developments (such as natural disaster, increased indebtedness, loss of industry) can undermine its ability to make the requisite periodic payments. By the same token, the sizable losses of a corporate obligor may affect its intention to make prompt payments of principal and interest when due.

These developments will affect the credit quality of the issues outstanding, and rating agencies are prompt to lower their quality rating. This, in turn, reduces investor appeal of the securities, with consequent implications upon their marketability. In the late 1970s, as the financial condition of Chrysler Corporation began to deteriorate, the rating of its bonds was lowered accordingly. This had a negative effect on the price of Chrysler's bonds and their marketability. Another example of change over time in the credit standing of the obligor is the case of railroad companies. At the turn of the twentieth century, many investors viewed favorably the purchase of railroad bonds with maturities of 100 years. The decline of the railroad industry in subsequent decades made apparent the danger involved in such long commitments.

Even though a bond may be free of credit risk, it is still subject to interest-rate risk. As stated before, this phenomenon is a result of the contractual rate of interest that bonds carry when issued, and of changes in the level of interest rates. When interest rates are low and the demand for loans is weak, banks usually have surplus funds for employment in the bond portfolio. Consequently, when banks enter the market to buy bonds, these bonds, reflecting the prevailing interest-rate trends, carry a low contractual rate of interest. Banks that purchase bonds when interest rates are low face the risk of a depreciation in the bond account when interest rates subsequently increase, for such an increase will adversely affect the market value of these bonds. Banks cannot, of course, afford to dispose of their bonds at such times, because they will sustain capital losses. They will try instead to hold them until maturity or until bond prices increase again, as a result of a reversal in interest-rate trends, and reach a level that will permit them to sell without realizing substantial losses. If, however, in response to unusual withdrawals or intense customer loan demands, banks are forced to sell a portion of their bond portfolios at low prices, they will sustain sizable losses.

There is, therefore, always uncertainty over the prospective level of interest rates both at the time when the obligation falls due and the funds are available for reinvestment, and (more so) throughout the period that the security is held. The longer the maturity, the greater the possibility that market value (and income) over the long run will be (favorably or unfavorably) affected by changes in the level of rates. An investment, for example, in a 32-year bond at 3.5 percent is tantamount to accepting that the average return on one-year funds will not exceed 3.5 percent over the next 32 years.*

It is apparent that the longer the term of maturity, the greater the potential for quality deterioration and market vulnerability. The question, therefore, that the policymaker faces is how far the maturities should be extended.

As depicted in Figure 15.2, it was not until the end of World War II that the general movement in interest rates turned upward. Based on the rising trend in interest rates that the market has shown since, it is easy to conclude that there should be some fairly short-term limit to the maturities of commercial bank investments. Bank experience with longer-term bonds has not been favorable; a number of banks have found themselves with substantial depreciation on holdings of such bonds acquired 15 to 20 years ago. If a bank is purchasing securities

---

*Such was the case, for instance, in February 1958, when the U.S. Treasury re-funded five issues, amounting in total to $16.8 billion, by offering holders in exchange three new issues, one of which was a 32-year bond maturing in 1990 and yielding 3.5 percent per annum.

Figure 15.2. Long- and Short-Term Interest Rates, 1911-83 (percent per annum)

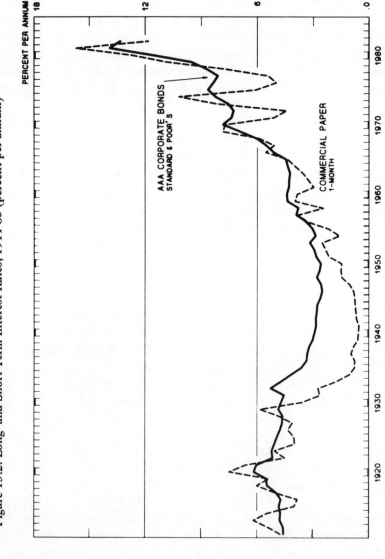

Source: Board of Governors of the Federal Reserve System, *Historical Chart Book* (Washington, D.C.: Federal Reserve System, 1983), p. 96.

412

for income to maturity, it should be prepared to accept receiving the stated income over a period of years. If it cannot live with it, then it should never buy the securities. Obviously, forecasting the state of the market and the demand for bank loans in the decade ahead, in planning for bond portfolio maturities, is a hard task. In light of the uncertainties involved in a rapidly changing world, many banks limit the maximum maturity of securities in the bond portfolio to 10 or 15 years, even though this may be considered a long time. Although there is important variation from one bank to another on this subject, establishing a maturity limit sets the framework for addressing another related issue—that of determining the maturity composition of the bond portfolio. This issue constitutes the subject of a bank's investment strategy.

INVESTMENT STRATEGY

Interest-rate fluctuations and their effect on bond portfolio profitability have led to the emergence of three basic strategies for structuring or scheduling maturities: spaced or staggered maturities, riding the yield curve, and the barbell maturity structure.

Spaced or Staggered Maturities

Although there are variants, the concept of a strictly spaced maturity structure provides for the even allocation of funds among various bond maturities within the established maximum maturity limits. For example, if, because of the uncertainties involved with long-term investments, the bond portfolio manager of a given bank wants to limit maturities to no longer than ten years, the funds may be spread evenly within this maturity range. This approach to allocating funds gives the bond portfolio the appearance of a ladder of maturities, hence the reference to this strategy as "laddered portfolio." As securities approach their maturity, the bank is provided with a convenient source of supplemental liquidity on an ongoing basis. The proceeds of maturing securities are reinvested at the longest maturity admitted to the account. The even spacing of maturities assures the bank of an average portfolio maturity of half the maximum and an income of average yields over an interest-rate cycle. This yield performance is true as long as banks continue their investment pattern (such as reinvesting maturing issues) over the course of the business cycle. As indicated in Chapter 14, on many occasions since World War II, commercial banks—prompted by a strong demand for credit—have reduced their security holdings in order to make more loans. To the extent, therefore, that securities are sold, or the proceeds from maturing securities are not reinvested, the rate of return of the bond portfolio will be lower than the average market returns over a complete interest-rate cycle.

The spaced approach is simple and requires little investment expertise. As a result a large number of banks are using it in their portfolio operations. Some apply this treatment only to a sector of the investment portfolio, such as the secondary reserves, while others apply it to the entire portfolio. In the former instance a bank has little choice to act differently. However, to apply this approach to the entire investment account undermines its profitability potential. For bank managers who are not sufficiently versed in a more flexible portfolio policy or do not wish, for one reason or another, to introduce and frame such a policy, the results of maturity spacing are doubtless better than those of intuitive judgment. Maturity spacing is an acceptable portfolio approach for small banks. But for the banks that are willing to replace a static rule with an analytical procedure and informed judgment, it will certainly make no sense, for instance, to reinvest the funds derived from maturing securities at the longest end of the maturity schedule when the economy is sluggish and monetary authorities pursue a policy of easy money. For if they do, they will find themselves with sizable book losses in their portfolios when the economy eventually recovers and interest rates start rising.

For management to adhere to the spaced maturities method rigidly and in all kinds of economic weather is to close its eyes and ignore the market opportunities that exist for portfolio improvement and added long-run income for the bank.

Riding the Yield Curve

This approach, also referred to as flexible investment policy, provides for an aggressive employment of funds by taking advantage of interest-rate movements. The essence of this approach is that if managers believe that interest rates will decline, they should lengthen maturities in their portfolios in order to "lock in" some of the currently high long-term rates and to generate potential capital gains when interest rates fall and security prices increase. If they anticipate that interest rates will increase, they should shorten portfolio maturities to avoid potential capital losses. This is tantamount to saying that it is advisable to hold short-term securities when business activity starts picking up slowly and the credit demand is expected to grow, and to lengthen maturities when the first indications of an approaching recession start setting in and the credit demand is expected to fall.

As implied, aggressive employment of funds in the bond portfolio relies heavily upon management ability to forecast interest-rate movements. The most useful predictive device available is the yield curve, which depicts the maturity distribution of yields (often called the term structure of interest rates) in the market at a particular time. This curve can be constructed by plotting graphically the yields of outstanding securities of comparable quality (or credit standing) but of different maturities.* A yield curve for U.S. government securities is published regularly in the *Treasury Bulletin*, a monthly publication of the U.S. Department of the Treasury. Yield curves for agency securities, municipal obligations, and corporates are published on a regular basis by various major investment banking houses.

Since the yield curve represents the pattern of yields in the market at a specific point in time, it is a useful tool in investment decision making because it permits investors to spot any deviations of individual securities from such curves. If a security's rate of return lies above the curve, this implies that the particular security is underpriced relative to others of the same maturity. This is a buy signal that many investors will try to take advantage of. The strong demand for the security will drive its price up and bring its yield down in line with others in the yield curve. By the same token, a yield below the curve would indicate an overpriced security; investors holding it will be quick to sell it, thus driving its price down and raising its yield toward the curve.

More important, the scope of the yield curve is critical for the planning of investment strategy. Its shape depicts the influence on financial markets of such forces as Federal Reserve monetary policy, maturity preferences of borrowers, and investors' expectations. Study of the shape of the yield curve thus enables portfolio managers to prepare their own interest-rate forecasts and attempt to pattern their activities in financial markets accordingly. There are four distinct types of yield curves: increasing, flat, decreasing, and humped. Examples of each of these types are depicted in Figures 15.3 through 15.6.

Figure 15.3 illustrates an increasing or upward-sloping yield curve for U.S. government securities as of September 30, 1982. An increasing yield curve is typical of a period of depressed business activity and a low demand for funds relative to the supply. Consequently the entire rate structure is at a lower level than during other phases of the

---

*A yield curve is simple to construct. The vertical axis of the graph represents the yield in percent, and the horizontal scale the number of years to maturity. The curve can be constructed from the information presented on a daily bond quotation sheet. The yield and corresponding maturity of the issues to be included in the curve are plotted on the chart and a curve is drawn to connect them. If there are several yield variations, a curve can be drawn to connect at the greatest concentration of points.

Figure 15.3. Yields of Treasury Securities, September 30, 1982 (based on closing bid quotations)

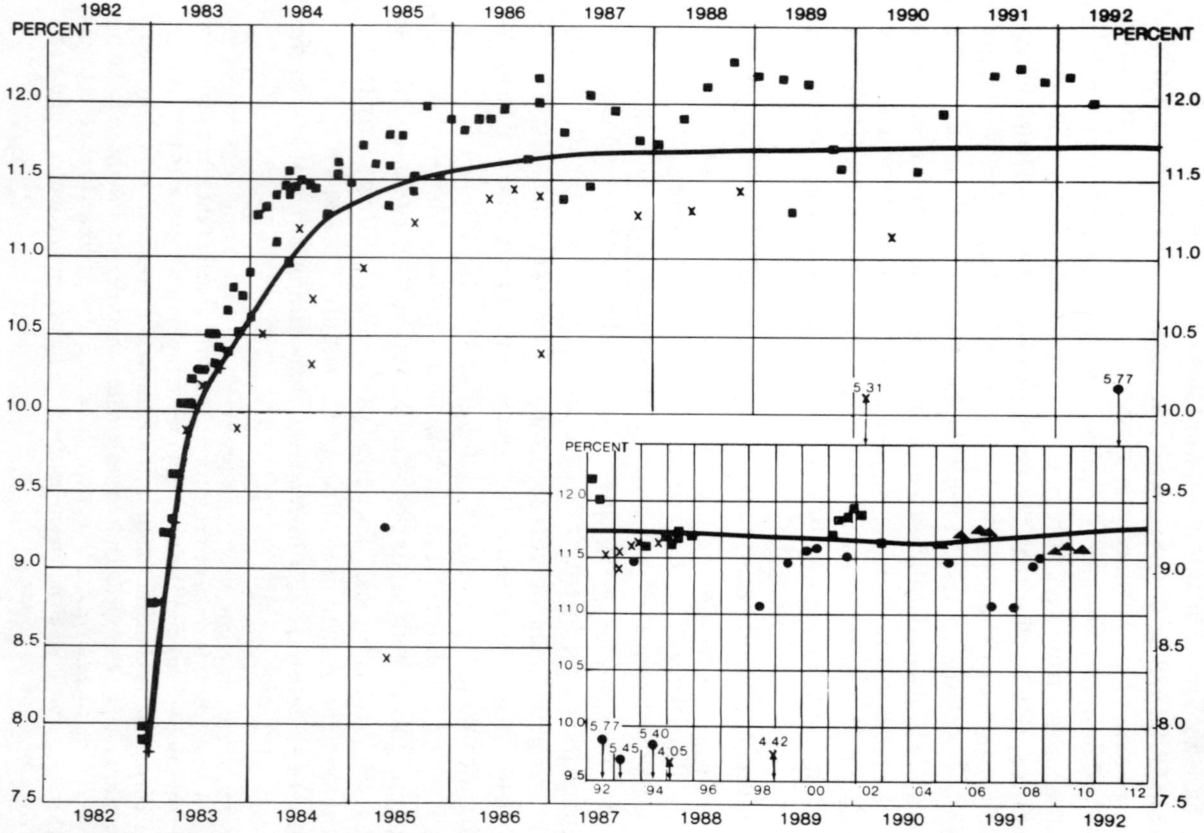

LEGEND
× Fixed coupon issues.
■ High coupon issues - 9% and higher fixed maturity issues.
● Callable issues. ▲ High coupon callable issues - plotted to earliest call date when prices are above par and to maturity date when prices are at par or below.
∗ 1¼% exchange notes.
+ Bills - coupon equivalent of 3mo., 6mo., and 1yr. bills.

Note: The curve is fitted by eye and based only on the most actively traded issues
Market yields on coupon issues due in less than 3 months are excluded

416

business cycle. Although rising yield curves vary in degree of steepness,* they are invariably characterized by lower short-term rates vis-à-vis other rates prevailing in the market. This reflects investor expectation that interest rates will be rising in the near future. Banks and other investors, in anticipation of the lending and investing opportunities during the ensuing expansionary phase of the business cycle, are unwilling to buy long-term securities at the present prices, but are willing to place their surplus funds in short-term issues. Thus a premium is paid for short-term maturity outlets in the form of lower yields, while sellers and issuers of long-term securities are forced to offer more favorable yields to attract buyers.

From the preceding discussion it follows that when the shape of the yield curve is upward-sloping, banks following a flexible investment policy place available funds in short-term issues. As the economy recovers and the expansionary phase of the cycle sets in, the proceeds of maturing short-term securities will be available to take advantage of lending and investing opportunities as these arise. To do otherwise— that is, to buy long-term issues during recession—would adversely affect the liquidity of the portfolio and undermine its profitability.

Figure 15.4 shows a flat yield curve for U.S. government securities as of March 31, 1981. A flat yield curve indicates a fairly even distribution in investor preferences among instruments of different maturities. It is generally observed during transitional periods—that is, either as the economy proceeds out of a recession into a cyclical peak and increased tightness, or vice versa. Because this stage is usually short-lived, no investment strategy may be devised.

Figure 15.5 illustrates a decreasing or downward-sloping yield curve for U.S. government obligation as of January 30, 1981. This curve, also referred to as inverted yield curve, is typical of a period of monetary tightness. As business expansion approaches a peak, investors expect rates at all maturities to decline. Investing in short-term securities—even at present high rates—will only entail opportunity losses later, since at maturity investors will have to reinvest the funds at the going lower rates. By contrast, investing in long-term bonds will permit investors to "lock in" some of the prevailing high long-term yields and realize capital gains when interest rates fall and bond prices increase. This expectation will induce investors to adjust their portfolio

---

*The bend, known as "shoulder," is a reflection of the relationship of inter-mediate interest rates to the short and long ends of the curve. In Figure 15.3 intermediate-term rates are closer to long-term rates, and hence there is quite a bit of shoulder.

Figure 15.4. Yields of Treasury Securities, March 31, 1981 (based on closing bid quotations)

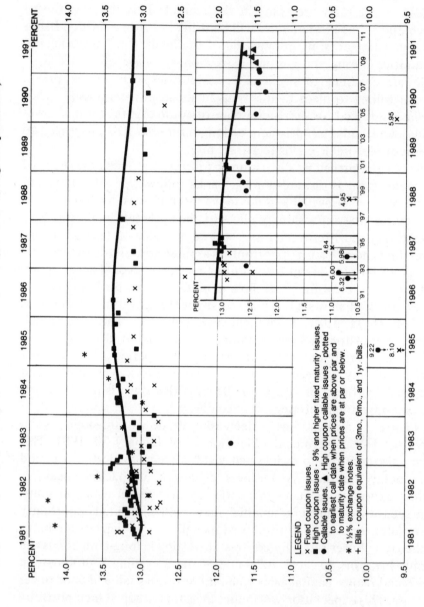

Note: The curve is fitted by eye and based only on the most actively traded issues. Market yields on coupon issues due in less than three months are excluded.

Source: U.S. Department of the Treasury, *Treasury Bulletin*, April 1981, p. 70.

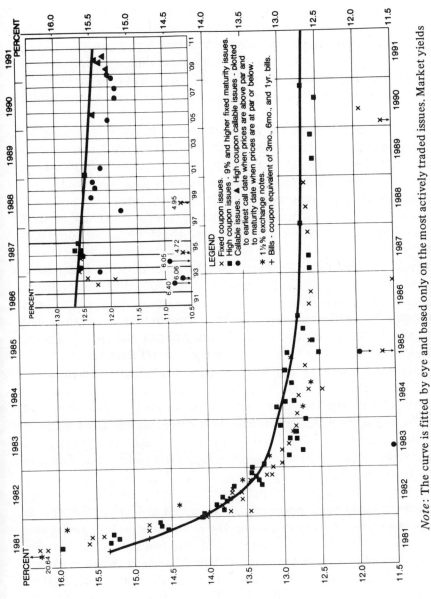

Note: The curve is fitted by eye and based only on the most actively traded issues. Market yields on coupon issues due in less than three months are excluded.

Source: U.S. Department of the Treasury, *Treasury Bulletin*, February 1981, p. 71.

and will affect the supply of funds in the money and capital markets accordingly. As investors become active sellers of short-term securities, they will drive the prices of these instruments down, thus contributing to an increase in their yields. This development, along with a reduced flow of short-term funds and a tight monetary policy, will push short-term rates above long-term rates. At the same time, as investors shift to longer-term maturities, the supply of funds will exceed the demand. Prices for bonds will thus be driven up and yields will consequently fall.

As is evident, when the shape of the yield curve is downward-sloping, banks following a flexible investment policy invest in long-term securities. Although the availability of investable funds at the peak of the cycle is minimal, downward-sloping curves usually persist for several months because of the protracted state of cyclical tightness. Thus, until economic activity begins to slow down and interest rates to decrease, portfolio managers may invest funds generated from loan repayments and declining liquidity needs in long-term securities. To avoid entering the market prematurely, alert managers should monitor certain key financial indicators. These include a decreasing reliance of banks on Federal Reserve borrowing, a drastic decline in short-term interest rates (which usually precedes a drop in long-term rates), and increases in the rates of growth of bank reserves and money supply, which signal an easy money policy by the Federal Reserve.

Figure 15.6 shows a humped yield curve for U.S. government issues as of September 30, 1981. Its name is derived from the formation of a peak between the very short end and the long end of the curve—that is, in the intermediate-term range. This curve, also referred to as an inverted yield curve, characterizes a period of high interest rates and is generally observed at the stage where the flat yield curve gives way to a downward-sloping curve.

There are two basic explanations of this hump. One has to do with Treasury's issuance of notes, which, as stated in Chapter 14, are exempt from any interest-rate ceiling. The increased supply of such notes in financial markets forces their prices down, and their yields up. Another explanation deals with banks' liquidity needs. When banks are faced with a growing reserve pressure from the Federal Reserve System or by a continued demand for loans, they are forced to liquidate some of their government securities. To minimize their capital losses in the face of rising yields and falling prices, they concentrate on the selling of securities with relatively short maturities. To the extent that they hold large amounts of intermediate-term maturities as they enter this phase of the business cycle, their sale of these intermediate securities creates a hump in the yield curve.

Figure 15.6. Yields of Treasury Securities, September 30, 1981 (based on closing bid quotations)

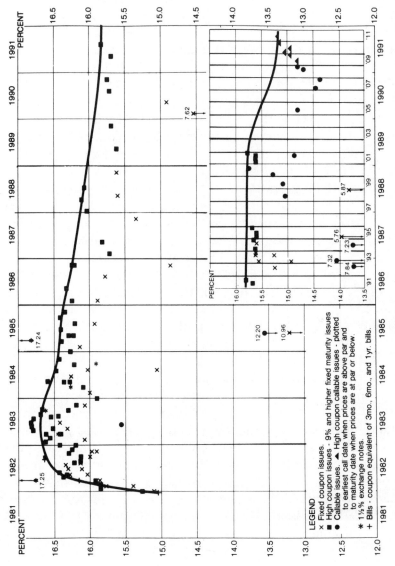

Note: The curve is fitted by eye and based only on the most actively traded issues. Market yields on coupon issues due in less than three months are excluded.

Source: U.S. Department of the Treasury, *Treasury Bulletin*, October 1981, p. 67.

Barbell Maturity Structure

This strategy provides for the splitting of the portfolio into two parts—the very short maturities and the very long. The resulting two "bulges" at the ends of the maturity spectrum give this strategy its name.

The purpose of this strategy is to ensure the average performance of the portfolio. The short end of the portfolio provides the necessary liquidity, and the long end generates the high yields that come from investing in long-term issues. This approach requires short-term securities to be rolled over as they mature, and long-term issues to be sold as they approach the midpoint of the maturity schedule. The proceeds from this sale are reinvested at the long end of the maturity spectrum. To lock in the necessary high yields in the long end of the portfolio, the purchase of long-term securities must be made in tight-money periods when the yield curve is downward-sloping. If interest-rate forecasts prove wrong and rates continue to rise, the long end of the portfolio will fail to produce as expected and will suffer significant depreciation. However, as short-term securities mature and their proceeds are reinvested at the prevailing higher market rates, the profitability of the portfolio will increase. If, on the other hand, interest-rate forecasts prove correct and rates decline, the high income (and potential capital gains) on the long portion of the portfolio will offset the low income on the short portion where maturing securities are reinvested at the prevailing low yields.

In a strict sense the barbell strategy calls for the splitting of the portfolio into two equal parts. In practice, however, advocates of this strategy recognize that the relative importance of each part will vary, depending upon the emphasis that different institutions place upon their need for supplementary liquidity and income. Banks using the barbell approach tend to trade portfolios depending upon the prevailing economic conditions. In tight-money periods these banks allow a higher concentration of long-term bonds in order for the portfolio to produce a higher level of current income. This process is reversed in periods of monetary ease, as long-term bonds are sold to reap capital gains and the proceeds are invested in the short end of the portfolio.

As implied by the preceding discussion, the barbell approach requires the same degree of sophistication and expertise as the flexible investment policy, since part of the portfolio is shifted to take advantage of expected major movements in interest rates. For bank managements that possess the necessary competence, either of these two approaches is preferable to the spaced portfolio. For banks lacking such competence, the spacing of maturities outperforms a haphazard or intuitive approach.

ORGANIZATION OF THE INVESTMENT FUNCTION

A bank's investment policy should provide for the internal organization to carry out the investment function. The size and form of such organization exhibits significant variation from one bank to another, reflecting, among other things, differences in the size of the bank, the type of securities purchased and held, involvement in underwriting activities, and the latitude of the authority delegated by the board of directors.

As with lending, the legal responsibility for bank investing rests with the entire board of directors. Here, too, however, it is customary for the board to assign the responsibility for supervising the investment function to a senior management member or to an investment committee, which will ensure that investments are made in accordance with legal prescription and the bank's own policies.

In small banks, where the relative importance of the investment portfolio is limited, the investment function is likely to be part-time. In such instances this function is usually delegated to the leading full-time executive officer, the president, who may also be the principal lending officer. In such banks a number of alternative approaches may be used to overcome the lack of proficiency in investment portfolio management. One approach is to concentrate on risk-free securities— that is, to invest in and hold U.S. government securities. On many occasions such holdings may be combined with local municipals. Another approach is to include nongovernment securities, on the basis of the information available from rating agencies. Obviously the availability of such information substitutes for the lack of individual knowledge and judgment. Such reliance can be detrimental, since ratings trail market developments, cannot claim to be faultless, and do not include very small issues that may be of high quality. A final, and in all respects better, approach is to use the services of the large-city correspondent, which ordinarily has the specialized staff to effectuate its investment policy. Reliance upon correspondent expertise will complete transactions at opportune times and generally provide important guidance in the management of the portfolio.

In large banks there is usually more delegation of authority. As with lending, it is customary for the board to assign responsibility for effecting the investment policies of the bank to an investment committee. In the larger of these banks, the investment committee serves as the liaison between the board of directors and the bank's investment or bond department, which carries out the investment function. In such banks the investment department gathers, records, and analyzes data with the objective of determining the degree of risk (credit and interest-rate risk) among alternative investment opportunities and evaluating the bank's ability to assume such risk. This information is made available to investment officers, who are customarily authorized to trade in securities. Like loan officers, investment officers too are assigned maximum dollar trading limits that give them the authority to purchase or sell securities up to a certain amount independent of the investment committee. However, they are required to report periodically to this committee about the bank's investment position.

Once securities are bought and become part of the bank's investment portfolio, the investment department is expected to assess these securities on a continuing basis. This aspect of the investment function, and the research and analysis aspects mentioned above, are carried out by a group of individuals specializing in the various phases of the investment program. The investment department staff, however, is small compared with the staff of the credit department. This is to be expected, since a bank's investments are the obligations of a few, while loans are made to thousands of individuals, business firms, and others. Furthermore, bank investments, and especially national bank investments, are generally limited by legal prescription to specified classes of issues, of which default-free federal government obligations have been a long-time favorite and convenient holding.

Whatever the form of organization of the investment function, the execution of portfolio policy should not be overburdened with constraints and limitations. An excess of either of these, whether it pertains to quality, maturity, or income, can negate the benefits of a flexible policy. Flexibility in investment policy, therefore, must be understood to extend to the working aspects of a portfolio policy and not just to its broader perspectives. Failure to realize this may render the portfolio manager a passive spectator of market developments as they shape and influence the financial world around him.

SUGGESTED REFERENCES

Anderson, Robert Bernerd. *Treasury-Federal Reserve Study of the Government Securities Market*. 3 pts. Washington, D.C.: Board of Governors of the Federal Reserve System, 1959-60.

Atkins, Paul. *Bank Bond Investment and Secondary Reserve Management*. Boston: Bankers Publishing Co., 1940.

Bradley, Stephen P., and Dwight B. Crane. *Management of Bank Portfolios*. New York: John Wiley, 1975.

Dince, Robert R., and James C. Fortson. "Maturity Structure of Bank Portfolios." *Bankers Magazine*, Autumn 1974, pp. 96-102.

Hempel, George H., and Stephen R. Kretschman. "Comparative Performance of Portfolio Maturity Policies of Commercial Banks." *Journal of Business and Economics*, Fall 1973, pp. 55-75.

Homer, Sidney. *A History of Interest Rates*. New Brunswick, N.J.: Rutgers University Press, 1963.

Lyon, Roger A. *Investment Portfolio Management in the Commercial Bank*. New Brunswick, N.J.: Rutgers University Press, 1960.

Pulliam, Kenneth P. "A Liquidity Portfolio Management Strategy Approach." *Journal of Bank Research*, Spring 1977, pp. 50-58.

Vining, James L. "Higher Yields from the Bond Portfolio." *Bankers Magazine*, Summer 1977, pp. 56-62.

16
SUMMARY:
BANK MANAGEMENT IN
PERSPECTIVE

This book has sought to identify the changes in the competitive environment in which banks operate and to describe the impact of these changes on banking activity. The emphasis has been on the management of commercial banks through the formulation and implementation of sound and flexible policies. Although these policies are the same for all banks, it is necessary that each individual bank's directors and management put their own variety of flesh and blood on the bare bones of the policies outlined in this discussion. Once this is done, the finer details of finished policy will evolve. Blind adherence to a banking practice, or to any policy shaped abstractly, does not serve the bank, its depositors, or its stockholders. Ignoring the need for continuous adjustments in banking policies that reflect changing economic conditions is courting trouble, frequently in the form of significant losses. The function of portfolio management, therefore, must be to relate internal banking requirements to the external, and ever-changing, economic conditions via the medium of portfolio policy.

Beyond the adoption of some minimum but perhaps essential requirements, which may be altered as the underlying conditions change, few absolute and arbitrary limitations should be placed upon bank operations. While in a given period certain criteria may be laid down as guidelines to bank activity, the cyclical nature of the economy and the results of its impact upon the monetary system and financial markets may frequently require not only shifts of emphasis in bank policy but also a close and continuing supervision of existing guidelines in recognition of changing relationships.

The book has postulated that a commercial bank has access to three sources of funds: invested and senior capital, deposits, and institutional borrowing. Banks rely heavily on debt to finance the acquisition of bank assets. The most important form of such debt is deposit liabilities—demand deposits, and time and savings deposits, competitively attracted. Stated differently, banks rely heavily on debt sources to finance the acquisition of bank assets, the vast majority of which constitute in fact the debts of others. This situation has earned banks the reputation of being dealers in debt. The origin and nature of bank funds have rendered their management a critical aspect of bank efficiency. Efficient management of funds is crucial for the efficient performance of banking functions. Efficient funds management implies the most effective use of all sources of bank funds in attaining optimum portfolio balance among liquidity, solvency, and profitability, consistent with the constraints imposed by law, regulation, and interests of the community. These portfolio objectives suggest a certain order of priorities in the employment of bank funds.

In the employment of bank funds, and hence in the formulation of bank policies, four priorities must be observed: maintaining primary reserves, providing secondary reserves, meeting customer credit demands, and investing for income.

Primary reserves are generally maintained in the form of cash, and hence constitute the most liquid assets of commercial banks. The bulk of the primary reserves consists of the legally required reserves held as deposit balances at the Federal Reserve or as vault cash, plus balances in correspondent banks. Because these are cash assets, banks, for obvious reasons, try to maintain, beyond their required reserves, only what is necessary to assure efficient day-to-day operations and compensate correspondent banks for their services.

Secondary reserves, or protective investments, perform precisely the role suggested by their name: they are basically designed to provide liquidity. Bank acceptance of funds repayable upon demand or within a given period of time, and the necessity to meet legitimate loan demands, focus upon the need for liquidity, rendering it of primary importance. Because of this need, probable liquidity requirements cannot be made subservient to other considerations. The investment portfolio, constituting the main source of liquidity, must be so arranged that such requirements will be met at all times with the least possible risk.

There are, of course, various levels of potential liquidity needs—levels of high, medium, and low probability. Because investments entail only two major categories of risk—the credit or default risk, and the market or interest-rate risk—those investments creating liquidity against the probable needs must be of the highest quality and shortest maturity. As the degree of probability declines, standards can be broadened somewhat to include possibly slightly greater default and interest-rate risks. The secondary reserves, long a byword in banking circles, are usually considered that portion of the portfolio providing a broad liquidity base. It has become increasingly useful to see this as a two-part base containing seasonal and nonseasonal or cyclical secondary reserves. The former should include investments aimed at covering the probable needs; the latter, portfolio assets aimed at covering the less probable liquidity needs. Such a division of investment or liquidity accounting provides the banker with a more accurate picture of his or her needs and investment position, and may result in a more economical use of investment funds.

As a rule, seasonal secondary reserves should never be allowed to fall below a minimum desirable level based upon probable liquidity requirements. If a shortage occurs, steps should be taken to rebuild the liquidity base as rapidly as possible. On the other hand, nonseasonal or cyclical secondary reserves are more flexible but should generally be allowed to decline below a desirable level only in the event of a concurrent increase in excess funds in the seasonal secondary reserves. This might well be the case when flexible portfolio policy considerations suggest that investment emphasis fall upon the short-term portion of the portfolio.

Once a bank has made itself liquid and safe, it should devote itself to the business for which it is best qualified, the granting of loans. Loans are the leading earning asset of commercial banks. Until at least the 1920s, the leading type of loan in the United States was the commercial loan. Since it was short-term and self-liquidating (that is, it generated the wherewithal for its own repayment), the commercial loan was considered the appropriate earning asset for banks, in view of the fact that banks had most of their obligations in the form of deposits redeemable on demand. Little by little, however, it was elbowed out of its place of prominence by other types of loans: by consumer loans, mortgage loans, securities loans, term loans, and, later, by the appearance and spread of bank credit-card lending, and even the beginnings of bank leasing to business (which amounts to lending productive assets rather than money per se). Thus, although nowadays some classes of borrowers and loan arrangements are more characteristic than others in bank lending, there is no such thing as a standard bank loan or borrower.

This evolution in bank lending was an outcome of several factors. First, there has been considerable change in the thinking and attitudes of bankers and regulatory authorities concerning liquidity as applied to earning assets. It became apparent, for example, that it was not so much the maturity of the assets that affected a bank's liquidity position as it was the quality of the assets themselves, their marketability (or shiftability), and the bank's own ability to issue acceptable liabilities to provide liquidity when needed. Second, as banks obtained more experience in meeting their liquidity needs, they gained more confidence in their ability to design portfolios with an asset mix that offered the greatest utility to the bank. This led to substantial improvements and refinements in the techniques of funds management. The third development, which in a sense was a cause of the other two, stemmed from the strong economic pressures for new outlets and improved earnings performance. Commercial banks were under strong economic pressures for new sources of earnings, especially after the depression and the sharp decline in the demand for commercial loans. In addition to this internal pressure for earnings, which forced banks to extend the maturities of their assets, the banking industry in the twentieth century has witnessed the development of another kind of competitive pressure: Nonbank financial institutions, which grew rapidly in size and number, began to perform functions similar to some of those performed by commercial banks. Commercial banks found that if they were to keep attracting funds, they would have to offer interest rates on savings deposits that were competitive with those offered by these other financial institutions (savings and loan associations and mutual savings banks). The payment of higher interest rates in turn required higher returns on bank portfolios if earning levels were to be maintained. Although both of the pressures described above, internal and external, were important, it was especially the last one that pushed banks more vigorously into consumer loans, real estate loans, and term loans, and subsequently—in the World War II years—into the market for government securities, federal as well as state and local.

In the postwar years a new factor arose to cause the process of change in commercial bank operations to gain new momentum. This time a phenomenal expansion in private loan demand exerted important pressures toward changes in the asset structure of commercial banks. Sustained by the postwar growth of the U.S. economy, this credit demand created new opportunities, which banks have been very resourceful in exploiting. Thus the postwar period has been characterized by shifts between and within categories of commercial banks' earning assets. At the same time new uses of bank loans have proliferated.

The pattern of commercial bank operations has thus been changing in response to changes in the tastes of customers, improvements in the techniques of funds management, and, to the extent that banks are permitted by laws and regulations to respond, the changing needs of the economy. Despite ever-expanding bank activities, lending continues to be the core of the commercial banking function. Formulation and implementation of sound and flexible lending policies are among the major concerns of bank directors and managers. Well-planned lending policies and carefully established lending practices are crucial if a bank is to perform its credit-creating role effectively, and develop and grow in response to community needs. The soundness of these policies will be reflected in the effectiveness with which a bank meets the credit needs of the community or markets involved. Policy decisions must be established in regard to the type and volume of bank loans, the maturity distribution of these loans, and the overall size of the loan portfolio. Policy decisions must also determine to whom the bank will lend and what the loan terms will be.

Loanable funds in excess of local loan demand are employed in the investment market. This constitutes the fourth and last priority in the use of commercial bank funds. Residual loanable funds can be employed in the longer end of the investment portfolio, to generate supplementary liquidity and income. The use of the secondary reserves, under a flexible policy, assists the portfolio manager in controlling the longer-term bond portfolio. The effect of time on such a portfolio position is often overlooked; should too large a portion of longer-term funds shift into the short-intermediate or intermediate-term range, it will become evident in reviewing the position of the nonseasonal reserves. Steps can then be taken to remedy the problem.

The secondary reserve and bond accounts, therefore, provide a context for a flexible investment policy, with such a policy centered on the considerations that determine the basic employment of funds in these areas. The flexibility of policy is geared to respond to the cyclical nature of the economy, changes in monetary policy, and probable fluctuations in the financial markets. The essential aim is, on the one hand, to emphasize the short-term area of the portfolio in employing new funds, maturing funds, and proceeds from profit realization transactions during periods of low yields and high bond prices (which normally coincide with business recession and monetary ease under conditions of a flexible monetary policy), and, on the other hand, to emphasize longer maturities in employing new funds, maturing funds, and proceeds of loss transactions, designed to reconstruct the portfolio balance during periods of higher yields and lower bond prices (which normally coincide with business improvement and monetary restraint). The liquidity sector of the investment portfolio, however, serves as a limiting factor when policy determines that emphasis is to be placed upon longer maturities, thus protecting the basic requirements of the investment portfolio from an overly aggressive policy of maturity extension.

A bank's loan policy must be equally flexible. Taking cognizance of the business cycle is equally important in the development of a flexible loan policy. It is essential to emphasize the short-term area of the loan portfolio during periods of slackened loan demand, which usually coincide with business recession and monetary ease. Conversely, one must emphasize longer loan maturities (that is, term lending) during periods of peak loan demand, which normally coincide with high business activity and monetary restraint. Such a pattern of loan maturity policy allows a bank to substantially improve its long-range rate of income.

Flexibility, therefore, must characterize both the loan and the investment policies of commercial banks. This flexibility of policy, geared to the cyclical nature of the economy, stresses that the maturity characteristics for both loan and investment portfolios must be synchronized with the phases of the business cycle. The stress is on the short-term area of the loan and investment portfolios during periods of business recession and monetary ease, and on the long-term area of the portfolios during periods of high business activity and monetary restraint. Guidelines for the pursuit of a flexible loan and investment policy are provided by the trends of monetary policy. More specifically, the reserve position of the banking system may be considered as a basic guideline for the direction of monetary policy and, hence, for the appropriate development of the portfolio.

The practice of a flexible loan and investment policy, as described, raises portfolio operation out of the "average" category, and thus should produce the best possible results, for it enhances the effectiveness of portfolio management. While flexibility as to maturity represents the essential part of a flexible policy, successful portfolio management demands that flexibility exist also in the use of the various type of loan and investment outlets. Yield differentials must guide the placement of funds in particular sectors of the market, and as these differentials change, portfolio policy should be sufficiently liberal to allow for response to more attractive opportunities as they develop. Maximizing portfolio benefits from many market opportunities demands flexibility in all respects rather than dogmatic adherence to one type of outlet.

Over the years, efforts have been made to assist bankers in the management of their portfolios by means of quantitative analysis. Important models have been developed that concentrate on the allocating of funds among various alternatives, with the purpose of securing the highest expected earnings consistent with the degree of risk the bank is willing to accept. In other words, what these quantitative analyses have in common is that they attempt to develop an optimum portfolio mix. Clearly the techniques available today are much more practical and pertinent than the best efforts of only a few years back.

Nevertheless, the world in which the banker operates is an increasingly uncertain, complex, and competitive world, and an optimum portfolio policy will require the exercise of considerable judgment. The attainment of an optimum portfolio, then, will be a continuous process of adjustment carried on by each individual bank under conditions of economic change, uncertainty, and risk. The actual results are likely to be optimal only in a relative sense.

EMMANUEL N. ROUSSAKIS is a professor of finance at Florida International University, Miami. Concurrently he is director of the Certificate in Banking Program, the Certificate in Savings and Loan Program, and the Certificate in International Bank Management Program, designed by the Finance Department of Florida International University in cooperation with Miami's financial community for the training of bank and savings and loan personnel.

Dr. Roussakis received a Florida State Research (STAR) grant for the study of international banking legislation and taxation; study recommendations were the basis for legislative changes implemented in July 1979 and June 1980.

Dr. Roussakis has taught at American universities in the United States and Europe, worked for American and European banks, and served in an advisory capacity to government agencies, both in the United States and abroad. He participated in the negotiations for Greece's admission to the European Economic Community in the area of commercial banks and banking policy. He has published widely on banking subjects, his articles having appeared in academic and professional journals in the United States, Belgium, France, Germany, Greece, and Italy.

Dr. Roussakis is the author of *Friedrich List, the Zollverein and the Uniting of Europe* (College of Europe Press, 1968), *Managing Commercial Bank Funds* (Praeger, 1977), and *Miami's International Banking Community: Foreign Banks, Edge Act Corporations and Local Banks* (Peat, Marwick, Mitchell, 1981). He is also editor of and contributor to *International Lending by U.S. Commercial Banks: A Casebook* (Praeger, 1981) and *International Banking: Principles and Practices* (Praeger, 1983).

Dr. Roussakis holds a B.A. from Athens University; an M.B.A. from Atlanta University; a Graduate Certificate in Advanced European Studies from the College of Europe, Bruges; and a Ph.D. from the Catholic University of Louvain. While pursuing his education he lived in the Middle East, in Europe, and in the United States. He speaks English, French, Greek, and Arabic.